A New Generation in International Strategic Management

Dedicated to Marcia and Tess

A New Generation in International Strategic Management

Edited by

Stephen Tallman

The E. Claiborne Robins Distinguished Professor in Business
University of Richmond, USA

Edward Elgar

Cheltenham, UK • Northampton, MA, USA

Published by
Edward Elgar Publishing Limited
The Lypiatts
15 Lansdown Road
Cheltenham
Glos GL50 2JA
UK

Edward Elgar Publishing, Inc.
William Pratt House
9 Dewey Court
Northampton
Massachusetts
01060
USA

Paperback edition 2008

A catalogue record for this book is available from the British Library

Library of Congress Cataloguing in Publication Data
A new generation in international strategic management / [edited by] Stephen
Tallman.
    p. cm.
    Includes bibliographical references and index.
    1. Strategic planning. 2. International business enterprises — Management.
I. Tallman, Stephen B.
    HD30.28.N483 2007
    658.4'092 — dc22   2007019455

ISBN 978 1 84720 038 9 (cased)
ISBN 978 1 84844 365 5 (paperback)

Printed by Biddles Ltd, King's Lynn, Norfolk

Contents

Figures

Tables

Contributors

Ruth V. Aguilera (PhD, Harvard University) is Associate Professor of Management at University of Illinois at Urbana-Champaign, USA. Her research interests include comparative corporate governance, institutional analysis, inter-organizational networks, organizational studies, economic sociology, and cross-border mergers and acquisitions.

Brent B. Allred (PhD, Pennsylvania State University) is Associate Professor of Strategic Management and International Business at the College of William & Mary, Williamsburg, VA, USA. He specializes in global competitive strategy and the international management of technology and innovation.

Victor Almeida (PhD, Federal University of Rio de Janeiro) is Professor of Marketing and International Business at the Federal University of Rio de Janeiro, Brazil. His research interests include internationalization strategies, channels of distribution and retail management.

Björn Ambos (PhD, University of Hamburg) is Professor of International Management at Vienna University of Economics and Business Administration, Austria. His research interests revolve around innovation, strategy and the management of technology-driven multinational firms.

Tina C. Ambos (PhD, WU-Wien) is Assistant Professor at the Vienna University of Economics and Business Administration, Austria. Her research and teaching interests include knowledge management, innovation and strategic management of the multinational corporation.

Veneta Andonova (PhD, Universidad Pompeu Fabra) is Professor of Management at the Universidad de los Andes School of Management, Colombia. Her research interests include information and communication technologies, business strategy and emerging markets, and institutional effects.

Daniel W. Baack (PhD, St Louis University) is Assistant Professor of Marketing at Ball State University, Muncie, IN, USA. His research interests include international advertising, cognitive theory, and culture's influence on marketing strategy and consumer behavior.

Chris Changwha Chung (PhD, University of Western Ontario) is Assistant Professor of Management at Florida International University, USA. His research interests are in real options during times of uncertainty, international joint venture evolution, and foreign subsidiary management.

Alvaro Cuervo-Cazurra (PhD, University of Salamanca; PhD, MIT) is Assistant Professor of International Business at the University of South Carolina, USA. His primary research interests include firm competitiveness and internationalization. He also studies issues of governance and corruption.

Jonathan Doh (PhD, The George Washington University) is Associate Professor of Management at Villanova University, PA, USA. His primary research interests include the study of emerging markets and their institutions, non-governmental organizations and their interactions with MNCs, and corporate responsibility to include corruption and CR strategies.

Manuel Portugal Ferreira (PhD, University of Utah) is an assistant professor at the Escola Superior de Tecnologia e Gestão – Instituto Politécnico de Leiria, Portugal. His primary research interests are in the areas of global strategic management, capabilities-based strategies of MNCs, and strategic and entrepreneurial issues in industry clusters.

Ricardo G. Flores is a doctoral candidate at University of Illinois at Urbana-Champaign, USA. His research interests include organizational adaptation to different environmental shocks, such as technological discontinuities and globalization.

Anthony Goerzen (PhD, University of Western Ontario) is Assistant Professor of Management at the University of Victoria, Canada. His primary research interests include the strategic management of multinational enterprises with a focus on the organizational and performance effects of inter-firm networks, cross-border alliances, and geographic location.

Seung-Hyun Lee (PhD, Ohio State University) is Assistant Professor of Management at the University of Texas at Dallas, USA. His main research interests concern real options, property rights theory, institutional change, and corruption.

Dan Li (PhD, Texas A & M University) is Assistant Professor of International Business at the Kelley Business School at Indiana University, USA. Her research focuses on the management of multinational enterprises and international strategic alliances.

Jing Li (PhD, Indiana University) is an assistant professor of international business at Simon Fraser University, Canada. Her research focuses on the application of real options theory in strategy and alliance activities in emerging economies.

Ronaldo Parente (PhD, Temple University) is Assistant Professor of Management at Rutgers University, NJ, USA. His research interests include global sourcing strategies, modularization, international strategy, supply chain management, and issues related to new product development.

Anupama Phene (PhD, University of Texas at Dallas) is Associate Professor of Strategy and David Eccles Faculty Fellow at the University of Utah, USA. Her research examines firm innovation and learning in high technology industries.

Roberto Ragozzino (PhD, Ohio State University) is Assistant Professor of Strategy at the University of Illinois at Chicago, USA. His research is in the area of mergers and acquisitions and strategic alliances, with an emphasis on how these corporate events apply to entrepreneurial ventures.

Robert Salomon (PhD, NYU) is Assistant Professor of Management and Organizations at the Stern School of Business, New York University, USA. His research focuses on the management and economics of international expansion.

Petra Sonderegger is a PhD candidate at Columbia University, USA. Her research focuses on changes in innovative collaboration across large distances and how they affect the geographical distribution of innovation networks.

Silviya Svejenova (PhD, IESE) is Assistant Professor of Management at ESADE in Barcelona, Spain. Her research interests include issues of relationship management (from social networks to inter-organizational arrangements), the careers and work of top managers, and the role they play in the transformation and internationalization of their companies.

K. Scott Swan (PhD, University of Texas at Austin) is Associate Professor of International Business and Marketing at The College of William & Mary, Williamsburg, VA, USA. His research interests include product design, sourcing strategies, cooperative strategies, global product development, and the interaction of innovation and culture.

Stephen Tallman (PhD, UCLA) is the E. Claiborne Robins Distinguished Professor in Business at the University of Richmond, USA. His research interests include international strategy, multinational diversification, alliances and joint ventures, and industry clusters.

Florian A. Täube (PhD, Johann Wolfgang Goethe-University, Frankfurt, Germany) is a lecturer at Imperial College, London, UK. His research focuses on the internationalization of knowledge-intensive global industries and the inter-organizational governance of innovation.

Tony W. Tong (Ohio State University) is an assistant professor of strategy at the State University of New York at Buffalo, USA. His research focuses on the application of real options theory in strategy and the dynamics of alliance activities.

C. Annique Un (PhD, MIT) is Assistant Professor of International Business at the University of South Carolina, USA. Her primary research interests include the management of technology and innovation in large multinational firms, and the international expansion and competition of developed country multinational firms in developing countries.

Paul Vaaler (PhD, University of Minnesota) is Assistant Professor of Management at University of Illinois at Urbana-Champaign, USA. His research interests include technology management in international business, and risk and investment in emerging-market countries.

Gurneeta Vasudeva (PhD, George Washington University) is Assistant Professor of strategy at the Indian School of Business in Hyderabad, India. Her research interests include comparative national institutions and their influence on firms' capabilities, knowledge-building in new technology development, geography of innovation and R&D internationalization.

Luis Vives (PhD, IESE) is Assistant Professor of Management at ESADE in Barcelona, Spain. His research focuses on the management of the firm's corporate scope, the processes, paths and positions of firm internationalization, and the co-evolution of corporations with their institutional environment.

Zheying Wu is a doctoral student in the University of Southern California, USA. His research interests include international strategy, knowledge and learning, and firm responses to environmental contexts.

Preface

In years of working with doctoral students and junior colleagues at the University of Utah and after serving on doctoral and junior faculty workshops at conferences, I became convinced that an increasing number of young researchers were working in the area of international or global strategic management, even though many of these individuals might not consider themselves primarily as international business scholars. These emerging scholars offer growing interest in theoretical ideas such as real options theory, agency theory, or knowledge-based strategy theory. They address new phenomena such as the rising strategic importance of alliances and networks, the potential for regional clusters replacing nations as the primary units of location economics, or the role of non-governmental organizations (NGOs) in the global marketplace. They are interested in the interactions of social, cultural, and other humanistic concerns with the economic focus of traditional international business (IB) studies. They have discovered a variety of new empirical data sources and empirical methods unfamiliar to many more established scholars.

Unfortunately for our field, the long delays in moving scholarly work to publication in influential academic journals, the challenge of publishing truly innovative ideas in blind-reviewed outlets, and the limited opportunities for invited publication by less known researchers all combine with the pressures of teaching and beginning a career to force the most original and innovative ideas from these individuals to be disseminated slowly at best and perhaps to never see the light of day. When I was approached by Alan Sturmer of Edward Elgar Publishing to do an edited volume, I determined to limit contributors to the junior faculty and doctoral candidates whom I was meeting. The consequence is that the lead authors in this book were all pre-tenure at the time the project began – though several of them have been promoted since then. A few of them have become widely appreciated in the last few years, but I think their contributions to this volume show that all of them have interesting ideas and great potential for important contributions. And they are not unique – rather, I think, they are quite typical of a much larger set of their contemporaries. They happened to come to my attention at the time that I was recruiting authors, but I hope their contributions will give readers pause to consider both the ideas presented here and the potential embodied in their own junior colleagues. They give me great hope for the future of both strategic management and international business.

The contributions in this volume are meant to offer new perspectives on international business strategy. Most edited volumes with invited authors seem to be opportunities for the 'usual suspects' among established scholars to offer variations on their already well-known concepts or to state opinions supported more by reputation than by research. The hope behind this book is that new perspectives stated in less practiced tones will both inform and inspire others among the emerging generation of international strategy scholars. The authors are new and emerging scholars, and the only guidance given them was to address a topic that interested them, was not well developed in the literature, and that they felt was sufficiently beyond current thinking to be difficult to publish in peer-reviewed journals. The result is a set of chapters with truly original thinking – concepts that won't be seen in the journals for years. After reading these contributions, I came to the conclusion that often stated fears of the demise of meaningful scholarship addressing international strategy are misdirected. Traditional concepts may be mature, even declining, but new ideas are evolving as fast as the global market itself. We just need to pay more attention to the new generation of scholars.

Steve Tallman
University of Richmond, 2007

PART I

New approaches to international strategy

1. Peripheral vision for international strategy: exploring vistas of the field's future

Luis Vives and Silviya Svejenova

According to the Merriam-Webster dictionary, peripheral vision relates to the outer part of the field of vision and encompasses a broad set of non-central points. When a subject is set in motion, points that have been peripheral may enter the center of vision and capture attention. In this chapter we use peripheral vision to explore emerging themes in International Strategy (IS) that may become more central in the future. We sketch out a number of changes which, taken together, could redefine the field's center of gravity in the coming years.

The IS field has had trouble converging around a single fundamental question. Different streams have posed and pursued different questions including, 'Why do countries differ?' (Ghemawat, 2003), 'What determines the international success and failure of firms?' (Peng, 2004), or 'How do internal and external forces interplay in the strategic process of MNCs?' (Melin, 1992). These streams run through a variety of levels of analysis, such as the environment, the industry, the firm, and the manager (Buckley and Lessard, 2005).

Furthermore, the field has encompassed different views of the world. There have been voices maintaining that the world is round (Gray, 2005), with countries and religions being the strongholds of identities. And while some have noticed the world's flattening (Friedman, 2005), others have seen new peaks rising, with certain cities and geographical regions standing out and making it look spiky (Florida, 2005). In the meantime, the field has continued debating how global the world and the business world really are. As part of that conversation, some scholars have suggested that intermediate states between the local and the global, such as semi-globalization (Ghemawat, 2003) or regionalization (Rugman, 2005), are worthy of exploration. It has also been argued that the pace of globalization differs not only across geographies, but also across markets, with capital markets being relatively integrated into a single global capital market, while labor markets remain rather separate at the national level (Buckley and Ghauri, 2004).

This chapter argues for a forward-looking, dynamic, phenomena-based, multidimensional, eclectic perspective on International Strategy. It consists of two main sections. First, we outline a number of well-received views in the field and suggest ways in which current and future trends can challenge and change them. Second, we offer a discussion of how these challenges could shift the center of gravity in IS and conclude with some implications for the field's future research agenda.

INTERNATIONAL STRATEGY'S NEW VISTAS

Our peripheral vision of the field has identified nine shifts that have, in our opinion, the potential to change the direction of IS in the future. These shifts are related to some basic tenets of the field, such as focal actors, role of location, strategies, organization forms, or power. They are listed below under two sections that indicate the level at which the change is expected to take place: the firm–context interaction or the firm itself (see Table 1.1).

Table 1.1   New vistas for international strategy

Firm–context interaction level
- From home/host country imprints to multi-country or no-country pedigree
- From established multinational enterprises (MNEs) as IS's focal actor to focusing on a variety of organizations that pursue international opportunities
- From developed countries to emerging markets
- From MNE–government interactions to coordinated market and political strategies

Firm level
- From a single sequential and linear process of international expansion to numerous viable paths and positions
- From entry strategies to a portfolio management of a firm's international activities
- From modularity of the internal value chain across locations to morphing in a network of virtual relations
- From the power of the HQ to the degrees of freedom and the impact of subsidiaries
- From international human resources management to global talent management

---

FIRM–CONTEXT INTERACTION

From Home/Host Country Imprints to Multi-country or No-country Pedigree

Locations and their specificities are the centerpiece of IS's distinctive domain. 'L' for location has been at the heart of Dunning's renowned ownership–location–internalization (OLI) paradigm (Dunning, 1977). With spikes rising and valleys flattening, and vast areas of the world still being excluded from the flows of internationalization, disagreements on the meaning of location become even more pronounced. Some authors affirm that globalization in its third version (3.0) has arrived (Friedman, 2005), while others see a world of semi-globalization (Ricart et al., 2004) or one with clearly pronounced regional influences and activities, in which global companies are rare species in a sea of regional multinationals (Rugman, 2005). In this changing context, the meaning of country of origin is worth clarifying, and so is the nature and strength of its impact on a firm's internationalization behaviour.

According to IS studies, the MNE's home country is expected to leave an imprint on the organization and internationalization of the company. As Bartlett and Ghoshal (1998) put it, a company's home country is a powerful shaper of its administrative heritage. However, as an MNE gains experience and knowledge of its host markets, not only home but also host markets may leave an imprint on a company's internationalization behaviour. The increasing international experience of firms and the learning processes that they develop when growing internationally can lead to the modification of a company's foundational imprints. Furthermore, major strategic events such as mergers and acquisitions can also alter a company's geographical make-up and scope of international activities, as in the case of IBM's PC Division becoming part of the Chinese company Lenovo, or the Indian-led steel making company, Mittal, acquiring the pan-European steel maker, Arcelor.

In addition to home country, notions such as cultural distance (Hofstede, 1980) or psychic distance (Vahlne and Wiedersheim-Paul, 1973) have been used to explain MNEs' internationalization behavior and the likelihood of success for their international operations. Cultural and business differences between home and host markets constitute the psychic distance (Johanson and Vahlne, 1977) and are expected to play a significant role in the selection of markets to enter and the degree of a firm's local responsiveness in each of those markets.

However, in recent years we have witnessed the birth and growth of an increasing number of international new ventures, also known as born-global firms. Either from inception or shortly afterwards, those firms start operating simultaneously from a number of geographical locations. In those cases, a single home country may have a weaker imprint on an organization's structure and its internationalization practices. Instead, multiple countries may have a joint imprint effect and, as such, affect the future internationalization processes and operations of the firm. Further, for web-born and web-based ventures that offer service worldwide, there may not be an easily identifiable home country imprint. The World Wide Web (www) itself may offer its particular imprints. In those cases, the meaning of cultural or psychic distance could be difficult to specify.

While some authors announce that distance is dead (Cairncross, 1997), others claim geography is still alive and that it matters (Buckley and Ghauri, 2004). For the latter, virtual space reinforces rather than substitutes spatial dispersion. Further, the geography of innovation and the spatial boundaries and role played by regional groupings of firms, such as clusters, are seen as promising lines for further research (Tallman et al., 2004). In that area, IS's collaboration with Economic Geography may offer useful insights.

From Established Multinational Enterprises (MNEs) as IS's Focal Actor to Focusing on a Variety of Organizations that Pursue International Opportunities

For a long time, MNEs have been the centerpiece of IS's research agenda (Ricart et al., 2004). In fact, becoming a multinational company has been considered a natural evolution for any firm with aspirations to pursuing growth through international opportunities. The IS literature has painstakingly documented MNEs' activities and structures. Scholars have provided detailed accounts of their organization, strategy, stuffing, knowledge flows and mindsets.

A number of recent studies have pointed out that IS should open up its field of inquiry to other kinds of organizations that pursue international opportunities and employ international resources. Since the 1980s, for example, growing attention has been focused on international new ventures, a stream of research promoted largely by the work of Oviatt and McDougall (1994). That stream has not only paved the way for IS's opening to studies of organizations that are much smaller, more agile, and at earlier stages of organizational development than established multinational corporations, it has also endorsed a prolific boundary-crossing collaboration between the fields of IS and Entrepreneurship.

Additionally, in the swiftly changing context of the twenty-first century, not only new ventures but also (perhaps paradoxically) anti-globalization movements seek to internationalize and become global players. Non-governmental organizations (NGOs) have risen as an important actor in the global arena and, through processes of internationalization and a variety of collaborations, have achieved global reach. For example, Oxfam International is a confederation of 13 organizations that seek to provide solutions to poverty, suffering and injustice in different parts of the world. For these purposes it collaborates with over 3000 partners located in more than 100 countries. As an acknowledgement of the growing influence and reach of NGOs, a novel IS trend argues for their inclusion as a relevant and influential focal actor in the IS's domain (Teegen et al., 2004). How such non-profit networks emerge, operate and expand around the globe requires further exploration. It also invites collaboration between IS and the field of Corporate Social Responsibility (CSR).

Hence, what we envisage for the future is a much richer and a more complex ecology of focal actors that IS has to take into consideration and examine. This ecology consists of organizations of different sizes (big and small), at distinct stages of their lifecycle (start-ups and incumbents), and of dissimilar natures (profit-seeking and non-profit). However, they all look for resources and pursue opportunities in foreign contexts, and partake in value creation on a domestic, international, regional, semi-global or global scale. In this new ecology, MNEs need to understand and interact with international NGOs (Teegen et al., 2004) and other relevant stakeholders. What's more, they may also serve as conduits for smaller firms' innovations and intermediaries in their internationalization (Acs et al., 1997; Rugman and Verbeke, 2003).

From Developed Countries to Emerging Markets

Traditionally, the focus has been on MNEs that have been born in a developed country and how they have built or transferred their competitive advantage predominantly to other developed markets (e.g. Vernon, 1966; Hymer, 1976; Dunning, 1988). In that stream of research, emerging economies have been considered as 'delayed markets' and, as such, companies have sought to reach them only after they had exhausted growth opportunities in available developed countries' markets, following what has been referred to as 'waterfall strategies' (Ayal and Zif, 1979; Kalish et al., 1995).

In recent years, emerging markets have become increasingly important destinations for MNEs, not only as a source of inexpensive labor, but also as a source of market growth. Furthermore, some of those companies have come to the realization that emerging markets offer opportunities beyond the limited layer of customers at the top of the pyramid. They have started addressing the needs of the majority of clients – that is, the great numbers that reside at the base of the pyramid and which, because of their low income, require distinct approaches and value propositions. The pursuit of such opportunities demands that companies foster innovation and come up with novel business models (Prahalad and Hart, 2002).

Furthermore, and in addition to the MNEs that have been established in developed countries, an increasing number of companies founded in emerging countries are accelerating their efforts to integrate into the global economy (Hoskisson et al., 2000). Among the most notable examples are Mexico's Cemex, Brazil's Embraer, India's Infosys Technologies, and the China-born Lenovo Group. Far from targeting only other emerging countries, these new multinationals enter developed economies' markets and, at times, take them by storm. IS needs to offer a better understanding of these new global challengers that employ new business models and other innovations that redefine the playing field (Aguiar et al., 2006). They are increasingly gaining size and power by acquiring companies with international presence from the developed world, forging partnerships, and challenging some of the traditional patterns of internationalization observed in MNEs in developed countries.

From MNE–Government Interactions to Coordinated Market and Political Strategies

Another issue at the heart of the IS research agenda is the role of governments in companies' internationalization and international operations, mainly through their regulatory competencies. However, countries are not uniform in their adoption of reforms. For example, they differ in their adoption of neoliberal, market-oriented reforms in their infrastructure industries (Henisz et al., 2005).

By making use of their competencies, governments have been able to affect both the international activities of national companies and the local opportunities available to foreign firms. As a consequence, a lot of attention has been paid to institutional environments and their impact on MNEs.

However, this impact is not necessarily unidirectional; that is, from a particular government to a given firm. A growing number of IS studies recognize the importance of interplay between a firm and its context (Noda and Collis, 2001; Dobrev et al., 2003). MNEs are not passive actors in their respective institutional arenas. They have the size and power, at times greater than that of a single nation state, that permits them to shape a given institutional context and, at times, to enforce their will. On numerous occasions they actively lobby or try to influence certain institutions that can hamper or enhance their opportunities, relative to those of their competitors, and their strategic position in a given market.

Along with the ongoing interest in MNEs' market strategies, scholars have been intrigued by the role these companies play in filling institutional voids as well as using political or non-market strategies to proactively manage multiple stakeholders and relevant contexts (Baron, 1995). Thus, a thriving international business requires a coordinated effort of both market and non-market strategies. Researchers should pay attention to how these two types of strategies are integrated into a harmonic whole that guarantees both competitiveness and political support to the corporation.

It is also worth recognizing that present and/or previous relationships and actions of an MNE may influence the success of its future market and non-market strategies. Further research should aim to disentangle those complex stakeholder relationship networks and offer insights into the strategies used by MNEs to influence and shape the institutional contexts in which they operate. It is of particular interest to examine the coordinated action of MNEs and other stakeholders, such as NGOs, that can significantly contribute to the ability of MNEs to enforce their will in a given market or country, while taking into account and addressing a wider range of interests. For example, in its 2005 General Business Principles, Royal Dutch Shell plc, the global group of energy and petrochemicals companies, stated this bridging of business and broader interests as follows: 'As part of the Business Principles, we commit to contribute to sustainable development. This requires balancing short- and long-term interests, integrating economic, environmental and social considerations into business decision making.'

FIRM-LEVEL CHANGES

From a Single Sequential and Linear Process of International Expansion to Numerous Viable Paths and Positions

Historically, international business has been defined as 'any firm that engages in international trade or investment' (Hill, 2003, p. 29). Studies have used different measures to capture a firm's degree of internationalization, such as the percentage of foreign sales over total sales, or the size of investment and labor in foreign countries. In their seminal paper, 'The Internationalization Process of Firms – a Model of Knowledge Development and Increasing Foreign Market Commitments', Johanson and Valhne (1977) outlined a sequential perspective of a firm's internationalization process. Based on the evidence they had collected, they concluded that companies follow a stepwise process of increasing commitments in international markets that starts with irregular exports, followed by regular exports. The process continues with the opening of commercial subsidiaries in host markets and then proceeds with the establishment of production subsidiaries.

Complementary to the sequential perspective of a firm's internationaliz-ation process is Johanson and Wiedersheim-Paul's (1975) notion of psychic distance, or 'the sum of factors preventing the flow of information from and to the market'. That notion helps explain why companies tend to start their international expansion from countries that are at a smaller psychic distance, followed by more psychically distant markets. Since then, the IS literature has devoted little attention to the processes of firm internationalization (Vermeulen and Barkema, 2002), with the 'Uppsala Model' remaining a dominant framework in both teaching and research.

Thus, despite criticism of the sequential model, the field has come up with a limited number of alternatives to it. Observation of the strategic behaviors of diverse international actors, from MNEs to born-global firms, as well as firms that distribute the activities of their value chain across different countries to those that concentrate them in a limited number of specific locations, suggest that there are multiple viable internationalization paths and milestone positions along these paths. Hence, it is important to understand and depict heterogeneity in firms' international behavior (Koza et al., 2004). The arena of wireless telecommunication providers, with cases as diverse as Japanese NTT DoCoMo and UK-born Vodafone, is an example of such dissimilar internationalization trajectories.

In this context, we argue, the notions of 'path' and 'position' acquire specific significance for the IS field. An internationalization 'path' represents the sequence of actions and directions followed by a company in the process of internationalization. A company's internationalization path involves decisions and compromises regarding what resources and capabilities to build, which can significantly alter the set of options available to it over time. A 'position', in turn, is a milestone on that path and accounts for the company's level of internationalization at any given moment in time in terms of breadth and depth of activities in foreign markets. Organizations competing in the international arena could experience equifinality; that is, they may follow different paths, yet over time reach the same or similar international positions.

The understanding and assessment of how and why companies make particular strategic bets, and how, through different internationalization paths, they could achieve comparable international positions can shed light on the implications and results that the use of different processes has on the firm's internationalization. Future research should examine these different paths and the internationalization-related results to which they can lead.

From Entry Strategies to a Portfolio Management of a Firm's International Activities

Studies on entry strategies have abounded in the IS literature. They have examined alternative entry modes and the criteria used in the modes' selection, as well as the results achieved through their implementation. Acquisitions, joint ventures or alliances, as well as greenfield subsidiaries are different means of entry.

Along with the thoroughly addressed issue of entry modes in the process of foreign expansion, there is a parallel and equally important phenomenon of exits and divestitures away from unprofitable or non-strategic foreign activity locations. Unlike the volumes written on entry modes, however, there continues to be a dearth of research on international exits and divestitures. The lack of balance in terms of the attention given to entry and exit when studying a firm's international activities is probably linked to the positive value that is usually assigned to growth and expansion and the negative connotations associated with the decision to reduce size and scope.

We argue that, for IS scholarship and practice, it is essential not only that both international entry and exit decisions are studied, but also that they are examined together, as interconnected and complementary parts of a company's overall international portfolio. If we push this line of reasoning further, this portfolio view needs also to account for decisions that have to do with activities, such as offshoring and offshore outsourcing.

As Chang (1996) argued, in the corporate strategy literature 'diversification and divestment [...] have been treated as separate and independent areas of study' and so 'the temporal sequence of entry and exit activities has remained unexplored' (p. 587). Decisions to acquire and divest businesses and subsidiaries in foreign locations and in the home market shape the evolution of a corporation's scope and have implications for the way the corporation creates value. For example, in early 2007, while exiting from some of its US-based operations, Hershey Co, the largest US candy maker, was reported to be opening a new factory in Monterrey, Mexico, thus coordinating its entry–exit activities. Similarly, at the end of 2006, the French car manufacturer Peugeot set up a new factory in Slovakia, after closing down a factory in the British Midlands. Therefore, we think that the IS diversification decisions need to be studied in a longitudinal and dynamic context (Pennings et al., 1994; Bergh, 1997) and in relationship to other critical decisions that affect the international scope of a firm.

From Modularity of the Internal Value Chain across Locations to Morphing in a Network of Virtual Relations

Scholars of IS have argued that as firms develop their international presence, in order to maximize the creation and appropriation of value, they may choose to distribute their activities across locations. This is a process usually orchestrated by a company's headquarters. As a company increases its international presence and gains international competitive advantage, its internal value chain is reconfigured and divided organizationally into more or less autonomous units that interact with one another. Some companies opt for value chain configurations whereby each local subsidiary replicates the full value chain in its local context, while others choose to place different activities of the value chain in diverse locations.

In recent times, there has been a wealth of opportunities for international new ventures and MNEs to offshore part of their activities, thus remaining focused and in control of the core or value-adding activities of their value chain. In such cases, a firm's international activities move towards a virtual network of partnerships, in which a company may have less ownership and direct control over its international operations. These practices suggest a move from a modularity-based view of the value chain across locations towards a morphing-based view of the MNE.

According to dictionary definitions, modularity is a feature of a system that has been split into sub-systems that interact with each other, while morphing originates in metamorphosis and is about the transformation of one image into another. As defined by Rindova and Kotha (2001), 'continuous morphing' captures the ongoing transformations through which a firm regenerates its competitive advantage. For example, Yahoo! morphed from an internet search engine into an internet portal. For large multinationals, offshoring requires an entirely new set of organizational capabilities 'as they morph into more porous web-based network structures. As these dynamics unfold, the role of location may diminish' (Lewin and Peeters, 2006b, p. 234). Hence, 'In the longer run, corporate management is faced again with the first question. Is it indeed more efficient to perform autonomous activities inside the MNE, or should such activities be spun off?' (Rugman and Verbeke, 2003, p. 133).

How do companies develop these new capabilities to manage a distributed network of activities? How do they organize and manage the coordination of these activities? Is the traditional role of headquarters modified in the new situation? These are just some of the questions IS research could explore in the future to improve knowledge of how MNE organizations evolve.

From the Power of the HQ to the Degrees of Freedom and the Impact of Subsidiaries

Several studies in the International Strategy field have centered on how MNEs are managed. Although such studies cover a wide range of topics, the analysis of the way subsidiaries are run has been historically neglected. More than 25 years ago, Prahalad and Doz (1981) illustrated the increasing power of some subsidiaries that allowed them to make decisions that 'they believe are in the best interests of the corporation as a whole, but not always in conformance with the expressed wishes of head office managers' (p. 2).

The parent company has continued to be the focus of attention in the field, probably because firm-specific advantages have been considered to originate there (Rugman and Verbeke, 1992). At the end of the 1990s, most of the literature on subsidiary management had focused mainly on 'understanding aspects of subsidiary context (how the subsidiary related to its parent, its corporate network, its local environment) [rather] than of understanding what really happens *inside* the subsidiary' (Birkinshaw et al., 1998, p. 223; italics in the original). However, critical knowledge in the MNE is not always developed by its headquarters. Subsidiaries can be a source of capabilities and expertise that can be transferred to the parent company as well as to other subsidiaries. For example, in the case of the Spanish-born telecommunications MNE, Telefónica, knowledge and experience in deregulation processes was generated by its subsidiaries in Latin America and then applied to its home country operations, as Spain's telecommunications market entered deregulation at a later stage.

Unlike the relatively small amount of attention paid to subsidiary management in IS research, it has proven to be a critical issue for managers of MNEs, even those who aim to reach the top in their headquarters, since in a large number of cases they are required to first demonstrate their talent at the subsidiary level.

Part of the difficulty in running subsidiaries stems from the fact that they rarely control the full range of activities in an MNE's value chain. In their performance, there are usually a number of areas in which they depend on subsidiaries in third countries or services provided by the company's center. Furthermore, with a long-term perspective in mind, the question 'Is it indeed more efficient to perform autonomous activities inside the MNE, or should such activities be spun off?' (Rugman and Verbeke, 2003) remains open to the corporate center. The spread of practices, such as offshoring or outsourcing, for example, is changing the configuration of MNEs towards a virtual network of international operations, in which the subsidiary rather than the parent takes control and responsibility for management. In such scenarios, the way subsidiaries are run, and how they can contribute to the competitive advantage of the multinational company, are critical questions that call for further exploration.

From International Human Resource Management to Global Talent Management

International Human Resource Management (IHRM), another distinctive stream in the IS field, has argued that people are the basis for the development and sustainability of a firm's competitive advantage in the international arena. Thus MNEs have been pushing forward expatriation and repatriation practices as a means of transferring key processes and resources from headquarters to subsidiaries as well as of maintaining control.

A number of scholars in the IHRM area have studied the advantages and disadvantages of establishing a local CEO in the subsidiary versus a foreign CEO coming from headquarters. While a local CEO helps the subsidiary in gaining local legitimacy, an expatriate CEO facilitates the coordination and implementation of practices from headquarters to the subsidiary (Gong, 2003). In addition, a large body of literature has examined the challenges involved in expatriating management: from how to find the best candidates and their adaptation and acceptance in a subsidiary, to how to relocate them once their assignment has finished.

Certain regions and countries in the world have benefited from their ability to attract and retain talent. A recent article in *The Economist* highlighted the importance of that ability in sustaining the competitiveness and historical success of the United States, in light of the increasing opportunities some of these people may encounter in their countries of origin:

> Half the Americans who won Nobel prizes in physics in the past seven years were born abroad. More than half the people with PhDs working in America are immigrants. A quarter of Silicon Valley companies were started by Indians and Chinese. Intel, Sun Microsystems and Google were all founded or co-founded by immigrants. But now India and China are sucking back their expats, and America's European competitors have woken up to the importance of retaining their talent. To cap it all, the immigration authorities are making life harder for foreigners. (Prestowitz, 2006, p. 8)

In a flattening world, Friedman (2005) had argued, people won't need to emigrate to have access to opportunities. That could lead to a shift from a demand-driven to a supply-based model of talent management.

MNEs need to foster practices that help identify talent around the world and develop structures and systems to attract and retain it. Thus, offshoring becomes 'a giant component in sourcing and locating human capital anywhere in the world' (Lewin and Peeters, 2006a, p. 24). However, MNEs are not alone in this '*global talent management war*'. Other actors in the global arena, such as international new ventures or NGOs, are increasingly competing for and attracting good talent. Moreover, intermediary companies also connect MNEs to a large pool of independent talent distributed around the world. This is the case of Innocentive, for example, which connects large companies that need solutions to particular research problems to a network it has built with over 100 000 researchers, working in different capacities and institutions around the world.

In our peripheral vision of the field's future, IS has to move from a focus on the management of human resources by MNEs across countries and locations towards the attraction and grooming of the best talent wherever it may be globally. Hence, as explained by Pfeffer (2005), 'Executive search firms increasingly share both candidates and job openings internationally in order to locate the best talent, no matter where it's to be found' (p. 56). In this move, people and talent may displace countries as the focal base for human resources practices.

RESEARCH FRONTIERS BASED ON INTERNATIONAL STRATEGY'S NEW VISTAS

This chapter has employed the metaphor of peripheral vision to identify and advance avenues for future research in IS. To foster the pursuit of the suggested new vistas, in this section we argue for the need for a forward-looking, dynamic, phenomena-based, multidimensional, and eclectic perspective of the IS field. We believe these characteristics constitute the basis for a relevant and rigorous research agenda in the area.

IS research has developed a substantial body of work that scrutinizes the challenges faced by MNEs. This research has been fertile ground for the development of frameworks and theories that advance the understanding of behaviors and structures in MNEs. Although we acknowledge the importance and insights brought by those frameworks and theories, at a certain point in time these may become obsolete. At times, the long research and publishing cycles result in ideas that, by the time they reach their audience, have to confront changes in context that may reduce their validity. We believe that, without renouncing rigor, future IS research should aim at being forward-looking, identifying problems and issues 'ahead of their time'. In this way the field could offer theoretical developments of emerging phenomena related to the variety of actors involved in international business.

We also call for a more dynamic view of the issues that constitute the core of IS's current and future agenda. Management research has been strongly influenced by neoclassical economics with its search for equilibrium. However, 'equilibrium can be understood only within a dynamic framework that explains how it comes about (if in fact it does)' (Young, 1998, p. 4). Scholars in the IS field should put their efforts into understanding the contingencies or levers that can disrupt these equilibria. In this way, we will be able to develop a more dynamic view of IS that allows us to understand the evolution of international strategies (Porter, 1991), as well as their sustainability.

The dynamic view and its theoretical constructs will continue to be challenged by the realities of all kinds of organizations that play a role in the international arena. To live up to the challenge, the field needs to continuously evaluate its theories and frameworks through the prism of changing context and firms' behaviour. This makes us suggest that the field should maintain a phenomena-based approach that allows it to keep up with an international arena that is constantly in motion.

By its very nature, IS is devoted to the examination of multidimensional phenomena possibly more than any other area of scholarly research. Actors developing activities in more than one country may experience external influences from a variety of significant players, such as supra-national institutions, national institutions, and major stakeholder groups. Therefore, to address the complexity in which international organizations develop their strategies, IS research needs to offer multidimensional approaches capable of coping with the existing complexity.

Finally, we believe that there is no single best theory that could serve as a foundation for IS research. Rather, IS should draw on an eclectic mix of theories, each allowing us to gain different, yet complementary, insights into the complex phenomena at the heart of the IS research agenda. Together, those pieces of insight will help us to gain a better understanding and appreciation of the dynamic, multidimensional puzzle that IS scholarship has set itself to resolve.

REFERENCES

Acs, Z., R. Morck, J.M. Shaver and B. Yeung (1997), 'The internationalization of small and medium-sized enterprises: a policy perspective', *Small Business Economics*, **9**, 7–19.
Aguiar, M., A. Bhattacharya, T. Bradtke, P. Cotte, S. Dertnig, M. Meyer, D.C. Michael and H. Sirkin (2006), 'The new global challengers: how 100 top companies from rapidly developing economies are changing the world', The Boston Consulting Group Report, Boston, MA.
Ayal, I. and J. Zif (1979), 'Market expansion strategies in multinational marketing', *Journal of Marketing*, **43** (2), 84–94.
Baron, D.P. (1995), 'Integrated strategy: market and nonmarket components', *California Management Review*, **37**, 47–65.

Bartlett, C.A. and S. Ghoshal (1998), *Managing across Borders: The Transnational Solution*, 2nd edn, London: Random House.

Bergh, D.D. (1997), 'Predicting divestiture of unrelated acquisitions: an integrative model of ex-ante conditions', *Strategic Management Journal*, **18** (9), 715–31.

Birkinshaw, J., N. Hood and S. Jonsson (1998), 'Building firm-specific advantages in multinational corporations: the role of subsidiary initiative', *Strategic Management Journal*, **19** (3), 221–41.

Buckley, P.J. and P.N. Ghauri (2004), 'Globalisation, economic geography and the strategy of multinational enterprises', *Journal of International Business Studies*, **35**, 81–98.

Buckley, P. and D.R. Lessard (2005), 'Regaining the edge for international business research', *Journal of International Business Studies*, **36**, 595–9.

Cairncross, F. (1997), *The Death of Distance*, Boston, MA: Harvard Business School Press.

Chang, S.J. (1996), 'An evolutionary perspective on diversification and corporate restructuring: entry, exit, and economic performance during 1981–89', *Strategic Management Journal*, **17** (8), 587–611.

Dobrev, S., T.Y. Kim and G. Carroll (2003), 'Shifting gears, shifting niches: organizational inertia and change in the evolution of the U.S. automobile industry, 1885–1981', *Organization Science*, **14**, 264–82.

Dunning, J.H. (1977), 'Trade, location of economic activity and the MNE: a search for an eclectic approach', in B. Ohlin, P. Hesselborn and M. Wijkman (eds), *The International Allocation of Economic Activity*, London: Macmillan, pp. 395–418

Dunning, J.H. (1988), 'The eclectic paradigm of international production: a restatement and some possible extensions', *Journal of International Business Studies*, **19** (1), 1–31.

Florida, R. (2005), 'The world is spiky', *The Atlantic Monthly*, October, available online at http://www.creativeclass.org/acrobat/TheWorldIsSpiky.pdf

Friedman, T. (2005), *The World is Flat*, New York: Farrar, Straus and Giroux.

Ghemawat, P. (2003), 'Semi-globalization and international business strategy', *Journal of International Business Studies*, **34** (2), 138–52.

Gong, Y.P. (2003), 'Subsidiary staffing in multinational enterprises: agency, resources, and performance', *Academy of Management Journal*, **46** (6), 728–39.

Gray, J. (2005), 'The world is round', *The New York Review of Books*, **52** (13), 13–15.

Henisz, W.J., B.A. Zelner and M.F. Guillén (2005), 'The worldwide diffusion of market-oriented infrastructure reform, 1977–1999', *American Sociological Review*, **70** (6), 871–97.

Hill, C.W.L. (2003), *International Business: Competing in the Global Marketplace*, New York: McGraw-Hill.

Hofstede, G. (1980), *Culture's Consequences: International Differences in Work-related Values*. Beverly Hills, CA: Sage.

Hoskisson, R., L. Eden, C. Lau and M. Wright (2000), 'Strategy in emerging economies', *Academy of Management Journal*, **43** (3), 249–67.

Hymer, S. (1976), *The International Operations of National Firms: A Study of Direct Investment*. Boston, MA: MIT Press

Johanson, J. and J. Vahlne (1977), 'The internationalization process of the firm: a model of knowledge development and increasing foreign commitments', *Journal of International Business Studies*, **8** (1), 23–32.

Johanson, J. and F. Wiedersheim-Paul (1975), 'The internationalization process of the firm: four Swedish case studies', *Journal of Management Studies*, **12** (3), 305–22.

Kalish, S., V. Mahajan and E. Muller (1995), 'Waterfall and sprinkler: new product strategies in competitive global markets', *International Journal of Research in Marketing*, **12**, 105–19.

Koza, M., S. Svejenova and L. Vives (2004), 'Wireless apostles and emperors: strategies for domination in a global arena', in A. Ariño, P. Ghemawat and J.E. Ricart (eds), *Creating Value through International Strategy*, London: Palgrave Macmillan, pp. 238–53.

Lewin, A.Y. and C. Peeters (2006a), 'The top-line allure of offshoring', *Harvard Business Review*, **84** (3), 22–4.

Lewin, A.Y. and C. Peeters (2006b), 'Offshoring work: business hype or the onset of fundamental transformation?', *Long Range Planning*, **39** (3), 221–39.

Melin, L. (1992), 'Internationalization as a strategy process', *Strategic Management Journal*, **13**, 99–118.

Noda, T. and D.J. Collis (2001), 'The evolution of intraindustry firm heterogeneity: insights from a process study', *Academy of Management Journal*, **44** (4), 897–925.

Oviatt, B. and P.P. McDougall (1994), 'Toward a theory of international new ventures', *Journal of International Business Studies*, **25** (1), 45–64.

Peng, M.W. (2004), 'Identifying the big question in international business research', *Journal of International Business Studies*, **35**, 99–108.

Pennings, J.M., H. Barkema and S. Douma (1994), 'Organizational learning and diversification', *Academy of Management Journal*, **37**, 608–41.

Pfeffer, J. (2005), 'Recruiting for the global talent war', *Business 2.0*, 1 August, 56.

Porter, M. (1991), 'Towards a dynamic theory of strategy', *Strategic Management Journal*, **12**, 95–117.

Prahalad, C.K. and Y.L. Doz (1981), 'An approach to strategic control in MNCs', *Sloan Management Review*, **22** (4), 5–14.

Prahalad, C.K. and S. Hart (2002), 'The fortune at the bottom of the pyramid', *Strategy + Business*, Issue 26, pp. 54–67.

Prestowitz, C.V. (2006), 'A survey of talent: nightmare scenarios', *The Economist*, 7 October, pp. 8–9.

Ricart, J., M. Enright, P. Ghemawat, S. Hart and T. Khanna (2004), 'New frontiers in international strategy', *Journal of International Business Studies*, **35**, 175–200.

Rindova, V. and S. Kotha (2001), 'Continuous morphing – competing through dynamic capabilities, form, and function', *Academy of Management Journal*, **44** (6), 1263–80.

Rugman, A.M. (2005), *The Regional Multinationals*, Cambridge: Cambridge University Press

Rugman, A.M. and A. Verbeke (1992), 'A note on the transnational solution and the transaction cost theory of multinational strategic management', *Journal of International Business Studies*, **23** (4), 761–71.

Rugman, A.M. and A. Verbeke (2003), 'Extending the theory of the multinational enterprise: internalization and strategic management perspectives', *Journal of International Business Studies*, **34** (2), 125–37.

Tallman, S., M. Jenkins, N. Henry and S. Pinch (2004), 'Knowledge, clusters and competitive advantage', *Academy of Management Review*, **29** (2), 258–71.

Teegen, H., J.P. Doh and S. Vachani (2004), 'The importance of nongovernmental organizations (NGOs) in global governance and value creation: an international business research agenda', *Journal of International Business Studies*, **35** (6), 463–83.

Vahlne, J.E. and F. Wiedersheim-Paul (1973), 'Economic distance: model and empirical investigation', in E. Hornell, J.E. Vahlne and F. Wiedersheim-Paul (eds), *Export and Foreign Establishments*, Uppsala: University of Uppsala, pp. 81–159.

Vemon, R. (1966), 'International investment and international trade in the product cycle', *Quarterly Journal of Economics*, **80** (May), 190–207.

Vermeulen F. and H. Barkema (2002), 'Pace, rhythm, and scope: process dependence in building a profitable multinational corporation', *Strategic Management Journal*, **23**, 637–53.

Young, H.P. (1998), *Individual Strategy and Social Structure: An Evolutionary Theory of Institutions*, Princeton, NJ: Princeton University Press.

2. Geographic diversification: risk reduction or operational flexibility

Seung-Hyun Lee and Chris Changwha Chung

The dominant characteristic of the global economy is uncertainty. Macroeconomic changes cause unpredictable and fundamental shifts in market demand, causing multinational corporations (MNCs) to rush to adjust or even to radically reconfigure their international investments to sustain competitive advantage (Allen and Pantzalis, 1996; Kogut and Kulatilaka, 1994; Tang and Tikoo, 1999). The challenge for the MNC is to reconfigure its current investments to address unknown future contingencies. Indeed, managing uncertainty is one of the primary objectives of MNCs that operate across international borders (Ghoshal, 1987). MNCs may be able to manage uncertainties by ensuring that dispersed foreign subsidiary operations are collectively more successful than if each were acting individually. In this way, MNCs can take advantage of flexibility and respond advantageously to unknown future changes in the environment (Foss, 1998).

Research on MNCs emphasizes that firms geographically diversify to either reduce risk through global risk diversification or exploit upside potential through operational flexibility (Campa, 1994; Kim et al., 1993). The risk reduction literature argues that MNCs can reduce the risk of uncertainty by not having all their investments in one country (Agmon and Lessard, 1977; Hisey and Caves, 1985). When an MNC is dispersed across multiple countries, risk in one of its subsidiaries only requires the MNC to divest that subsidiary. With this structure, MNCs with more dispersed subsidiaries enjoy greater risk reduction benefits than MNCs that have concentrated subsidiary locations or MNCs that compete only in domestic markets. On the other hand, real options theory suggests that MNCs have the opportunity to shift production from one subsidiary to other subsidiaries when uncertainty prevails (Allen and Pantzalis, 1996; Tong and Reuer, 2007), without closing the subsidiary that is in trouble. The real options literature emphasizes the value of operational flexibility under conditions of uncertainty (Reuer and Leiblein, 2000; Tang and Tikoo,

1999). Thus each theory ascribes different benefits to the dispersed foreign subsidiary structure. Past research suggests that diversification benefits are created by reducing performance variance in the portfolio of subsidiaries; real options flexibility benefits come from shifting production from one location to another (Hisey and Caves, 1985; Tang and Tikoo, 1999).

Past research, however, has not simultaneously examined these two concepts; thus it has been unclear whether MNCs geographically diversify to reduce performance variability via risk diversification or to increase operational flexibility by shifting production. On the one hand, geographic risk diversification theory suggests that MNCs will close their subsidiary operations in economically troubled areas when demand decreases in these regions (Benito, 1997, 2005). On the other hand, MNCs may shift production to subsidiaries in economically troubled locations when sudden currency devaluations lower their costs of production (Allen and Pantzalis, 1996; Kogut and Kulatilaka, 1994).

Furthermore, previous research has been restricted to examining the performance benefit of the geographically diversified subsidiary structure, rather than examining the actual behavior of the MNC (e.g. Allen and Pantzalis, 1996; Kim et al., 1993; Reuer and Leiblein, 2000; Tang and Tikoo, 1999). For example, Allen and Pantzalis (1996) and Tang and Tikoo (1999) used stock market performance to measure the benefits of having geographically dispersed subsidiaries. However, we cannot assess whether the relative performance benefit arises more from geographic risk diversification or from operational flexibility, unless we examine the actual behavior of the MNC. In particular, it is difficult to discern the operating mechanism of the MNC by only investigating aggregated performance measures such as stock market performance and return on sales. We attempt to address this research gap by examining the actual behavior of the MNC at the subsidiary level during times of uncertainty. In the next section, we examine how the predictions of real options theory differ from those of geographic risk diversification theory.

GEOGRAPHIC DIVERSIFICATION AND SUBSIDIARY DIVESTMENT

Extant research suggests that global diversification is often propelled by either the risk reduction logic of geographic risk diversification theory or the operational flexibility logic of real options theory (Campa, 1994; Kim et al., 1993).[1] Firms may diversify internationally to minimize the negative effects of fluctuating supply and demand in any one market and thus reduce the variability of their earnings (Mansi and Reeb, 2002; Rugman, 1979).

Firms may also establish subsidiaries in different countries so they can shift production to more favorable areas when conditions in any one location become uncertain or unstable in order to try to maximize earnings over time (Allen and Pantzalis, 1996; Tang and Tikoo, 1999). The following section compares the differing relationships between international geographic diversification and subsidiary divestment. Here, subsidiary divestment is defined as the closure or sale of a subsidiary by the foreign parent firm. This definition has been widely used in the foreign divestment literature (Benito, 1997, 2005; Boddewyn, 1979; Kindleberger, 1969; Li, 1995; Torneden, 1975).

Geographic Risk Diversification Theory

A sizeable literature has examined the effect of international diversification on performance (Grant et al., 1988; Kim et al., 1993; Tallman and Li, 1996). In general, a firm's level of international diversification is typically reflected in the number of different countries in which it operates. In the presence of barriers to capital flows, MNCs have an advantage over single-country firms in their ability to diversify risks across economic settings (Agmon and Lessard, 1977; Errunza and Senbet, 1984). An MNC's configuration of internationally dispersed operations can contemporaneously reduce its risk by offsetting the increased risk it is exposed to in one market by potentially reduced risk in others. Therefore, given non-correlated economic cycles, increased operations across overseas markets may help the MNC diversify its risk. Geographically diversified firms may benefit from more stable earnings and less variable revenue streams, compared to domestic competitors that do not have such an efficient means of lowering risk (Hisey and Caves, 1985). In principle, the notion of geographic risk diversification theory is analogous to not putting all one's eggs in one basket. In this sense, geographic risk diversification theory is based on a financial risk reduction model (Agmon and Lessard, 1977; Mansi and Reeb, 2002). In an uncertain global market, firms diversify internationally to reduce risk by minimizing performance variance (Dess et al., 1995; Levi and Sarnat, 1970). Rugman (1979) studied Fortune 500 firms and found that indeed as international geographic diversification increased, earnings variability, and hence risk, decreased.

In finance, dynamic asset allocation is an important concept in portfolio risk diversification. Dynamic asset allocation has been argued to be crucial for controlling and balancing the overall risk of the global portfolio (Grinold and Kahn, 1999; Madura, 1996). Similarly, strategic management scholars approach corporate investment and divestment decisions from a portfolio perspective and argue that the portfolio of company assets should be continuously under review, both financially and strategically (Chow and Hamilton, 1993; Duhaime and Grant, 1984; Hamilton and Chow, 1993).

Most importantly, and directly related to this study, international business scholars also suggest that the MNC needs to control and balance the overall risk to which it is exposed by periodically reconfiguring its portfolio of foreign subsidiaries in response to environmental changes (Benito, 1997; Benito and Welch, 1997; Boddewyn, 1979; Van Den Bulcke et al., 1979; Wilson, 1980). Boddewyn (1979) suggested that for every two foreign subsidiaries added to an MNC network, one is divested. More recent studies have found a similar ratio of foreign investment to divestment. These include Padmanabhan's study (1993) of UK MNCs; Barkema et al.'s study (1996) of Dutch MNCs; and Benito's study (1997) of Norwegian MNCs.

In terms of dynamic asset allocation, keeping a troubled subsidiary open in a country with drastic economic problems creates more troublesome risk than eliminating the subsidiary. For example, Japanese MNCs experienced dramatically reduced demand in countries stricken by the Asian economic crisis of the late 1990s (Chung and Beamish, 2005). The economic devastation was so severe that the region was considered a dead economy (*Euromoney*, 1998). In such circumstances, the value of having a subsidiary may be reduced dramatically and the MNC may reach a point where the risk of maintaining the subsidiary is beyond a tolerable level (Benito and Welch, 1997; Drummond, 1995). Given these circumstances, MNCs that had undertaken geographic diversification to reduce risk would have closed their subsidiaries in the troubled area because there was no benefit in retaining them (Benito, 1997, 2005; Boddewyn, 1979; Van Den Bulcke et al., 1979; Wilson, 1980). In these crisis-stricken countries, the goodwill attached to real assets was close to zero, if not negative, and it would have made sense to divest the assets (Clarke and Gall, 1987; Duhaime and Grant, 1984). The experience of Japanese firms in the Asian economic crisis illustrates that when an MNC is highly geographically diversified, it enjoys more diversification benefits from its non-troubled subsidiaries than its operations in crisis-stricken countries; thus the MNC has little incentive to maintain troubled operations. This logic is in line with the divestiture literature, which states that environmental changes lower the benefits of diversification, thus making divestiture one of the most viable corporate actions for diversified MNCs (Borde et al., 1998; Johnson, 1996; Thompson and Wright, 1995). This is why past research argues that divestiture is a reversal of past diversification (Benito and Welch, 1997; Haynes et al., 2003; Mueller, 1969).

The propensity for a geographically diversified MNC to divest a troubled subsidiary operation arises in part from its degree of freedom (Benito, 2005). In principle, when MNCs diversify, the risk of the overall portfolio is supposed to be less than the weighted sum of the risks contributed by each individual subsidiary (Grubel, 1968; Mansi and Reeb, 2002). To paraphrase a popular cliché, the whole is *less* than the sum of its parts.

This portion of risk that disappears in the process of constructing the portfolio is called diversifiable risk (Mikhail and Shawky, 1979). The risk that remains is called nondiversifiable risk (Mikhail and Shawky, 1979). An MNC can only diversify its diversifiable risk up to a certain point. After this point, only non-diversifiable risk exists. Therefore, the most cost-effective approach for an MNC is to configure its global portfolio so that it diversifies away diversifiable risk. There will be higher pressure to divest the troubled subsidiary when the benefit of diversification is questionable because of lower performance or when the benefits of diversification are not well understood (Benito and Welch, 1997; Chang, 1996). When the MNC's global portfolio moves closer to the maximum level of diversifiable risk, the marginal benefit of adding more subsidiary operations dramatically declines at an increasing rate, and the marginal cost of keeping the additional subsidiary greatly increases because there is only a small benefit to be realized by holding onto these additional operations (Agmon and Lessard, 1977). Beyond the maximum level of diversifiable risk diversification, the marginal benefit of additional subsidiary operations becomes null and the cost of maintaining the additional subsidiaries becomes prohibitively expensive. Therefore, a highly diversified MNC is more likely to divest its troubled subsidiary operations – it simply costs less to divest than to maintain (Benito, 1997, 2005; Boddewyn, 1979; Van Den Bulcke et al., 1979). In contrast, closing a subsidiary greatly reduces the benefits of global risk diversification for less globally diversified firms. As such, the more diversified the MNC's portfolio, the greater the degree of freedom it has to rationalize troubled subsidiary operations in crisis-stricken countries. In sum, we propose that from the geographic risk diversification perspective, more globally diversified MNCs are more likely to divest their troubled subsidiary operations in crisis-stricken countries than less globally diversified MNCs.

Real Options Theory

The operational flexibility that arises from shifting production is different from the risk reduction that arises from investing in geographic risk diversification. From the geographic risk diversification standpoint, a portfolio of international indices should theoretically create the same return as a portfolio of MNC stocks. However, Mikhail and Shawky (1979) found that the actual portfolio of MNC stocks generated a higher return than the international indices. The returns for both investments should have been the same, unless there are other benefits to diversified subsidiaries. Geographic risk diversification theory does not explain Mikhail and Shawky's (1979) findings, suggesting that firms have other reasons for operating subsidiaries in diversified international locations. Their decision may be explained by the real options logic of operational flexibility (Bowman, 1980).

Real options theory arises from finance and is applied to strategic management; it focuses on the real business applications of financial option models (Bowman and Hurry, 1993). In financial options, upside potential increases and downside risk declines as uncertainty increases (Fama and Miller, 1972). This logic also applies to real options theory; the more the variance in possible outcomes, the higher the value of the option investment (McGrath, 1999; Sanchez, 1993). Early real options studies applied complex mathematical formulae to individual projects in order to derive a specific dollar value for the degree of flexibility afforded by a particular real option (Majd and Pindyck, 1987; Trigeorgis and Mason, 1987). As the field developed, real options research moved beyond valuing individual projects to promoting real options thinking as a normative framework for corporate strategy. In particular, real options thinking helps firms battle (McGrath, 1997), capitalize on (Amram and Kulatilaka, 1999), and even befriend, uncertainty. As Coy said, make uncertainty 'your friend, not your enemy' (1999, p. 118). One of the main implications of applying real options theory to multinational corporate strategy is that it suggests that the firm can benefit from geographically dispersed subsidiaries by being able to shift production among subsidiary locations in uncertain times (Allen and Pantzalis, 1996). Thus the MNC can benefit by having the right, but not the obligation, to shift production across borders as market environments change.

MNCs with subsidiaries in various locations can benefit by shifting their operations across borders in response to environmental changes such as fluctuating foreign exchange rates or abrupt changes in factor and product market conditions (Kogut, 1985; Tang and Tikoo, 1999). When a currency sharply depreciates in value and demand in the region also dramatically slows, the MNC can shift production to the newly lower cost location and export products to other more lucrative high-demand markets. For example, at the onset of the Asian economic crisis, devalued currencies in crisis-stricken countries reduced the costs of labor and locally purchased inputs in Japanese yen, while increasing the competitiveness of local export sectors. For example, Matsushita upgraded its export-oriented operations in Malaysia, and Patlite (a Japanese indicator-light manufacturer) took advantage of the collapsed Indonesian rupiah to set up or expand export-oriented manufacturing facilities in Indonesia (Lim, 1999).

The main advantage of the MNC structure is that it allows firms to switch operations from one location to another, an option that is not available to rivals with purely domestic operations. The MNC also benefits from intra-firm trade when one subsidiary gets the opportunity to reduce its production costs. Little (1986, p. 46) argues that firms with production facilities in many countries

> possess an extra degree of flexibility in adjusting to a new competition situation. These multinationals can ... expand output where relative production costs are falling ... Accordingly, intra-firm trade might be expected to adjust more quickly to an exchange rate change than would trade between unaffiliated and noncooperating firms.

Little's (1986) argument holds weight, given that intra-firm trade currently accounts for one-third of world trade (Tang and Madan, 2003). Approximately 40 percent of US trade stems from the transfer of goods among subsidiaries (Kogut, 1985); in 1999, 28.6 percent of Japanese trade was intra-firm (Kiyota and Urata, 2005; OECD, 2002). MNC intra-firm trading behavior is consistent with McGrath's (1997, p. 975) argument that 'the distinguishing characteristics of an options approach lies in firms making investments that confer the ability to select an outcome only if it is favorable'. For example, during the Asian economic crisis, Asea Brown Boveri (ABB) restructured its global intra-firm network to reduce productive capacity in high-cost Europe and expand it in newly low-cost Asian countries. ABB's Malaysian unit conducted project engineering work for Latin American plants – work previously handled by ABB's Swiss unit. Japanese MNCs such as Matsushita and Hitachi also moved their research and development (R&D) operations to facilities in Malaysia and Singapore, where relatively less expensive, English-speaking, and Western-trained engineers help to integrate global R&D activities with other subsidiaries in the global network (Lim, 1999). In each of these instances, the MNCs took advantage of their ability to shift production to lower-cost venues. Based on the real options rationale above, we propose that the greater the extent of an MNC's international geographic diversification, the less likely it will be to divest a subsidiary in a crisis-stricken country.

JOINT OWNERSHIP AND SUBSIDIARY DIVESTMENT

A number of MNC scholars have emphasized that there are obstacles to realizing the benefits of multinational operations (e.g., Rugman and Verbeke, 2004; Tong and Reuer, 2007). As Kogut (1989, p. 388) stated, 'having the potential to exercise is a far cry from having the management system to do it'. Unlike a global portfolio of pure financial instruments, the risk reduction benefit of geographic diversification does not automatically accrue to MNCs, simply by spreading subsidiary operations in different countries; the MNCs also have to establish mechanisms to reduce risk during times of uncertainty

(Burgman, 1996; Reeb et al., 1998). Similarly, the flexibility benefit of real options does not arise automatically. An MNC that establishes subsidiaries in many different countries may be overloaded by information processing and overwhelmed by the complexity of coordinating different operations. This may reduce the operational flexibility benefits that the MNC had hoped to gain from diversifying internationally (Doukas and Pantzalis, 2003; Roth et al., 1991; Tong and Reuer, 2007). To date, these organizational constraints have been under-researched.

The central tenet of geographic risk diversification theory is that dispersing subsidiaries across different locations diversifies the MNC's exposure to risk. In this model, the MNC decides the destiny of each subsidiary, case by case, based on whether the subsidiary helps diversify and reduce risk. Each subsidiary is viewed as part of a risk reduction mechanism, making joint ventures valuable because they require less coordination from MNC headquarters. The cooperative logic underlying joint venture arrangements enables the MNC to reduce risks in the global marketplace. Cooperating with other firms greatly helps MNCs to achieve the risk reduction benefits of diversifying geographically, but coordinating subsidiaries is more important for realizing operational flexibility. From the real options standpoint, an MNC has dispersed subsidiaries in order to take advantage of uncertainty by shifting production from one location to another (Tang and Tikoo, 1999), but production shifts can only occur when the subsidiaries are viewed as a whole, rather than individually (Kogut, 1985). We examine cooperation and coordination issues by looking at the relationship between joint ownership and subsidiary divestment, based on the two competing theoretical perspectives described earlier.

Geographic Risk Diversification Theory

Joint ownership in crisis-stricken countries
Earlier, we argued that there is a greater tendency for the MNC to divest its troubled subsidiaries in crisis-stricken countries during times of uncertainty. However, wholly-owned subsidiaries and joint ventures do not have the same likelihood of being divested. In the presence of environmental uncertainty, predictions of future environmental conditions are prone to error (North, 1990). In addition, foreign ventures experience higher failure rates because of the liability of foreignness (Hymer, 1976; Zaheer, 1995). Political risk research also shows that the liability of foreignness is a source of additional risk for MNCs in foreign countries (Brewer, 1983).

Strategic foresight regarding the likely incidence, instigators, severity, and type of environmental change leads MNCs to implement risk mitigation strategies to reduce the impact of environmental uncertainty on the viability

of foreign ventures. Risks can be mitigated by partnering with a local firm
that has better knowledge of managing in the host environment (Beamish
and Banks, 1987); therefore MNCs often form joint ventures with partners.
The international joint venture literature states that reducing risk is one of
the most important reasons for sharing ownership with partners (Root,
1988). During times of uncertainty, MNCs can buffer the negative impacts
of abrupt environmental change by sharing risk with their joint venture
partners (Anderson and Gatignon, 1986). This lower risk enables MNCs
to better tolerate joint venture subsidiaries during times of uncertainty
(Contractor and Lorange, 1988; Harrigan, 1985). Thus, joint ventures can
be viewed as a 'hedging vehicle' against environmental risks (Shan, 1991,
p. 559). On the other hand, wholly-owned subsidiaries bear the negative
impact of environmental uncertainty alone, so they are exposed to greater
risks when markets in crisis-stricken countries collapse. As such, MNCs are
less tolerant of troubled wholly-owned subsidiaries than of joint ventures.
This argument is consistent with the divestiture literature, which states that it
is more valuable for MNCs to divest foreign operations that are larger, such
as wholly-owned subsidiaries (Borde et al., 1998). Therefore, an MNC would
be less likely to divest its joint ventures than its wholly-owned subsidiaries
in crisis-stricken countries during times of uncertainty.

Joint ownership in non-crisis-stricken countries
The extent to which an MNC has joint ventures in non-crisis-stricken
countries also influences its decision about whether to divest struggling
subsidiaries in economically troubled countries. The MNC that has pursued
geographic diversification via joint ventures is likely to have a greater reservoir
of organizational resources and managerial capacity than the MNC that has
diversified via wholly-owned subsidiaries (Contractor and Lorange, 1988).
This is because partnering with other firms requires fewer organizational
resources and less managerial capacity, leaving a reservoir of capacity that
can be used for troubled subsidiary operations in crisis-stricken countries.
As such, the MNC that makes greater use of a joint venture strategy in
non-crisis-stricken countries is likely to be more tolerant of its troubled
subsidiaries in crisis-stricken countries, and so less likely to divest those
subsidiaries in times of economic crisis. On the other hand, if the MNC
pursues geographic diversification primarily through a wholly-owned mode
of entry, the complexity of managing dispersed subsidiary operations may
exhaust its organizational resources and managerial capacity (Siddharthan
and Lall, 1982). This reduces the MNC's tolerance for troubled subsidiaries
in crisis-stricken countries and makes it more likely that these subsidiaries
will be rationalized because they are prohibitively expensive to maintain
during times of economic crisis.

In addition, while geographic risk diversification is achieved by having subsidiaries in various countries that do not have perfectly correlated economies, MNCs still need to have a risk-mitigating mechanism that buffers them from risks arising in non-crisis-stricken countries (Delios and Henisz, 2000). Political risk may increase when host country governments unexpectedly change the business environment of the foreign firm, such as through boycotts, fund remittance control, and expropriation (Boddewyn, 1988). Financial risk, such as exchange rate fluctuation and inflation (Reeb et al., 1998) may offset the earnings stability advantages of globally diversified portfolios. If affiliated subsidiaries in non-crisis-stricken countries fail to mitigate these sorts of risks, and as a result fail to diversify the MNC's risks, the MNC may have to exit its subsidiaries in crisis-stricken countries. This is because maintaining high-risk foreign operations in both crisis-stricken and non-crisis-stricken countries is extremely costly, and thus greatly reduces the benefits of diversifying internationally. Based on the rationale above, we expect that the greater extent to which an MNC uses joint ventures (versus wholly-owned subsidiaries) in non-crisis-stricken countries, the less likely the MNC is to divest its subsidiaries in a crisis-stricken country.

Interaction effect of joint ownership between crisis-stricken and non-crisis-stricken countries

Joint ownership of subsidiaries in crisis-stricken countries interacts positively with joint ownership of ventures in unaffected countries, thereby further reducing the likelihood that the MNC will divest subsidiaries in crisis-stricken countries during times of uncertainty. Sharing ownership buffers an MNC from the uncertainties and risks of the contextual environment (Contractor and Lorange, 1988; Root, 1988). As such, MNCs are less likely to close down joint ventures in crisis-stricken countries during times of uncertainty. MNCs are most able to bear the downside risk of troubled joint venture operations in collapsed economies when they make greater use of a joint venture strategy in unaffected countries. The interaction effect occurs because these MNCs have greater reservoirs of organizational resources and managerial capacity to support their troubled joint ventures (Siddharthan and Lall, 1982) and because they gain more diversification benefits from non-crisis-stricken countries (Reeb et al., 1998). Therefore, compared with MNCs that globally diversify via a wholly-owned mode of entry, the MNC that makes greater use of a joint venture strategy in non-crisis-stricken countries tends to be more tolerant of joint ventures in crisis-stricken countries, and so less likely to divest these operations during times of uncertainty. Therefore, we expect that the interaction between the use of a joint venture in a crisis-stricken country and the extent to which an MNC makes use of joint ventures in non-crisis-stricken countries will have a negative effect on the divestment likelihood of the joint venture in the crisis-stricken country.

Real Options Theory

Joint ownership in crisis-stricken countries

An MNC has to control its foreign subsidiaries in order to shift production among them. Helleiner (1981, p. 3) emphasizes that intra-firm trade usually takes place 'in consequence of central commands rather than in response to price signals'. Thus, even under conditions of uncertainty, MNCs may have differing levels of flexibility, depending on how much control they have over their foreign subsidiary operations. This is why Rangan (1994) used a sample of majority-owned or wholly-owned subsidiaries to examine intra-firm trade.

When it comes to real options flexibility, an MNC only benefits from its subsidiary's presence when it shifts production. When production shifts between two locations, for example, one subsidiary has to decrease its production level, which typically entails firing some workers and selling off some assets, and the other subsidiary has to hire more workers and expand its facilities to increase production. It is easier for the MNC to decide at headquarters level how to enact change during times of uncertainty when it solely owns the subsidiary in the crisis-stricken country (Hennart et al., 1998; Li, 1995). In jointly-owned subsidiaries, shifting production requires the consent of the other partner, which reduces the potential benefit of operational flexibility (Rugman and Verbeke, 2004; Tong and Reuer, 2007). In addition, real options research suggests that a shared ownership stake provides firms with the flexibility of put option (i.e. selling off the subsidiary) when the value of keeping the option is low (McGrath, 1999). In this case, it is wiser for the MNC to divest a subsidiary, especially when high coordination costs make it difficult to achieve the potential benefits of shifting production. On the other hand, MNCs with wholly-owned subsidiaries may not have the option of a low-cost exit from a troubled economy (Williamson, 1979). This reluctance to divest wholly-owned subsidiaries is an example of economic hysteresis (Dixit and Pindyck, 1994). In sum, we propose that an MNC is more likely to divest joint ventures than wholly-owned subsidiaries in crisis-stricken countries.

Joint ownership in non-crisis-stricken countries

Likewise, an MNC may not be able to fully use its operational flexibility in response to uncertainty, unless it can easily and readily reconfigure resource flows across its dispersed subsidiaries. The potential benefit of operational flexibility can be particularly constrained if the dispersed subsidiary operations involve joint venture partners (Hennart et al., 1998; Li, 1995; Tong and Reuer, 2007). It may not be easy for an MNC to readily change the operational direction of a subsidiary that is controlled by joint venture partners. In fact, it may have to renegotiate the original partnership agreement and obtain partner consent before it can fully benefit from the operational flexibility that resides in being part of the multinational network. Even when it is possible to divest subsidiaries in crisis-stricken countries, if a shift of production to other locations is hampered, firms would have a problem with the call option. In other words, even if the joint venture partners consent to changing subsidiary operations, the MNC is likely to incur significant coordination costs. The difficulty of fine-tuning the firm's production activities may also lead to inefficient resource allocation among subsidiaries (Goerzen and Beamish, 2003).

On the other hand, if the firm has full control of operations across its dispersed subsidiaries, it does not have to coordinate change with other partners, and thus can readily shift production and products across dispersed subsidiaries in different locales. Control enables the MNC to integrate the operations of its subsidiaries in different locations, in terms of information sets, intermediate and final product portfolios, and physical and human assets that are compatible across borders (Rangan, 1998). When an economic downturn calls for a change in operational focus, the MNC with greater control over its dispersed international operations can more easily reconfigure its value chain activities since it already has a system in place for intra-firm product and information flows across affiliated subsidiaries dispersed in different markets (Miller, 1992). This built-in operational flexibility allows the MNC to control and manage the demands imposed by dynamic environments during times of uncertainty (Bowman and Hurry, 1993). However, it may be difficult for an MNC with joint ventures in non-crisis-stricken countries to realize the aforementioned benefits of operational flexibility; thus it may divest the subsidiary operation in the crisis-stricken country. MNCs that make more use of joint ventures will experience higher coordination costs and be more likely to divest subsidiaries during times of uncertainty, therefore we expect that the greater the extent to which an MNC makes use of joint ventures (versus wholly-owned subsidiaries) in non-crisis-stricken countries, the more likely the MNC is to divest its subsidiaries in crisis-stricken countries.

Interaction effect of joint ownership between crisis-stricken and non-crisis-stricken countries

Real options theory suggests that the more an MNC controls its internationally dispersed subsidiary operations, the greater operational flexibility benefit it extracts during times of uncertainty (Tong and Reuer, 2007). As a logical converse, shared control of a subsidiary operation makes it difficult for an MNC to use the potential operational flexibility that resides in being part of the multinational network. This coordination problem means that the MNC that jointly owns a subsidiary in a crisis-stricken country will be more likely to divest the subsidiary during the period of uncertainty. The coordination problem is worse if the MNC also has joint ventures in non-crisis-stricken countries. Joint ownership structures in both crisis-stricken and unaffected countries greatly limit the upside potential of using operational flexibility under conditions of uncertainty, therefore we expect that the interaction between joint venture usage in a crisis-stricken country and the extent to which an MNC makes use of joint ventures in non-crisis-stricken countries will have a positive effect on the divestment likelihood of the joint venture in the crisis-stricken country.

DISCUSSION AND CONCLUSION

Since Hymer's (1960) seminal work on MNCs, scholars have delved into the competitive advantage of MNCs, and a number of them have suggested that MNCs possess superior resources and have competitive advantages that purely domestic firms do not have (Buckley and Casson 1976; Dunning 1980; Dunning and Rugman 1985). However, growing uncertainties are the very reality that MNCs face in today's global economies. For this reason, what is required for MNCs most in today's uncertain environment is gaining and sustaining the competitive advantage that effectively deals with the heightened uncertainties of the global economy. During times of uncertain environmental conditions, such as abrupt changes in foreign exchange rates, and factor and product market conditions, MNCs may extract benefits from their geographically dispersed subsidiaries by either reducing the risk via dispersed investments or adjusting and shifting their value chain activities across different subsidiary locations. Geographic diversification theory suggests that MNCs, by having dispersed investments in various countries, can benefit from risk reduction, therefore when any location is considered as not adding value to the whole portfolio, it is important to get back to the optimal risk reduction structure by diverting investments in troubled locations. On the other hand, the real option logic of operational flexibility suggests that MNCs do not simply divest the presence of a foreign subsidiary because of risk prevailing in the host country, but rather they attempt to make the best use of existing subsidiaries to take advantage of uncertainty during times of economic crisis. MNCs with subsidiaries in various locations can benefit by shifting their operations across borders in response to environmental changes. This real options approach can refocus managerial attention on the strategic value of operational flexibility in increasingly turbulent environments.

The theoretical prediction made in this study provides a positive normative view of the behavior of MNCs. Real options reasoning has often been criticized for lacking real-world application and treating the management of foreign subsidiaries like a game of chess. This criticism may have arisen because the real options approach to strategic management was born out of the financial option pricing model, thus real options theory unrealistically treats foreign subsidiaries like financial instruments rather than real assets. In this study, we compared real option reasoning with another well-established derivative of finance theory that has been applied to the management of foreign subsidiaries – geographic risk diversification theory. Indeed, the geographic risk diversification theory takes an even more finance-oriented view of managing foreign subsidiaries because it treats each foreign subsidiary as a financial instrument. If geographic risk diversification theory is a rather blunt portfolio approach to reducing risk, real options theory is a more fine-grained approach that gets to the level of subsidiary change. This study took into consideration such strategic value of real options approach at the subsidiary level, and attempted to provide a positive normative implication of real options approach on subsidiary management.

In this chapter, we also investigated the implications of organizational constraints in order to respond to criticisms that finance-based theories have a simplistic view of complicated multinational management issues. We propose that both geographic risk diversification theory and real options theory can have more meaningful managerial implications if we examine the two theories in conjunction with the choice of ownership. From the viewpoint of geographical risk diversification theory, it is imperative that MNCs treat each subsidiary as independent from one other; otherwise, the intention of preserving uncorrelated risk among subsidiaries is violated. In this sense, it makes more sense for MNCs to be locally responsive to ensure that each subsidiary further reduces the risk of being similar. By treating each subsidiary independently, higher risk reduction can be achieved. Joint venture relationships, having to share ownership and decision rights with local partners, inevitably lead to more locally responsive subsidiaries, which in turn provides stronger risk reduction for the whole portfolio of the MNC. This is why it is more valuable from the risk diversification perspective to keep joint ventures rather than wholly-owned subsidiaries in the troubled regions, since joint ventures tend to be more locally responsive.

Real options reasoning, on the other hand, may opt for wholly-owned subsidiaries since the wholly-owned mode enables MNCs to have better control when it is needed most, such as when the region or the country is in economic trouble. The real options theory suggests that MNCs can benefit from the operational flexibility that resides in being part of a multinational network, but their latent operational flexibility to respond to uncertainty may not be fully exploited if they cannot easily adjust or change the strategic and operational directions of the dispersed subsidiaries in their multinational network. It is particularly difficult for an MNC to modify and reconfigure operating options if its subsidiary is a joint venture. Unless the MNC has full control over the operation of the subsidiary, it has to negotiate strategic and operational changes with its partners. Substantive conflict and relationship conflict may arise between partners who disagree about how to operate the subsidiary. These conflicts may significantly increase coordination costs, thereby limiting the benefit of operational flexibility. The negative effect of joint ownership can manifest in subsidiaries in both crisis-stricken and unaffected countries. In crisis-stricken countries during times of uncertainty, MNCs are more likely to divest their joint venture than their wholly-owned subsidiary. The greater use the MNC makes of joint ownership in non-crisis countries, the more likely it is to divest its subsidiary in the crisis-stricken country, under conditions of uncertainty.

Strategy selection may be less a matter of measuring relative amounts of various input variables and more an issue of how management sees the world. Therefore, different international expansion strategies may follow different risk logics (Rangan, 1998; Bartlett and Ghoshal, 1989). For example, global integration strategy may follow the risk logic of real options, whereas multidomestic strategy follows the logic of geographic risk diversification. If MNCs strategize based on the risk logic of real options, they are likely to utilize global strategies by striving for a high level of global integration through their global networks. To capture economies of scope and scale, MNCs use their subsidiaries as pipelines for their global networks. In doing so, they generally employ a high level of control through such mechanisms as a high level of equity ownership and a high use of expatriates (Rangan, 1998). As such, MNCs pursuing global integration strategy tend to utilize the wholly-owned subsidiary mode because this makes it easier to incorporate the organizational practices of the parent firm and to integrate with the parent's global production networks. Therefore, for the shift of production to take place, it is important that the MNC has established its subsidiaries based on the risk logic of real options before economic crisis occurs. The caveat is that the real options risk logic requires a path dependent strategy to enable MNCs to operate flexibly during times of uncertainty (Teece et al., 1997).

On the other hand, if MNCs strategize based on the logic of geographic risk diversification, they are more likely to engage in multidomestic strategies and to strive for a high level of local responsiveness in host countries. In particular, they adapt and conform to the requirements of the local markets such as products and policies. As such, these MNCs generally give their subsidiaries a high level of autonomy by exercising a low control mechanism. Thus MNCs exploiting multidomestic strategies tend to use the entry mode of joint venture, because partnering with local firms that have locally relevant capabilities makes it easier for them to integrate into the local markets. For example, some local subsidiaries not only modify products, but also modify 'even manufacturing processes to meet local needs' (Bartlett and Ghoshal, 1989, p. 46). If an MNC did not have operational flexibility in mind at the time of subsidiary establishment, it would be more likely that the MNC would have focused on localization. This is why, for operational flexibility to work optimally, pre-existence of intra-firm linkages should proceed (Rangan, 1998).

NOTE

1. Other reasons for having subsidiaries in diversified international locations may include economies of scale, economies of scope, internalization, internationalization, and retaliation against competitors that move to an untapped market. In this study, we focus on risk reduction and operational flexibility.

REFERENCES

Agmon, T. and D. Lessard (1977), 'Investor recognition of corporate international diversification', *Journal of Finance*, **32**, 1049–55.

Allen, L. and C. Pantzalis (1996), 'Valuation of the operating flexibility of multinational corporations', *Journal of International Business Studies*, **27**, 633–53.

Amram, M. and N. Kulatilaka (1999), *Real Options: Managing Strategic Investment in an Uncertain World*, Cambridge, MA: Harvard Business School Press.

Anderson, E. and H. Gatignon (1986), 'Modes of foreign entry: a transaction cost analysis and propositions', *Journal of International Business Studies*, **17**, 1–26.

Barkema, H., J. Bell, and J. Pennings (1996), 'Foreign entry, cultural barriers, and learning', *Strategic Management Journal*, **17**, 151–66.

Bartlett, C. and S. Ghoshal (1989), *Managing Across Borders: The Transnational Solution*, Boston, MA: Harvard Business School Press.

Beamish, P.W. and J.C. Banks (1987), 'Equity joint ventures and the theory of the multinational enterprise', *Journal of International Business Studies*, **18**, 1–16.

Benito, G. (1997), 'Divestment of foreign production operations', *Applied Economics*, **29**, 1365–77.

Benito, G. (2005), 'Divestment and international business strategy', *Journal of Economic Geography*, **5**, 235–51.

Benito, G. and L. Welch (1997), 'De-internationalization', *Management International Review*, **37**, 7–25.

Boddewyn, J.J. (1979), 'Foreign divestment: magnitude and factors', *Journal of International Business Studies*, **10**, 21–6.

Boddewyn, J.J. (1988), 'Political aspects of MNE theory', *Journal of International Business Studies*, **19**, 341–63.

Borde, S., J. Madura and A. Akhige (1998), 'Valuation effects of foreign divestitures', *Managerial and Decision Economics*, **19**, 71–9.

Bowman, E. (1980), 'A risk/return paradox for strategic management', *Sloan Management Review*, **21**, 17–31.

Bowman, E. and D. Hurry (1993), 'Strategy through the option lens: an integrated view of resource investments and the incremental-choice process', *Academy of Management Review*, **18**, 760–82.

Brewer, T.J. (1983), 'Political sources of risk in the international money markets: conceptual, methodological, and interpretive refinements', *Journal of International Business Studies*, **19**, 161–4.

Buckley, P. and M. Casson (1976), *The Future of Multinational Enterprises*, London: Macmillan.

Burgman, T. (1996), 'An empirical examination of multinational capital structure', *Journal of International Business Studies*, **27**, 553–70.

Campa, J. (1994), 'Multinational investment under uncertainty in the chemical processing industries', *Journal of International Business Studies*, **25**, 557–78.

Chang, S.J. (1996), 'An evolutionary perspective on diversification and corporate restructuring: entry, exit and economic performance during 1981–89', *Strategic Management Journal*, **17**, 587–612.

Chow, Y.K. and R.T. Hamilton (1993), 'Corporate divestment: an overview', *Journal of Managerial Psychology*, **8**, 9–13.

Chung, C.C. and P.W. Beamish (2005), 'The impact of institutional reforms on characteristics and survival of foreign subsidiaries in emerging economies', *Journal of Management Studies*, **42**, 35–62.

Clarke, C. and F. Gall (1987), 'Planned divestment: a five-step approach', *Long Range Planning*, **20**, 17–24.

Contractor, F.J. and P. Lorange (1988), 'Why should firms cooperate? The strategy and economics basis for cooperative ventures', in F.J. Contractor and P. Lorange (eds), *Cooperative Strategies in International Business*, Lexington, MA: Lexington Books, pp. 3–30.

Coy, P. (1999), 'Exploiting uncertainty: the real options revolution in decision-making', *Business Week*, 7 June, 118–24.

Delios, A. and W.J. Henisz (2000), 'Japanese firms' investment strategies in emerging economies', *Academy of Management Journal*, **43**, 305–23.

Dess, G., A. Gupta, J.F. Hennart and C. Hill (1995), 'Conducting and integrating strategy research at the international, corporate and business levels: issues and directions', *Journal of Management*, **21**, 357–93.

Dixit, A.K. and R.S. Pindyck (1994), *Investment under Uncertainty*, Princeton, NJ: Princeton University Press.

Doukas, J. and A. Patzalis (2003), 'Geographic diversification and agency costs of debt of multinational firms', *Journal of Corporate Finance*, **9**, 59–92.

Drummond, H. (1995), 'De-escalation in decision making: a case of disastrous partnership', *Journal of Management Studies*, **32**, 265–81.

Duhaime, I. and J.H. Grant (1984), 'Factors influencing divestment decision making: evidence from a field study', *Strategic Management Journal*, **5**, 301–18.

Dunning, J.H. (1980), 'Toward an eclectic theory of international production: empirical tests', *Journal of International Business Studies*, **11**, 9–31.

Dunning J.H. and A. Rugman (1985), 'The influence of Hymer's dissertation on the theory of foreign direct investment', *American Economic Review*, **75**, 228–32.

Errunza, V. and L. Senbet (1984), 'International corporate diversification, market valuation, and size-adjusted evidence', *Journal of Finance*, **39**, 727–43.

Euromoney (1998), 'Shrugging off the Asia effect', Issue 346, 98–104.

Fama, E.F. and M.H. Miller (1972), *The Theory of Finance*, New York: Holt Rinehart & Wilson.

Foss, N. (1998), 'Real options and the theory of the firm', in R. Sanchez (ed.), *Options Theory in Strategic Management*, London: Sage.

Ghoshal, S. (1987), 'Global strategy: an organizing framework', *Strategic Management Journal*, **8**, 425–40.

Goerzen, A. and P.W. Beamish (2003), 'Geographic scope and multinational enterprise performance', *Strategic Management Journal*, **24**, 1289–306.

Grant, R., A. Jammine and H. Thomas (1988), 'Diversity, diversification, and profitability among British manufacturing companies, 1972–84', *Academy of Management Journal*, **31**, 771–801.

Grinold, R.C. and R.N. Kahn (1999), *Active Portfolio Management*, New York: McGraw-Hill.

Grubel, H. (1968), 'Internationally diversified portfolios: welfare gains and capital flows', *American Economic Review*, December, 1299–314.

Hamilton, R.T. and Y.K. Chow (1993), 'Why managers divest: evidence from New Zealand's largest companies', *Strategic Management Journal*, **14**, 479–84.

Harrigan, K.R. (1985), *Strategies for Joint Ventures*, Lexington, MA: Lexington Books.

Haynes, M., S. Thomson and M. Wright (2003), 'The determinants of corporate divestment: evidence from a panel of UK firms', *Journal of Economic Behavior and Organization*, **52**, 147–66.

Helleiner, G. (1981), *Intra-firm Trade and the Developing Countries*, New York: St Martin's Press.

Hennart, J.-F., D.J. Kim and M. Zeng (1998), 'The impact of joint venture status on the longevity of Japanese stakes in U.S. manufacturing affiliates', *Organization Science*, **9**, 382–95.

Hisey, K. and R. Caves (1985), 'Diversification strategy and choice of country: diversifying acquisitions abroad by U.S. multinationals, 1978–1980', *Journal of International Business Studies*, **16**, 51–64.

Hymer, S. (1960), 'The international operations of national firms: a study of direct foreign investment', PhD dissertation, MIT, Cambridge, MA.

Hymer, S. (1976), *The International Operations of National Firms: A Study of Direct Foreign Investment*, Cambridge, MA: MIT Press.

Johnson, R. (1996), 'Antecedents and outcomes of corporate refocusing', *Journal of Management*, **22**, 439–83.

Kim, W., P. Hwang and W. Burgers (1993), 'Multinationals' diversification and the risk–return trade-off', *Strategic Management Journal*, **14**, 257–86.

Kindleberger, C.P. (1969), *American Business Abroad: Six Lectures on Direct Investment*, New Haven, CT: Yale University Press.

Kiyota, K. and S. Urata (2005), 'The role of multinational firms in international trade: the case of Japan', Research Institute of Economy, Trade, and Industry Discussion Paper Series (05-E-012), Tokyo, Japan: RIETI.

Kogut, B. (1985), 'Designing global strategies: profiting from operating flexibility', *Sloan Management Review*, Fall, 27–38.

Kogut, B. (1989), 'A note on global strategies', *Strategic Management Journal*, **10**, 383–9.

Kogut, B. and N. Kulatilaka (1994), 'Operating flexibility, global manufacturing, and the option value of a multinational network', *Management Science*, **40**, 123–39.

Levi, H. and M. Sarnat (1970), 'International diversification of investment portfolios', *American Economic Review*, **60**, 668–675.

Li, J. T. (1995), 'Foreign entry and survival: effects of strategic choices on performance in international markets', *Strategic Management Journal*, **16**, 333–51.

Lim, L. (1999), 'Challenges for government policy and business practice', in L. Lim, F. Ching, and B. Villegas (eds), *The Asian Economic Crisis: Policy Choices, Social Consequences and the Philippine Case*, New York: Asia Society, pp. 5–29.

Little, J. (1986), 'Intra-firm trade and United States protectionism: thoughts based on a small survey', *New England Economic Review*, Jan–Feb, 46–51.

McGrath, R.G. (1997), 'A real options logic for initiating technology positioning investments', *Academy of Management Review*, **22**, 974–96.

McGrath, R.G. (1999), 'Falling forward: real options reasoning and entrepreneurial failure', *Academy of Management Review*, **24**, 13–30.

Madura, J. (1996), *Global Portfolio Management for Institutional Investors*, Westport, CT: Quorum.

Majd, S. and R. Pindyck (1987), 'Time to build, option value, and investment decisions', *Journal of Financial Economics*, **18**, 7–27.

Mansi, S. and D. Reeb (2002), 'Corporate diversification: what gets discounted?', *Journal of Finance*, **57**, 2167–83.

Mikhail, A. and H. Shawky (1979), 'Investment performance of U.S.-based multinational corporations', *Journal of International Business Studies*, **10**, 53–66.

Miller, K.D. (1992), 'A framework for integrated risk management in international business', *Journal of International Business Studies*, **23**, 311–31.

Mueller, D. (1969), 'A theory of conglomerate mergers', *Quarterly Journal of Economics*, **83**, 643–51.

North, D.C. (1990), *Institutions, Institutional Change, and Economic Performance*, New York: Cambridge University Press.

OECD (2002), *Intra-industry and Intra-firm Trade and the Internalization of Production*, Paris: OECD Economic Outlook.

Padmanabhan, P. (1993), 'The impact of European divestment announcements on shareholder wealth: evidence from the UK', *Journal of Multinational Financial Management*, **2**, 185–208.

Rangan, S. (1994), 'Are transnational corporations an impediment to trade adjustment?', *Transnational Corporations*, **3**, 52–80.

Rangan, S. (1998), 'Do multinationals operate flexibly? Theory and evidence', *Journal of International Business Studies*, **29**, 217–37.

Reeb, D.M., C.Y. Kwok and Y.H. Baek (1998), 'Systematic risk of the multinational corporation', *Journal of International Business Studies*, **29**, 263–79.

Reuer, J. and M. Leiblein (2000), 'Downside risk implications of multinationality and international joint ventures', *Academy of Management Journal*, **43**, 203–14.

Root, F. (1988), 'Some taxonomies of international cooperate arrangements', in F.J. Contractor and P. Lorange (eds), *Cooperative Strategies in International Business*, Lexington, MA: Lexington Books, pp. 69–80.

Roth, K., D. Schweiger and A. Morrison (1991), 'Global strategy implementation at the business unit level: operational capabilities and administrative mechanisms', *Journal of International Business Studies*, **22**, 369–402.

Rugman, A. (1979), *International Diversification and the Multinational Enterprise*, Lexington, MA: Lexington Books.

Rugman, A. and A. Verbeke (2004), 'A perspective on regional and global strategies of multinational enterprises', *Journal of International Business Studies*, **35**, 3–18.

Sanchez, R. (1993), 'Strategic flexibility, firm organization, and managerial work in dynamic markets', *Advances in Strategic Management*, **9**, 251–91.

Shan, W. (1991), 'Environmental risks and joint venture sharing arrangements', *Journal of International Business Studies*, **22**, 555–78.

Siddharthan, N.S. and S. Lall (1982), 'Recent growth of the largest US multi-nationals', *Oxford Bulletin of Economics and Statistics*, **44**, 1–13.

Tallman, S. and J. Li (1996), 'Effects of international diversity and product diversity on the performance of multinational firms', *Academy of Management Journal*, **39**, 179–96.

Tang, C. and S. Tikoo (1999), 'Operational flexibility and market valuation of earnings', *Strategic Management Journal*, **20**, 749–61.

Tang, L. and V. Madan (2003), 'The relative efficiency of ownership structures and intra-firm trade', *International Trade Journal*, **17**, 177–203.

Teece, D., G. Pisano and A. Shuen (1997), 'Dynamic capabilities and strategic management', *Strategic Management Journal*, **18**, 509–33.

Thompson, S. and M. Wright (1995), 'Corporate governance: the role of restructuring transactions', *Economic Journal*, **105**, 690–703.

Tong, T.W. and J. Reuer (2007), 'Real options in multinational corporations: organizational challenges and risk implications', *Journal of International Business Studies*, Forthcoming.

Torneden, R. (1975), *Foreign Divestment by U.S. Multinational Corporations: With Eight Case Studies*, New York: Praeger.

Trigeorgis, L. and S.P. Mason (1987), 'Valuing managerial flexibility', *Midland Corporate Finance Journal*, **5**, 14–21.

Van Den Bulcke, D., J.J. Boddewyn, B. Martens and P. Klemmer (1979), *Investment and Divestment Policies of MNCs in Europe*, Farnborough, Hants: Saxon House.

Williamson, O. (1979), 'Transaction cost economics: the governance of contractual relations', *Journal of Law and Economics*, **22**, 233–61.

Wilson, B.D. (1980), *Disinvestment of Foreign Subsidiaries*, Ann Arbor, MI: UMI.

Zaheer, S. (1995), 'Overcoming the liability of foreignness', *Academy of Management Journal*, **38**, 341–63.

3. Is *Do what you do best and outsource the rest* an appropriate technology sourcing strategy?

Brent B. Allred and K. Scott Swan

Outsourcing has become increasingly necessary and difficult, particularly as global trade barriers drop and communication and transportation times improve. Additionally, companies are often faced with key 'make versus buy' decisions regarding necessary technology. While recent debates between the merits and costs associated with buying technology have been contentious, outsourcing and offshoring have become an important reality in many industries. A company's technology sourcing strategy is increasingly reliant on finding capable technological sources across the globe, whether offshoring from international subsidiaries within the organization, outsourcing from trusted international partners, or through market-based transactions. Since technology is becoming more readily available from a multitude of international sources, firms that fail to consider these options will not remain competitive.

Companies are finding that their sourcing strategy is not only an important aspect of gaining competitive advantages and improving performance, but may also be necessary for survival in the dynamic global marketplace. An example that serves to highlight the role of sourcing strategy is the actions of Dell. Dell's relentless push to become the leading player in the PC industry requires a technology sourcing strategy that supports its clear strategic objectives of low cost, high quality, and speed-to-market with relevant technology.

The PC industry is characterized by considerable sameness in technology, design of products and services, and general marketing approach. Dell has achieved superior strategy and performance primarily through advantages in direct customer relationships and value. Additionally, Dell is best at offering customers performance-proven technology at the best price before anyone else. Its made-to-order assembly and just-in-time parts delivery, along with design and manufacturing of key components, allow Dell to offer the latest proven technology within days as opposed to the weeks required by many of its competitors.

We examined the technology sourcing strategy of Dell as well as a couple of hundred other companies across various industries to determine critical factors that influence technology sourcing strategy. We found that Dell and many of these companies accomplish their objectives through a range of sourcing options that have changed and expanded over time. Despite being a late entrant in a tough, competitive industry, Dell took a leading position in the 1990s by buying standardized components and assembling computers to order; elements important to its early success. To expand its market and broaden its appeal, Dell then partnered with firms such as Xerox, Unisys, and Geotronics to offer services, peripherals (e.g. printers), and higher end products (e.g. servers). These moves provided more complete solutions for individual, corporate and government accounts and added significantly to Dell's success. While Dell now designs and manufactures its own motherboards and cases, it continues to leverage relationships with partners. In a recent shift from selling third-party branded products, Dell now offers its own branded products, such as printers, cartridges, PDAs and plasma TVs (Lashinsky, 2004). Dell continually assesses its own capabilities, as well as those of existing and potential partners, in crafting a technology sourcing strategy that balances internal development with external acquisition to achieve cost, quality and speed advantages.

Dell's strategic focus is not unique. Indeed, many companies strive to seek advantages across a mix of all three of these areas. To further explore effective technology sourcing strategies, we present an overview of the strategic objectives of low cost, high quality, and speed-to-market achieved through three technology sourcing options: internal development, joint development with cooperative partners, and market-based transactions. We view these alternatives from different perspectives to better understand how companies achieve their desired objectives. We also evaluate factors in the technology environment (e.g. the level of product design dominance, the technology protective system and access to complementary assets) that affect the sourcing strategy and conclude with actionable insights and recommendations.

THE PURSUIT OF COST, QUALITY AND SPEED OBJECTIVES

The purpose of technology sourcing strategy is to improve performance. The strategic objective the company chooses to pursue will influence its selection of the appropriate sourcing option, since a cost strategy typically leads to price leadership, while high quality and speed-related strategies lead to differentiation. Low cost, high product quality and speed-to-market have traditionally been recognized as important, yet conceptually distinct objectives. The common belief has been that there are significant trade-offs among the three and that when one of these objectives is emphasized, it comes at a cost to the others. For example, speed-to-market is generally expected to raise costs and have a negative effect on quality. In another traditional trade-off, high quality is usually associated with increased costs and long development times.

The perceived differences among these objectives and their outcomes have begun to diminish (Wheelwright and Clark, 1992). There is evidence that even with faster product development cycles, companies may be able to simultaneously lower costs, improve customer satisfaction and enhance quality (Bower and Hout, 1988). For Dell, the abilities to reduce inventories and to leverage partner relationships allow it to offer customers faster, smaller and lower cost computers by integrating proven technology into products faster. These actions have allowed Dell to lower its average inventory turnover to less than four days. In contrast, data indicate that Gateway's average is closer to 10 days, IBM's is 21 days (before being sold to Lenovo), and HP holds 42 days in average inventory. In fact, analysts measure Dell's inventory turnover in terms of hours instead of days. Dell effectively demonstrates that low cost, high quality and speed can be concurrently achievable. Despite the blurring of boundaries between these objectives, it is still important to understand each of them individually.

Low Cost Objective

While cost reduction is important, behaviors associated with low cost leadership are often difficult to implement. Low cost advantages require constant attention to 'process' development, sourcing, manufacturing and distribution activities. Additionally, having the lowest costs may not result in a competitive advantage if achieving it requires too great a sacrifice of quality and speed. Because of the concern for sacrificing quality, the ability of the technology sourcing strategy to balance competing objectives is important. While it has been suggested that internal development of technology is cheaper than external acquisition (Capon and Glazer, 1987), high costs and risks have been cited in a growing movement towards the acquisition of new technologies (Noori, 1990). Both outsourcing and offshore sourcing have grown in popularity as a solution to decrease costs. The difficulty in control, communication and coordination across great physical and cultural distances is real. Another problem occurs when external technology provides some crucial advantage – the company may be compelled to purchase it from others at an exorbitant price, sacrificing its low cost position.

While it is important to consider cost implications during design, efficiencies and economies are realized during the production stage. For example, Ford's executives rave about their plant in Brazil for the Fusion automobile. 'It's our lowest-cost plant in the world', Nick Scheele said (Zaun et al., 2002, p. A1). It is a combination of offshoring and outsourcing, since the cost savings are a result of heavy reliance on two dozen outside suppliers who operate directly on the Ford assembly line, that means the Brazilian plant is producing some of the best quality in Ford's global network.

The pursuit of low cost typically requires technology investments focused on process steps along the value chain. While a high degree of technological control allows the firm the greatest potential benefits, it can also come with higher development costs. Process technology requires less control because it is harder for competitors to copy. As a result, for a low cost objective, there is only an intermediate need to control the technology.

High Quality Objective

Whereas cost objectives involve an emphasis on process, a high quality objective is rooted in the firm's ability to differentiate its product in a manner that generates customer loyalty, satisfaction and/or a price premium. Unlike a low cost objective, where cost is the only basis of advantage, a quality position can be achieved in many different ways, providing functional, experiential and symbolic customer value. High quality objectives require investments in both design and manufacturing, with an emphasis on product technology.

General Motor's (GM) Zafira automobile, which is made for Subaru in the Japanese market and for Opel in the European market, highlights the challenge of achieving a high quality objective (Zaun et al., 2002). For GM, quality issues were considered at both development and production levels since the Zafira's design needed to appeal to demanding Japanese and European customers. A challenge was the alignment between the front and rear doors. In Japan, where lower speeds and appearance are primary concerns, they are expected to be flush. Alternatively, in Europe the front door typically sticks out slightly to reduce wind noise at autobahn speeds. GM wound up splitting the difference in its final product. Once the design was created, quality issues moved to production. To ensure manufacturing quality matched the car's design, GM invested heavily in cutting-edge equipment in its Thailand plant, which makes the Zafira for both markets.

The pursuit of a high quality objective usually raises concerns about longer development cycles. While the firm may possess the ability and resources to design high quality products, it must avoid delays that could result in missed market opportunities and undercut early mover advantage. In addition, to achieve the greatest benefits from a high quality objective, the firm needs to maintain a high level of control over the technology. Since competitors quickly attempt to imitate or copy successfully differentiated products, the greater the control the firm has over core technology, the longer the sustainability of its competitive advantage. While internal technology development provides the greatest degree of control, it also yields a higher risk of other technologies pre-empting or establishing the standard. Outsourcing can provide an immediate and acceptable technological solution, but limits the competitive advantage since such solutions are generally available to competitors.

Speed-to-Market Objective

The final objective is the speed with which the firm develops its technology and subsequently brings its products to market. George Stalk (1988, p. 41) states that, 'as a strategic weapon, time is the equivalent of money, productivity, quality, even innovation'. Geoffrey Moore goes even further by claiming that in emerging markets, time wins hands down in the trade-off with money and you would buy time at practically any price (Moore, 2002). The importance of speed makes the effective management of new product innovation and technological development a critical source of advantage. International firms must not only bring new products quickly to the market, but also must do so over and over again to maintain momentum (Kotabe and Swan, 1995).

As the length of the product life cycle continues to shrink, speed-to-market has become even more important to the success of the firm. Risks of delay and associated increases in costs from internal development are major concerns. As a result, the speed-to-market objective may drive the firm to outsource its technology to sources that provide quick and complete technological solutions. For example, Northrop Grumman wanted technology to make stealthier ships. Instead of developing the technology itself, it turned to Kockum AB, the Swedish unit of the German submarine maker HDW. Northrop's spokesman states, 'What this will do is shave off years of time it would take to develop these ships. This will be a savings of time and cost. The technology has already been paid for' (Fabey, 2002, p. E1).

For a speed-to-market objective, the primary area of investment is at the design stage. The technology emphasis is at both the product and the process level, since it is important not only to rapidly design the product, but also to achieve a reliable level of production quality and sufficient volume to achieve the desired early mover status. Because the advantage is gained by quick market entry, there is a low to intermediate need for control over the technology.

The complex trade-offs among these three strategic objectives make managerial decision-making difficult. For example, while the pursuit of a low cost objective is intended to lead to price leadership, high quality and speed-to-market objectives may also produce cost advantages. The decision to internally develop or externally acquire technology to achieve these objectives is not obvious, since there are both advantages and disadvantages. In fact, the challenge is that it really isn't a simple *make versus buy* decision. Instead, the firm has a range of technology sourcing strategy options to consider and balance. Further complicating the technology sourcing decision, the benefits of the desired objectives must be understood within the context of both environmental and internal factors.

TECHNOLOGY SOURCING STRATEGY OPTIONS

The objective of a technology sourcing strategy is to guide the firm in developing, acquiring and applying technology to gain competitive advantages and improve performance (Kotabe, 1992). It is not easy to create an advantage though technology sourcing. George Shultz (1988), former US Secretary of State, pointed out the difficulties experienced with technology development and production with an example of his favorite shipping label for integrated circuits:

> Made in one or more of the following countries. Korea, Hong Kong, Malaysia, Singapore, Taiwan, Mauritius, Thailand, Indonesia, Mexico, Philippines. The exact country of origin is unknown.

Because of technology, Dell knows with certainty where every circuit, wire and screw within every computer came from. Unfortunately, there are many uncertainties surrounding technology sourcing strategy formulation, so a better understanding of the options and contexts that affect both strategy and outcomes is essential.

Throughout the 1990s, outsourcing of non-critical functions and peripheral technology became a competitive necessity for many companies. With increased pressures to improve profitability, firms focused limited resources on developing and enhancing core capabilities. Outsourcing provided increased flexibility, allowing the firm to do more with less (Insinga and Werle, 2000). The attitude, '*Do what you do best and outsource the rest*', led firms to rely more on joint development with cooperative partners, and market-based transactions.[1]

The firm is generally presented with three technology sourcing strategy options. First, internal development involves development within the organization and offers the highest degree of control over the technology. This option allows the firm to draw not only on its own resources, but also on those across other business units within the corporation, broadening both its technological and its geographic reach. This extends the resources needed to both develop desired technology and achieve strategic objectives, yet stays within the boundaries of the larger organization. Second, as an attractive alternative, the firm can acquire technology from external partners with which it already has established experience and trust. Experience and mutual commitments may serve as a mechanism for control (Das and Teng, 1998), and allow the firm to draw on a broader set of skills and resources. While the level of control over such technology development is only intermediate, the costs associated with contract monitoring and concerns with opportunistic behavior are less than with market-based transactions, the third sourcing option. Market-based outsourcing provides the lowest level of control over the technology and its proliferation. Since competitors are likely to have access to the same or similar technology, it may be necessary to use widely available technology only if the other two options are not feasible and depending on the strategic objectives of the firm. Unfortunately, it is difficult to create a competitive advantage from technology acquired from outsourcing.

While we have presented a discussion of different technology sourcing options and strategic objectives, it is not apparent which option is most appropriate to achieve desired results. To make this decision, it is necessary to recognize the factors that influence strategy selection. We next present three perspectives that highlight critical factors for determining which sourcing option produces the desired strategic objective. We also offer actionable insights.

THREE PERSPECTIVES ON SOURCING

The factors that influence the technology sourcing decision can be viewed from three complementary perspectives: the *resource* view, the *transaction* view, and the *relational* view (see Table 3.1 for an overview). These perspectives are essential to this discussion because, first, it is easy to focus on only one view and forget other dimensions of the technology sourcing strategy. Second, these perspectives are theoretically derived from successful management practice and offer holistic, complimentary sets of issues that

Table 3.1 Comparison of resource, transaction and relational perspectives

Primary concepts	Resource perspective	Transaction perspective	Relational perspective
Key focus	Firm	Transaction	Pair/network of firms or subsidiaries
Emphasis	Knowledge of resources and physical assets	Minimization of costs	Relationships
Source of competitive advantage	Scarce/valuable and difficult to imitate/substitute resources	Efficiency	Leveraging experience and relationships
Mechanisms for maintaining positional advantage	Barriers to resource imitation or substitutability	Internalization versus contracts	Partnership barriers to imitation
Ownership/control	Firm	Firm	Collective with partners
Concerns	Uncertainty	Imperfect information, bounded rationality, tacitness, opportunism	Goal incongruence, monitoring, incentives
Managerial prescription	Review competencies and physical assets and benchmark. With uncertainty, competencies take a higher priority	Monitor costs/risks of innovation versus outsourcing. Pursue option that minimizes costs.	Identify and leverage capabilities and physical assets across partner network. Manage through relationships and experience

affect the technology sourcing decision. Third, these perspectives provide general managerial insights for how a technology sourcing strategy should be created and most importantly, their likely performance outcomes.

According to the *resource* view (Wernerfelt, 1984), technology sourcing strategy is driven by knowledge and physical assets that can best be converted into competitive advantages such as low cost, high quality or speed-to-market. Attention is focused on resources that are valuable, rare and difficult to either substitute or imitate (Barney, 1991). Although firms retain ownership of the developed technology, those that best exploit the resources across their partner network should have superior performance. Since uncertainty surrounding the sustainability of competitive position is a concern, firms must attempt to raise barriers to imitation and substitutability. For example, pharmaceutical companies attempt to build their advantage when confronted with a highly unpredictable innovation process and a short, uncertain patent protection period. These companies attempt to fend off imitators, generic versions, and even substitutes in order to maximize their return. Based on this discussion, the first insight is:

> *Insight 1*: Firms should focus on creating knowledge-based and physical assets while leveraging those available throughout their partner network. As uncertainty increases, knowledge-based resources are more important than physical assets. Firms should consistently review their resources and benchmark against key competitors. This requires developing skills to manage resources. Outsourcing requires skills in selecting, contracting and monitoring partners. Offshore sourcing requires skills in cross-cultural communication and coordination.

From the *transaction* view (Williamson, 1985), anything bought generally cannot be the source of long-lived advantage (Dierickz and Cool, 1989). A firm exists because of its ability to transfer and exploit knowledge more effectively within the corporate context than through external markets (Gupta and Govindarajan, 2000). Competitive advantage is gained through efficiency and cost minimization. Because of a range of possible barriers (e.g. imperfect information, limited ability to understand and absorb knowledge (bounded rationality), difficulty with transferring knowledge to others (tacitness), or an incomplete understanding of how the knowledge can be used to bring about success), it is generally difficult to successfully integrate externally acquired technology. Since innovating firms retain greater ownership and control of the technology's value, firms that use external sources via contracting must be concerned about self-seeking behavior. The risk of opportunistic behavior is confounded by the usually short-term inability of management to fully distinguish between firms that are committed to cooperative actions versus those engaged in self-interested behavior. These limitations push firms toward internalization. For example, firms entering developing countries are often reluctant to use local R&D partners, because of concerns that proprietary technology and product knowledge may be stolen or misappropriated (Cannic et al., 2004). This concern often outweighs the benefit of gaining a partner with a better understanding of the local market. Therefore:

> *Insight 2*: Monitor costs and risks to your firm of innovation versus outsourcing. Anticipate when the point of transition from one source to another is likely to occur, and respond by developing the firm's abilities or by negotiating contracts to minimize costs. This requires developing skills to manage transactions, which requires a deep understanding of the international cost structure in the industry to allow managers to know when outsourcing offshore sourcing is likely to improve their risk/reward trade-off.

The *relational* view of technology sourcing focuses on the network of organizations and relationships the firm uses to create its competitive advantage (Dyer and Singh, 1998). Access to critical resources can span firm boundaries and may be embedded in inter-firm relationships and routines. Competitive advantage can be acquired through relationships and experience with cooperative partners. Effectively managing the relationship, access to complementary resources across the partners, and inter-firm knowledge-sharing routines can be a primary source of competitive advantages. This is highlighted in our introductory example. Dell's entry into the printer and cartridge market did not occur through creating its own printer technology. Instead, it partnered with Lexmark to create a line of Dell branded products and pooled resources to compete with Hewlett-Packard (H-P), the industry leader whose products Dell previously sold (Morrison, 2002). Not content with just this relationship, Dell announced it was collaborating with Samsung, Kodak and Fuji Xerox on new printers. Regarding these strategic moves, Michael Dell said, 'We've got access to more intellectual property than any single competitor out there by leveraging a network of partners who have technology, but didn't necessarily have customer relationships or an understanding of what features needed to be in the products' (Lashinsky, 2004, p. 115). Thus:

> *Insight 3*: Identify knowledge-based capabilities and physical assets of existing and potential partners. Leverage them to complement your own resources and buttress your weaknesses. Manage relationships and experience to increase competitive advantages. Outsourcing requires developing skills to manage partners. Offshore sourcing requires cross-cultural skills to manage 'partners' such as government officials and other foreign stakeholders.

The resource, transaction and relational views offer implications regarding the possession and acquisition of technology within the contexts of outsourcing and offshore sourcing. The resource view suggests that competitive advantages are derived from combining current and incremental resources to create distinctive capabilities. The transaction view indicates a less important role for 'what the firm has' as opposed to 'what a firm needs'. The development or acquisition of technology focuses on transactions and cost minimization as key to efficiency. Organizations exist because they can bring together desirable exchange benefits from within at lower costs than from the external market (Williamson, 1975). A firm with low levels of necessary technology will need to augment them with a stock of specialized knowledge and physical assets in order to achieve gains in cost, quality and speed. According to the relational view, competitive advantage-enhancing technology is not only available within the firm, but across the network of cooperative partners.

By considering the above perspectives, technology sourcing can be viewed as managing resources to achieve objectives. The ability of the firm to create positive and unique value is complemented by activities that seek to minimize costs of production, search, information and monitoring, as well as enforcing contractual performance (Robins, 1987). In addition, relationships and experience with cooperative partners allow the firm access to a broader network of competencies and physical assets, while attempting to minimize opportunistic behavior and costs. These perspectives lay the foundation for understanding the influence of strategic objectives on appropriate technology sourcing strategies, given environmental and internal factors.

To summarize what we have discussed so far: (1) we have introduced alternative objectives and have shown that firms pursue these with different sourcing mechanisms, and (2) we have presented three perspectives that offer complementary opportunities and concerns for making sourcing decisions. Now we add a third area of importance in technology sourcing strategy: the technology environment both external and internal to the firm.

INFLUENCES ON TECHNOLOGY SOURCING STRATEGY

Although the pursuit of low cost, high quality or speed-to-market objectives may favor one sourcing strategy over the others, other factors also influence that decision. David Teece suggests that three basic influences, representing both environmental and internal factors, determine the firm's ability to profit from innovation (Teece, 1986). These influences, the *level of product design dominance*, the *technology protective system*, and the *level of complementary assets*, affect the relationship between the firm's strategic objectives and the appropriate technology sourcing strategy.

Product Design Dominance

The degree to which a product design is dominant in an industry plays a key role in technology development and organizational outcomes (Hill, 1997). New technology is considered emergent, while older technology is probably more established as an industry standard. As new technologies emerge they create uncertainty, with competing standards hindering the diffusion process. Alternatively, a dominant design enhances this process by reducing consumer purchase risk and thus provides some degree of stability in the industry. Once a dominant design is established, the prevailing standard remains in force until it is replaced with a new, usually superior standard. While the lack of a dominant design encourages the development of proprietary technology for firms hoping to establish the industry standard, the existence of a dominant design leaves the firm with one of two choices. The firm could either adopt the existing technological standard by acquiring it from the most appropriate source, or could invest in the development of disruptive technologies with the expectation of establishing a new dominant product design.

If managed well, firms that control the dominant design should reap the greatest benefits, as is the case with Microsoft and its Windows operating system. In fact, Microsoft's dominance in this category has led to its ability to gain a strong position in numerous other technology categories. Unfortunately, commercial success and sustained high returns are not guaranteed to firms that create a dominant design. Firms such as Xerox, IBM and Intel may have let high initial development costs, neglect and uncompetitive factor costs detract from significant long-term gains for products that they originally established as the standard (Christensen, 1997).

The manner in which a firm manages its technology strategy influences its success or failure in the marketplace – Sony's Betamax versus VHS video recording formats and the IBM PC versus Apple's Macintosh computer exemplify this challenge. Similar issues are presently being played out in cellular telephone platforms, high definition television (HDTV), and hybrid automotive engines (Shirouzu, 2003). For example, although the DVD format is the current standard for high quality digital video, a battle is raging over what standard will emerge for DVD writers (Gomes, 2002).

DVD+RW, DVD-RW, and DVD-RAM are competing designs among the current technologies promoted by companies such as Apple, Panasonic, Phillips, HP and Dell. Sony, in spite of being a co-creator of the core DVD technology, is hedging its bet by offering products that recognize multiple, competing formats. High-definition DVD (HD-DVD), supported by Toshiba and NEC Corp., is going head to head with Blu-ray, backed by Sony, H-P, and ten other major electronics companies (Dvorak, 2004). Firms that are left outside the standard usually leave the market or quickly adopt the dominant design. This suggests that firms must decide whether to attempt to be a standard-setter or a standard-adopter. This decision has clear implications for technology sourcing strategy and competitive advantage. As with the above example of Sony, LG Electronics and H-P are taking the proactive position of offering products that incorporate both technologies, which may only prolong the battle for the dominant format to emerge (Ramstad and McBride, 2007).

The product design dominance also influences the type of technology being developed. With a lack of a dominant design, investments focus primarily on product technology instead of process technology. While both product and process technology are important for new product development, investments in process technology are typically premature at this stage because of uncertainty and cost, as the product standards on which the process technology depends have yet to emerge. Instead, firms should either invest heavily in developing technology with hopes of establishing the industry standard, or wait and adopt after the standard emerges.

Once the product standard emerges, investments shift to concentrate more on process technology as competition focuses more on cost factors. At this stage, large investments in the core product technology should have a less direct effect on competitive advantage and may draw away critical resources required in other areas. Instead, incremental product improvements, rather than radical changes, characterize the industry until the next significant technological breakthrough is achieved. Speed-to-market concerns give way to technology investments that now center on process improvements to improve cost and quality. Product uncertainty is reduced, while experience with manufacturing allows better investment decisions in process technology development or acquisition. Consequently:

> *Insight 4*: Firms must decide on a standard-setting or standard-adopting strategy. Before a dominant product design emerges, investments focus primarily on product technology. Once a dominant product design is established, investments focus on process technology. If the firm is attempting to create a new standard, internal innovation is emphasized, while a cost objective is likely to lead to an increasing use of outsourcing and offshore sourcing.

During the emergent stage of the dominant design, if the firm is vying to create the industry standard, it is best to develop technology internally. With the lack of a standard, there are no external providers of adequate solutions, so the firm must rely on internal capabilities to develop the technology. In the case of a speed-to-market objective, the firm may be motivated to work with cooperative partners to rapidly create a new technology.

Once a product design becomes dominant, the appropriate sourcing option changes. A greater percentage of the technology is more likely to be outsourced in order to pursue a low cost objective. Developing all the technology internally may be inefficient since it is difficult to do all things well, and while innovations are possible for all components and processes, critical technology tends to be developed internally. A speed-to-market objective is not applicable at this stage, since the standard and early movers have already been established. Only when a firm is attempting to develop the next generation of technology would internal development support a speed-to-market objective (see Table 3.2).

Table 3.2   Technology sourcing strategy: dominant design

Strategic goal	Level of dominant design	
	Emergent	Established
Low cost	Internal	Outsource
High quality	Internal	Internal or partner
Speed-to-market	Internal or partner	Not applicable

Technology Protective System

The technology protective system indicates how easily others can appropriate or copy the technology – legally or otherwise. The level of protection influences how the technology is developed or acquired and the ability of the innovating firm to guard and benefit from its investments. In a weak technology protective system, where legal and other technology protection is limited, the firm's sourcing strategy is likely to promote heightened secrecy and control over the technology. Countering other firms' opportunistic behavior is important and may be achieved by developing technology internally and reducing costs through offshore sourcing. Unfortunately, if the protection for technology development cannot be assured, the incentive for internal development decreases. Simply outsourcing from the lowest total cost provider often becomes the best option.

If protective mechanisms fail, the firm may rely on more tacit means to control the technology. Tacit knowledge (i.e. not easily communicated or replicated) is not embodied in physical items such as equipment, but is best used by those in possession of the knowledge (Reed and DeFillipi, 1990). For example, the skills and knowledge of a master craftsman are difficult to imitate because these capabilities are not learned from a textbook or class, but through years of experience and apprenticeship. For firms, trade secrets may be preferred when patents are not well protected or enforceable. Since patents require a full disclosure of the technology, they are easier to copy.

A strong technology protective system requires the firm to consider both internal development and acquisition of technology from the most advanced sources. Not all innovation may be resident, which would require the firm to outsource. Unfortunately, we must reiterate, it is difficult to create a competitive advantage from technology acquired from outsourcing. Internal development presents the opportunity for superior performance and control, since external mechanisms are in place to protect innovations. It also poses the challenge of being expensive and time-consuming, and risks not producing the desired technological outcomes. In fact, the result may be a loss of competitive advantage, since scarce resources (i.e. money and time) are spent inventing wholly new products or processes when adequate external solutions may not only be available but established as market standards. Accordingly, with strong technology protective systems, firms depend on the resources of cooperative partners when they are unable to develop their own technologies.

Further, when the technology protective system is weak, firms tend to outsource if they are pursuing low cost and speed-to-market objectives. Since there is limited protection for internally developed technology, firms look to acquire solutions that will either be most efficient or allow for a rapid response. If the firm has a high quality objective and the technology can be shielded by a protective mechanism, trade secrets, technology tacitness, internal development or cooperative partners, are popular options. With a strong technology protective system, internally developed technology is afforded protection and the firm receives benefits by pursuing all three strategic objectives. In the case of a low cost, the firm should consider offshore sourcing that could offer the potential for greater cost efficiencies or, with a speed-to-market objective, using a cooperative partner that promises quicker development times (see Table 3.3).

Table 3.3   Technology sourcing strategy: technology protective system

	Technology protective system	
Strategic goal	Weak	Strong
Low cost	Outsource	Internal or partner
High quality	Internal or partner	Internal
Speed-to-market	Outsource	Internal or partner

Technology protection differs significantly across nations. Although the inflow of investments and technology is critical for progress and development, developing countries often have poor legal mechanisms for protecting technology ownership. These critical flows are encouraged as countries strengthen their protective system. Accordingly, entering countries with weak legal protection, firms generally rely on internal resources or draw on relationships with trusted partners. As the technology matures or when entering countries with strong legal protection, outsourcing within the local market may offer the best solution. Hence:

> *Insight 5*: When the technology protective system is weak, firms that can develop proprietary technology should rely on internal development when they can create mechanisms of protection; otherwise, they should outsource technology from cooperative partners. Be cautioned that when the technology protective system is weak, competing firms tend to appropriate technology through legal or other means.

Complementary Assets

While the technology protective system and product design dominance are external factors, the level of complementary assets is influenced by firm actions. Although not core technology, complementary assets are knowledge-based and physical resources that foster product innovation through the further development of efficiency gains, quality improvements, quicker development cycles and successful commercialization (Teece, 1986). While ownership of complementary assets provides the greatest control, a firm could use cooperative partners to create a broad base of resources on which to establish competitive advantages. Complementary assets might include its stock of product and process technology, newness of plant and equipment, financial resources and marketing capabilities.

A key challenge is how to deploy limited resources in a complementary way to achieve the greatest competitive benefits. The issue is whether investment in additional resources will improve competitive advantage. On one hand, when a firm lacks complementary assets, additional investments, appropriately combined with existing resources, are more likely to result in substantial improvements. On the other hand, for a firm that possesses critical and abundant complementary assets, the cost of development or acquisition of additional resources may not result in gains commensurate to that cost. At this stage, limited resources may be better utilized by the firm for developing the next generation of technology.

For example, in response to anticipated customer demands, Taiwanese bicycle makers such as Sunrace, Merida and Giant, whose local market fostered a strong research base from which to dominate the world market, developed fancy gears and brakes, and new aluminum alloys. These technologies have since diffused to less expensive bikes offered at mass retailers such as Wal-Mart in the US and Asda in Britain (*The Economist*, 2002). In search of complementary assets, these bicycle makers are switching to cheaper production locales like China. In order to gain greater access to an American brand name and its distribution network, Merida purchased a stake in Specialized, a US-based bicycle manufacturer. Sunrace bought Sturmey Archer, a well-known British component maker to complement its existing capabilities and market presence.

Lacking an abundance of critical resources and relationships with external partners, a firm within an industry characterized by emerging technology is generally more dependent on market transactions to acquire technology and build its complementary asset base. As a result, even though the internal development of new technology and complementary assets might provide the greatest control and competitive advantages, the size of the needed investment and cost of delay for such development may be prohibitive. As the technology becomes more established, firms typically build up their stock of complementary assets, as well as their capabilities for internal technology development. In addition, established firms are better able to form important external partnering relationships on which they can draw for future technology development.

Accordingly, firms with a low level of complementary assets need to look to cooperative partners, or even outsource, to achieve low cost and speed-to-market objectives. For a high quality objective, achieving competitive advantage tends to be developed through proprietary technology, either internally or with cooperative partners. While a high level of complementary resources might allow the firm to pursue all strategic objectives internally, it might consider using a cooperative partner to improve speed-to-market (see Table 3.4). Therefore:

> *Insight 6*: When a firm possesses a low level of critical complementary assets, investments should focus on developing, partnering, or acquiring appropriate resources to achieve desired outcomes. The firm should also foster relationships with cooperative partners in order to broaden its complementary asset base.

Table 3.4   Technology sourcing strategy: complementary assets

Strategic goal	Level of complementary assets	
	Low	High
Low cost	Partner or outsource	Internal
High quality	Internal or partner	Internal
Speed-to-market	Partner or outsource	Internal or partner

TOWARDS AN INTEGRATION

An integrative framework is likely to be helpful at this point, since technology maturity is a critical factor influencing the prescriptions of the resource, transaction and relational views for technology sourcing strategy (see Figure 3.1). The importance of the technology as well as the level of difficulty in developing the technology influences the sourcing decision. Technology that is difficult to develop encourages the use of external means, yet there may be limited sources available. Additionally, both the age of the technology and the firm's experience with the technology help determine the mix of technology sourcing options that offers a superior competitive advantage.

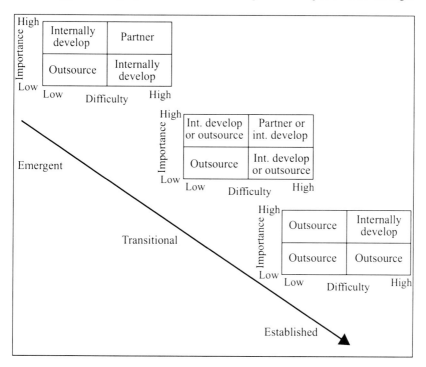

Figure 3.1   Effects of technology maturity on the outsourcing decision

In the emergent stage, firms typically have scarce resources, little experience and few partners. In addition, there are either inadequate market solutions available or numerous competing standards. The resulting uncertainty presses firms with limited internal capabilities to concentrate on developing technology that (1) is not available from external sources, and (2) offers an advantage. In such an environment with technology that is easily developed but highly important, internal development is best. If the technology is highly important and highly difficult to develop, the firm is likely to develop the technology internally in an attempt to set the standard. Alternatively, it may outsource to a trusted partner with an attractive technology to leverage resources. When the technology is of low importance but difficult to develop, the firm is likely to outsource from a partner or even transactional companies unless no external options exist and it is compelled to develop internally. When the technology is of low importance and easily developed, it should be obtained from the market and internal development adds no advantage.

During the transitional stage, standards are becoming more entrenched and the technology development focus shifts. More external sources become available and the uncertainty of the technology decreases, while competitive uncertainty increases. Subsequently, the general prescriptions remain from the emergent stage, but are supplemented by the need to move in the direction of the suggested strategies in the established stage. The technology and environment are in a state of flux. Firms must respond to the current environment but maintain an eye toward a future sourcing strategy. The firm typically moves toward internally developing technologies that are important for offering a differentiating advantage and for raising barriers to their competitors (usually associated with difficult development). The firm is also transitioning to outsourcing for all but highly important technologies, since availability is improving and there is little need to invest the firm's scarce resources in technology that won't create an advantage.

During the emergent and transitional stages, investments emphasize product technology. Once the standard has emerged, technology investments tend to shift towards process technology where improvements in cost and quality occur in manufacturing. This pushes the firm toward offshore sourcing. Key sourcing challenges include determining (1) the importance of the technology, and (2) the different natures and outcomes of product and process technologies, and (3) managing the transition as technology matures.

By the established stage, firms typically have improved resources, experience and partners. This means that they can draw on a large range of internal capabilities, and concentrate on developing technology that offers the greatest competitive advantage, since standardized technological solutions are now more widely available. At this point, the firm should concentrate its efforts on highly important core technology that is difficult to develop. Such technology supplies the firm with a differentiable advantage and increases the protective system around the technology. All other technologies are either less critical or less difficult to develop, and should be outsourced, since they are more widely available externally.

As can be seen, the dominance of product design changes over time, and influences where technology should be developed or acquired. Before the product standard is established, technology developed internally or with cooperative partners provides the greatest control and can reap the greatest competitive advantages if the technology emerges as the standard. Once the technological standard is established, market-based transactions are often most appropriate, except in the case where the firm itself has developed a core technology that offers a competitive advantage. As the product technology matures, additional product investments become less efficient, unless the purpose is for overthrowing the dominant technology standard.

CHALLENGES AND CONCLUSIONS

Masaaki Kotabe, a leading expert in the field, states that the complex nature of technology sourcing strategy spawns many barriers to its successful execution (Kotabe, 1998). It increasingly requires considering a wider range of sourcing options and making trade-offs among strategic objectives and outcomes. When developing a technology sourcing strategy, the benefits and costs among (1) internal development, (2) cooperative partners, or (3) market-based outsourcing must be understood. Internal development provides greater control over technology use and a chance for improved performance outcomes. With increased control, flexibility and adaptability may be sacrificed, which is particularly disastrous in times of high uncertainty. Outsourcing may result in a quicker or more cost-effective solution, but is less likely to provide long-term advantages, since externally acquired technology is likely to be available to competitors as well.

The resource, transaction and relational views provide complementary perspectives on the firm's organization and management of its technology sourcing strategy. Combined, these perspectives generally indicate that internal development of technology will improve the desired competitive advantage. They also offer additional insight into this complex decision. First, while pursuing a preferred strategic objective influences the choice of technology sourcing strategy, an advantage based on only one of these objectives (i.e. cost, quality, or speed) will be more easily negated by competitors. Accordingly, while multiple objectives are increasingly being pursued, there is a rise in the difficulty of implementation. Second, there are environmental and internal issues that influence the appropriateness and potential benefits of the technology sourcing options. Understanding the role of the degree of product design dominance, the technology protective system, and complementary assets is critical for profiting from technology. Thus managers must determine (1) the standard-setting context within the industry, (2) the ability to appropriate technology, (3) the complementary knowledge-based and physical resources possessed by themselves and their partners, and (4) how the objectives and strategy will affect their competitive advantage and performance. This must be considered in a turbulent, global environment that continues to put barriers in the path of a good technology sourcing strategy.

In conclusion, is 'Do what you do best and outsource the rest' really a good technology sourcing strategy? As with many such bromides, there is a ring of truth and a practical ability of these decision tactics to be correct in many circumstances. We have examined the contexts and demonstrated the complexity of the technology sourcing strategy that a simple heuristic does not capture. Managers with responsibilities related to technology development and sourcing understand that their decisions and strategies are intricate, more situational, and more subtle than simple.

'Do what you do best' is good advice, but what you do best is dependent on your ever-changing resources, partners and environmental context. Specifically, as technology matures different actions are required to capture the intended strategic positions of low cost, high quality, and/or speed-to-market. Additionally, relationships with cooperative partners offer options that are worth considering. Dell originally outsourced the manufacturing of components and concentrated on the assembly of computers and on developing direct relationships with their customers. They now are (1) selectively adding printers, services and other products, (2) wisely using complementary outside partner competencies and physical assets, and (3) cautiously remaining flexible within an uncertain environment. While Dell could not have done all this initially, they must do it now. In strategy, context is critical.

NOTE

1. The use of each of the three sourcing strategies is not mutually exclusive; a combination of strategies is often engaged. Whether as a clear attempt to optimize performance or more a function of limited resources, we found in a study conducted earlier that (a) 55.6 percent of technology was internally developed and 17.2 percent was sourced from other units within the same firm, (b) 9.1 percent of technology was contracted/licensed from cooperative third-parties, and (c) 18.1 percent was obtained through the market or other sources. All sources had great variation.

REFERENCES

Barney, J. (1991), 'Firm resources and sustained competitive advantage', *Journal of Management*, **17** (1), 99–120.

Bower, J.L. and T.M. Hout (1988), 'Fast-cycle capabilities for competitive power', *Harvard Business Review*, **66** (6), 110–18.

Cannic, M.V., R. Chen and J.D. Daniels (2004), 'Managing international technology transfer risk: alternatives and complements to ownership structure', *Management International Review*, **44** (Special Issue 1), 129–52.

Capon, N. and R. Glazer (1987), 'Marketing and technology: a strategic coalignment', *Journal of Marketing*, **51** (3), 1–14.

Christensen, C.M. (1997), *The Innovator's Dilemma*, Boston, MA: Harvard Business School Press.

Das, T.K. and B. Teng (1998), 'Between trust and control: developing confidence in partner cooperation in alliances', *Academy of Management Review*, **23** (3), 491–512.

Dierickx, I. and K. Cool (1989), 'Asset stock accumulation and the sustainability of competitive advantage', *Management Science*, **35** (12), 1504–13.

Dvorak, P. (2004), 'DVD-Standard panel approves format backed by Toshiba, NEC', *Wall Street Journal*, 26 February, p. B6.

Dyer, J.H. and H. Singh (1998), 'The relational view: cooperative strategy and sources of interorganizational competitive advantage', *Academy of Management Review*, **23** (4), 660–79.

The Economist (2002), 'Rough ride', 1 June, p. 62.

Fabey, M. (2002), 'Northrup finds latest technology in Sweden', *Daily Press*, 3 November, p. E1.

Gomes, L. (2002), 'Movie copying goes mainstream (sort of)', *Wall Street Journal*, 15 April, p. R8.

Gupta, A.K. and V. Govindarajan (2000), 'Knowledge flows and the structure of control within multinational corporations', *Academy of Management Journal*, **16** (4), 768–92.

Hill, C.W. (1997), 'Establishing a standard: competitive strategy and technological standards in winner-take-all industries', *Academy of Management Executive*, **11** (2), 7–25.

Insinga, R.C. and M.J. Werle (2000), 'Linking outsourcing to business strategy', *Academy of Management Executive*, **14** (4), 58–70.

Kotabe, M. (1992), *Global Sourcing Strategy: R&D, Manufacturing, and Market Interfaces*, New York: Quorum.

Kotabe, M. (1998), 'Efficiency vs. effectiveness orientation of global sourcing strategy: a comparison of U.S. and Japanese multinational companies', *Academy of Management Executive*, **12** (4), 107–19.

Kotabe, M. and K.S. Swan (1995), 'The role of strategic alliances in high technology new product development', *Strategic Management Journal*, **16** (8), 621–36.

Lashinsky, A. (2004), 'Where Dell is going next', *Fortune*, 18 October, p. 115.

Moore, G.A. (2002), *Living on the Fault Line, Revised Edition: Managing for Shareholder Value in Any Economy*, New York: HarperBusiness.

Morrison, S. (2002), 'Dell takes first step into printer market', *Financial Times*, 25 September, p. 30.

Noori, H. (1990), *Managing the Dynamics of New Technology*, Englewood Cliffs, NJ: Prentice Hall.

Ramstad, E. and S. McBride (2007), 'How dual-format DVD players may prolong duel', *Wall Street Journal*, 9 January, p. B4.

Reed, R. and R.J. DeFillipi (1990), 'Causal ambiguity, barriers to imitation, and sustainable competitive advantage', *Academy of Management Review*, **15** (1), 88–102.

Robins, J.A. (1987), 'Organizational economics: notes on the use of transaction cost theory in the study of organizations', *Administrative Science Quarterly*, **32** (1), 68–86.

Shirouzu, N. (2003), 'When hybrid cars collide', *Wall Street Journal*, 6 February, p. B1.

Shultz, G. (1988), 'The winning hand: American leadership and the global economy', address given in Washington, DC, 28 April.

Stalk, G. (1988), 'Time – the next source of competitive advantage', *Harvard Business Review*, **66** (4), 41–51.

Teece, D.J. (1986), 'Profiting from technological innovation: implications for integration, collaboration, licensing, and public policy', *Research Policy*, **15** (6), 285–305.

Wernerfelt, B. (1984), 'A resource-based view of the firm', *Strategic Management Journal*, **5** (2), 171–80.

Wheelwright, S.C. and K.B. Clark (1992), *Revolutionizing Product Development: Quantum Leaps in Speed, Efficiency, and Quality*, New York: The Free Press.

Williamson, O.E. (1975), *Markets and Hierarchies: Analysis and Antitrust Implications*, New York: The Free Press.

Williamson, O.E. (1985), *The Economic Institutions of Capitalism: Firms, Markets, Relational Contracting*, New York: The Free Press.

Zaun, T., G.L. White, N. Shirouzu and S. Miller (2002), 'Auto makers look for another edge farther from home', *Wall Street Journal*, 31 July, p. A1.

4.   Types of difficulties in internationalization and their consequences[1]

Alvaro Cuervo-Cazurra and C. Annique Un

International expansion provides the firm with many benefits, but it is challenging. The company views foreign markets as a good place to increase sales and draw on the firm's advantages (for a review of these arguments, see Tallman and Yip, 2001). However, once the firm moves abroad, in many cases it faces difficulties, regardless of how successful it may be at home. For example, the US retailer Wal-Mart entered the German market in 1997, viewing expansion into a large developed country as relatively easy and profitable. However, after losing money for several years, it decided to withdraw from the country in 2006. Despite being the largest retailer in the world, a leading user of information technologies and despite its cost-cutting, it could not overcome the challenges of understanding German shoppers and of needing to be better than German retailers (*The Economist*, 2006).

In this chapter we analyze types of difficulties in internationalization and discuss the direct consequences associated with each. The separation of difficulties in internationalization by their causes and specificity leads to the identification of three main groups (Cuervo-Cazurra, 2004; Cuervo-Cazurra and Un, 2004; Cuervo-Cazurra et al., 2007): the inabilities to transfer advantage and create value, the disadvantages of transfer and of foreignness, and the liabilities of expansion, newness, foreignness, and infrastructure. Each type of difficulty is associated with distinct consequences. However, this is an area that has not been explored in the literature, which has tended to analyze the difficulties as a single concept. Therefore, this chapter explores the specific consequences associated with each type of difficulty in internationalization.

The chapter is organized as follows. In the next section we briefly review the main theoretical concepts and key empirical findings. We then discuss the types of difficulties in internationalization, and connect each to their specific consequences. We conclude with some suggestions for future research.

EXISTING THEORETICAL CONCEPTS AND EMPIRICAL FINDINGS

The challenges faced by firms as they expand into foreign markets have traditionally been analyzed using three concepts: (1) cost of doing business abroad, (2) liability of foreignness, and (3) difficulties in internationalization. Although these concepts are related, they are not identical. The initial identification of the challenges was made in the economic-based international business literature under the heading of 'the cost of doing business abroad' (Hymer, 1976). This refers to the additional costs that a firm incurs in order to operate in a foreign market, and that domestic companies do not have to incur. The sources of these additional costs are the investments needed to operate at a distance, to deal with unfamiliarity with the economic, political and social characteristics of the country, and to deal with discrimination by the host government (Buckley and Casson, 1976; Dunning, 1977; Hennart, 1982; Hymer, 1976; Vernon, 1977).

A second stream of analyses, taking an organization studies viewpoint, refers to these challenges using the term 'liability of foreignness' (Zaheer, 1995). The liability of foreignness was initially defined as 'the cost of doing business abroad that results in a competitive disadvantage for a MNE subunit' (Zaheer, 1995, p. 342), but later studies moved away from costs and highlighted institutional differences as the distinguishing characteristics of the liability of foreignness (Zaheer, 2002). The sources of liability of foreignness are lack of adaptation to local institutional requirements, lack of legitimacy, and lack of membership of information networks (Kostova and Zaheer, 1999; Zaheer, 1995, 2002; Zaheer and Mosakowski, 1997).

A recent stream of research uses the concept of 'difficulties in internationalization' to refer to the challenges that multinationals face when they expand across countries (Cuervo-Cazurra, 2004; Cuervo-Cazurra and Un, 2004; Cuervo-Cazurra et al., 2007). The concept has been used to systematically identify the causes of the difficulties, which we discuss below. This concept incorporates the cost of doing business abroad as part of the solution to some of the difficulties. It also incorporates the liability of foreignness as one of the difficulties the firm faces when it has to deal with a new institutional environment. Therefore, in this chapter we use the concept of 'difficulties in internationalization'.

The empirical literature has focused primarily on analyzing the performance consequences of these difficulties in internationalization. The studies can be separated into two types: those that compare the performance of subsidiaries of foreign firms to that of domestic companies, and those that analyze the performance of multinationals with different international presence. Studies of the first type try to test for the existence of difficulties in internationalization. These studies found that, in general, subsidiaries of foreign firms have lower performance levels than domestic firms, especially when they are first beginning to operate abroad. For example, Zaheer (1995) compared the performance of US and Japanese foreign exchange trading firms in the US and Japan and found that foreign firms have lower financial performance. Zaheer and Mosakowski (1997) compared the survival rate of foreign exchange trading rooms around the world and found that subsidiaries of foreign firms have a lower probability of survival than domestic firms, although after several years their probability of survival is equal. However, other studies have not found that foreign firms have lower performance than domestic ones. For example, Li and Guisinger (1991) found that failure rates of foreign firms were lower than those of domestic ones, while Mata and Portugal (2002) separated new domestic firms from established ones and found that foreign firms and new domestic firms had similar probabilities of survival.

Studies of the second type present an indirect test of the difficulties in internationalization, since they do not compare the multinational firm's performance with that of local firms, but rather with that of other multinationals. They nevertheless capture one of the types of difficulties in internationalization, the liability of expansion. This literature focuses on problems associated with managing increasingly dispersed operations, rather than the difficulties faced by subsidiaries in a foreign country. These studies have found that the performance of multinationals varies according to their international presence. For example, Tallman and Li (1996) found that international expansion was associated with higher performance levels, while Hitt et al. (1997) found that very high levels of international expansion were associated with lower performance levels. Contractor et al. (2003) and Lu and Beamish (2004) found that performance levels increased with international presence in a curvilinear way, with performance being low at the beginning of the international expansion, increasing with further international presence, but diminishing with high international presence.

In sum, there is support for the idea that firms face difficulties in internationalization that reduce their performance, but there is a need for more nuanced analyses to resolve the empirical inconsistencies. We argue that some of the conflict originates in using a single concept that captures multiple types of difficulties. Separating difficulties in internationalization into several types reveals that some of them are not related to international expansion. At the same time, this separation helps establish direct consequences, some of which will not necessarily have an influence on performance or be revealed in a comparison between foreign and domestic firms. We discuss these ideas in the remainder of the chapter.

TYPES OF DIFFICULTIES IN INTERNATIONALIZATION AND THEIR CONSEQUENCES

Although many studies list several causes of the difficulties in internationalization, few analyze them in depth. The exception is recent work from a resource-based perspective that separates the causes of difficulties in internationalization into three main groups based on their relationship with advantage. Cuervo-Cazurra et al. (2007) provide an overarching analysis of the types of difficulties in internationalization. Cuervo-Cazurra (2004) discusses strategies that managers can use to identify and solve the difficulties. Cuervo-Cazurra and Un (2004) study how developed country MNEs, which tend to have many advantages, still face difficulties when they enter developing countries, and discuss strategies to solve these difficulties.

These studies separate difficulties into several types based on their resource-based cause. This yields three groups: (1) inabilities to transfer advantage and to create value, originating when resources lose their advantageous nature when transferred to a new country; (2) disadvantages of transfer and of foreignness, which occur when resources generate a disadvantage when transferred to a new country; and (3) liabilities of expansion, newness, foreignness and infrastructure that emerge when firms lack the complementary resources required to operate in the new country. A second classifying variable is the specificity of the difficulty; that is, whether the difficulty is firm-specific or common to a set of firms.

Table 4.1 summarizes the types of difficulties resulting from this classification, which we now discuss in detail. In addition to describing the types of difficulties, we discuss how each is associated with specific consequences, and present some strategies for identifying these consequences. In so doing, we extend the analysis of the liability of foreignness and its identification presented in Mezias (2002a). Here we analyze all types of difficulties in internationalization and discuss the identification of their associated consequences.

Loss of Advantage: Inability to Transfer Advantage and Inability to Create Value

The advantage provided by resources is relative to the competitive environment in which the firm operates (Tallman, 1992). The environment in a new country will differ from a firm's home country because of variations in physical characteristics, such as geography and climate, or in the characteristics of its people and institutions, such as government, businesses,

Table 4.1 Types of difficulties in internationalization and their consequences

Classification dimensions		Type of difficulty by its cause	Direct consequences of the type of difficulty	Identification strategy
Relationship to advantage	Specificity			
Loss of advantage: resources transferred lose advantageous nature in new country	Specific to a firm	*Inability to transfer advantage:* A resource that was the source of advantage in existing operations loses its advantageous characteristic when transferred to the new country	Lower than expected revenues, lower performance than existing operations	Internal analysis of firms' attempt to transfer advantage, and of the sustainability of the advantage in comparison to domestic competitors
	Common to a set of firms	*Inability to create value:* A set of firms in an industry do not obtain value from the transferred resources that were a source of advantage in existing operations because their products are not useful in the new country	No revenues	Existence of competitors in industry
Creation of a disadvantage: resources transferred generate disadvantage in new country	Specific to a firm	*Disadvantage of transfer:* A resource becomes disadvantageous when transferred to the new country	Inefficiencies in operations, revenue and performance below potential, independent of competitors, domestic or foreign	Comparison to existing operations
	Common to a set of firms	*Government-based disadvantage of foreignness:* A set of firms from the same country are discriminated against by the host government because it dislikes their country of origin	Reduced revenues, limited operations, higher costs, lower profitability, higher taxes, exclusion from subsidies or government contracts	Comparison to domestic firms and to firms from other foreign countries
		Consumer-based disadvantage of foreignness: A set of firms from the same country are discriminated against by consumers because they dislike their country of origin	Lower than expected revenues, lawsuits, violence against facilities	Comparison of products with different countries of origin

Table 4.1 continued

Classification dimensions		Type of difficulty by its cause	Direct consequences of the type of difficulty	Identification strategy
Relationship to advantage	Specificity			
Lack of complementary resources: need complementary resources to operate in the new country	Specific to a firm	*Liability of expansion*: The firm lacks the complementary resources needed to operate at a larger scale required by the expansion into the new country	Inefficiency at headquarters, lower overall performance for firm	Compare efficiency and performance before and after expansions
		Liability of newness: The firm lacks the complementary resources required to compete in the industry in the new country	Reduced revenues and performance in comparison to established firms, but not in comparison to new domestic entrants, increased costs to obtain missing resources	Compare foreign firms and newly created domestic firms to established domestic firms
		Liability of foreignness: The firm lacks complementary resources required to operate in the institutional environment of the new country	Lower than expected revenues, higher costs after investment in complementary resources to operate in country	Compare institutions in host country and those in countries of operation
	Common to a set of firms	*Liability of infrastructure*: A set of firms do not obtain value from transferred resources because customers in the new country lack the complementary assets needed to use their products	Zero or reduced revenues	Analyze need for complementary resources or knowledge to use firm's products

Source: Adapted and extended from Cuervo-Cazurra and Un (2004) and Cuervo-Cazurra et al. (2007).

religion, language, wealth or culture (Ghemawat, 2001). When competitors and customers differ across countries, a resource that supported a firm's advantage in one country may lose its ability to support that advantage in a new country (Hu, 1995).

Inability to transfer advantage

A firm suffers from the *inability to transfer advantage* when it faces a firm-specific loss of advantage; that is, when a resource that is advantageous in existing operations is transferred to a new country but the advantage provided by the resource is not transferred. A resource that is rare (i.e. that few competitors possess) in one country may not be rare in another because of differences in the countries' endowments (Kogut, 1985); thus a resource that supported advantage in one country may not do so in another country. Alternatively, domestic competitors may already have the resource, have imitated it, or have substituted it with another that provides a similar or improved benefit. Of course, not all firms face this difficulty when they enter a new country. In many cases the impetus for entry into a new country is precisely the fact that local competitors are weak or non-existent. The inability to transfer advantage is not exclusive to the firm's internationaliz-ation. The advantage provided by an advantageous resource is limited to a specific period of time (Miller and Shamsie, 1996).

The main consequence of the inability to transfer advantage is lower-than-expected revenues. A firm that suffers from this difficulty does not have a unique value proposition for customers in the new market, hence customers in the new country will not pay a premium for the firm's products, or will not buy them because there are better domestic alternatives. As a result of not being able to transfer its advantage to the new country, the firm does not achieve higher-than-normal profits. This does not mean that the firm will experience losses, however, as it can still be profitable in the new country, but it will not achieve the level of profitability it is accustomed to in other operations. Nevertheless, if the firm has to incur additional costs to solve other difficulties, these investments will increase its costs and reduce its profitability, which can result in losses. Moreover, if the firm faces aggressive competitors that react to its entry into the market with actions that reduce the profitability of the newcomer in order to deter further entry, such as lowering their own prices, it may incur losses (Tirole, 1988).

The identification of this difficulty requires, first and foremost, an internal analysis of the basis of the firm's competitive advantage and whether the firm has tried to transfer its advantage abroad. Not all firms do this. For example, the US welding-machine manufacturer Lincoln Electric did not even try to transfer the source of its advantage, its piece-rate incentive system, to the new operations in Germany. As a result, it could not achieve the level of efficiency and quality it was used to achieving in the USA and suffered losses (Hastings, 1999). Second, once the firm has identified the basis of its advantage and tried to transfer it, the firm must evaluate this advantage in existing operations and determine whether it is valuable, rare, difficult to imitate or challenging to substitute in the new country. This requires evaluating existing competitors in the country, analyzing their source of advantage and whether the firm offers something different.

Inability to create value

Some firms will suffer from the *inability to create value* when the environment in a new country is so different that the industry or industry segment in which they operate is not viable in the country. As a result, they are not able to transfer an advantage to the new country. In this extreme case, customers cannot use, do not need, or will not pay for the firms' products or services. There are multiple reasons for this, including cultural norms such as prohibition of certain foods, geographic characteristics such as the weather, or factor markets such as abundant low-cost labor; all of which may limit the need for some products. For example, a firm that produces pork products will not have a market in Israel or in Muslim countries where the consumption of pork is prohibited by religion. It is unlikely that firms would choose to enter a country when such conditions exist, but there are many cases of firms doing inadequate up-front planning, and overestimating the value they can potentially create in a new country (Ricks, 2000). The inability to create value is not necessarily exclusive to internationalization – again, in an extreme case, a firm could theoretically diversify into an unrelated industry that is not viable in its home country.

The consequence of the inability to create value is a lack of revenue in the new country. The industry or segment in which the firm operates is not viable in the new country, which means that not only the firm in question but other firms, both foreign and domestic, will not be able to sell their products there. The identification of this difficulty is relatively straightforward. The firm can evaluate whether there are companies in their particular line of business operating in the country. A lack of foreign presence in the industry may indicate that it is not viable in the country. Exploring further the reasons for the lack of firms in the industry will reveal which characteristics, such as weather, religion or culture, preclude the existence of the industry there.

Creation of Disadvantage: Disadvantage of Transfer and Disadvantage of Foreignness

On some occasions resources may not simply cease to provide an advantage in the new country, but actually become liabilities, or disadvantageous, when transferred. This can be specific to one firm or common across multiple companies that share a common resource.

Disadvantage of transfer

A firm suffers from the disadvantage of transfer when some of the resources transferred to the new country conflict with existing practices in the country, creating a disadvantage relative to other firms, and resulting in the destruction of value created by other resources. The firm develops resources adapted to the characteristics of the environment in which it operates (Penrose, 1959). Such resources and the knowledge associated with their use are then codified into routines to facilitate the retrieval and replication of resources over time and across locations (Kogut and Zander, 1993; Nelson and Winter, 1982). As the company transfers them to another country, however, routines that were embedded in technical and managerial systems and supported by values and norms prevailing in the original context may be incompatible with the characteristics of new host-country environment, so creating a disadvantage. Even firms that are not internationalizing can face a disadvantage of transfer. Resources that were a source of advantage at one point in time can become a source of disadvantage at another (Leonard-Barton, 1992).

The consequence of the disadvantage of transfer is difficulty in operating in the new country. The firm transfers resources and capabilities that clash with some norms in the country and create disadvantages. For example, the operations of the US fast food firm Kentucky Fried Chicken in Japan had problems because headquarters continued to impose dishes and practices that worked in the US, but that were contrary to taste and norms in Japan (Bartlett and Rangan, 1986). These problems in the operation can be contained internally and result only in lower efficiency in the operation, with little impact on revenues, as long as the firm can generate products that clients want. In such a case, the firm may have lower profitability than expected because its work practices clash with existing norms in the country. However, its profitability may not be lower than that of competitors in the new country; the firm may generate the product differently from competitors and still be competitive in the marketplace. Nevertheless, the inefficiencies created by the disadvantage of transfer may be severe and result not only in internal problems, but also in problems interacting with customers, which can affect revenues and result in losses.

The identification of this difficulty requires a comparison of the new operation with existing ones to identify whether the practices that are being used in the new operation are creating problems there, and whether the firm is as efficient in the new operation as in existing ones. The disadvantage of transfer depends on whether the practices transferred to the new country clash there or not. As a result, it is independent of what domestic competitors are doing. Domestic competitors are relevant insofar as the disadvantage of transfer can reduce the firm's relative advantage.

Disadvantage of foreignness

The firm is suffering from the *disadvantage of foreignness* when its nationality puts it at a disadvantage relative to domestic firms. One resource that is common to several firms, the country of origin, creates a disadvantage because people in a host country discriminate against the nationality of the foreign firms. Unlike other difficulties that are common to other expansions of the firm, the disadvantage of foreignness, together with the liability of foreignness, discussed below, are the only two types of difficulties that are exclusive to the cross-border expansion of the firm.

We distinguish between two types of disadvantage of foreignness, based on whether it is the host government or the consumers that discriminate against the country of origin. These two groups differ in their knowledge of the true country of origin of the company, and on the impact of their actions on the firm. The government is in a position to know the country of origin of the firm, and it can impose a wide number of costs and constraints on the firm, including preventing entry. In contrast, consumers in the host country react more to the perceived country of origin than to the real one. Their actions are usually limited to the sales of the firm. We discuss government-based and consumer-based disadvantages of foreignness separately.

The *government-based disadvantage of foreignness* appears when a host-country government discriminates against foreign firms in general or firms from one country in particular because these companies pose a threat to their sovereignty (Hymer, 1976; Stopford and Strange, 1992). To reduce such threat, the government in the host country establishes limitations on the activities of foreign firms there (Buckley and Casson, 1976), increasing the risk of operating in the host country (Kobrin, 1979). Unlike other difficulties that tend to be higher at the beginning of operations, and then decline as the foreign firm learns and undertakes needed investments, the disadvantage of foreignness can increase or decrease quickly with changes in the government or in the relationship between the host-country and home-country governments. A firm that did not face a disadvantage of foreignness when it entered a given country may come to face it later on because, for example, a new government that dislikes foreign firms comes into power and reneges on previous contracts (Henisz and Williamson, 1999).

The consequences of the government-based disadvantage of foreignness vary depending on the type of limitations that the government establishes on the behavior of foreign firms or firms from certain countries. First, the government can exclude foreign firms from operating in the country. It has control over entry in the form of approval of foreign investments. This exclusion can affect all foreign firms, or those in sectors of the economy that are considered to be of national interest. Second, the government can allow foreign firms entry into the country, but establish constraints on their operations there, such as requiring smaller operations than desired, imposing the need to have a local firm as a joint-venture partner to facilitate the transfer of technology to the country, requiring the investment to be located in a region that needs development, or limiting the scope of activity to certain segments within the industry, among others. These constraints affect the revenues, costs and profitability of the subsidiary in comparison with domestic competitors that have the freedom to decide the characteristics of their operations. An example is the behavior of the Chinese government regarding foreign participation in the banking industry. Until 2006 it did not allow foreign participation above 25 percent of capital and no single shareholder could have more than 20 percent of capital. It also limited the services foreign-owned banks could offer to local customers. This, in effect, excluded the majority of the population from banking with foreign firms. In late 2006 it opened up the industry and established regulations to allow foreign banks to provide full services to local customers, but required local incorporation and high levels of operating funds for each branch. Foreign bankers viewed these constraints as overly onerous and believed them to be designed to slow down their expansion (Dickie and Tucker, 2006). Third, the government may impose additional taxes and fees on foreign firms, or tax foreign firms at higher rates than domestic ones. These additional taxes can not only lower the profits of the operation in the new country, but in some cases may drive it to losses, such as when taxes are imposed on revenues rather than on profits. Fourth, the government may indirectly discriminate against foreign firms by excluding them from receiving benefits such as subsidies, contracts and governmental support, which are given to domestic firms. The consequences of these actions will be lower revenues in the case of exclusion from contracts and relatively higher costs in the case of exclusion from subsidies or government support.

The identification of the government-based disadvantage of foreignness requires two comparisons, one between foreign and domestic firms and another among foreign firms from different foreign countries and domestic firms. The first comparison helps establish the existence of a disadvantage of foreignness that affects all foreign firms. In this case, it is the foreign nature of the firm that is discriminated against. The second comparison helps establish the existence of a disadvantage of foreignness against certain countries of origin. In this case, it is not the foreignness of the firm, but rather the particular country of origin that is discriminated against. Additionally, the timing of comparison matters because the disadvantage of foreignness does vary across time with changes in the political situation of the home country, the host country, and the relationship between the home and host countries. A comparison at one point in time may reveal no disadvantage, but the same comparison at a later period may reveal it.

The *customer-based disadvantage of foreignness* appears when consumers, acting independently of their government, discriminate against the firm either because it is foreign or because of the specific country of origin of the firm. Consumers may dislike the country of origin for nationalistic reasons, or may have a negative perception of the quality of products generated in the foreign country. As a result, consumers will buy products coming from other nations independent of product or service quality (Bilkey and Nes, 1982; Peterson and Jolibert, 1995). As in the case of government-based discrimination, this difficulty can vary according to current events. However, unlike in the previous case, consumers react to the *perceived* country of origin of the firm rather than to the *actual* country of origin. As a result, some foreign firms may not suffer from this. For example, in May 1999, demonstrations in China against the bombing of the Chinese embassy in Belgrade by US planes affected the Chinese franchises of the fast food restaurants Kentucky Fried Chicken (KFC) but not of Pizza Hut, even though both were owned by the US firm Tricon. Managers of Tricon argued that maybe the Chinese viewed the Pizza Hut outlets as being Italian (Ruggless, 1999). Nevertheless, a little over a year after the attacks, KFC was already planning a further expansion of 100 new outlets in China (*New York Times*, 2001).

The consequences of the consumer-based disadvantage of foreignness are felt primarily in marketing and sale of products, while an effect on operations is less common. Consumers that dislike the foreignness of the product or the firm, or its particular country of origin, will choose products from their own country or other foreign countries. As a result, the firm will have lower revenues than expected. This does not mean that the firm will necessarily have lower performance than domestic companies; the firm may still be able to sell to consumers that do not care about the country of origin, or take advantage of low costs of production to provide a better price–quality offer. Nevertheless, the firm will attain a lower level of performance than it could attain if it were not suffering a consumer-based disadvantage of foreignness. This disadvantage can be a constant source of discrimination for the firm, or can increase with events in the home or host country, as the case of KFC in China illustrates. Although the main consequence of the consumer-based disadvantage of foreignness is felt on the revenue side, it can have other impacts on the operations. These include more lawsuits against foreign firms (Mezias, 2002b), or even attacks on the facilities of foreign firms.

The consumer-based disadvantage of foreignness can be identified by conducting a comparison of views about the country of origin. The firm can place products with an indication of the country of origin and ask consumers to rank them by preference. Additionally, one can compare negative actions of individuals against firms, such as lawsuits or violence, and compare the incidence of such events for foreign and domestic companies, making sure to take into account the perceived foreignness or country of origin rather than the actual one, since consumers may not be aware of the actual country of origin of the firm. As indicated previously, the timing of the comparison is also relevant. The firm may face a customer-based disadvantage of foreignness at one point but not at another.

Lack of Complementary Resources: Liability of Expansion, Liability of Newness, Liability of Foreignness, and Liability of Infrastructure

The firm can also suffer from a lack of complementary resources. Because of differences across countries, some resources cannot be transferred to the new country (Rugman and Verbeke, 1992). As a result, additional resources, such as knowledge, may be required in the new country but not the home country (Eriksson et al., 1997). These are complementary resources, in the sense that they complement the advantage provided by other resources (Teece, 1986). Nevertheless, the lack of such resources can negatively affect the operations in the new country in comparison to local competitors because the internationalizing firm will need to incur expenses that are not incurred by established local competitors.

Liability of expansion

A firm suffers from the *liability of expansion* when it lacks complementary resources to operate at a larger scale. Internationalization is accompanied by an increase in the scale of a firm's activities, requiring the firm to deal with additional transportation, communication and coordination (Tallman and Li, 1996; Hitt et al., 1997). To manage this increase in scale and complexity, the firm needs slack resources, otherwise, it may have to stretch its existing resources so thinly as to be ineffective (Penrose, 1959). The liability of expansion is not exclusive to internationalization: a firm faces similar difficulties when it grows in scale and complexity as it moves from being a local competitor to being a national one, or when it diversifies into multiple industries.

The consequences of the liability of expansion are inefficiencies at headquarters rather than at the new subsidiary. The increases in size and complexity that accompany the expansion across countries result in existing activities, information systems and management teams being overwhelmed by the requirements of the new operation in terms of the need for products, for information processing, or for coordination with the new operations. As a result, current activities, systems and management are stretched thin and show signs of inefficiency, such as delays in processing orders, improper information management, or excessive overtime hours. For example, the US welding firm Lincoln Electric had difficulty managing its rapid internationalization in the 1980s because managers at headquarters did not have the expertise, and in some cases not even the passports, needed to deal with foreign operations (Hastings, 1999).

This problem appears at the beginning of the firm's internationalization or after a large foreign expansion, where the firm's existing capacity is insufficient to cope with the new addition. Thus identification of the liability of expansion requires an internal analysis of the efficiency and effectiveness of the existing operation before and after the expansion, examining whether there was spare capacity that the new expansion has absorbed, and whether there is a need for more capacity than the firm currently possesses. As discussed above, this difficulty is reflected in the change in performance with the expansion of operations, where the multinational has lower performance in the initial expansion, higher performance as it continues its expansion, but then a drop in performance with high levels of international expansion (Contractor et al., 2003; Lu and Beamish, 2004).

Liability of newness

A firm encounters a *liability of newness* when it lacks complementary resources to compete in a new competitive environment. A firm's existing competitive environment induces it to develop certain strategies and resources to compete against other firms within a particular industry structure (Porter, 1985). When the firm moves to another country, the competitive environment often differs, requiring additional resources that the firm does not possess in that market, either because it cannot transfer them across countries or because it has not developed them (Anand and Delios, 1997). The liability of newness is not exclusive to the internationalization process. New entrants to an industry lack some complementary resources that established competitors already have, and as a result they are at a disadvantage relative to established firms (Lieberman, 1989).

The consequences of the liability of newness are, primarily, low revenues and, secondarily, high costs. The firm may not be able to sell its products because it lacks value chain segments that are necessary in the host country, such as a distribution channel or a production facility. The firm may still be able to sell its products but will achieve lower levels of sales than expected when the complementary resources it lacks are more intangible in nature but still important for competing in the industry, such as reputation in the marketplace, managerial knowledge of the nuances of the industry, or established relationships with clients. This was the case, for example, of the US welding firm Lincoln Electric in its European operations, where its poor reputation and relationships with clients limited its ability to sell its technologically superior products (Hastings, 1999). The firm will have higher costs than competitors when it has to invest in developing or acquiring the complementary resources it needs to compete in the industry. However, the foreign firm will not have higher costs than new domestic competitors that are entering the industry. Both the foreign firm and the new domestic competitor lack complementary resources and incur higher costs than established competitors. The result is that foreign firms and new domestic entrants have similar chances of failure (Mata and Portugal, 2002).

The liability of newness can be identified by comparing the foreign firm to domestic companies, separating newly created companies and established firms. Both the foreign firm and the newly created domestic companies will suffer from the liability of newness and have lower profitability than established domestic firms. However, the foreign firm is likely to have higher performance than the newly created firm because it is already operating in the industry in other countries. Thus it is only required to obtain complementary resources and learn how to compete under the particularities of the industry in the new country. Newly created firms, in contrast, have to obtain all resources needed to operate in the industry as well as learning how to compete there.

Liability of foreignness
A firm suffers from a *liability of foreignness* when it lacks the complementary resources to operate in a new institutional environment. The institutional environment (i.e. the set of norms and rules that influence human behavior, such as culture, language, religion, and the political, legal, and economic systems) affects all firms operating in the country (North, 1990). A firm's home-country institutional environment induces the firm to develop certain resources to operate effectively in that environment and interact with other social actors (Tallman, 1992). When the firm moves into a new country with a different institutional environment, it will lack the resources needed for dealing with other entities and understanding the prevailing rules of behavior (Johanson and Vahlne, 1977; Zaheer, 2002). Similar to the disadvantage of foreignness, the liability of foreignness only affects firms that internationalize, since it originates in the differences in social and institutional contexts that exist across countries.

The consequences of the liability of foreignness tend to be lower sales than expected. The lack of resources arises from differences in institutional environment between the new host country and the countries where the foreign firm operates. The resources that the firm lacks can take multiple dimensions, affecting revenues differently. Language is one common and obvious difference among countries. Poor translations can result in a lack of understanding or the creation of problems when the translation has a negative connotation; similarly, the failure to translate the name may create problems. For example, the US automobile company GM was unable to sell many of its Chevy Novas in Central and South America because it did not change the name, which means 'it does not go' in Spanish (Ricks, 2000). The legal system is another obvious institutional difference. In common-law countries contracts are lengthier and more detailed than in civil-law countries, where one relies on the existing codes (La Porta et al., 1998). Norms of behavior are less obvious but still important differences, which can create havoc in international operations. For example, in some countries building a relationship requires the exchange of gifts; not following these gift exchange ceremonies will limit the firm's ability to operate in the country because it will not be able to build the trust needed to operate (Donaldson, 1996). The liability of foreignness can also appear in the products that the firm generates, which are developed to operate under certain institutional conditions. For example, electronic products are developed to use a certain electrical standard in terms of hertz and volts; they will not operate without modification in countries that have a different standard.

Identifying the liability of foreignness can be done through a comparison of institutions in the host country with those where the firm operates. A multinational that comes from a home country that differs greatly from the host country is more likely to suffer a liability of foreignness. However, this multinational may operate in other countries that are more similar to the host country. Hence, to properly identify the liability of foreignness, one must analyze the differences between the institutions in the host country and the institutions of not only the home country, but also other foreign countries where the foreign firm operates. The foreign firm can use the knowledge acquired in these other countries to facilitate entry into the new host country (Barkema and Vermeulen, 1998).

Liability of infrastructure
In addition to these firm-specific liabilities, a set of foreign firms in the same industry entering the new country may suffer from the *liability of infrastructure*, whereby customers lack the complementary resources needed to use the firm's products. The liability of infrastructure affects all firms, both foreign and domestic, seeking to market a similar product or service to customers in the country. The complementary resources necessary may be tangible (e.g. the availability of refrigeration for products that need to be kept cold), or intangible (e.g. knowledge about how to use an innovative product). They may

also arise from 'institutional voids' that may, for example, make it difficult for firms to handle logistics, or enforce contracts (Khanna et al., 2005). The liability of infrastructure is not exclusive to the firm's internationalization. Firms may face similar problems when they move across market segments in their home country; some lower level customers may not have the knowledge or complementary assets needed to use the firm's product.

The consequences of the liability of infrastructure are low sales of products. The firm's product may be useful in addressing customers' unmet needs, but customers cannot use it because they do not have the required complementary resources. As a result, the firm will have lower sales than in countries in which customers have the required resources to use the product. For example, a firm that sells frozen foods will have difficulty selling their product in a country where the majority of the population does not have freezers. Moreover, this difficulty can appear not only with the end consumers, but also with the distribution channels. For example, a Western frozen food company encountered difficulties when expanding into India because retailers' freezers did not reach the low temperatures necessary for the products to stay frozen (Prahalad and Lieberthal, 1998).

In sum, to identify the liability of infrastructure one must first analyze the firm's products and determine whether they require complementary resources for their use, and then assess whether the new country has customers that possess these complementary assets.

CONCLUSIONS

Firms face difficulties when they expand into other countries. We discussed how these difficulties may be categorized into various types and how each type is associated with different consequences. Our analysis reveals new insights in the relationship between difficulties in internationalization and their consequences; these may serve as guidelines for future research. First, each of the causes has different consequences associated with them. As a result, analyzing one consequence will detect only a limited set of difficulties, and will thus yield predictions that may not be applicable to other consequences. Second, our review of the consequences of difficulties in internationalization reveals that lower revenues are the most common consequence. However, empirical studies have not explored this consequence. Third, this study reveals that identification of the consequences of the different types of difficulty does not always require comparison with domestic competitors; in some cases, a comparison across operations in different countries may be more appropriate. As indicated above, few of the difficulties faced in a firm's international expansion are exclusive to the cross-border expansion.

Many affect both foreign and domestic firms as they expand. Empirical studies, however, do not separate these different difficulty types. The ideas discussed here may also be of use for managers. The framework highlights the multiplicity of difficulty types that the firm may encounter when it internationalizes, and demonstrates that each type is associated with different consequences. This may assist managers in identifying the existence of a particular difficulty that the firm is facing, and designing specific solutions that target the root cause of the type of difficulty.

NOTE

1. We thank Steve Tallman for helpful suggestions and the Center for International Business Education and Research at the University of South Carolina for providing financial support for this research. All errors are ours.

REFERENCES

Anand, J. and A. Delios (1997), 'Location specificity and the transferability of downstream assets to foreign subsidiaries', *Journal of International Business Studies*, **28**, 579–603.
Barkema, H.G. and F. Vermeulen (1998), 'International expansion through start-up or acquisition: a learning perspective', *Academy of Management Journal*, **41**, 7–27.
Bartlett, C. and U.S. Rangan (1986), '*Kentucky Fried Chicken (Japan)*', Harvard Business School Case Study 9-387-043, Boston, MA: Harvard Business School.
Bilkey, W.J. and E. Nes (1982), 'Country-of-origin effects on product evaluations', *Journal of International Business Studies*, **13**, 89–99.
Buckley, P. and M. Casson (1976), *The Future of the Multinational Corporation*, London: Macmillan.
Contractor, F.J., S.K. Kundu, and C.C. Hsu (2003), 'A three-stage theory of international expansion: the link between multinationality and performance in the service sector', *Journal of International Business Studies*, **34**, 5–18.
Cuervo-Cazurra, A. (2004), 'Dificultades en la internacionalización de la empresa' [Difficulties in the internationalization of the firm], *Universia Business Review*, **4** (4), 18–29.
Cuervo-Cazurra, A. and C.A. Un (2004), 'The bald eagle cannot find its way in the rainforest: sources and solutions to the difficulties in the internationalization of developed country MNEs into developing countries', in S.B. Prasad and P.N. Gauri (eds), *Global Firms and Emerging Markets in the Age of Anxiety*, Westport, CT: Praeger.
Cuervo-Cazurra, A., M. Maloney and S. Manrakhan (2007), 'Difficulties in internationalization: A resource-based analysis', *Journal of International Business Studies*, forthcoming.

Dickie, M. and S. Tucker (2006), 'China issues rules for foreign banks', *Financial Times*, 16 November.

Donaldson, T. (1996), 'Values in tension: ethics away from home', *Harvard Business Review*, **74** (5), 48–56.

Dunning, J. (1977), 'Trade, location of economic activity and the MNE: a search for an eclectic approach', in B. Ohlin, P.O. Hesselborn and P.M. Wijkman (eds), *The International Allocation of Economic Activity*, London: Macmillan.

The Economist (2006), 'Global retailing. Trouble at till', 4 November, p. 18.

Eriksson, K., J. Johanson, A. Majkgard and D.D. Sharma (1997), 'Experiential knowledge and cost in the internationalization process', *Journal of International Business Studies*, **28**, 337–60.

Ghemawat, P. (2001), 'Distance still matters', *Harvard Business Review*, **79** (8), 137–45.

Hastings, D.F. (1999), 'Lincoln Electric's harsh lessons from international expansion', *Harvard Business Review*, **77** (3), 162–78.

Henisz, W.J. and O.E. Williamson (1999), 'Comparative economic organization within and between countries', *Business & Politics*, **1**, 261–77.

Hennart, J.F. (1982) *A Theory of Multinational Enterprise*, Ann Arbor, MI: University of Michigan Press.

Hitt, M.A., R.E. Hoskisson and H. Kim (1997), 'International diversification: effects on innovation and firm performance in product-diversified firms', *Academy of Management Journal*, **40**, 767–98.

Hu, Y.S. (1995), 'The international transferability of the firm's advantages', *California Management Review*, **37**, 73–88.

Hymer, S. (1976), *The International Operations of National Firms: A Study of Direct Investment*, Cambridge, MA: MIT Press.

Johanson, J. and J.E. Vahlne (1977), 'The internationalization process of the firm: a model of knowledge development and increasing foreign market commitments', *Journal of International Business Studies*, **8**, 23–32.

Khanna, T., K.G. Palepu and J. Sinha (2005), 'Strategies that fit emerging markets', *Harvard Business Review*, **83** (6), 63–76.

Kobrin, S.J. (1979), 'Political risk: a review and reconsideration', *Journal of International Business Studies*, **10**, 67–80.

Kogut, B. (1985), 'Designing global strategies: comparative and competitive value-added chain', *Sloan Management Review*, **26** (Summer), 15–28.

Kogut, B. and U. Zander (1993), 'Knowledge of the firm and the evolutionary theory of the multinational corporation', *Journal of International Business Studies*, **24**, 625–45.

Kostova, T., and S. Zaheer (1999), 'Organizational legitimacy under conditions of complexity: the case of the multinational enterprise', *Academy of Management Review*, **24**, 64–81.

La Porta, R., F. Lopez-de-Silanes, A. Shleifer and R.W. Vishny (1998), 'Law and finance', *Journal of Political Economy*, **106**, 1113–55.

Leonard-Barton, D. (1992), 'Core capabilities and core rigidities: a paradox in managing new product development', *Strategic Management Journal*, **13**, 111–26.

Li, J. and S. Guisinger (1991), 'Comparative business failures of foreign-controlled firms in the United States', *Journal of International Business Studies*, **22**, 209–224.

Lieberman, M.B. (1989), 'The learning curve, technology barriers to entry, and competitive survival in the chemical processing industries', *Strategic Management Journal*, **10**, 431–47.

Lu, J. and P.W. Beamish (2004), 'International diversification and firm performance: the s-curve hypothesis', *Academy of Management Journal*, **47**, 598–609.

Mata, J. and P. Portugal (2002), 'The survival of new domestic and foreign-owned firms', *Strategic Management Journal*, **23**, 323–43.

Mezias, J.M. (2002a), 'Reexamining the liability of foreignness construct, creating a framework for identification, and assessing its role in managing multinational corporations', *Journal of International Management*, **8**, 407–22.

Mezias, J.M. (2002b), 'Identifying liabilities of foreignness and strategies to minimize their effect: the case of labor lawsuits judgments in the United States', *Strategic Management Journal*, **23**, 229–44.

Miller, D. and J. Shamsie (1996), 'The resource-based view of the firm in two environments: the Hollywood film studios from 1936 to 1965', *Academy of Management Journal*, **39**, 519–43.

Nelson, R.R. and S.G. Winter (1982), *An Evolutionary Theory of Economic Change*, Cambridge, MA: Belknap Harvard.

New York Times (2001), 'Tricon to open 100 more KFC franchises in China', 6 February.

North, D.C. (1990), *Institutions, Institutional Change, and Economic Performance*, New York: Cambridge University Press.

Penrose, E. (1959), *The Theory of the Growth of the Firm*, Oxford: Oxford University Press.

Peterson, R.A. and A.J.P. Jolibert (1995), 'A meta-analysis of country-of-origin effects', *Journal of International Business Studies*, **26**, 883–900.

Porter, M.E. (1985), *Competitive Advantage*, New York: The Free Press.

Prahalad, C.K. and K. Lieberthal (1998), 'The end of corporate imperialism', *Harvard Business Review*, **76** (4), 69–79.

Ricks, D.A. (2000), *Blunders in International Business*, 3rd edn, Malden, MA: Blackwell.

Ruggless, R. (1999), 'US operators close Chinese units after NATO bombing', *Nation's Restaurant News*, 24 May.

Rugman, A.M. and A. Verbeke (1992), 'A note on the transnational solution and the transaction cost theory of multinational strategic management', *Journal of International Business Studies*, **23**, 761–71.

Stopford, J.M. and S. Strange (1992), *Rival States, Rival Firms: Competition for World Market Shares*, New York: Cambridge University Press.

Tallman, S.B. (1992), 'A strategic management perspective on host country structure of multinational enterprises', *Journal of Management*, **18**, 455–71.

Tallman, S.B. and J. Li (1996), 'Effects of international diversity and product diversity on the performance of multinational firms', *Academy of Management Journal*, **39**, 179–97.

Tallman, S.B. and G.S. Yip (2001), 'Strategy and the multinational enterprise', in A.M. Rugman and T.L. Brewer (eds), *The Oxford Handbook of International Business*, New York: Oxford University Press.

Teece, D.J. (1986), 'Profiting from technological innovation: implications for integration, collaboration, licensing and public policy', *Research Policy*, **15**, 285–305.

Tirole, J. (1988), *The Theory of Industrial Organization*, Cambridge, MA: MIT Press.

Vernon, R. (1977), *Storm Over the Multinationals: The Real Issues*, Boston, MA: Harvard University Press.

Zaheer, S. (1995), 'Overcoming the liability of foreignness', *Academy of Management Journal*, **38**, 341–63.

Zaheer, S. (2002), 'The liability of foreignness, redux: a commentary', *Journal of International Management*, **8**, 351–8.

Zaheer, S. and E. Mosakowski (1997), 'The dynamics of the liability of foreignness', *Strategic Management Journal*, **18**, 439–64.

5. R&D internationalization: building organizational capabilities to balance exploration and exploitation

Gurneeta Vasudeva and Petra Sonderegger

Increasingly, multinational enterprises (MNEs) from both industrialized and emerging market economies are internationalizing their research and development (R&D) activities (Cantwell, 1995; Carlsson, 2006; Zhao 2006). A recent study by Booz Allen Hamilton and INSEAD (2006) suggests, for instance, that the share of overseas R&D sites for multinational firms increased from 45 per cent in 1974 to 66 per cent in 2004. The level of dispersion however varies both by home country and technology sector. For instance, firms based in Western Europe are the most international, though their dispersion has a distinctively regional flavour with most R&D sites located within Europe itself. Technology sectors such as information technology hardware and software are less internationalized than the pharmaceutical, biotechnology, automotive and chemical sectors, where knowledge is relatively more codified.

But what is more impressive is the fact that combined, China and India are on the brink of overtaking Western Europe as locations for foreign R&D, especially for US multinational firms (Booz Allen Hamilton and INSEAD, 2006). Patents assigned to Indian subsidiaries of multinational firms such as Intel, Oracle, Texas Instruments, Cisco and General Electric, for example, indicate that a significant amount of innovation now stems from India. The drivers for this trend towards R&D internationalization include access to technology clusters, qualified manpower, proximity to new markets, cost-cutting or simply herd instincts that are not uncommon among multinational firms (Khanna et al., 2005).

While on the one hand, internationalization of R&D presents opportunities for firms to widen their knowledge inputs and access new skills, technologies and customers; on the other hand, managing and integrating these activities requires new organizational structures, processes and capabilities. Firms face serious difficulties in assessing the value of new knowledge embedded in unfamiliar contexts, for example, and this problem is more pronounced for firms dealing in complex knowledge (Cohen and Levinthal, 1990; Lane and Lubatkin, 1998). Dispersion also brings with it greater costs and, therefore, leveraging projects to enable sharing and re-using knowledge across the network can be key to efficient and effective global innovation.

In addition, in the context of emerging market economies it appears that multinational firms are internationalizing their R&D activities despite weak institutions for contract enforcement or protection of intellectual property (Zhao, 2006; Khanna et al., 2005) and although considerable differences persist in the organizational practices between the multi-nationals' subsidiaries and domestic firms (Kostova and Roth, 2002). Given these institutional and technological challenges, we ask: what kind of organizational capabilities do multinational firms need to conduct R&D in emerging market economies?

The literature on dynamic capabilities suggests that adapting and reconfiguring organizational processes and routines (Teece et al., 1997) and developing 'architectural competence' by integrating specialized technological knowledge in novel and flexible ways (Henderson and Clark, 1990), allows multinational firms to acquire and assimilate resources, shed resources or recombine them (Eisenhardt and Martin, 2000). Dynamic capabilities of firms, therefore, are reflected in the extent to which they balance coordination and recombination of knowledge across geographical units and external knowledge acquisition.

The organizational learning perspective deploys the exploration and exploitation framework to draw attention to the fundamental tension in organizational adaptation (March, 1991). According to March (1991, p. 85) exploitation is characterized by the 'refinement and extension of existing competencies, technologies and paradigms', so that the organization is likely to rely on its established routines and problem-solving heuristics. March (1991) described exploitation as learning from an organizational code that reflects best practices to produce rapid conformity of beliefs and practices throughout the organization. However, conformity to the code drives out intra-organizational heterogeneity, resulting in lower long-run performance. Exploration is characterized by experimentation with new alternatives, the returns from which are 'systematically less certain, more remote in time and organizationally more distant than the locus of action and adaptation' (March, 1991, p. 73). Exploration occurs to the extent that non-conforming beliefs and practices persist despite information about proven best practices available from the code. The organizational learning perspective emphasizes the merits of balancing the conflicting needs for exploration and exploitation (Rivkin and Siggelkow, 2003). Similarly, firms are seen to possess dynamic capabilities to the extent that they can integrate new knowledge with the existing knowledge base (Zahra and George, 2002).

Building on recent research that examines how firms balance exploration and exploitation over time and within organizational domains as well as across these domains (Lavie and Rosenkopf, 2006), we suggest that R&D activities in emerging market economies that are both geographically and institutionally distant constitutes an exploratory strategy. However, to balance such exploratory learning, MNEs are more likely to pursue exploitative strategies for building organizational capabilities in other important domains of their R&D internationalization strategy.

Previous literature has examined how MNEs balance exploration and exploitation within the technological domain. As an extension to these studies, we suggest that MNEs that have located R&D units in India seek to balance exploration in geographically, culturally and institutionally distant contexts, by adopting exploitation strategies for developing organizational capabilities. Our framework is motivated by the experiences of MNEs' R&D units located in India. In the sections that follow we elaborate on the tension between exploration and exploitation in pursuing R&D in emerging market economies. We begin by explaining why conducting R&D in an emerging market economy such as India constitutes an exploratory strategy and then proceed to suggest that firms that succeed in their R&D internationalization efforts tend to balance this kind of exploratory approach by adopting more exploitative approaches across at least three dimensions of organizational capabilities – intra-organizational coordination, staffing practices and inter-organizational alliances.

R&D INTERNATIONALIZATION: AN EXPLORATORY STRATEGY

Opening a new R&D unit involves significant investments, and conducting international R&D across large distances in general carries high inherent risks, communication hurdles and transaction costs (von Zedtwitz and Gassmann, 2002). Despite these risks and costs, firms are rapidly internationalizing R&D. R&D internationalization, however, has followed very different paths across industrialized and emerging market economies. In industrialized countries, overseas research facilities were set up in order to gain access to cutting edge technology in 'centres of excellence', and development facilities were opened only in the largest markets (Voelker and Stead, 1999). Often, such development facilities focused on an exploitative strategy or the adaptation of the firm's existing products and technologies to local conditions, rather than an exploratory approach focused on acquiring and building on locally available knowledge. Only access to new technologies or large existing markets justified the high risks and costs associated with distributing R&D and opening new facilities.

The course of the new Indian R&D laboratories set up by multinational firms from the USA, Japan and Western Europe is quite different. These decisions do not manifestly follow the older model of seeking access to existing markets and/or new technologies. Despite rapid economic growth, the Indian markets for high-technology products have not yet reached a critical mass that can challenge the dominance of western (especially US) markets.[1] Further, notwithstanding their impressive success in applying and adapting existing technologies in the software services and manufacturing industries, respectively, India is not yet on a par with industrialized countries as 'centres of excellence' in the development of new high technologies. Furthermore, a recent survey on R&D internationalization revealed that many institutions important for industrial R&D are either weak or missing in these countries (Economist Intelligence Unit, 2004a). Protection for intellectual property rights is often ineffective; university–industry linkages are rarely as strong as in industrialized countries; and local entrepreneurship is often restricted by a lack of venture financing, inadequate property rights and an excessive bureaucratic burden (Economist Intelligence Unit, 2004a).

Recent research has suggested that organizational capabilities and strategies of firms are at least partially contingent on the national institutional context within which innovation occurs (Lewin and Kim, 2004). Orru et al. (1991) observed, for example, that firms in Japan, Taiwan and South Korea display dissimilar intra- and inter-organizational practices that reflect the unique institutional characteristics of these countries. National institutions reflected in the legal, financial, cultural and educational systems of a country define the nature of problems that firms have to solve, affect technological learning, shape the incentives and constraints for innovation and, therefore, exercise a strong influence on the basic organizational processes involving technology development (Nelson and Winter, 1982; Nelson and Rosenberg, 1993). Thus, MNEs that adopt an exploratory approach for R&D internationalization must also possess the capabilities to meld the characteristics of the diverse institutional contexts within which they operate.

The example of Siemens's telecommunications R&D unit in India illustrates our point well. Even though the Indian R&D unit set up in Bangalore was expected to develop global products and was envisioned as a 'centre of excellence' carrying out breakthrough innovations, much like Siemens's R&D unit in Boca Raton, Florida, the organizational strategy was crafted independent of the social, political and cultural setting. Thus the organizational model was driven primarily by economic efficiencies that could be gained from cutting resource and labour costs, around-the-clock innovation taking advantage of the different time zones, and proximity to customers in a new and emerging market. Since the organizational strategy relied solely on local resources, it was not long before the headquarters in Munich was confronted with differences in research cultures and problem-solving approaches between the Indian and the German engineers, contributing to technological glitches and consequent embarrassment with large clients like Deutsche Telekom. Despite these problems, management decided that it would not impose on the Bangalore unit the organizational practices of its German counterpart in Munich. The approach adopted to realize the exploratory R&D strategy allowed for greater organizational autonomy but ignored the need for a balance between exploration and exploitation across domains within an organization.

In view of the significant difficulties involved in coordinating long-distance research within the globally integrated multinational firm and the institutional weaknesses of national innovation systems in emerging market economies, it may seem somewhat surprising that multinational firms choose to conduct R&D in emerging market economies beyond the bare minimum required for localization efforts or demanded by host country governments. As it turns out, several MNEs have changed their strategy mid-stream and a few have closed or sold R&D units soon after setting them up. The recent failure of Intel's high-profile Whitefield microprocessor project in Bangalore that made use of Intel's cutting-edge mobile chip technology highlights some of the problems in developing technologies in R&D units in emerging market economies. According to media reports, the project's failure in large measure was linked to engineering delays and a financial fraud, resulting in the sudden lay-off of key employees.

The preceding example illustrates how, in the process of transcending geographical boundaries and technological communities, the MNE is confronted with enormous technological and institutional diversity (Frost, 2001). At the same time, it is this unique structural position across institutional and technological boundaries that gives an MNE its competitive advantage as a knowledge-creating organization (Cantwell, 1995). As Almeida (1996) observed in a study of knowledge flows in Silicon Valley, MNE subsidiaries can and do take advantage of technological diversity and subsequently draw more from local knowledge resources than comparable domestic firms in the same region. But less clear are the organizational processes that MNEs deploy to achieve this objective in the context of institutional and technological diversity, or for that matter in the context of weak or altogether missing institutions.

In summary, many MNEs seek to internationalize their R&D with little or no prior experience in emerging markets in general or the specific country chosen for the new R&D unit. MNEs that conduct R&D in emerging markets, therefore, must deal with the higher management risks and costs associated with long-distance collaboration; they must adapt to radically different or entirely missing institutions; and they must integrate new technological communities while pursuing an internationalization strategy that doesn't have the traditional goals of improved access to new technologies or existing markets.

Based on the risks, uncertainty, novelty and longer term pay-offs associated with R&D conducted in emerging markets, we conclude that MNEs that pursue such a strategy follow an exploratory approach in terms of their R&D geography. We suggest that MNEs balance the stresses of geographical exploration by following a more exploitative approach in the technological and/or organizational capability domains of their R&D. Technological exploitation has been defined as refining existing technologies for an existing customer base or adapting them for new customers (Kuemmerle, 1998). In this chapter we offer a framework for understanding how firms adopt an exploitative approach for building organizational capabilities in the context of R&D internationalization.

BUILDING ORGANIZATIONAL CAPABILITIES: AN EXPLOITATIVE APPROACH

Frost (2001) noted that the extent to which an MNE follows an exploratory or exploitative R&D mandate in a host country is a function of its own technological capabilities and those of the local firms. As an extension to this argument we suggest that the choice of an exploratory versus exploitative R&D mandate is driven by not only the MNEs' and local firms' technological capabilities, but also their organizational capabilities. In other words, MNEs will be more likely to adopt exploratory mandates in R&D internationalization when they possess the organizational capabilities to exploit their existing practices and processes.

Such an exploitative organizational strategy encompasses intra-organizational coordination, staffing and inter-organizational alliances. It will allow for combining existing knowledge across various R&D units with local knowledge through the provision of a common experimental platform. MNEs must also possess appropriate search capabilities to identify and engage with local firms and research institutions, and to build on the knowledge they acquire as a result of such inter-organizational relationships. Within the firm, the staffing practices of firms must allow for integrating new knowledge with existing knowledge. Thus, not only will firms need to hire locally, but they will also benefit from sending experienced expatriates to take up senior managerial positions. Others may hire locals with sufficient global experience gathered either through prior international assignments and/or through employment with local multinational firms (mostly software and business process outsourcing organizations in the case of India) that train them to suit the needs of US or European MNEs.

Intra-organizational Coordination

An exploitative organizational approach applies existing processes and practices to the new R&D unit, and this new unit is tightly linked to others through joint projects, policies and platforms. Rather than pursuing independent research projects, this type of unit will typically collaborate closely with other units on existing projects at first. As it takes on leadership of new projects, it will continue to collaborate with other units around the world. Harmonization of organizational practices across R&D units also requires a synthesis of institutions that are reflected in the organiz- ational practices. Local policies, such as staffing guidelines or intellectual property safeguards, will be strongly aligned with overall company policies. Information technology systems will support these linkages; for example, project management systems or intranet-based knowledge management. Shared experimental platforms and testbeds in the software industry allow rapid diffusion of knowledge and standardization of research parameters. An explorative approach is much more likely to encompass local policies and practices from the outset. It will also be more likely that the new R&D unit pursues independent, less collaborative projects with somewhat less access to company systems and knowledge.

At SAP, a German software firm, the NetWeaver project, for example, is being developed by 2500 researchers in five locations around the world, but the project is led by the Palo Alto R&D unit, which sets the goals and verifies that the plans are on track (Economist Intelligence Unit, 2004b). ABB also conducts around-the-globe development and has implemented a common project management instrument that provides highly detailed and near-instant information on progress and bugs in order to facilitate coordination between sites. At STMicrolectronics, a leading semiconductor firm that has 16 advanced research and 39 design centres around the world, global integration of organizational practices is achieved through clear communication and constant reiteration of R&D goals. Similarly, at Ericsson standard R&D approaches – down to the units of measurement – are regarded as key to R&D success, regardless of where the R&D unit is located. Milestones and deliverables are monitored during the life cycle of the project so that researchers around the globe know how they and their colleagues are progressing.

Thus firms like SAP, ABB, STMicrolectronics and Ericsson have adopted a globally integrated organizational platform for conducting R&D in India. However, standardizing organizational routines and bridging the cultural divide across R&D units must be balanced with maintaining the independence of R&D units so that they are different enough to make a novel contribution, but similar enough so that the contribution is on target. This balance is difficult to achieve, as the Ericsson example illustrates. Despite decades of sales and manufacturing experience in India, its first attempt at opening a globally integrated R&D facility in the country was not a clear success. The company opened several labs in India, but later sold them to Wipro, an Indian software and R&D outsourcing firm. Ericsson retained some national R&D activities, but opened a new internationally focused R&D facility again only four years later.

Staffing Practices

In order to tap the competence of existing employees and to integrate new employees efficiently, the MNE will place a strong focus on sending experienced senior management to supervise the new R&D unit. These managers play a strong role in transferring the MNE's existing management styles, work practices and process definitions to the new unit. Relocating staff at other levels may also be desirable. An exploitative approach may also involve a strong emphasis on staff induction and sending new staff to previously existing R&D units to meet colleagues and absorb tacit knowledge and established best practices. By contrast, an exploratory strategy would focus on local recruitment practices and networks to hire local staff and management.

As an exemplar of an exploitative staffing strategy, Google standardizes hiring criteria across its R&D units (Google Labs) around the world. Its international 'Code Jam' hiring competitions are legendary among software professionals. Once employees are hired, Google Labs offers them comparable career paths across all locations. The goal is to encourage knowledge sharing based on the understanding that all engineers have similar levels of competence. Ultimately, Google hopes that employees can shift between labs frequently and seamlessly. Short of outright relocation, Google Labs encourages frequent travel between locations to integrate its worldwide workforce.

For both Intel and SAP, innovating in Bangalore rests on hiring engineers trained in their proprietary software on the books of Indian IT-services firms such as Wipro, Infosys and Tata Consultancy Services. Even though firms like Intel and SAP have benefited from the congenial workforce ecosystem developed by trail-blazers such as Texas Instruments, their staffing practices in the R&D units in Bangalore include hiring and training university graduates and supplementing them with senior expatriate engineers from the USA and Germany, respectively.

Intel has also announced the formal opening of the Intel Software College in Bangalore – a training school that will support India's software developer community by expanding their skills on Intel software and microprocessor technologies. Other firms, such as ABB and Philips, donate equipment to engineering colleges to encourage them to teach students about their particular platforms; Microsoft and several pharmaceutical firms offer summer schools or summer training programmes so that students can develop specific skills not taught in academic programmes before joining the workforce. HP Labs will offer fellowships that allow PhD students to complete their research within HP; and Philips is developing a joint MTech programme with the Sri Jayachamarajendra College of Engineering in Mysore.

At Accenture Technology Labs, the R&D unit established in Bangalore in 2006 will 'shape the future and invent the next wave of cutting-edge business solutions and new ways to develop those solutions'. To accomplish this objective of carrying out exploratory R&D at the new unit in Bangalore, Accenture's strategy involves staffing its Bangalore unit with R&D professionals from India's leading universities, and at the same time infusing Accenture's research culture.

To overcome cultural differences, firms like Ericsson and Microsoft encourage cross-pollination of ideas across R&D units. Similarly, General Motors offers cultural classes and Agilent has sent researchers from its Scottish labs to Beijing and vice versa (Economist Intelligence Unit, 2004b). Thus firms such as Google, Intel and SAP pursue an exploitative approach in their staffing practices, seeking employees who have a similar knowledge base and similar work practices. New employees are recruited from firms with similar work cultures and are assimilated into the firm's work practices rapidly through induction training and site visits to other R&D units. Where skills or knowledge are lacking in the labour market, these firms seek to fill the gap through university programmes, internal training, or by relocating staff from existing R&D units.

Even firms such as HP that have operated in India for decades before setting up their R&D unit in Bangalore in 2002 have emphasized the need for exploiting existing organizational capabilities. At HP, Anil Gupta, a veteran researcher of Indian origin, spent many years with HP Labs in the UK, set up HP's global offshoring unit in India and formed the EHPT alliance with Ericsson in India, before heading the R&D lab in Bangalore. In this manner, HP Labs drew on Gupta's knowledge of both internal practices and local institutions and his experience in bridging the two. HP Labs India has chosen to grow slowly (it has 12 research and one support staff), making it easier to train employees intensively. In addition, all employees are South Asian or of South Asian origin, most have several years of research experience in the USA or Western Europe and received their PhDs abroad,[2] thus forming a cultural bridge between the Indian and foreign institutional contexts. Most who were hired locally worked for MNEs in India before joining HP. The international or MNE experience provided a shared understanding of research and general work practices, and the PhD training abroad allowed for greater conformity with research standards in other industrialized countries.

Based on field evidence, we find that the research groups of multinational R&D units in Bangalore have a particularly high percentage of returnees, mostly researchers and managers of Indian origin who completed their postgraduate education in the USA or Europe and acquired several years of work experience there. Quite often they have worked for a particular MNE in its home country before transferring to India. Their familiarity with both western work practices and Indian culture is considered particularly valuable in bridging cultural differences. Some firms such as SAP have even instituted a formal 'returning Indians' programme to encourage such internal transfers.

Inter-organizational Alliances

Koza and Lewin (1998) distinguished between alliances designed to explore new opportunities and those designed to exploit existing resources. Typically, exploitation alliances focus on shared revenue collection or marketing. R&D alliances are considered to be exploratory by their very nature. Lavie and Rosenkopf (2006) added further dimensions to this definition; alliances can also be exploratory if the partners have no previous history of cooperation or if the partnering firms are radically different.

Faced with unfamiliar institutions in an emerging market, an MNE will need to rely on local partners to adjust to the institutional context. These partners will often, by definition, be new and different. A firm that seeks a more exploitative approach may choose to partner with other MNEs (local and foreign) that have more experience in the local context – such firms are likely to be more similar, and the two MNEs may even have a past history of alliances in other locations. In the Indian information technology and telecommunications industries, the large software outsourcing firms – especially Wipro and HCL, which have a strong R&D focus – often play such a bridging role.

To illustrate the nature of exploitative alliances, let us consider Intel's platform definition centre in Bangalore, which is engaged in developing locally relevant computing solutions based on Intel technology. According to the senior management at Intel (*The Economist*, 2004), the engineers employed by the firm in its Bangalore unit are engaged in R&D challenges as complex as any other project in the world. They use the fastest supercomputer in India and are divided into four product-design divisions covering ultra-wideband radio, enterprise processors, mobile and wireless chip-sets and communications. Intel's efforts in India, however, are largely aimed at adapting existing technologies to local needs. As an example, Intel is bringing its Discover the PC initiative to India and has formed alliances with firms including HCL, Millennium, PCS, Wipro and Zenith Computers to make available a low-cost, fully featured, high quality desktop PC, with an easy-to-use interface designed to introduce a new set of people to the world of technology for the first time. The PCs will be will be priced 20 per cent below the lowest priced Intel-based PCs in India with similar feature-rich configurations.

MNEs naturally also partner with local universities and government institutions. These alliances are generally highly explorative in all dimensions. Universities and government laboratories are per se different from large corporations; in emerging markets they are often also organizationally and culturally quite different from similar organizations in the MNEs' home countries. IBM's Indian research facility, for example, is located on the campus of the elite Indian Institute of Technology in Delhi in order to facilitate collaboration, and several MNEs are collaborating on projects with the Indian Institute of Science, located in Bangalore. In another instance, Alcatel[3] partnered with the Centre for Development of Telematics (C-DOT), the Indian government's telecommunications technology development centre, to open a WiMax research centre in Chennai. To hedge against the uncertainties inherent in such alliances, MNEs tend to focus on the ultra-elite universities at least initially, but are known to expand their ties with other smaller and internationally less well known universities for a variety of purposes that range from research to recruitment and public relations.

In its collaborative efforts, HP Labs follows a fairly low-risk endeavour encompassing formal ties with six major institutions and sponsoring PhD fellowships, all of which are at least partially targeted at fostering MNE-style research practices. In this manner HP Labs India is exploiting its existing organizational capabilities to acquire new knowledge and develop a recruiting base of similar-minded researchers.

MNEs in India are also participating in cooperative arrangements at the industry level. In 2004, ABB, for example, helped to found the Indian Automation Industry Association, aimed at sharing knowledge of cutting-edge technologies and leveraging these technologies for the Indian market.[4] Members of the association include Emerson, Siemens, Larsen and Toubro

(L&T), Tata Honeywell, Rockwell Automation, Yokogawa India Ltd and Invensys India, among others. Most large multinational members have at a minimum been co-members of other industry associations. Facilitating new alliances is therefore a highly compatible second-order objective of such association memberships.

Our findings, therefore, suggest that even in instances where MNEs' alliances are exploratory, they find ways to balance the strains of excessive exploration by reducing the technological complexity of projects (e.g. pure localization efforts), partnering with 'bridging' organizations and cooperating in less intensive ways with familiar MNEs.

DISCUSSION

Organizational learning theory posits the need for a balance between exploitation and exploration as firms adapt to new or changing environments. Within any domain, however, feedback loops will tend to reinforce either exploitation or exploration (March, 1991). While it is sometimes possible to achieve a balance within a domain, there is some evidence suggesting that achieving balance *across* domains is the more likely route for firms. Our analysis of Indian R&D labs of MNEs suggests there are greater performance benefits for firms that possess dynamic capabilities that allow them to combine external and internal knowledge through strategies for intra-organizational coordination, staffing practices and inter-organizational collaboration.

Even an MNE like HP Labs that initiated R&D internationalization as early as 1983 and has gained extensive experience in India since 1989 through manufacturing, development, sales and marketing activities, faced significant difficulties when it first established its R&D lab in Bangalore in 2002. In the initial years, HP's R&D expansion into India was highly explorative along both the technological and the organizational dimensions, but the results from this R&D effort were largely disappointing, leading to a radical readjustment geared towards an exploitation orientation. The HP Labs mandate was thus adjusted to focus on more familiar urban customers (reducing exploration on the technological side) and to work on global products with an emerging markets emphasis, rather than pure emerging markets products (enabling closer coordination with the rest of the firm and allowing researchers to draw more heavily on existing knowledge and technologies).

Similarly, SAP's success in establishing a large R&D unit in India (second only to the home country R&D unit in Germany) is derived in large measure from its ability to integrate and standardize organizational processes worldwide, thereby establishing close coordination and modularity of applications to enable their use across projects. Such an approach encourages researchers and developers to work in a highly coordinated fashion and draw on the centres of excellence worldwide for specific problems. SAP Labs in India has relied heavily on local recruitment to facilitate its rapid expansion from 80 to 3000 employees since its inception in 1998. But to make the induction and integration of new employees seamless, the staffing strategy relies on intensive training for six to eight weeks covering technical areas as well as 'soft' skills, including communication skills and cross-cultural sensitivity. In addition, SAP Labs strives to build an innovation ecosystem around its Netweaver platform by encouraging external developers to adopt the platform for innovation, engages in collaborative projects with Indian systems integrators and extends global alliances with Accenture and others to India.

The organizational capabilities developed by both HP and SAP in India represent an exploitative strategy that balances the exploration inherent in carrying out R&D in emerging market economies. R&D in an emerging market is, by its very nature, an exploratory step for a western MNE because the risks and uncertainties associated with conducting R&D are exacerbated by the unfamiliarity with the institutional and cultural context (all the more so when the MNE has no prior experience through sales or manufacturing activities in the host country). Furthermore, by locating R&D in an emerging market the MNE is pursuing novel goals, often different from the traditional ones of access to new technologies or existing markets.

While an exploitative approach for building organizational capabilities provides one strategy for balancing the exploratory nature of R&D in emerging market economies, future research could investigate other forms of firms' strategies that help overcome the technological and institutional distance associated with emerging market contexts. Our study can also be extended to understand how firms devise strategies for building organizational capabilities in the context of emergent R&D clusters in cities such as Bangalore, Beijing and Taipei. The paradox of geographical proximity and institutional distance in emerging market economy clusters raises some important questions. A central tenet of the institutional perspective is that organizations sharing the same environment will employ similar practices and thus become isomorphic with each other (DiMaggio and Powell, 1991). The emergence of shared organizational practices, as well as norms, ideas and regulations is even more likely when firms are geographically proximate (Saxenian, 1994; Tallman et al., 2004). When applied to clusters in emerging market economies, these observations beg the question of which organizational practices and institutions will be likely to emerge as the norm – the ones characterizing the domestic firms or MNE subsidiaries, or some hybrid of the two types of firms represented in the cluster? Is it plausible that clusters within emerging market countries represent institutional voids that MNEs come to occupy? Or is there evidence of institutional collision as divergent norms, rules and ideas compete for dominance? Given this interplay between varied institutional forms and organizational capabilities, what kind of organizational and institutional evolution might one expect to see in clusters?

While previous research has addressed the diffusion of organizational practices within MNEs under conditions of institutional duality (Kostova and Roth, 2002), clusters in emerging market economies provide an appropriate context to extend these arguments to a setting where multiple institutions intersect.

NOTES

1. One possible exception is the mobile telephony industry. According to one estimate two million subscribers are added each month, representing one of the fastest growth rates of 55 per cent per year in the telecommunications sector.
2. Over two-thirds of the staff hold PhDs.
3. Prior to its merger with Lucent.
4. Similarly, MNEs in the pharmaceutical industry have formed an association called the Organization of the Pharmaceutical Producers of India, which is responsible for engaging with the government and non-governmental actors to protect the interests of the pharmaceutical industry in India.

REFERENCES

'Accenture launches new R&D facility in Bangalore, India', accessed at http://careers3.accenture.com/Careers/India/AboutAccenture/Career+News/0608_acc_launch_new_fac_india on 15 January 2006.

Almeida, P. (1996), 'Knowledge sourcing by foreign multinationals: patent citation analysis in the United States semiconductor industry', *Strategic Management Journal*, **17** (Winter), 155–65.

Booz Allen Hamilton and INSEAD (2006), 'Innovation: Is global the way forward?', A joint study by INSEAD, Fontainebleau France and Booz Allen Hamilton.

Cantwell, J. (1995), 'The globalisation of technology: what remains of the product cycle model?', *Cambridge Journal of Economics*, **19** (1), 155–74.

Carlsson, B. (2006), 'Internationalization of innovation systems: a survey of the literature', *Research Policy*, **35** (1), 56–67.

Cohen, W.M. and D.A. Levinthal (1990), 'Absorptive capacity: a new perspective on knowledge spillovers and innovation', *Administrative Science Quarterly*, **35** (1), 128–52.

DiMaggio, P.J. and W.W. Powell (1991), *The New Institutionalism in Organizational Analysis*, Chicago: University of Chicago Press.

Economist Intelligence Unit (2004a), 'Harnessing innovation: R&D in a global growth economy', an Economist Intelligence Unit white paper sponsored by Agilent Technologies.

Economist Intelligence Unit (2004b), 'Scattering the seeds of invention: the globalization of research and development', an Economist Intelligence Unit white paper sponsored by Scottish Development International.

Economist, The (2004), 'India's growing strength in innovation', accessed at http://www.economist.com/business/displaystory.cfm?story_id=E1_NVVRNGJ on 23 May 2007.

Eisenhardt, K.M. and J.A. Martin (2000), 'Dynamic capabilities: what are they?', *Strategic Management Journal*, **21** (10/11), 1105–21.

Frost, T.S. (2001), 'The geographic sources of foreign subsidiaries' innovations', *Strategic Management Journal*, **22** (2), 101–23.

Henderson, R. and K.B. Clark (1990), 'Architectural innovation: the reconfiguration of existing product technologies and the failure of established firms', *Administrative Science Quarterly*, **35** (1), 1–30.

Khanna, T., K.G. Palepu and J. Sinha (2005), 'Strategies that fit emerging markets', *Harvard Business Review*, **83** (6), 63–76.

Kostova, T. and K. Roth (2002), 'Adoption of an organizational practice by subsidiaries of multinational corporations: institutional and relational effects', *Academy of Management Journal*, **45** (1), 215–33.

Koza, M.P. and A.Y. Lewin (1998), 'The co-evolution of strategic alliances', *Organization Science*, **9** (3), 255–64.

Kuemmerle, W. (1998), 'Strategic interaction, knowledge sourcing and knowledge creation in foreign environments: an analysis of foreign direct investment in R&D by multinational companies', in M.A. Hitt, J.E. Ricart and R.D. Nixon (eds), *Managing Strategically in an Interconnected World*, Chichester: John Wiley, pp. 149–66.

Lane, P.J. and M. Lubatkin (1998), 'Relative absorptive capacity and interorganizational knowledge spillovers', *Strategic Management Journal*, **19** (5), 461–77.

Lavie, D. and L. Rosenkopf (2006), 'Balancing exploration and exploitation in alliance formation', *Academy of Management Journal*, **49** (4), 797–818.

Lewin, A.Y. and J. Kim (2004), 'The nation state and culture as influences on organizational change and innovation', in M.S. Poole and A.H. Van de Ven (eds), *Handbook of Organizational Change and Development*, Oxford: Oxford University Press, pp. 324–53.

March, J.G. (1991), 'Exploration and exploitation in organizational learning', *Organization Science*, **2** (1), 71–87.

Nelson, R.R. and N. Rosenberg (1993), 'Technical innovation and national systems', in R.R. Nelson (ed.), *National Innovation Systems: A Comparative Analysis*, Oxford: Oxford University Press, pp. 3–22.

Nelson, R.R. and S.G. Winter (1982), *An Evolutionary Theory of Economic Change*, Cambridge, MA: Belknap Harvard.

Orru, M., N.W. Biggart and G.G. Hamilton (1991), 'Organizational isomorphism in East Asia', in W.W Powell and P.J. DiMaggio (eds), *The New Institutionalism in Organizational Analysis*, Chicago: University of Chicago Press, pp. 361–89.

Rivkin, J.W. and N. Siggelkow (2003), 'Balancing search and stability: interdependencies among elements of organizational design', *Management Science*, **49** (3), 290–311.

Saxenian, A.-L. (1994), *Regional Advantage: Culture and Competition in Silicon Valley and Route 128*, Cambridge, MA: Harvard University Press.

Tallman, S., M. Jenkins, N. Henry and S. Pinch (2004), 'Knowledge, clusters and competitive advantage', *Academy of Management Review*, **29** (2), 258–71.

Teece, D.J., G. Pisano and A. Shuen (1997), 'Dynamic capabilities and strategic management', *Strategic Management Journal*, **18** (7), 509–33.

Voelker, R. and R. Stead (1999), 'New technologies and international locational choice for research and development units: evidence from Europe', *Technology Analysis & Strategic Management*, **11** (2), 199–209.

von Zedtwitz, M. and O. Gassmann (2002), 'Market versus technology drive in R&D internationalization: Four different patterns of managing research and development', *Research Policy*, **31** (4), 569–88.

Zahra, S.A. and G. George (2002), 'Absortive capacity: a review, reconceptualization and extension', *Academy of Management Review*, **27**, 185–203.

Zhao, M. (2006), 'Conducting R&D in countries with weak intellectual property rights protection', *Management Science*, **52** (8), 1185–99.

6. Real options theory and international strategic management

Jing Li and Tony W. Tong

The international business (IB) and strategic management literature has long recognized uncertainty as a persistent feature in international investment. Uncertainty in the international environment, which often exposes multinational enterprises (MNEs) to unfavorable conditions yet potential opportunities, plays an important role in influencing MNEs' investment decisions. Existing theories in IB such as internalization theory (Buckley and Casson, 1976; Rugman, 1981) tend to view uncertainty as an unfavorable condition that often complicates the decision-making process and exposes MNEs to potential risks and losses. As a result, these theories propose various means to minimize the potential negative outcomes related to uncertainty. As a complement to these theories, real options theory suggests a new way to deal with uncertainty in international investment. The core concept is that although uncertainty may impose unfavorable business conditions on MNEs, it may also present valuable opportunities for MNEs to take advantage of; accordingly, instead of focusing solely on strategies to minimize potential downside, as emphasized in the existing theories, MNEs can create real options to access upside opportunities and manage investments sequentially as uncertainty is resolved (Kogut, 1983, 1985; Kogut and Kulatilaka, 1994; Chi and McGuire, 1996; Reuer and Leiblein, 2000). This new perspective of dealing with uncertainty has added useful insights to the IB literature, and the influence of real options theory on IB research is beginning to take shape. To explore the usefulness of real options theory in developing future IB theory and research, we provide a review of existing applications of real options theory in IB as well as offering several directions for future studies.

REAL OPTIONS THEORY AND INTERNATIONAL BUSINESS

Real Options Theory

The concept of real options originates from financial options (Myers, 1977). Financial options afford option holders the right but *not* the obligation to sell or buy a financial security at a price (i.e. exercise price) for a predetermined period of time. Options allow the investor to pursue opportunities that have significant upside potential while containing downside risk, suggesting an asymmetrical performance distribution for the investment. Such asymmetry, derived from having the right but not the obligation to exercise the option, lies at the heart of an option's value and real options theory (Trigeorgis, 1996).

Real options are based on real assets instead of financial assets. Myers (1977) first recognizes that capital investments can possess option-like features; for example, current sunk investments create real options because they can provide investors discretionary opportunities to benefit from upside potentials. Two characteristics determine whether an investment provides real options: first, there must be volatility regarding future payoffs of the investment; second, there must be managerial flexibility in increasing or decreasing commitment according to the resolution of uncertainty in the business environment.

Real options theory provides a systematic tool to conceptualize and quantify the factors that contribute to the value of real options, which shapes firms' investment decision making under uncertainty (Dixit and Pindyck, 1994). Among the factors that may influence the real option value of an investment (Copeland and Antikarov, 2001), the followings are the most important ones: (1) an increase in the uncertainty regarding future payoffs of the investment increases the value of managerial flexibility embedded in the investment, and therefore the real option value of the investment; (2) an increase in potential cash flows lost to competitors decreases the option value of the investment; (3) a longer time to expiration of the real option embedded in the investment allows decision makers to learn more about the uncertainty and therefore increases the option value; (4) an increase in the option's exercise price reduces the option value of the investment.

Real options are often embedded in international investments, because of the high levels of uncertainty confronting such investments. For example, a multinational operating network provides an MNE with real options because the firm can obtain *the option to switch* sourcing, production, or distribution within the network contingent on how uncertainty is resolved in the institutional and economic environment of different countries comprising the network (Kogut, 1983; Kogut and Kulatilaka, 1994). Another example is that international joint ventures (IJVs) can be viewed from a real options perspective because an IJV can position a firm to exploit upside potentials by acquiring additional equity stakes from its partner if uncertainty is resolved in a favorable fashion (i.e. *the option to grow*), or to limit downside loss by selling its equity to its partner or dissolving the venture, when uncertainty turns out to be unfavorable (i.e. *the option to abandon*) (Chi and McGuire, 1996; Chi, 2000; Tong et al., 2007). A third example relates to the timing of investment. Specifically, delaying investment into an international market surrounded by high levels of uncertainty has a high option value as a result of *the option to defer* investment (Campa, 1993; Rivoli and Salorio, 1996).

The Value of Real Options Theory to IB

When entering an overseas market, MNEs face a variety of uncertainties, which generally fall into two types: exogenous and endogenous uncertainty (Roberts and Weitzman, 1981). Exogenous uncertainty is not affected by a firm's actions and can only be revealed over time. Uncertainty in the macroeconomic environment (such as political and economic conditions) usually falls into this type. Endogenous uncertainty can be decreased by the firm through investments. Uncertainty in the microeconomic environment (such as consumer needs and competitive conditions) and at the firm level (such as partner behaviors) often falls into this type. For example, an MNE can invest in an IJV to reduce uncertainty about the amount of complementary knowledge local partners can provide (e.g. distribution channels and relationships with the government), and to reveal the extent to which local partners may behave opportunistically.

Given the prevalence of uncertainty in international business operations, two streams of IB research – research based on transaction cost economics (Buckley and Casson, 1976; Rugman, 1981; Hennart, 1982; Anderson and Gatignon, 1986) and research based on internationalization theory (Johanson and Vahlne, 1977) – have proposed alternative means to deal with uncertainty in international investment. Real options theory can add to each of the two theories, as discussed below.

IB research based on transaction cost economics pays particular attention to one type of uncertainty – behavioral uncertainty – and emphasizes the need for using high-control governance structures *ex ante* to minimize transaction costs arising from potential partner opportunism. Partner opportunism may arise because of asset specificity, which refers to the investments a firm makes that are highly specific to a transaction and can be redeployed only by sacrificing their productive value (Williamson, 1985).

This stream of research emphasizes that an MNE should employ high-control market entry modes such as wholly owned subsidiaries to curb potential opportunistic behaviors (Buckley and Casson, 1976; Rugman, 1981; Anderson and Gatignon, 1986).

Different from transaction cost economics, real options theory can incorporate the impact of various types of exogenous and endogenous uncertainty, where behavioral uncertainty is considered to be one type of endogenous uncertainty. Instead of focusing on ex ante control mechanisms to deal with uncertainty, real options theory emphasizes maintaining flexibility ex ante and implementing strategic actions ex post to take advantage of new information (Dixit and Pindyck, 1994; Trigeorgis, 1996). For example, MNEs can use low-control, low-commitment entry modes when facing high uncertainty, which cannot only limit MNEs' downside losses when the future unfolds unfavorably but also serve as platforms for expansion when future opportunities arise. A key concept is that uncertainty implies risks as well as opportunities, and firms can engage with uncertainty and benefit by creating real options (such as the option to defer, the option to grow, and the option to learn) to maintain flexibility in response to new information (Rivoli and Salorio, 1996; Buckley and Casson, 1998). This perspective is useful in extending existing IB research based on transaction cost economics, as this research does not fully consider potential opportunities that may accompany uncertainty or managerial flexibility in adjusting investment decisions in response to the resolution of uncertainty.

Another important stream of IB research that deals with uncertainty is based on internationalization theory. The staged model of internationalization theory proposes that firms gradually increase commitments to foreign markets when facing uncertainty. Specifically, firms often begin by exporting to a foreign market, then set up a selling or distribution subsidiary, and finally form a production subsidiary such as a joint venture or a wholly owned subsidiary (Johanson and Vahlne, 1977; Sullivan and Bauerschmidt, 1990). However, one can easily find exceptions to the staged path of expansion suggested by internationalization theory, thereby reducing its empirical validity or generality (Benito and Gripsrud, 1992; Fina and Rugman, 1996). Real options theory can complement this research by providing an economic rationale for incremental internationalization and by prescribing boundary conditions under which it is optimal to internationalize sequentially (Seth and Chi, 2005).

Real options theory suggests that low-commitment market entries at an early stage of internationalization provide an MNE with the option to defer investments, which is valuable when the MNE faces high levels of uncertainty. However, real options theory also suggests that delaying high commitment to the target market may lead to a lower value of *the option to grow* because the MNE may lose potential benefits arising from strategic advantages associated with timely commitment and the reduction of endogenous uncertainty (Kulatilaka and Perotti, 1998). If the value of growth options is salient, the MNE may deviate from the incremental internationalization process and skip to high-commitment entry modes or make greater investments even if it is facing high levels of uncertainty. Hence, a careful examination of the trade-offs between the option to defer and the option to grow could add insights to internationalization theory.

In sum, real options theory provides a more systematic way of analyzing the role of uncertainty in international investments, and the theory can be valuable in extending existing IB research, such as research based on transaction cost economics and internationalization theory.

EXISTING APPLICATIONS OF REAL OPTIONS THEORY IN IB

Existing applications of real options theory in IB fall into two broad categories that seek to answer two questions: (1) How do MNEs create and exercise real options in the face of exogenous and endogenous uncertainty? and (2) What are the performance implications of real options for MNEs?

The Creation and Exercise of Real Options

Existing applications of real options theory in IB have developed along three broad paths:

- Multinationality and operational flexibility: Maintaining a multinational operating network provides MNEs with valuable growth options and switching options.
- IJVs as a market entry mode: Compared with other entry modes, IJVs offer a valuable combination of growth options and abandonment options.
- The timing of international investment: The optimal timing of international investment depends on considerations reflecting both deferral options and growth options.

Multinationality: switching and growth options

Kogut (1983) first presents that the value of a global network lies in the ability of the MNE to operate flexibly in an uncertain world. The MNE is uniquely positioned to exploit uncertainties surrounding international environments by arbitraging institutional restrictions; for example, tax systems, antitrust provisions and financial limitations. The MNE can also capture externalities in information and economies of scale in marketing and manufacturing on a global scale. Therefore, national boundaries do not just represent the costs of tariffs and transport, but they also represent profitable opportunities that can only be exploited by an MNE (Kogut, 1983, p. 43). Hence, the evaluation of a multinational network should include the value of holding the options to switch sourcing, production, distribution and profits within the network.

Since a multinational network provides the options to switch and grow, the choice of locations and organization of a multinational network should be strategic in order to enhance the MNE's operational flexibility. Buckley and Casson (1998) provide the following example to illustrate how MNEs could strategically choose locations to increase operational flexibility. MNEs can choose a regional production and distribution hub, where several neighboring countries are serviced from the same location. Because the hub is closer to each market than is the home location, it reduces transportation costs and offers better local information. Meanwhile, because the hub is close to several markets, it avoids exclusive commitments to any one of them. Thus, even if one of these markets declines, products can still be switched to other markets. The option to switch therefore enhances an MNE's operational flexibility while limiting its losses.

To more accurately capture the value of an MNE as a network of subsidiaries, Kogut and Kulatilaka (1994) build a real options model to demonstrate that the value of the network lies in the opportunity to benefit from uncertainty through coordination of geographically dispersed subsidiaries. Specifically, they develop a dynamic programming model to examine the option value of a multinational network in response to exchange rate shocks. Their results show that having the option to switch production to a location with lower input prices helps the MNE to ensure against detrimental movements of the real exchange rate. This insurance benefit derived from operational flexibility is greater in periods of increased volatility in exchange rates. Hence, the value of multinationality increases with greater volatility.

Rangan (1998) finds some empirical evidence to support the switching options embedded in a multinational network. Specifically, he examines whether firms substitute inputs from other countries in the production process when the exchange rate changes. Using data on US MNEs' operations abroad as well as foreign MNEs' operations in the USA from 1977 to 1993, Rangan finds that MNEs systematically exploit currency shifts, though to a relatively modest degree overall. Campa (1994) compares capacity expansion decisions of MNEs and domestic firms and finds some evidence for the option value of a multinational network. Based on a sample of chemical processing industries from 1977 to 1988, his findings show that exchange rate uncertainty has a negative effect on capacity expansions of domestic firms, whereas exchange rate uncertainty has no such effect on those of MNEs. The findings suggest that MNEs are better able to manage exchange rate uncertainty by shifting their production among different countries.

Given prior work's focus on the industry level of analysis, more research is needed to investigate switching options at the firm level to provide more granular evidence. For instance, switching options, as well as growth options, can affect the location choice of MNEs' subsidiaries and thus can shape the geographic composition of a multinational network.

International joint ventures: growth and abandonment options

Among different market entry modes, such as wholly owned subsidiaries (WOSs), IJVs, export and licensing, IJVs have drawn the largest amount of attention in existing research on real options. This research has mainly sought to answer two sets of questions: (1) To what extent can IJVs be viewed as real options? and (2) What determines the option value of IJVs?

Real options theory suggests that the choice of market entry mode should not be a static decision; a market entry mode should be evaluated according to not only the net present value that the investment would generate, but also the option value that the investment could bring about; that is, the value from adjusting investment decisions in response to uncertainty and new information. An IJV can provide option value because an MNE maintains the flexibility to adjust decisions by acquiring the partner's equity or divesting its own equity, depending on how the future unfolds (Chi and McGuire, 1996; Tong et al., 2007). In a certain sense, export, licensing and WOSs can also offer the option to expand/contract capacity or switch to other high–low-commitment market entry modes. Therefore, these market entry modes can also have similar types of real options, such as the option to grow (exploit market opportunities) and the option to abandon (withdraw from the market).

Despite the similarities among different entry modes, an IJV probably provides a higher option value than a WOS, licensing or export, as suggested by Buckley and Casson (1998). Compared to licensing or export, an IJV provides more information about the host country's environment since ownership of assets confers valuable information, which implies that if uncertainty resolved favorably and the market grew unexpectedly, the foreign investor with an IJV could recognize the growth and respond more quickly, resulting in a higher option value. Moreover, in exercising the option to grow, the MNE with an IJV faces lower costs of capacity expansion than does an exporter or licensor who decides to switch to foreign production. Hence, an IJV provides a higher option value to grow than export or licensing. Compared with a WOS, an IJV does not require as much initial investment, and thus the investor will find it less costly to exit the market. Moreover, the IJV partner provides a ready market for divested assets that a WOS lacks. It follows that an IJV provides a higher option value to abandon than a WOS.

Chi and McGuire (1996) use a real options model to investigate the conditions under which options provided by IJVs are valuable. Their findings show that the real options value of an IJV depends on how the partners forecast the expected value of the IJV; specifically, the option value of the IJV is higher when the partners have divergent expectations of the value of the joint assets. Intuitively, the partner with a higher valuation is willing to pay a higher price than the other partner does, resulting in a mutually beneficial trade in their equity. On the contrary, if the partners have similar valuations of the IJV, they cannot benefit from any trade in equity, therefore leading to a lower value of the option to grow.

There have been few empirical examinations that use real options theory to predict MNEs' entry mode decision. Kouvelis et al. (2001) examine the impact of exchange rate volatility on MNEs' choice of governance structure for overseas production. Based on the information from 187 US MNEs, they find that a strongly depreciated home currency encourages the use of export, whereas a strongly appreciated home currency encourages the use of IJVs or WOSs. However, the high costs of switching between different strategies force a period of inaction or hysteresis during which the MNE continues to use its existing mode, even if the immediate profits would favor switching strategies. Such inaction is reinforced when the volatility of exchange rates is high.

Reuer and Tong (2005) draw from real options theory and transaction cost economics to investigate the factors that motive IJV partners to have explicit call option clauses in their agreement. They argue that the transaction cost perspective suggests that a firm is more likely to use option clauses in IJVs situated in its core business because such clauses can help to protect its proprietary knowledge during the collaboration; real options theory, however, predicts that it is more attractive to have explicit call options in non-core IJVs because the firm faces greater uncertainty about the operation of the businesses, and having such options provides the flexibility to expand investments. Their results provide more support for the transaction cost perspective, that is, MNEs are more likely to use explicit call options in IJVs in their core businesses.

The limited empirical studies in this category indicate that more empirical studies are needed to examine MNEs' choice of market entry mode. In particular, two types of empirical studies will be valuable. First, future studies can empirically examine how exogenous and endogenous uncertainty separately and jointly influence the choice of market entry mode and governance structure (e.g. whether the existence of exogenous and endogenous uncertainty encourages the establishment of IJVs). Second, research can also analyze whether the resolution of uncertainty triggers changes in market entry modes (e.g. whether resolution of uncertainty triggers ownership changes in IJVs).

Market entry timing: deferral and growth options

Market entry timing refers to the time to initiate or increase an investment in a foreign market. Studies on this topic support the following ideas: on the one hand, the option to defer an investment is valuable under conditions of uncertainty and irreversibility; on the other hand, the option to grow may also be valuable because of strategic advantages following timely investment and strategic commitment (Buckley and Casson, 1981; Kester, 1984; Kulatilaka and Perotti, 1998; Smit and Trigeorgis, 2004). Hence, the optimal investment timing may depend on the relative importance of the two types of options; that is, the option to defer and the option to grow.

Rivoli and Salorio (1996) apply real options theory to analyze the optimal timing of foreign direct investment (FDI), and they compare the benefits and costs of immediate investment and late investment. Delaying investment provides an MNE with an opportunity to wait for more relevant information to make informed decisions regarding whether to enter the market and how much to invest. This deferral option is particularly valuable if the MNE is likely to maintain its ownership position over a long period and if the investment is difficult to reverse. However, when the market becomes competitive and the option exercising right is not proprietary (i.e. many MNEs have similar options to enter the market), the MNE is more willing to exercise the option earlier rather than delay it. This is because doing so creates a growth option that may generate first-mover advantages as well as reduce competitors' preemptive threats. In addition, immediate investment can also contribute to information collection and endogenous uncertainty reduction, thus facilitating MNEs' sequential decision making.

Existing empirical studies on this topic are limited to studying the relationship between uncertainty and the timing of foreign investments at the aggregate *industry* level, and few studies have examined this relationship at the *firm* level. For example, Campa (1993) studies whether firms exporting to the USA defer their direct investments in the country during the 1980s because of the fluctuations of the USA's real exchange rate. He uses a sample of foreign investments in 60 US wholesale industries and finds that exchange rate volatility is negatively correlated with the number of foreign investments that occur in these industries. This negative effect is most pronounced for industries where sunk investments in physical and intangible assets are relatively high; that is, when the investments are more irreversible.

Real Options and MNE Performance

Existing studies on how the creation and exercise of real options contribute to MNE performance have mainly focused on the relationship between multinationality and MNE performance measured by market valuation, corporate risk and corporate exposure. These studies have shown mixed findings: multinationality increases market valuation under certain conditions, but it does not appear to reduce corporate risks.

Allen and Pantzalis (1996) focus on multinationality and measure the value derived from operating flexibility as the difference in the market value between MNEs and a sample of matched domestic firms. They use two variables to capture the network structure of MNEs: breadth (number of foreign countries in which MNEs have operations) and depth (the concentration of foreign subsidiaries in a few countries). Based on the information on domestic and foreign affiliates of US firms in 1991, they find that returns to multinationality are maximized for firms with networks that have breadth but not depth. The findings suggest that the value of multinationality increases as firms expand their holdings of real options by widening the breadth of their network, but the value decreases with the acquisition of redundant real options by increasing the number of subsidiaries in each country. Consistent with this idea, Tang and Tikoo (1999) find that the stock market responds more to earnings changes of US MNEs that have breadth, compared to those that have depth. In another study, Pantzalis (2001) finds that the market value of MNEs whose network of subsidiaries does not include operations in developing countries is substantially lower than that of MNEs with operations in such countries, suggesting that the value of the real options portfolio that MNEs possess increases when they operate across segmented markets.

Miller and Reuer (1998) compare the effect of export with the effect of FDI on MNEs' economic exposure to exchange rate movements. Economic exposure refers to the sensitivity of a company's real value to environmental contingencies, such as changes in foreign exchange rates. Using data on US manufacturing firms, they find that FDI reduces MNEs' economic exposure to foreign exchange rate risks, whereas export does not have such an impact. Reuer and Leiblein (2000) examine the impact of multinationality and IJVs on corporate downside risk, which is measured as the probability of firms failing to meet a performance objective. They find that US manufacturing firms' investments in dispersed FDI and IJVs do not have a general, negative impact on downside risk, which is inconsistent with predictions from real options theory. Furthermore, Tong and Reuer (2007) employ models to control for unobserved firm resources or other characteristics that might have an impact on the relationship between multinationality and downside risk. Their finding of a curvilinear relationship suggests that MNEs benefit from the switching options embedded in dispersed FDI up to certain level, and then incur significant organization and other costs that may arise as a result of the need to manage a portfolio of switching options. In another study, Tong et al. (2007) examine the value of growth options embedded in IJVs and investigate the growth options that have often been attached to emerging economies in particular. They find that IJVs in emerging economies generally do not enhance MNEs' growth option values, unless the venture is either in a product market outside the firm's core business or the firm takes on less than 50 percent ownership in it. These contingent effects of product-market focus and ownership structure applied to IJVs in developed countries as well.

The mixed empirical findings (multinationality may increase market valuation but does not necessarily reduce corporate risks) call for a more careful examination of the conditions under which a multinational network brings extra value to MNEs. It appears that the creation of real options (e.g. building a multinational network) does not always lead to value creation or risk reduction. Existing findings imply that multinationality is more likely to lead to higher market values and lower corporate risks when the multinational network could effectively allow the firm to switch sourcing, production and distribution across country borders. As we will discuss below, some organizational and institutional barriers may prevent the realization of the option value of maintaining a multinational network. In addition, MNEs vary in their abilities to recognize, create, evaluate and exercise the real options embedded in multinational operations.

REAL OPTIONS THEORY AND FUTURE IB RESEARCH

The previous section reviews existing applications of real options theory in IB research. In this section, we propose several avenues for future IB research on real options theory.

Measurement of Uncertainty

Although abundant research opportunities exist, as specified in previous sections, empirical applications of real options theory in IB are still at an initial stage. One challenge that faces IB scholars is to develop appropriate measures for the various uncertainties facing MNEs. Recall that uncertainties fall into two general types – exogenous and endogenous. Compared with endogenous uncertainty, exogenous uncertainty is relatively easier to capture, and the literature has provided several measures that can proxy for institutional uncertainty (Brunetti and Weber, 1998), such as political hazards (Henisz and Delios, 2001) and political risks (Kobrin, 1979); for economic fluctuation, such as exchange rate volatility (Campa, 1993); and for industry volatility, such as market and technological uncertainty (Folta, 1998).

Endogenous uncertainty facing MNEs, however, is relatively more difficult to capture because such uncertainty is often idiosyncratic to an individual firm. Some measures of endogenous uncertainty used in the IJV literature include business overlaps (Folta, 1998) and cultural distance between partners; higher business overlaps or lower cultural distance probably lead to lower levels of endogenous uncertainty within the IJV. However, these measures may have some bias, because as MNEs' experience in a country or a business sector increases and as their relationships with business partners develop, such endogenous uncertainty is likely to decrease (e.g., Barkema et al., 1997). Hence, these measures might not be able to capture the dynamic component in endogenous uncertainty. In view of this argument, an indirect measure of endogenous uncertainty can be a firm's experience in an international market or its prior collaborations with business partners in that market. As experience increases, it stands to reason that an MNE is likely to face lower levels of endogenous uncertainty (Chang and Rosenzweig, 2001; Mitra and Golder, 2002).

It can be argued that one limitation in the above measures is that they do not directly incorporate managers' perceptions of uncertainty in international investment, even though they are the actual decision makers who create and exercise real options. Therefore, there is much value to use qualitative methods such as surveys or interviews to directly capture managers' perceptions of various exogenous and endogenous uncertainties (e.g. Guiso and Parigi, 1999).

Uncertainty and International (Dis)Investment Decision

Since real options theory deals with firms' decision making under uncertainty and their subsequent actions when uncertainty is revealed, the theory can shed some light on an MNE's sequential decision making in a foreign country. On this topic, internationalization theory has suggested incremental commitment to a foreign market in order to accumulate experience and minimize risks. Real options theory can help to bound predictions of internationalization theory by systematically examining the conditions under which the MNE adjusts its decisions on the level of commitment to the foreign market.

The main factors that may influence the internationalization process suggested by real options theory include levels of uncertainty (high or low) and types of uncertainty (exogenous or endogenous). When the level of uncertainty (including both types) is high, an MNE may not want to increase commitment because the option to defer is more valuable. When exogenous uncertainty is revealed unfavorably, an MNE may not increase commitment either; in fact, it may even exercise the option to reduce resource commitment to the foreign market. When exogenous uncertainty resolves favorably, an MNE is positioned to exercise the growth option by increasing resource commitment to the market. However, whether an MNE is able to exercise the option to grow and exploit the upside potential also depends on the extent to which it can reduce endogenous uncertainty through learning and experience accumulation. Thus an increase in resource commitment depends on the reduction of both exogenous and endogenous uncertainty in a favorable fashion. Kogut and Chang's (1996) study provides some supporting evidence for this assertion. They find that initial investments of Japanese firms in the USA help to accumulate experience (reduce endogenous uncertainty) and serve as platforms for sequential investments; when uncertainty surrounding real exchange rates resolves favorably (exogenous uncertainty resolves favorably), Japanese firms choose to increase their commitment by undertaking greater investments.

The above argument emphasizes the value of the option to defer when facing high levels of uncertainty and thereby supports low commitment to a foreign market under this condition. Not considered in this argument is the countervailing effect of the value of the option to grow that can be generated by high-commitment market entries. To the extent that the value of the option to grow is important, an MNE may have incentives to make high-commitment investments even when the level of uncertainty is high. For example, MNEs may decide to skip, or shorten the time period of, export and licensing, and adopt high-commitment entry modes in order to gain first-mover advantages, preempt competition, and obtain valuable growth options ahead of their competitors (Buckley and Tse, 1996; Kulatilaka and Perotti, 1998).

In summary, real options theory suggests that the speed of the internationalization process depends on the balance between the option to defer and the option to grow, since switching from low-commitment to high-commitment entries reduces the value of the deferral option but increases the value of the growth option. In general, when exogenous and endogenous uncertainty are unresolved, the option to defer becomes relatively more valuable; by contrast, the option to grow becomes more salient when uncertainty resolves favorably, or when firms are able to reduce uncertainty or achieve strategic advantages by making timely commitment.

Managerial and Organizational Dimensions of Real Options

Currently one of the most neglected areas of IB research on real options concerns the implementation of real options. International strategic management researchers have long suggested that various challenges can surround the evaluation and implementation (i.e. creation, maintenance, and exercise) of real options in MNEs. For example, Kogut (1985) points to the difficulty that an MNE's managers may have in recognizing valuable options embedded in the firm's investments. Moreover, just because a firm recognizes the embedded options does not mean that it has the management and organizational system to support the implementation of options (Kogut, 1989). In addition, managers might not use the correct information to assess real options or might evaluate them incorrectly because of the lack of suitable proxies (Kogut and Kulatilaka, 1994; Bowman and Moskowitz, 2001). Finally, managerial and organizational factors might further alter option maintenance and exercise decisions: managers may be prone to escalation of commitment, they may not follow the optimal exercise policies because of incentive problems, and they may find it hard to monitor the complex cues for exercise because of bounded rationality (Kogut, 1991; Bowman and Hurry, 1993; Trigeorgis, 1996; Kogut and Kulatilaka, 2004).

Future research can begin to examine some of the organizational aspects of real options in IB. For instance, Tong and Reuer (2007) find that while downside risk initially falls as firms enter more foreign countries, the complexity that accompanies extensive multinational operations leads to higher downside risk levels as the firm's FDI becomes even more dispersed. They also find that downside risk levels are increasing in the average cultural differences between the firm's home base and its foreign subsidiaries in its portfolio, and this finding is consistent with the idea that organizational complexity and coordination costs can limit the firm's ability to implement and benefit from such switching options. An interesting question this study raises is how MNEs can dynamically configure their subsidiary networks in response to the resolution of different sources of uncertainty in the environment. For instance, under conditions of uncertainty, an MNE may value particular country locations that can help to broaden rather than deepen its operating network. This consideration therefore may affect the location choice for establishing a new subsidiary or divesting an existing one. Research along such lines can also help to address potential interaction effects in a portfolio of options, such as the option portfolio possessed by MNEs (e.g. Trigeorgis, 1996).

Future IB research on real options can also address questions such as these by obtaining primary data on firms, and even on actual decision-makers' investment motives and preferences for real options analysis, given that the empirical developments to date have largely relied on secondary data. For instance, in the case of multinational business operations, managers need to attend to different sources of uncertainty, and it would be interesting to understand which cues managers attend to and how management matters (e.g. Guiso and Parigi, 1999).

CONCLUSION

An emerging area of research in international strategic management is the application of real options theory to MNEs' international investment under uncertainty. Compared with existing theories in international business strategy, real options theory provides a more recent and novel treatment of uncertainty, and it has made important contributions to extant research in international strategic management. In this chapter, we review key applications of real options theory in the field and highlight several future research opportunities. We believe that international strategy scholars are well positioned to advance real options theory by paying attention to unique sources of uncertainty and by addressing some of the managerial and organizational dimensions of real options in the international business context. We hope this chapter will stimulate more theoretical and empirical research on real options theory in the field of international strategic management.

REFERENCES

Allen, L. and C. Pantzalis (1996), 'Valuation of the operating flexibility of multinational operations', *Journal of International Business Studies*, **27** (4), 633–53.
Anderson, E. and H. Gatignon (1986), 'Models of foreign entry: a transaction cost analysis and propositions', *Journal of International Business Studies*, **17** (3), 1–26.
Barkema, H.G., O. Shenkar, F. Vermeulen and J.H.J. Bell (1997), 'Working abroad, working with others: how firms learn to operate international joint ventures', *Academy of Management Journal*, **40**, 426–42.
Benito, G.R.G. and G. Gripsrud (1992), 'The expansion of foreign direct investment: discrete rational location choices or a cultural learning process', *Journal of International Business Studies*, **23** (2), 461–76.
Bowman, E.H. and D. Hurry (1993), 'Strategy through the options lens: an integrated view of resource investments and the incremental choice process', *Academy of Management Review*, **18** (4), 760–82.

Bowman, E.H. and G.T. Moskowitz (2001), 'Real options analysis and strategic decision making', *Organization Science*, **12**, 772–7.

Brunetti, A. and B. Weber (1998), 'Investment and institutional uncertainty: a comparative study of different uncertainty measures', *Weltwirtschaftliches Archiv*, **134**, 513–33.

Buckley, A. and K. Tse (1996), 'Real operating options and foreign direct investment: a synthetic approach', *European Management Journal*, **14** (3), 304–14.

Buckley, J.P. and M. Casson (1976), *The Future of the Multinational Enterprise*, New York: Holmes & Meier Publishers.

Buckley, J.P. and M. Casson (1981), 'Optimal timing of a foreign direct investment', *Economic Journal*, **91** (361), 75–87.

Buckley, J.P. and M. Casson (1998), 'Models of multinational enterprise', *Journal of International Business Studies*, **29** (1), 21–44.

Campa, J.M. (1993), 'Entry by foreign firms in the United States under exchange rate uncertainty', *Review of Economics and Statistics*, **75** (4), 614–22.

Campa, J.M. (1994), 'Multinational investment under uncertainty in the chemical processing industries', *Journal of International Business Studies*, **25** (3), 557–78.

Chang, S.-J. and P.M. Rosenzweig (2001), 'The choice of entry mode in sequential foreign direct investment', *Strategic Management Journal*, **22** (8), 747–76.

Chi, T. (2000), 'Option to acquire or divest a joint venture', *Strategic Management Journal*, **21** (6), 665–87.

Chi, T. and D.J. McGuire (1996), 'Collaborative ventures and value of learning: integrating the transaction cost and strategic option perspectives on the choice of market entry modes', *Journal of International Business Studies*, **27** (2), 285–307.

Copeland, T.E. and V. Antikarov (2001), *Real Options: A Practitioner's Guide*, New York: Texere.

Dixit, A.K. and R.S. Pindyck (1994), *Investment under Uncertainty*, Princeton, NJ: Princeton University Press.

Fina, E. and A.M. Rugman (1996), 'A test of internalization theory and internationalization theory: the Upjohn company', *Management International Review*, **36** (3), 199–213.

Folta, T.B. (1998), 'Governance and uncertainty: the tradeoff between administrative control and commitment', *Strategic Management Journal*, **19** (11), 1007–28.

Guiso, L. and G. Parigi (1999), 'Investment and demand uncertainty', *Quarterly Journal of Economics*, **114**, 185–227.

Henisz, W.J. and A. Delios (2001), 'Uncertainty, imitation, and plant location: Japanese multinational corporations, 1990–1996', *Administrative Science Quarterly*, **46** (3), 443–75.

Hennart, J.-F. (1982), *A Theory of Multinational Enterprise*, Ann Arbor, MI: University of Michigan Press.

Johanson, J. and J. Vahlne (1977), 'The internationalization process of the firm: a model of knowledge development and increasing foreign commitments', *Journal of International Business Studies*, **8** (1), 23–32.

Kester, W.C. (1984), 'Today's options for tomorrow's growth', *Harvard Business Review*, **62** (2), 153–60.

Kobrin, S.J. (1979), 'Political risk: a review and reconsideration', *Journal of International Business Studies*, **10** (1), 67–80.

Kogut, B. (1983), 'Foreign direct investment as a sequential process', in C.P. Kindelberger and D. Audretsch (eds), *The Multinational Corporations in the 1980s*, Cambridge, MA: MIT Press.

Kogut, B. (1985), 'Designing global strategies: profiting from operational flexibility', *Sloan Management Review*, **27** (1), 27–38.

Kogut, B. (1989), 'A note on global strategies', *Strategic Management Journal*, **10**, 383–9.

Kogut, B. (1991), 'Joint ventures and the option to expand and acquire', *Management Science*, **37** (1), 19–33.

Kogut, B. and S.-J. Chang (1996), 'Platform investments and volatile exchange rates: direct investment in the US by Japanese electronic companies', *Review of Economics & Statistics*, **78** (2), 221–31.

Kogut, B. and N. Kulatilaka (2004), 'Real options pricing and organizations: the contingent risks of extended theoretical domains', *Academy of Management Review*, **29**, 102–10.

Kogut, B. and N. Kulatilaka (1994), 'Operating flexibility, global manufacturing and the option value of a multinational network', *Management Science*, **40** (1), 123–39.

Kouvelis, P., K. Axarloglou and V. Sinha (2001), 'Exchange rates and the choice of ownership structure of production facilities', *Management Science*, **47** (8), 1063–80.

Kulatilaka, N. and E.C. Perotti (1998), 'Strategic growth options', *Management Science*, **44** (8), 1021–31.

Miller, K. and J.J. Reuer (1998), 'Firm strategy and economic exposures to foreign exchange rate movements', *Journal of International Business Studies*, **29** (3), 493–513.

Mitra, D. and P.N. Golder (2002), 'Whose culture matters? Near-market knowledge and its impact on foreign market entry timing', *Journal of Marketing Research*, **39** (3), 350–65.

Myers, S.C. (1977), 'Determinants of corporate borrowing', *Journal of Financial Economics*, **5** (2), 147–75.

Pantzalis, C. (2001), 'Does location matter? An empirical analysis of geographic scope and MNC market valuation', *Journal of International Business Studies*, **32** (1), 133–55.

Rangan, S. (1998), 'Do multinationals operate flexibly? Theory and evidence', *Journal of International Business Studies*, **29** (2), 217–37.

Reuer, J.J. and M.J. Leiblein (2000), 'Downside risk implications of multinationality and international joint ventures', *Academy of Management Journal*, **43** (2), 203–14.

Reuer, J.J. and T.W. Tong (2005), 'Real options in international joint ventures', *Journal of Management*, **31** (3), 403–23.

Rivoli, P. and E. Salorio (1996), 'Direct investment and investment under uncertainty', *Journal of International Business Studies*, **27** (2), 335–54.

Roberts, K. and M.L. Weitzman (1981), 'Funding criteria for research, development, and exploration projects', *Econometrica*, **49** (5), 1261–88.

Rugman, A. (1981), *Inside the Multinationals: The Economics of Internal Markets*, New York: Columbia University Press.

Seth, A. and T. Chi (2005), 'What does a real options perspective add to the understanding of strategic alliances?', Working Paper, University of Illinois at Urbana Champaign.

Smit, H.T.J. and L. Trigeorgis (2004), *Strategic Investment: Real Options and Games*, Princeton, NJ: Princeton University Press.

Sullivan, D. and A. Bauerschmidt (1990), 'Incremental internationalization: a test of Johanson and Vahlnes's thesis', *Management International Review*, **30** (1), 19–30.

Tang, C.Y. and S. Tikoo (1999), 'Operational flexibility and market valuation of earnings', *Strategic Management Journal*, **20** (8), 749–61.

Tong, T.W. and J.J. Reuer (2007), 'Real options in multinational corporations: organizational challenges and risk implications', *Journal of International Business Studies*, **38**, forthcoming.

Tong, T.W., J.J. Reuer and M.W. Peng. (2007), 'International joint venture and the value of growth options', *Academy of Management Journal*, **50**, forthcoming.

Trigeorgis, L. (1996), *Real Options: Managerial Flexibility and Strategy in Resource Allocation*, Cambridge, MA: MIT Press.

Williamson, O.E. (1985), *The Economic Institutions of Capitalism: Firms, Markets, Relational Contracting*, New York, London: The Free Press.

PART II

New organizational forms for multinational companies

7. International business theory, multinational enterprise, and new organizational forms

Jonathan Doh

International business (IB) research has recently come under criticism for a number of shortcomings. Debates over whether the IB research agenda is 'running out of steam' have prompted reconsideration of the relevance of the IB research theories and thrusts (Buckley, 2002; Peng, 2004; Shenkar, 2004). Buckley (2002) highlights a range of issues that the IB research community has overlooked, including, for example, knowledge management, geography, and the role of NGOs in global affairs. Peng (2004) argues that there are a number of evolving aspects of IB, such as emerging economies, that have received inadequate exploration, but rejects the notion that IB is in need of a 'big issue', arguing that the fundamental question in IB research is (and has always been) the relative performance of the firm in international markets. Shenkar (2004), however, criticizes the excessive focus of IB research on narrow definitions of performance. He calls for a broader and more inclusive consideration of a range of relevant variables at multiple levels, and examination of the role and impact of multinational enterprises (MNEs) on broader global conditions.

In this chapter, I add to this list of IB research areas and topics ripe for reconsideration by arguing that the evolution of new organizational forms has rendered obsolete some of the basic understandings of IB theory and practice, including the definition of the multinational enterprise, the central organizing construct of the IB field. I propose that both IB generally, and multinational strategy specifically, are due for reconsideration and potential reconceptualization to reflect the realities of the contemporary global business environment. Specifically, I argue that some of the assumptions surrounding the relationship between strategy and structure in both domestic and international contexts are under question. In particular, new organizational forms – some of which do not seem to be a direct result of a conscious corporate strategy – have emerged, and network structures, arising spontaneously or at least unpredictably, have materialized as viable counterpoints to traditional corporate organizational forms.

I begin by reviewing classic literature on the IB and the MNE, especially research focusing on the relationship between strategy and structure in the global business environment. I then introduce literature from strategy and organizational management on the co-evolution of firms and contexts and the new organizational forms that emerge from those dynamic interactions. I use that literature to frame a critique of traditional IB theory and assumptions. I explore three organizational phenomena – cross-sectoral networks, offshore outsourcing, and 'born-global' firms – to demonstrate that aspects of current IB theory are anachronistic and in need of reconceptualization. I close by arguing that the traditional concept and definition of the MNE may itself be antiquated, as many organizations, small and large, have international dimensions to their scope, either as a direct part of the business or through the many networks in which they operate. Hence, I conclude with a respecification of the definition of MNEs in the current global political and economic environment.

INTERNATIONAL BUSINESS THEORY AND MNE ORGANIZATION

For decades, international strategy scholars have been concerned with the organizational implications and consequences of international strategic choices. Indeed, according to Kogut (1988), research on the rationale for multinational activity can be divided into two basic schools: the strategic behavior explanation and the transaction cost explanation. In the broader strategy literature, two of the main frameworks that have characterized economic approaches to strategy research are the industrial organization (I/O) perspective and the resource-based view (RBV).

The I/O perspective (Porter, 1980) has focused on the interaction of firms within industries characterized by particular structures and dynamics, while the RBV (Barney, 1991; Penrose, 1959; Nelson and Winter, 1982) has focused on the resources firms possess and deploy, and the strategies that permit the firm to acquire, generate, and deploy those resources. These two perspectives have influenced IB strategy and its extension to the structure of the internationalizing firm (Johanson and Vahlne, 1977, 1990).

Bartlett and Ghoshal's (1989) classic integration–responsiveness framework in which MNEs were viewed as balancing pressure for global standardization and local responsiveness was developed from I/O concepts. It suggested that the strategy–structure relationship had relevance for international strategy as firms wrestled with how to align their organizational structure to best fit the strategic position that resulted from those dual pressures. Another aspect of this strategy–structure relationship concerns business–government interactions. IB strategy scholars have typically described a bilateral bargaining relationship between MNE and host government, with attendant organizational implications (Vernon, 1971).

Internationalization and Governance

The export behavior and internationalization processes of firms have been the topic of widespread research efforts during the past 30 years. Since the mid-1970s, two streams of research have emerged, one in Europe (e.g. Johanson and Vahlne, 1977) and one in North America (e.g. Bilkey, 1978; Cavusgil, 1980). Both research streams, however, conceptualize export development as taking place in gradual and sequential stages (learning sequences involving feedback loops), based on a series of incremental commitment decisions depending on perception, expectation, experience, managerial capacity, and so on. The firm is assumed to build a stable domestic position before starting international activities and to undertake a step-by-step series of action that lead to increasing international commitments.

Johanson and Vahlne (1977) were perhaps the first to examine the sequential internationalization process that distinguishes specific stages of gradually increasing foreign involvement that firms follow as they internationalize. Their model emphasizes incremental internationalization through acquisition, integration, and use of knowledge concerning foreign markets. The firm enters new markets with increasing 'psychic distance', defined as aspects of language, culture, business practices, and industrial development that tend to reduce the efficiency of information flows between the market and the firm (Johanson and Vahlne, 1977).

A related stream of IB research has examined how path dependent, mimetic learning and experience influence subsequent governance and entry mode options of firms as they internationalize (see Barkema and Vermuelen, 1998 for a review). Tallman (1992, pp. 462–3) explicitly discusses the importance of past decision-specific experience in MNCs' organizational structure decisions, by noting that

> The MNE (multinational enterprise) may reduce its uncertainty in a given situation by attempting to imitate either its own previously successful strategies and structures or those of its competitors in the new market.

In choosing an ownership structure, a firm with greater general international business and/or host country experience may prefer full ownership, because that experience may enable the firm to bear the risks associated with the extensive financial, managerial, technological and strategic resource requirements of full ownership, and the political risks associated with possible changes in host government policies or the political climate. However, greater general international business/host country experience may also enable the firm to deal effectively with the costs and uncertainties associated with accepting equity partners in shared ownership (such as limited operational flexibility, opportunistic behavior of partners, involuntary dissipation of proprietary assets, and loss of trust between equity partners) (Padmanabhan and Cho, 1999).

Padmanabhan and Cho (1999) summarize prior studies on the role of early decisions on international investment entry mode and ownership structure, and report that firms place much greater importance on prior decision-specific experience in selecting their ownership structure and establishment mode forms than they do on general international business experience and host country-specific experience. Makino and Delios (1997) argue that joint venture performance is positively related to the extent of joint venture experience of the parent firm. The results also indirectly support the conjectures of Tallman (1992), Tallman and Shenkar (1994), and Kogut and Zander (1992), namely that firms are able to generate value from past experiences with similar structures.

The TCE, OLI and Internalization Views of Structure

Since its inception, strategy and organizational theory, and its application in IB, have been concerned with basic questions about organization. Coase (1937) was one of the first to explore the extent to which firms should internalize transactions versus engaging in market exchanges. Transaction costs, which include search and information costs, bargaining and decision costs, and policing and enforcement costs, provided the basic framework for an important stream of research in management generally and international strategy in particular. Williamson (1975) extended this transaction cost economic (TCE) perspective by arguing that the existence of firms derives from 'asset specificity' in production, where assets required for a transaction are specific to each other such that their value is much less in a second-best use, raising the risk of market transactions.

IB scholars have borrowed heavily from the TCE view in examining issues of governance and entry mode in international business. For example, Dunning's eclectic owner–location–internationalization (OLI) framework (1981, 1988) of foreign direct investment (FDI) as applied to entry mode choice suggests that firms will select their entry mode by considering ownership advantages (control, and the costs and benefits of inter-firm relationships and transactions), location advantages (resource commitments and requirements, and the availability and cost of resources), and internalization advantages (the ability to reduce transaction and coordination costs and prevent opportunistic exploitation of tacit knowledge).

A related perspective is the notion of the MNE as a constellation of proprietary managerial and knowledge-based assets that, if properly secured, can be leveraged and deployed from one jurisdiction to another (Buckley and Casson, 1976). This perspective, generally known as internalization theory, argues that firms elect to adopt entry mode and governance forms designed to maximize the efficiency of their technological and knowledge assets. In particular, MNEs will adopt strategies that 'internalize' transactions by forgoing joint ventures and other exchange relationships that could lead to appropriation of knowledge assets (Buckley and Casson, 1976). Buckley and Casson (1976) focused especially on the issue of the problem of external markets, particularly in terms of governing and safeguarding the exploitation of knowledge and expertise. They argued that this challenge provided opportunities for the MNE to create internal markets for knowledge and expertise such that advantages could be developed and maintained that overcame the inherent costs in operating transnationally.

Institutional Perspectives

Institutions play a critical role in supporting markets (North, 1990). Two variations of institutional perspectives have emerged that are of relevance to IB research and its interest in the organizational structures of internationalizing firms. The first focuses on the role of an institution in lowering transaction and information costs by reducing uncertainty and establishing a stable structure that facilitates interactions (North, 1990). The second emphasizes the need for organizations to adapt to institutional conditions in various markets. DiMaggio and Powell (1983) explored the phenomenon of isomorphism: the tendency of one unit in a population to resemble others. Within IB, researchers have argued that MNEs should seek to become 'isomorphic' with the local institutional environment. This would include making adjustments in personnel, image, branding, government relations and other areas in order to seek legitimacy in these markets. As Kostova and Roth (2002, p. 215) suggest, 'Since it is vital for the MNC to achieve and maintain legitimacy in all its environments, the MNC will experience the pressure to adopt local practices and become isomorphic with the local institutional context.' This research has often advocated structural solutions to this problem, arguing that foreign firms can work to mitigate liabilities by hiring local staff, putting a local face on the firm, and otherwise seeking to become similar to or even engrained in the local society and culture.

Khanna and Palepu (2000) and Khanna et al. (2005) have termed the absence of institutions, such as financial markets, as 'institutional voids' and argued that these voids constitute severe liabilities for doing business in developing countries. Institutional voids arise in locations where specialized intermediaries on which a firm customarily relies – legal, financial, human resource – are absent. The reasons for such absences may result from poorly functioning institutional infrastructure and governance systems. One response of firms to these institutional deficits is to internalize functions through the development of business groups or conglomerates that provide internal capital and labor markets and protect property rights by not exposing them to partners. In essence, the MNE takes on the structure of an entire political economy in order to establish institutions internally that are absent in the broader environment.

More recently, research on the relationship between MNE headquarters and subsidiaries has examined the locus of control and influence between these two nodes of the MNE. As Birkinshaw (2000) has pointed out, subsidiaries can seek to extend their role by actively developing new products and charters. From the institutionalist perspective, however, the power of subsidiaries to extend their mandates is crucially dependent on the capabilities generated in the local setting and the degree to which these are valuable and scarce resources that the headquarters (or other subsidiaries) care about having access to. Such capabilities lead us to a fourth major stream in IB strategy.

Resource-based Perspectives

The RBV was proposed as an alternative to the industrial organization view of strategy, which focused on the competitive environment in industries and how a firm could/should respond to that environment. The RBV, by contrast, examined the economic returns to resources that a firm owns, acquires, or develops (Barney, 1991; Penrose, 1959; Nelson and Winter, 1982). Resources must demonstrate a specific set of characteristics to generate above-normal returns: they must be valuable in facilitating exploitation of an opportunity in the business environment, or at least contribute to neutralizing a threat; they must also be scarce, or must come together in a unique way as a result of how the firm packages or bundles them. In addition, resources must be immobile: imperfectly immobile resources include those that are idiosyncratic to the firm, those for which property rights are not well defined or those that are co-specialized with other assets. A related characteristic to that of imperfect mobility is that of imperfect imitation. Resources must provide some ex post limits to competition (Peteraf, 1993). Once a firm has gained an initial competitive advantage, there must be additional resources to freeze out competitors, allowing the firm to maintain the rent-earning for a period of time. For a firm to be in a position to fully exploit a valuable and rare resource there must be a resource position barrier – often in the form of some facet of organizational structure – preventing imitation by other firms.

In surveying three rationales for multinational strategy, Tallman (1992) contends MNEs use FDI when a structure providing more managerial control is required to better extract rents from the firm-specific resources in a host market. He suggests (1992, p. 462) that: 'The resource-based model provides for conditions under which firms can accrue higher profits if they have a resource advantage, but where close potential substitutes make cost efficiency vital to sustainable advantage.' Indeed, the structural forms themselves become part of the MNE's resource base as it learns and experiments with various structures so as to better apply them in other markets. In a related paper, Tallman (1991) tests domestic and international experience, as well as strategic group membership, to predict when firms will choose investment in direct production abroad versus trade (export). He finds that size and strategic group membership are strong predictors of the decision to undertake direct foreign production, while variables designed to capture the resources and capabilities acquired through experience are less predictive.

Recent extensions of the RBV literature have offered a dynamic capabilities perspective on strategy. The RBV had been criticized for lacking sufficient focus on how and why certain firms have competitive advantage in situations of rapid and unpredictable change (Eisenhardt and Martin, 2000) and for overlooking the managerial coordinative processes by which firms assemble and leverage knowledge assets. In response, building on the administrative and productive capabilities of the RBV, strategy researchers have offered an extension of the RBV and other strategy perspectives in the form of a 'dynamic capabilities' view of competitive strategy (Kogut and Zander, 1992; Teece et al., 1997). Dynamic capabilities refer to capabilities by which managers 'integrate, build, and reconfigure internal and external competencies to address rapidly changing environments' (Teece et al., 1997, p. 516). Kogut and Zander (1992) refer to 'combinative capabilities' as the ability to acquire and synthesize knowledge resources and build new applications from those resources, especially in a changing environment. The focus of the dynamic capabilities perspectives on rapid change captures the environment in which firms consider – often under intense pressure from competitors and the external environment – how and where to deploy and redeploy assets across geographic space.

In a related vein, the strategic management literature has struggled with how best to apply resource-based perspectives on strategy in international environments characterized by turbulence and change. Moreover, strategy researchers are now expanding their focus beyond the boundaries of the firm, as reflected in conceptual development and empirical testing of co-evolutionary theory. In particular, recent work in the area of dynamic, co-evolutionary processes in organizations (Volberda and Lewin, 2003) is relevant to the challenges for the firm of maintaining competitive advantage in the face of pressures to reduce costs and shift production brought about by changing technology, markets and competition.

In sum, the characteristics of the MNE as conceived in IB literature over the past three decades include a relatively fixed (although incrementally evolving and adapting) structure, a separation of functions and activities that take place inside rather than outside the organization, based primarily on ownership, and dyadic (bilateral ties) to host governments through which the MNE would negotiate issues of access, entry, and operations. These characteristics are summarized in Table 7.1.

NEW ORGANIZATIONAL FORMS IN INTERNATIONAL STRATEGY

Co-evolution and New Organizational Forms

Recent research on the co-evolution of organizations and their environment has often highlighted the new organizational forms that emerge from this adaptation process. Indeed, research on strategic adaptation and change has focused closely on the emergence of new organizational forms (Lewin and Koza, 2001; Lewin and Volberda, 1999; Volberda and Lewin, 2003). Research on new organizational forms illustrates the interrelated nature of strategy and structure. In this case, 'forms' is generally interpreted as new structures, but may also refer to strategies or both. Indeed, one view of these organizational forms views them as strategic choices among different configuration options. The traditional boundary of the organization also sought to delineate who is 'inside' and who is 'outside', and thus helped set the boundary of the firm. March and Simon (1958) noted that the legal boundary is fundamental, but also acknowledged its limitation for managerial purposes. Baligh and Burton (1981, 1982) argue that the managerial boundary of the organization and the legal boundary are frequently different, setting up the conceptual underpinnings of new organizational forms and structures.

Recent developments in the international business and broader international political-economic environment suggest that traditional notions regarding the boundaries of the firm must be relaxed. In particular,

Table 7.1 New organizational forms and examples of their challenge to IB theory

Phenomenon	Challenge to IB theory	Challenge to definition of multinational
Cross-sectoral (MNE–NGO) Collaboration	• TCE/internationalization/alliances/JVs: Alliance may be across sectors and for purposes distinct from those exclusively among with firms • RBV: Resources may be external to the firm and focused on acquiring capabilities such as reputation that MNE cannot build alone or in in conjunction with other firms • MNE–host government bargaining: Bilateral MNE–host government bargaining may include multiple actors (such as NGOs) and interactive relationships • Institutional theory: Isomorphic adaptation may be to civil society/NGO environment	'MNE' may be broadened to include non-profit NGOs and their networks with firms
Offshore outsourcing	• OLI: L factors less about hard infrastructure and more about human capital • OLI: Firms generally produce for foreign consumption; little or no local market activity • RBV: Resources, such as human capital, may be 'leased' abroad • Product life-cycle: In services, PLC may be abbreviated or circumvented • Institutional theory: Less need to adapt to local environment if output is exported	MNE may be 'virtual' with little or no physical presence or a physical presence that is disaggregated across geographic and conceptual boundaries
Born global firms	• Internationalization: Firms may not experience slow or even sequential internationalization but 'leapfrog' stages • RBV: Resources, such as human capital, may be 'leased' abroad	MNE may not have physical presence in other countries to be considered multinational

advances in network theory – which predicts that sharing resources with other organizations that are linked together through a pattern of inter-relationships will produce benefits for an organization – have begun to blur the traditional boundaries of the firm (Dacin et al., 1999; Granovetter, 1985; Wasserman and Faust, 1994). Dunning (1995) even offered a reappraisal of his OLI framework in light of the advent of 'alliance capitalism'.

In the international strategy area, offshore outsourcing, strategic alliances, joint ventures, franchising, network organizations, and other phenomena continue to challenge what we think of as a multinational firm, and which activities we associate with it. From the organizational perspective, co-evolutionary researchers would argue that organizations adapt to their environment, and that the environment, in turn, is affected by those adaptations. Hence, there is a natural reciprocal and dynamic aspect to the emergence of new organizational forms. These phenomena depart from the traditional concept of the organization with fixed boundaries to one in which entities operate in complex boundary relationships in dynamic environments in which each organization is managing in part the activities of the other. These evolving structures require new conceptualizations of authority, responsibility, command, control and how managerial actions will be realized. While Williamson (1975) argued that organization and transaction size and frequency will be determined by the optimal mix of activities inside the organization (hierarchy) and activities outside the firm (market), this new approach relaxes some of these assumptions and rigidities that go beyond either market or hierarchy.

In the following sections, I outline three 'new' organizational forms that reflect emergent and evolutionary structures in international business organizations. While there are many additional forms emerging, some of which may be more salient and relevant to this argument, I discuss these three as exemplars that illustrate how the IB environment is changing, and how organizations are changing with it.

Inter-sectoral Networks

Resource dependence theorists have suggested that the development of inter-organizational ties such as strategic alliances results from underlying resource dependencies (Pfeffer and Nowak, 1976). Several studies in the 1960s and 1970s showed that an important reason for ties between human service agencies was their perceived strategic interdependence with each other (for a review, see Oliver, 1991). This research suggested that organizations enter partnerships when they perceive critical strategic interdependence with other organizations in their environment (Schermerhorn, 1975). More recently, Gulati (1995) tested how the social context emerging from prior alliances and considerations of strategic interdependence influence partnership decisions between firms. He found that this social network facilitates new alliances by providing valuable information to firms about the specific capabilities and reliability of potential partners. He also found that connected firms would enter alliances more frequently if the firms were interdependent to begin with, and that there would thus be interactions between interdependence and common ties and between interdependence and distance.

Research on the antecedents of alliances among private or non-profit organizations also has compelling implications for understanding collaboration and cooperation among MNEs and civil society organizations or NGOs. Doh and Teegen (2003) report that NGOs are increasingly engaged in various connections with governments and private corporations in the global environment. More specifically, network relationships with NGOs may comprise an exchange of complementary resources not unlike those that occur in other types of alliances among private sector firms (Eisenhardt and Schoonhoven, 1996). Alliances involve resource complementarities among firms, some of which include social effects, including legitimacy (Eisenhardt and Schoonhoven, 1996). Such effects are especially relevant for MNEs operating across geographic boundaries where reputations may be critical to market entry and acceptance.

Alliances with NGOs, however, may also provide MNEs with access to different skills, competencies and capabilities than those that are otherwise available within their organization or that might result from alliances with for-profit organizations. According to Rondinelli and London (2003), cross-sector alliances may provide opportunities for MNEs to achieve the legitimacy and develop the capabilities needed to respond to increasing pressure from stakeholders to address environmental and other social issues (Waddock, 1988; Westley and Vredenburg, 1991). Even when an interaction begins with an NGO advocacy campaign, such as a public protest, media criticism or boycott, the relationship may evolve into a more collaborative exchange. Doctors without Borders, a strong advocate for the provision of lower cost medication to treat HIV/AIDS may subsequently offer a reliable, efficient and trustworthy partner for pharmaceutical companies in distributing medications in developing countries once they decide to participate in a program to deliver drugs at low prices. Oxfam is another organization that has developed networked relationships with companies. Oxfam's approach to these relationships could generally be characterized as 'engagements' as opposed to close partnerships. Lindenberg (2001, p. 605) reports that Oxfam has pursued an 'evolving, comprehensive strategy that is complex, dynamic and involves multiple corporate relationships'. Such partnerships may convey potential reputation benefits (or costs) that are idiosyncratic to its status as a non-firm, non-governmental stakeholder.

Participation in a cross-sector alliance, however, presents challenges. Corporations and NGOs have fundamentally different structures and values (Rondinelli and London, 2003). Relations between corporations and NGOs, especially in the emerging markets context, have often been characterized by hostility and mistrust. Cross-sector alliances face an additional challenge because organizational learning generally requires some level of common experience, a condition that is often weak or missing in alliances between profit-making and non-profit organizations (Rondinelli and London, 2003). This lack of common experience, trust and communication can sometimes result in conflict, even when partnerships have been established that appear to signal shared values and commitments. Indeed, partnerships with NGOs may sometimes open a path to escalating (and potentially unrealistic) demands for firms to upgrade their commitment to social development, placing greater, not lesser, regulatory pressure on the firm. Nonetheless, MNE–NGO collaborations have gained the attention of management researchers seeking to inform both theory and practice (Doh and Teegen, 2003; Spar and La Mure, 2003; Yaziji, 2004).

One reason why MNEs may be increasingly open to cross-sectoral network relationships that include NGOs is that they are under increasing pressure to account for – and mitigate – the perceived social and environmental consequences of their actions. Indeed, for some firms, demonstrated commitment to social development may be a precondition for market entry or a de facto requirement for maintaining market presence – a license to operate. As part of their response to these pressures, some MNCs pursue social development strategies involving partnerships with NGOs and other organizations as part of their overall market strategies. Indeed, NGOs may present firms with special opportunities to shape socially responsive non-market strategies, often in response to initial criticism by those NGOs (Teegen et al., 2004). Such strategies may help safeguard the firm from NGO activism and escalating condemnation. In some cases, firms appear to preempt negative pressure by developing proactive strategies that focus on social development.

Hence, in their assessment of the collaborations between corporations and non-profit environmental groups, Rondinelli and London (2003) also report increasing interest from corporations and non-profits to reconsider their past adversarial relationships and form new, cooperative relationships. In increasing numbers, executives point to these collaborations as important parts of their corporate social responsibility strategies. Teegen et al. (2004) propose that the emergence of civil society in general, and the activism of civic NGOs in particular, have broad implications for the role, scope and definition of corporations in the global economy. They suggest that traditional research paradigms, such as the historic conceptualization of MNE alliances with international or local private partners, must be relaxed as MNEs develop various alliance relationships with NGOs. Moreover, they also argue that the traditional dyadic approach to multinational corporation (MNC)–host government bargaining must be relaxed to account for these new actors.

Offshore Outsourcing Structures

Offshoring is an important economic and social phenomenon that has generated considerable attention in practitioner outlets (Corbett, 2004), the popular press (Baker and Kripalani, 2004) and in political circles (Drezner, 2004). According to the United Nations Conference on Trade and Development (UNCTAD, 2004), offshoring of services reached about $32 billion in 2001 and offshoring of IT-enabled services alone is expected to reach $24 billion in 2007, up from just $1 billion in 2002. Yet, IB scholars have only begun to explore the implications of services offshoring for research and practice (Doh, 2005; Kotabe and Murray, 2004). Offshoring of administrative and technical work (and, indeed, knowledge work generally) may challenge some of the established precepts of IB theory, especially theories related to internationalization and FDI. In response, some researchers are beginning to critique traditional IB theories in light of the increased mobility of services and the consequences of that mobility for decisions about whether and where to locate offshored facilities. Doh (2005) asserts that the phenomenon of offshoring directly challenges the relevancy and assumptions of both macro-level IB theories such as Porter's (1990) conceptualization of country-level comparative advantage, and more micro-level perspectives on international expansion and FDI (e.g. Johanson and Vahlne, 1990; Buckley and Casson, 1976).

Contrary to the slow, sequential internationalization anticipated by Johanson and Vahlne (1977), the inputs to final production of many services may be 'de-coupled' from intermediate inputs early in the internationalization process under offshoring schemes. Hence, the linkages between production location and core knowledge-based activities may be weak. Examples include film production, programming, back office and call centre functions in audio-visual, software, legal and accounting services. For production of these services, local demand is less (or un-) important, while specific country factors – land, labor, and infrastructure – are proportionately more important. IB researchers have begun to argue that traditional approaches to location behavior in the international business literature such as the OLI framework are no longer appropriate for describing the behavior of MNEs (McCann and Mudambi, 2004). In the context of offshoring, Doh (2005) has argued that ownership and internalization are less relevant because these two advantages can erode through the transfer and disintegration of production stages to other countries. Location advantages are still viewed as relevant in contemporary theory. However, these location advantages emphasize a broader portfolio of assets beyond lower input costs, availability of resources, or savings from tariff avoidance.

Schemenner (1979), Mudambi (1995), and various others have identified the factors that influence MNEs' location decisions for manufacturing. These include, inter alia, infrastructure, location-specific risk factors, government policy, and others (Mudambi, 1995). Because of better telecommunications technology, proximity to major markets is less crucial for services offshoring. Graf and Mudambi (2005) argue that human capital is more important for business process outsourcing than for manufacturing because of the role of the 'human touch'. More broadly, the factors that influence manufacturing and services offshoring location decisions are distinct. Services often depend more on knowledge and information and less on highly specialized machinery. As a result, services may be more easily relocated than manufacturing, and a principal differentiating factor among services offshoring locations is likely to be the skill level of the employees.

Finally, services investment does not suffer from the 'obsolescing bargain' as described by Vernon in that retention of the investment is as important to the host country as the investor, because of the employment and economic generation effects. Yet, a services investment is much more mobile than infrastructure or manufacturing, allowing investors to move investments as conditions change and the attractiveness of locations evolves.

'Born Global' Firms

Another organizational form that would appear to prompt a re-evaluation and/or respecification of IB theory, especially the conceptualization of the internationalization process as a slow, sequential series of steps that occur of a period of years (Johanson and Vahlne, 1990), is the increasing incidence of 'Born Globals' – firms that engage in significant international activity a short time after being established. Since the early 1990s, empirical studies of the export behavior of firms have challenged many findings of actual export behavior reported in the traditional internationalization literature. Again, supported by rapid advances in technology and transportation and the reduction of trade and investment barriers of all types, many small, 'local' firms are able to reach international markets easily and cheaply. It has been demonstrated that many firms now do not develop in incremental stages with respect to their international activities. Firms are often reported to start international activities right from their birth, to enter very distant markets right away, to enter multiple countries at once, to form joint ventures without prior experience, and so on. Such firms have been labeled International New Ventures (Oviatt and McDougall, 1994), High Technology Start-ups, and Born Globals (Knight and Cavusgil, 1996).

The explanation for this new picture of the internationalization of firms is based on more global market conditions, new developments in transportation and communication technologies, and the rising number of people with international experience. Some authors (Knight and Cavusgil, 1996; Oviatt and McDougall, 1994) have suggested that these empirical observations call for development of new theory, whereas others (Bell et al., 2001) argue that even though such firms overtly behave differently, they do not necessarily differ from other firms with respect to more fundamental processes. According to the latter argument, the phenomenon may not require new theories, but may be explained by already well-known constructs. However, it may still be relevant to categorize such firms as something unique from a structural or operational perspective.

Building on an empirical study of small firms in Norway and France, Oystein (2002) found that more than half of the exporting firms established there since 1990 could be classified as Born Globals. Examining the differences between newly established firms with high or low export involvement levels revealed that a decision maker's global orientation and market conditions are important factors in whether a firm moves early toward an international reach. Knight and Cavusgil (2004) highlighted the critical role of innovative culture, as well as knowledge and capabilities, in this unique breed of international, entrepreneurial firm. An analysis of case studies and surveys revealed key strategies that engender international success among these innovative firms (Knight and Cavusgil, 2004). Successful 'Born-Global' firms leverage a distinctive mix of orientations and strategies that allow them to succeed in diverse international markets. Firms that possess the fundamental capabilities of international entrepreneurial orientation and international marketing orientation engender the development of a specific collection of organizational strategies.

The most important business strategies employed by born-global firms are global technological competence, unique product development, quality focus, and leveraging of foreign distributor competences. Zahra et al. (2000) studied more than 300 private independent and corporate new ventures based in the United States. Building on past research about the advantages of large, established multinational enterprises, their results from 12 high-technology industries show that greater diversity of national environments is associated with increased technological learning opportunities, even for new ventures whose internationalization is usually thought to be limited. They also find that the breadth, depth and speed of technological learning from varied international environments is significantly enhanced by formal organizational efforts to integrate knowledge throughout a firm via structures like cross-functional teams and formal analysis of both successful and failed projects. Further, they show that venture performance is improved by technological learning gained from international environments, echoing the RBV and internationalization literature cited above.

In summary, in comparison to the traditional conceptualizations of MNE structure, these new and emerging trends suggest a relaxation in the notion of a fixed structure for the MNE; rather, the MNE may take on a fluid, complex, adaptive structure. The boundaries that define those activities conducted 'inside' and 'outside' the MNE are increasingly porous as a result of the network and other boundary-spanning activities that constitute an increasing share of MNE activity. Finally, relationships with governments are no longer dyadic, but involve multiple stakeholders at various levels, including civil society organizations and NGOs that are supplanting some of the traditional roles of host governments.

CONCLUSION: A NEW DEFINITION OF THE MULTINATIONAL ENTERPRISE?

Scholars have never fully agreed on what constitutes an MNE. In an early IB text, Blough (1966) summarized the methods by which a national manufacturing organization could operate internationally, ranging from simply soliciting purchases by foreign buyers in one or more countries, to establishing a factory in a foreign country, what we would generally term FDI. Operational definitions are complicated by differences in the forms that the relationship between the parent and the subsidiaries can take. Perlmutter (1969), of course, distinguished among the following categories of corporations (in what he considers to be an evolutionary chain): ethnocentric corporations (headquarters maintains responsibilities for principal decisions, priority is given to nationals of the home country for filling important posts in foreign subsidiaries, parent company considered superior and to have a monopoly on know-how); polycentric corporations (recognition that local situations are different from one another and from the parent country, subsidiaries operated by the nationals of each country; company becomes a confederation of loosely connected subsidiaries, many of which have access to all financial and research data; parent company remains in the hands of nationals of the headquarters country who occupy all important posts); and geocentric corporations (posts filled without regard to nationality; policies formulated without regard to national preferences;

subsidiary directors participate in the formulation of general policies; headquarters location considered to be an accident of history to be changed according to the convenience of tax laws).

Perlmutter's simple framework appears almost quaint in an era of global connectivity and significant migration and integration. As we consider the emergence of global networks, from anti-globalization activists to on-line communities such as MySpace.com and Youtube.com that arose from the grassroots but are now extremely valuable institutions and brands, the structured, hierarchical organizations that traditionally fall under the MNE are mostly anachronistic. At the same time, the traditional business–government relationship has given way to a much more complex multi-party (network-type) connection, with commensurate ramifications for organizational and institutional structures.

The Organisation for Economic Co-operation and Development (UNCTAD, 1974, p. 2) offers probably one of the simplest definitions of MNEs:

> Multinational enterprises include enterprises, whether they are of public, mixed or private ownership, which own or control production, distribution, services or other facilities outside the country in which they are based.

While broad and seemingly encompassing a wide range of activities, an even broader definition of a multinational organization could be advocated. Developments in the global business environment, as represented by cross-sectoral collaboration, the emergence of 'born-global' firms, and the rapid growth in offshore outsourcing may suggest an even more expansive definition. It may be that at the beginning of the twenty-first century, multinational organizations could include 'any organization that has substantial and ongoing reliance or dependence on developments and activities outside its home market'. Such a definition begins to capture and recognize the diversity and scope of internationalization among so many organizations operating in the world today.

REFERENCES

Baker, S. and M. Kripalani (2004), 'Software: will outsourcing hurt America's supremacy?', *Business Week*, 1 March pp. 84–91.

Baligh, H.H. and R.M. Burton (1981), 'Describing and designing organization structures and processes', *International Journal of Policy Analysis and Information Systems*, **5** (4), 251–66.

Baligh, H.H. and R.M. Burton (1982), 'The movable boundaries between organizations and markets', *International Journal of Policy Analysis and Information Systems*, **6** (4), 435–49.

Barkema, H.G. and F. Vermuelen (1998). 'International expansion through start-up or acquisition: a learning perspective', *Academy of Management Journal*, **41** (1), 7–26.

Barney, J. (1991), 'Firm resources and the theory of competitive advantage', *Journal of Management*, **17**, 99–120.

Bartlett, C. and S. Ghoshal (1989), *Managing Across Borders*, Boston, MA: Harvard Business School Press.

Bell, J., R. McNaughton and S. Young (2001), '"Born-again global" firms: an extension to the "born global" firms', *Journal of International Business Studies*, **9** (1), 33–46.

Bilkey, W.J. (1978), 'An attempted integration of the literature on the export behavior of firms', *Journal of International Business Studies*, **9** (1), 33–46.

Birkinshaw, J. (2000), *Entrepreneurship in the Global Firm*, Thousand Oaks, CA: Sage.

Blough, R. (1966), *International Business: Environment and Adaptation*, New York: McGraw-Hill.

Buckley, P. (2002), 'Is the international business research agenda running out of steam?', *Journal of International Business Studies*, **33** (2), 365–73.

Buckley, P.J. and M. Casson (1976), *The Future of the Multinational Enterprise*, London: Holmes and Meier.

Cavusgil, S.T. (1980), 'On the internationalization process of firms', *European Research*, **8**, 273–81.

Coase, R. (1937), 'The nature of the firm', *Economica*, **4** (16), 386–405.

Corbett, M.F. (2004), *The Outsourcing Revolution: Why it Makes Sense and How to Do it Right*, Chicago: Dearborn Trade Publishing.

Dacin, M.T., M.J. Ventresca and B.D. Beal (1999). 'The embeddedness of organizations: dialogue and directions', *Journal of Management*, **25** (3), 317–56.

DiMaggio, P.J. and W.W. Powell (1983), 'The iron cage revisited: institutional isomorphism and collective rationality in organizational fields', *American Sociological Review*, **48** (2), 147–60.

Doh, J.P. (2005), 'Offshore outsourcing: implications for international business and strategic management theory and practice', *Journal of Management Studies*, **42** (3), 695–704.

Doh, J.P. and H. Teegen (eds) (2003), *Globalization and NGOs: Transforming Business, Government, and Society*, Westport, CT: Praeger Publishers.

Drezner, D.W. (2004), 'The outsourcing bogeyman', *Foreign Affairs*, **83** (3), available at http://www.foreignaffairs.org/2004/3.html.

Dunning, J.H. (1981), *International Production and the Multinational Enterprise*, London: Allen and Unwin.

Dunning, J.H. (1988), 'The eclectic paradigm of international production: a restatement and some possible extensions', *Journal of International Business Studies*, **19** (1), 1–31.

Dunning, J.H. (1995), 'Reappraising the eclectic paradigm in an age of alliance capitalism', *Journal of International Business Studies*, **26** (3), 461–91.

Eisenhardt, K.M. and J.A. Martin (2000), 'Dynamic capabilities: what are they?', *Strategic Management Journal*, **21** (Special Issue), 1105–21.

Eisenhardt, K.M. and C.B. Schoonhoven (1996), 'Resource-based view of strategic alliance formation: strategic and social effects in entrepreneurial firms', *Organizational Science*, **7** (2), 136–50.

Graf, M. and S.M. Mudambi (2005), 'The outsourcing of IT-enabled business processes: a conceptual model of the location decision', *Journal of International Management*, **11** (2), 253–68.

Granovetter, M.S. (1985), 'Economic action and social structure: the problem of embeddedness', *American Journal of Sociology*, **91** (3), 481–510.

Gulati, R. (1995), 'Social structure and alliance formation patterns: a longitudinal analysis', *Administrative Science Quarterly*, **40**, 619–52.

Johanson, J. and A. Vahlne (1977), 'The internationalization process of the firm: a model of knowledge development and increasing foreign market commitments', *Journal of International Business Studies*, **8** (1), 23–32.

Johanson, J. and J.E. Vahlne (1990), 'The mechanism of internationalization', *International Marketing Review*, **7** (4), 11–24.

Khanna, T. and K. Palepu (2000), 'Is group affiliation profitable in emerging markets? An analysis of diversified Indian business groups', *Journal of Finance*, **55** (2), 867–91.

Khanna, T., K. Palepu and J Sinha (2005), 'Strategies to fit emerging markets', *Harvard Business Review*, **83**, 63–74.

Knight, G.A. and T.S. Cavusgil (1996), 'The Born Global firm: a challenge to traditional internationalization theory', *Advances in International Marketing*, **8**, 11–26.

Knight, G.A. and T.S. Cavusgil (2004), 'Innovation, organizational capabilities, and the born-global firm', *Journal of International Business Studies*, **35** (2), 124–41.

Kogut, B. (1988), 'Joint ventures: theoretical and empirical perspectives', *Strategic Management Journal*, **9**, 319–32.

Kogut, B. and U. Zander (1992), 'Knowledge of the firm, combinative capabilities, and the replication of technology', *Organization Science*, **3**, 383–97.

Kostova, T. and K. Roth (2002), 'Adoption of an organizational practice by the subsidiaries of the MNC: institutional and relational effects', *Academy of Management Journal*, **45**, 215–33.

Kotabe, M. and J. Murray (2004), 'Global sourcing strategy and sustainable competitive advantage', *Industrial Marketing Management*, **33** (1), 7–14.

Lewin, A.Y. and M. Koza (2001), 'Empirical research in co-evolutionary processes of strategic adaptation and change: the promise and the challenge', *Organization Studies*, **22** (6), v–xii.

Lewin, A.Y. and H.W. Volberda (1999), 'Prolegomena on coevolution: a framework for research on strategy and new organizational forms', *Organization Science*, **10** (5), 519–34.

Lindenberg, M. (2001), 'Reaching beyond the family: new nongovernmental organization alliances for global poverty alleviation and emergency response', *Nonprofit and Voluntary Sector Quarterly*, **30**, 603–15.

McCann, P. and R. Mudambi (2004), 'The location behavior of the multinational enterprise: some analytical issues', *Growth and Change*, **35** (4), 491–524.

Makino, S. and A. Delios (1997), 'Local knowledge transfer and performance: implications for alliance formation in Asia', *Journal of International Business Studies*, **27**, 905–27.

March, J.G. and H.A. Simon (1958), *Organizations*, New York: McGraw-Hill.

Mudambi, R. (1995), 'The MNE investment location decision: some empirical evidence', *Managerial and Decision Economics*, **16**, 249–57.

Nelson, R. and S. Winter (1982), *An Evolutionary Theory of Economic Change*, Cambridge, MA: Harvard University Press.

North, D.C. (1990), *Institutions, Institutional Change and Economic Performance*, Cambridge, MA: Harvard University Press.

Oliver, C. (1991), 'Strategic responses to institutional processes', *Academy of Management Review*, **16** (1), 145–79.

Oviatt, B.M. and P.P. McDougall (1994),'Toward a theory of international new ventures', *Journal of International Business Studies*, **25** (First Quarter), 45–64.

Oystein, M. (2002), 'The born globals: a new generation of small European exporters', *International Marketing Review*, **19** (2/3), 156–75.

Padmanabhan, P. and K.R. Cho (1999), 'Decision specific experience in foreign ownership and establishment strategies: evidence from Japanese firms', *Journal of International Business Studies*, **30**, 25–42.

Peng, M. (2004), 'Identifying the big question in international business research', *Journal of International Business Studies*, **35** (2), 99–108.

Penrose, E.T. (1959), *The Theory of Growth of the Firm*, London: Blackwell.

Perlmutter, H. (1969), 'The tortuous evolution of the multinational corporation', *Columbia Journal of World Business*, **4**, 9–18.

Peteraf, M. (1994), 'The cornerstones of competitive advantage: a resource-based view', *Strategic Management Journal*, **14**, 179–91.

Pfeffer, J. and P. Nowak (1976), 'Joint ventures and interorganizational interdependence', *Administrative Science Quarterly*, **21**, 398–418.

Porter, M. (1980), *Competitive Advantage*, New York: The Free Press.

Porter, M. (1990), *The Competitive Advantage of Nations*, New York: The Free Press.

Rondinelli, D. and T. London (2003), 'How corporations and environmental groups collaborate: assessing cross-sector collaborations and alliances', *Academy of Management Executive*, **17** (1), 61–76.

Schemenner, R.W. (1979), 'Look beyond the obvious in plant location', *Harvard Business Review*, **57**, 126–32.

Schermerhorn, J.R., Jr. (1975), 'Determinants of interorganizational cooperation', *Academy of Management Journal*, **18**, 846–56.

Shenkar, O. (2004), 'One more time: international business in a global economy', *Journal of International Business Studies*, **35** (2), 161–71.

Spar, D.L. and L.T. La Mure (2003), The power of NGOs activism: assessing the impact of NGOs on global business', *California Management Review*, **45**, 78–101.

Tallman, S. (1991), 'Strategic management models and resource-based strategies among MNEs in a host market', *Strategic Management Journal*, **12** (Summer), 69–82.

Tallman, S. (1992), 'A strategic management perspective on host country structure of multinational enterprise', *Journal of Management*, **18**, 445–71.

Tallman, S.B. and O. Shenkar (1994), 'A managerial decision model of international cooperative venture formation', *Journal of International Business Studies*, **25** (1), 91–112.

Teece, D.J., G. Pisano and A. Shuen (1997), 'Dynamic capabilities and strategic management', *Strategic Management Journal*, **18** (7), 509–33.

Teegen, H., J.P. Doh and S. Vachani (2004), 'The importance of nongovernmental organizations (NGOs) in global governance and value creation: an international business research agenda', *Journal of International Business Studies*, **35** (6), 463–83.

United Nations Conference on Trade and Development (UNCTAD) (1974), *Multinational Corporations and World Development*, New York: United Nations.

Vernon, R. (1971), *Sovereignty at Bay*, New York: Basic Books.

Volberda, J. and A. Lewin (2003). 'Co-evolutionary dynamics within and between firms: from evolution to co-evolution', *Journal of Management Studies*, **40**, 2111–136.

Waddock, S.A. (1988), 'Building successful social partnerships', *Sloan Management Review*, **29**, 17–23.

Wasserman, A. and K. Faust (1994), *Social Network Analysis: Methods and Applications*, Cambridge: Cambridge University Press.

Westley, F. and H. Vredenburg (1991), 'Strategic bridging: the collaboration between environmentalists and business in the marketing of green products', *The Journal of Applied Behavioral Science*, **27**, 65–90.

Williamson, O.E. (1975), *Markets and Hierarchies*, New York: The Free Press.

Yaziji, M. (2004), 'Turning gadflies into allies', *Harvard Business Review*, **82** (February), 110–15.

Zahra, S.A., R.D. Ireland and M.A. Hitt (2000), 'International expansion by new venture firms: international diversity, mode of market entry, technological learning, and performance', *Academy of Management Journal*, **43** (5), 925–50.

8. Organizing for discontinuous knowledge flows: a new perspective on the management of knowledge and innovation in MNCs

Björn Ambos and Tina C. Ambos

Over the last two decades, a growing body of literature has turned to knowledge as an intriguing and powerful explanation of why some firms are able to build sustainable competitive advantages and others are not. The rationale for this focus on knowledge is obvious: knowledge itself can be seen as a scarce, valuable and if not impossible, at least difficult to imitate resource, which may serve as the foundation of a firm's competitive advantage (e.g. Kogut and Zander, 1993). In an increasing number of industries, knowledge has been found to be globally dispersed, thus, companies seeking to draw competitive advantage from globally dispersed knowledge are forced to locate organizational satellites in the worldwide epicentres of innovation. The resulting dispersion and differentiation of knowledge within the firm leads to situations where, at least to some degree, local units possess *distinct* stocks of knowledge. Some of them are characterized by high tacitness or stickiness, which render them inert and difficult to move across locations. Thus sharing, transferring or recombining knowledge across the organization constitutes an important avenue to create such a competitive advantage (e.g. Kogut and Zander, 1992, 1993; Buckley and Carter, 2004).

The apparent difficulty of transferring knowledge across subunits separated by large geographical, cultural and organizational distances has spurred on much research among international business scholars (e.g. Leonard-Barton, 1995; Nonaka and Takeuchi, 1995; Szulanski, 1996; Inkpen and Dinur, 1998; Hansen, 1999; Gupta and Govindarajan, 2000). However, this research culminates in what we believe to be ill-guided conclusions, such as subsidiaries that do not share knowledge are disadvantaged or are 'not part of the in-crowd' (Monteiro et al., 2004), or normative prescriptions such as the need to increase the absorptive capacity, overcome barriers, and motivate units to share and stimulate flows.

In this chapter we argue that three (related) misconceptions lead to these conclusions. First, scholars hardly ever distinguish between the different aims of knowledge transfer: creation or exploitation. Second, stimulating knowledge flows may not always be the best option – there may be situations when organizational units benefit from isolation. Third, knowledge flows within organizations are generally assumed to take place on a continuous basis; that is, at an average high or low level. Based on this assumption, typologies created to capture the diverse and differentiated tasks of different units tend to suggest a static role and hardly ever take into account that the organizational unit may best contribute to the multinational corporation (MNC) as a whole by changing its role and its level of integration in the organization.

While most research acknowledges that knowledge flows are instrumental to stimulating innovation, it tends to ignore the vital link between the management of knowledge flows and the organizational embedding of innovation. By relaxing the assumption of continuous knowledge flows and by subscribing to a dynamic perspective, we attempt to advance our knowledge of innovation within the MNC. We argue that the nature of knowledge flows in practice is discontinuous and that organizations are well advised to shift between different modes of managing their overseas innovation units.

The research contributions of this chapter are threefold. First, this study suggests that dynamics are important and so far underexplored characteristics in the management of organizational knowledge. Second, it introduces a new approach to look at the role models assigned to organizational units and fosters an evolutionary approach for their management – beyond current models of subsidiary evolution. Third, it contributes to an understanding of the linkage between knowledge and innovation dynamics by re-embedding knowledge transfers within the firm in the larger context of structure and innovation.

In the next section, we describe several misconceptions in contemporary knowledge management literature and advocate a need for change in this area. Then we draw on insights from three existing streams of literature that partly address these problems. In an effort to reconcile these perspectives we develop a model of discontinuous knowledge flows, which helps us to better organize knowledge flows for innovation-intensive units. We conclude by suggesting a new research agenda for knowledge management.

A CRITICAL REVIEW OF KNOWLEDGE MANAGEMENT LITERATURE

During the last decade, research on organizational knowledge flows has received paramount emphasis. It is difficult to find any issue of an academic journal on organization or international business without a contribution in this field. While these studies offer a wide variety of issues and contexts, most seem to follow very similar assumptions. By critically reviewing the literature, we came to the conclusion that three misconceptions are found consistently in contemporary knowledge management literature. In the following, we address them in turn.

Knowledge Management: What For?

Different schools of thought have identified the ability to transfer knowledge on a global basis as the raison d'être of MNCs. According to Buckley and Casson (1976), the very existence of an MNC depends on its ability to internalize externalities by putting together resources and activities at a more efficient rate than markets do. The argument that firms create value through combining dispersed knowledge fits this perspective well, especially if one accepts that markets often fail to transfer this knowledge at a price (Caves, 1982; Hymer, 1976; Teece, 1998). Following different logic, Kogut and Zander (1993) come to a similar conclusion regarding the MNC as a knowledge integrating institution. Building an evolutionary theory of the firm, they state that knowledge exists as part of social relations among cooperating members of a community without fixed boundaries. In this vein, the MNC is seen as a social community, whose productive knowledge builds the basis for a competitive advantage. These assumptions are well in line with the emergent literature on transnational, heterarchical or multi-focal firms (Bartlett and Ghoshal, 1988; Forsgren, 1990; Ghoshal and Nohria, 1993; Hedlund, 1994; Ghoshal and Moran, 1996). Rather than seeing the MNC as a result of market failures, these authors emphasize the MNC's ability to integrate, combine and create new knowledge. They subscribe to the idea that the benefits from the sum of knowledge shared are larger than those accrued from its parts. Scholars have enthusiastically embraced this idea, but largely ignored that the outlined benefits from intra-organizational knowledge flows follow two distinct objectives: on the one hand, to disseminate and exploit existing knowledge, and on the other hand, to create new knowledge.

While a relatively large stream of literature has contributed to our understanding of the efficiency arguments for sharing and transferring knowledge within the firm, ironically there is not much evidence concerning the potential to create *new* knowledge (see also Nickerson and Zenger, 2004). During the last two decades, many studies have focused on the barriers and impediments of knowledge flows between organizational units (e.g. Leonard-Barton, 1995; Nonaka and Takeuchi, 1995; Szulanski, 1996; Inkpen and Dinur, 1998; Hansen, 1999; Gupta and Govindarajan, 2000). A lack of absorptive capacity (Tsai, 2001; Minbaeva et al., 2003), the inability to codify knowledge (Szulanski, 1996; Nonaka and Takeuchi, 1995; Kogut and Zander, 1993) and general motivations and power positions (Mudambi and Pedersen, 2006; Mudambi and Navarra, 2004) have been identified as the main obstacles to smooth knowledge transfer. Some of these studies focus explicitly on replication (Winter and Szulanski, 2001; Kogut and Zander, 1992; Szulanski and Jensen, 2006; Darr and Argote, 1995) – that is, exploitation of prior knowledge – but most others are agnostic about the aim of knowledge transfer and do not distinguish between creation or exploitation of knowledge. However, most arguments for knowledge transfer build on an efficiency logic and are geared towards exploiting the organization's knowledge potential on a global basis. Many authors forget that even Kogut and Zander's seminal article (1992) referred to 'replication' rather than knowledge creation. Collectively, we find very little empirical evidence that knowledge transfer actually creates new knowledge.

Selected studies recognize that certain processes are necessary in order to create new knowledge. Schulz (2003), for example, suggested a 'lock–key' mechanism: external knowledge, like a key, can connect to knowledge in a way that fits. Although Schulz talks about the creation of new knowledge through that combination of incoming and local knowledge, he argues that 'relevance affects how much and where knowledge travels in organizations' (Schulz, 2003, p. 441). As units that are about to create something new are not necessarily cognizant of the relevance of certain issues, Schulz's core argument also follows an efficiency logic. Another example is Buckley and Carter's work (2004), which theoretically distinguishes three different combination processes, among which 'sequential complementarity' bears the highest potential for the creation of new knowledge. But they did not model knowledge creation resulting from transfers. We may assume that knowledge creation is a 'derived' outcome, as the received knowledge may serve as the basis for creation of new knowledge, but studies usually fail to address this issue explicitly. Interestingly, the few contributions that do test the impact of knowledge flows on the creation of new knowledge (or innovation) come from studies using patent citations as a proxy for knowledge creation (e.g. Yamin and Otto, 2004). However, using patents as measures of either knowledge flows or knowledge outcomes has recently been heavily criticized (e.g. Brusoni et al., 2005).

Despite the lack of empirical evidence in this field, it is obvious that the variables that affect the exploitation of existing knowledge and the creation of new knowledge must be different. Thus we believe it is important to highlight the conceptual difference. As we argue in this chapter, distinguishing between the two objectives – transfer to exploit and transfer to create – has important implications for the organization of knowledge flows in MNCs. In order to shed more light on this phenomenon, future studies need to use different dependent variables to capture knowledge creation, investigate the combination of knowledge using interactions of senders and recipients, or target different phenomena, for example transnational teams versus Centres of Excellence (see Ambos and Schlegelmilch, 2005).

Stimulating Knowledge Flows: Always?

As outlined above, contemporary thinking suggests that knowledge flows are advantageous for any organization – even at the expense of redundancies (Bartlett and Ghoshal, 1989). Recently, selected studies have suggested that more knowledge transfer is not necessarily better (Chini, 2004; Mahnke et al., 2004; Haas and Hansen, 2005). Mahnke et al. (2004) suggested an inverted U-shaped effect of knowledge outflows on performance. Arguing that the value of obtaining and using knowledge should be assessed by evaluating the impact of that knowledge use, Haas and Hansen (2005) found that the performance of teams did not depend on how much they knew, but how they used what they knew. By including certain contingencies of the team and the task environment, this study shed some light on the question of *when* knowledge flows are warranted, but their sample from the consulting context was very specific and difficult to relate to other firm environments. While more and more scholars call for a limit on knowledge transfers from a cost–benefit perspective, other reasons to limit knowledge flows remain in the dark. What seems to be missing is a better understanding of the circumstances in which knowledge transfer is *not* beneficial to organizations.

For example, Leonard-Barton (1992) found that inconsistencies between core capabilities and innovation demands frequently led to more intensive use of extant strengths, resulting in teams repeatedly missing opportunities for creative breakthroughs. Asakawa (2001) suggested that an evolutionary process drives research and development (R&D) units that are decoupled from headquarters' knowledge flows to build ties with their local environments. In his analysis of overseas R&D units, Birkinshaw (2002) showed that units that possessed knowledge that was immobile and difficult to understand were often left alone in order to capitalize on and further develop their capabilities. Probably the most enlightening study in this area is Hansen's (1999), which showed that weak and strong relationships between organizational units have their respective weaknesses and benefits for search and transfer that are related to the complexity of the knowledge. His results highlight the dilemma innovative units face: weak ties are beneficial in order to search for new knowledge, but strong ties are more efficient if the knowledge to be transferred is complex.

In general, the literature on innovation suggests granting innovative organizational units autonomy and freedom in order to experiment and to build ties with host country stakeholders. Paradoxically, the knowledge management literature has a tendency to attribute more importance to units that are highly integrated through knowledge flows. For example, Gupta and Govindarajan's 'Global Innovator and Integrated Player', or Asakawa's units with 'connected freedom' are not only described as more innovation-intensive roles (i.e. geared towards knowledge creation), but also as somewhat more desirable from the subsidiary manager's perspective. Monteiro et al. (2004) even found that subsidiaries that are isolated, and are not intensively involved in knowledge in- and outflows, perform worse than highly integrated units. The normative but usually unconsidered implication of such studies is that more knowledge sharing is better for the organizations. They mostly ignore the contingencies that may recommend isolation rather than integration, especially for innovative units. While we do not claim that isolation is better per se, we argue in line with the literature on innovation that its merits are linked to the specific circumstances of knowledge creation. This leads us to the next section, where we explore further problems of continuous knowledge flows.

Continuous Knowledge Flows: Realistic?

A third misconception that is implicit in a large proportion of knowledge management studies is that knowledge flows are (or should be) conceptualized as a continuous state rather than a discrete event. In other words, knowledge flows continuously over time. Notwithstanding the purpose of knowledge transfer – creation or exploitation – this assumption seems unrealistic. Let us consider the transfer of a best practice, such as the introduction of incentive schemes, between two organizational units. It is equally unlikely that the adoption of such a new practice will be accomplished with one single interaction or transfer as through a continuous level of knowledge. More realistic is a pattern of intensive exchange followed by very low or no transfer at all. Despite the common-sense appeal of such examples, most studies on knowledge management talk about units with (average) high or low levels of knowledge flow. Usually, these units are assumed to have similar attributes or strategic directions (Gupta and Govindarajan, 1991, 1994; Asakawa, 2001; Monteiro et al., 2004). A partial explanation for this common research approach lies in the difficulty of measuring and comparing knowledge flows, but we hold that it is important to distinguish between very short intensive knowledge flows and continuous lower average level flows over a longer period of time. The assumption of continuous knowledge flows is unlikely to be reflected in practice and has led to over-simplified and even misleading conceptualizations of the knowledge transfer practices in organizational units.

Based on the assumption of continuous knowledge flows, some conceptualizations of the roles of organizational units are also problematic. Since the 1980s there have been various attempts to classify the roles and responsibilities different organizational unit take on (e.g. White and Poynter, 1984; Bartlett and Ghoshal, 1989; Martinez and Jarillo, 1989; Taggart, 1997; Gupta and Govindarajan, 1991; Paterson and Brock, 2002). The multitude of typologies is based on different criteria such as competences, market environment or autonomy. Also the level of a unit's knowledge (in- and out)flows has been used to characterize its strategic role in the company (e.g. Gupta and Govindarajan, 1991, 1994; Asakawa, 2001). Based on this literature, we may assume that, regardless of the initial purpose of knowledge transfer, some organizational units will engage more heavily in knowledge creation while others will exploit the existing knowledge.

If we acknowledge that knowledge flows are discontinuous, a subsidiary's knowledge sharing role will change depending on whether it is in a knowledge 'creation' or a knowledge 'dissemination' mode. In other words, static conceptualizations of units as Global Innovators (low inflows and high outflows) or Local Innovators (low in- and outflows) (Gupta and Govindarajan, 1994, 2000) are misleading in a sense that Global Innovators may also encounter times where it is more beneficial not to transfer. At the heart of the problem is the definition of roles through in- and outflows. This is problematic as units need to engage in and refrain from transfer at different points in time. Thus defining a role through the amount of outflows at one point or averaged over a certain period and correlating this with levels of control and so on (e.g. Gupta and Govindarajan, 1994) is misleading. This misconception may explain why Gupta and Govindarajan (1994) only find mixed results with regard to control and reward systems of their different roles. In the same vein, the conclusion that 'internal isolation' hurts performance (Monteiro et al., 2004) is problematic. Even though the authors limit their study to marketing units and argue that isolation is also a social phenomenon ('not part of the in-crowd'), the generalization that a low level of knowledge flows is associated with lower performance could probably be challenged in a longitudinal extension of this study.

These observations lead us to the conclusion that the current debate on knowledge flows is incomplete at best – if not misleading. While there are certainly many other problems, we posit that the misconceptions identified above are critical to our understanding (or misunderstanding) of knowledge creation and innovation in the MNC. Although they cannot be treated completely independently of each other, we believe that the assumption of discontinuous knowledge flows is the most important issue in this respect. If studies were to incorporate this thinking, the other issues would probably resolve themselves to a great extent. In order to mitigate these problems, a model of 'discontinuous knowledge flows', which helps us to understand how knowledge flows in MNCs can be organized, is warranted.

TOWARDS DISCONTINUOUS KNOWLEDGE FLOWS

Three streams of literature prove helpful in understanding the misconceptions and paradoxes in knowledge management research and in crafting an organizational model of discontinuous knowledge flows. In the following we draw on three different streams of literature – innovation, subsidiary evolution and ambidextrous organizational designs – and show how their insights may help us to mitigate the above mentioned problems. Pursuing this eclectic approach further, we then propose a model of discontinuous knowledge flows in order to rectify some of the problems addressed. First, we turn to innovation literature, then to research on subsidiary evolution, and last but not least to ambidexterity.

Lessons from Innovation Literature: Separating Creation and Exploitation

Recognizing the potential of dispersed knowledge in modern MNCs, the literature on innovation has proposed organizational structures that are geared for innovation at the international level and allow (1) the appropriation of (local) knowledge, (2) the combination of knowledge, and (3) the exploitation of this knowledge to enhance the firm's core competences (e.g. Asakawa, 2001). Common conceptualizations of these activities include exploration versus exploitation, sense–respond–implement, appropriate–mobilize–leverage and many others (Zaltman et al., 1973; Bartlett and Ghoshal, 1988; Doz et al., 2001; Ambos and Chini, 2005; Kuemmerle, 1999). Most authors acknowledge that there is a need for a sequencing in the innovation process, where it is vital to first sense, explore and understand new (combinations of) knowledge and, at a later stage, exploit and distribute this newly created knowledge.

In contrast to the studies of knowledge management, the innovation literature has long argued that exploration (creation) and exploitation are fundamentally different strategies (March, 1990; Kuemmerle, 1999; Ambos,

2005; Chiesa, 1996). Consequently, individual organizational units should be assigned distinct roles and their task environment must have an impact on how these units should be monitored and rewarded. To search for and create new knowledge, scholars usually recommend a low level of knowledge flows, as units need to search broadly for new activity configurations (Asakawa, 2001; Ambos and Reitsperger, 2004), whereas for embedding and scaling the innovation in the organization they suggest high levels of knowledge flows in order to coordinate across their independent activities. Facing this paradox, the question of how to integrate and coordinate innovation-intensive organizational units has received paramount attention during recent years (Nobel and Birkinshaw, 1998; Ambos, 2005; Frost et al., 2002). Especially in the context of R&D units, many scholars argued for a division between different processes.

In this stream of literature, organizational units are assigned clear objectives, which then imply a certain level of knowledge flows. However, knowledge in- and outflows to peer units are seen independently of the role assignment and hardly ever are integrated in these studies. Thus the distinction between exploration and exploitation advocated in innovation literature may help us to better distinguish knowledge flows for different purposes.

Lessons from Subsidiary Evolution: Dynamic Roles

The literature on subsidiary evolution has made great contributions to a dynamic understanding of different organizational roles, in particular how roles are assigned or assumed and how they may evolve, thus our criticism regarding the continuous and static nature of subsidiary roles has partly been addressed by the subsidiary evolution literature advocated by Birkinshaw (1997), Asakawa (2001) and others. These studies argue that the role of an organizational unit may change over time. There is a common understanding that this process may be either subsidiary-driven or parent-driven (Birkinshaw, 1997), but the predominant change agents in evolutionary models seem to be proactive subsidiaries, which recognize new opportunities and undertake initiatives (Birkinshaw et al., 1999; Birkinshaw and Fry, 1998). Organizational power or resource objectives drive this evolution, and knowledge flows are a means to an end in so far as they change in line with the different role assignment. Moreover, extant literature has mainly centred on the question of how the control mechanisms and the nature of headquarters–subsidiary relationships change.

While the insight that organizational units evolve and change over time is valuable to complement the current literature on knowledge management, two crucial points have not been addressed. First, the necessity of knowledge flows from an innovation point of view is not at the centre of this debate, as these flows seem to be a by-product of the unit's evolution. Second, there is a tendency to extend a development model to more powerful and influential roles or positions in the organization – in extreme words: a teleological development. Asakawa (2001) even described a life-cycle model for R&D units. At the time of their establishment, headquarters intervened strongly in order to help the units get started. Then the units were left alone to facilitate interaction with the local environment and avoid an over-reliance on headquarters. Having created new knowledge, these units were reintegrated in order to disseminate and share their knowledge with the rest of the organization. However, Asakawa portrayed a single life cycle and remained silent about the possibilities of a renewed cycle. There may be reasons to assume that this evolutionary process could take place on a more systematic basis in line with the tasks assigned to the unit.

Lessons from Ambidextrous Organizational Designs: Temporal Separation

The innovation literature traditionally recommended spatial separation between creative and exploitative activities throughout the organization. For example, Kuemmerle (1999) and Ambos (2005) identified strong location pulls that favour the establishment of exploitation as opposed to exploration units. Recently, scholars have suggested that firms can engage in a mix of creation and exploitation through structural ambidexterity (Brown and Eisenhardt, 1997; Tushman and O'Reilly, 1997; He and Wong, 2004). This concept has been developed at the broader organizational level and posits that firms need to develop a meta-capability that allows them to pursue new, exploratory initiatives and at the same time dedicate resources to the pursuit of existing initiatives within the same structure. In prior studies the idea of ambidexterity has been applied to innovation and efficiency pressures and mostly focused on the ability of entire organizations or the top management teams to shift between priorities. While organizational solutions to this dilemma are heatedly debated, a useful approach for organizational units that face different pressures seems to be temporal separation of activities – that is, an entire unit focuses on one set of tasks one day and on a different set of tasks on another day (Adler et al., 1999; Duncan, 1976; McDonough and Leifer, 1983). Using a simulation technique, Siggelkow and Levinthal (2003) also found that temporary decentralization yielded higher performance than pure centralization or decentralization of decision allocation. Their model suggests that temporary decentralization followed by reintegration is a helpful search strategy, even if the temporary aspect of decentralization was not intended. However, they focus on decomposable decision making and environmental changes and, thus, remain silent as to *when* the decoupling has to take place in the innovation cycle.

To the best of our best knowledge, intra-organizational knowledge transfer has not been explicitly considered in this context, but the level of knowledge flows is key to distinguishing different stages or modes taken by organizational units. Thus we believe that this model of ambidexterity, especially the form of temporal separation, fits the idea of discontinuous knowledge flows well.

In conclusion, the three streams of literature advocate different positions with regard to the importance and the aim of knowledge flows as well as their impact on organizational roles. Table 8.1 summarizes how these different literature streams address the questions outlined earlier. From innovation, we take away the differentiated needs of creation and exploitation tasks, from subsidiary evolution the dynamic perspective and the potential of organizational units to change, and from ambidexterity the challenge to organize for different tasks in one unit.

Table 8.1   Lessons from three streams of literature

Literature	Innovation	Subsidiary evolution	Ambidexterity
Knowledge flows	Not continuous; exploration vs. exploitation	Knowledge flows change in line with evolution of units	Unit has to switch between the creation and dissemination stage
Stimulating flows	Only for exploitation; 'weak ties' logic	Depends on power and resource goals of the unit in a particular stage	Depends on task priority
What for?	To exploit *or* to explore	To help the unit evolve into a more desirable stage	To exploit *and* to explore
Impact on unit roles	Separate role conceptualization from knowledge flow	Knowledge flow is dependent on (teleological) unit evolution	Role is dependent on knowledge flow stage

Modelling Discontinuous Knowledge Flows

In the last section, we showed how insights from three streams of literature suggest alternative solutions to the problems in current knowledge management literature. Drawing on the input from these streams of literature and our insights from managers in the field, we propose a model of discontinuous knowledge flows. This model tries to respond to the identified misconceptions and suggests a dynamic perspective for organizing knowledge flows within organizations. To reduce complexity, we depart from two assumptions: first, in line with contemporary literature, we posit that knowledge is dispersed and locally embedded, thus knowledge creation takes place locally. Second, for the purpose of our model, we assume that units are able create knowledge independently from other units.

Figure 8.1 shows the stylized development of an organizational unit over time, distinguishing between phases of high and low knowledge outflows. Stages 1, 3 and 5 depict a 'creation mode', while stages 2 and 4 depict a 'dissemination mode'. We start by explaining the two different modes and then elaborate on the potential evolution and development alternatives.

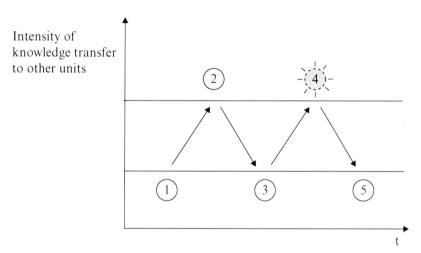

Figure 8.1   A model of discontinuous knowledge flow

Units that are geared for creation focus on searching for new knowledge locally. Local innovation requires a high degree of autonomy. To this end, roles and mandates are usually defined in broad terms and units work with little interference in their daily operations from others. Accessing and building ties with local stakeholders, such as research institutions, business partners or competitors is a preoccupation of organizational units during this stage. Given that the local context constitutes the primary source of innovation, innovative units are usually well integrated into the local community. Following the logic of innovation literature, we posit that these units benefit from isolation, thus knowledge flows are generally low, but selective inflows may be used to coordinate with other units that possess complementary knowledge (Andersson et al., 2006).

Units geared for dissemination, in contrast, focus on the distribution of knowledge and capabilities for exploitation within the larger firm. In this position, knowledge outflows should be high. We assume that there are also knowledge inflows taking place, as the developed innovation may have to be explained and/or adjusted according to other units' needs. During this stage, integration with the rest of the MNC becomes more important than embeddedness in the host country environment.

Obviously, there is nothing new about the identification and description of these two stages. MNCs have long differentiated between exploration and exploitation roles, but the critical process is the *transition* between the stages. How does a unit progress from a creative stage (1) to a dissemination stage (2)? It seems logical that units should first create and then disseminate. Few scholars have described a transition from stage 2 to stage 3: a de-integration of the unit. Asakawa (2001) and Siggelkow and Levinthal (2003) are among the few examples who recommended such a de-integration process. In fact, decoupling units, if only temporarily, from the corporate knowledge stream often helps to sustain their innovative momentum (see also Siggelkow and Levinthal, 2003). T-Mobile is a case in point.

After years of heavy expansion, T-Mobile sensed the need to redefine the tasks of their new business units. Given Europe's technological lead in voice, value added services and heavy investments into the UMTS standard, the US subsidiary was looking for new sources of competitive advantage. Departing from T-Mobile's relatively weak network coverage in the USA, and thus low pressures to conform with existing businesses, T-Mobile's US subsidiary decided to embrace W-LAN technology. The initial decision led to the formation of a new and geographically separated business unit mandated to take on this strategically important task. Working in relative isolation from the corporate knowledge stream while working closely with other firms in the local environment, T-Mobile's W-LAN branch was able to set its own innovative pace and became highly successful and innovative.

Another case was provided to us by a manager from General Electric. Having acquired a small European company with competence in medical imaging, they decided to leave them alone with a some of their scientists in order to come up with a new innovative technology. The directions for this project (and knowledge inflows) were very vague in order to allow them to experiment and aim for a solution 'out-of-the-box'. After some years, this unit was integrated again in order to link their knowledge with the rest of the organization.

Similar examples are described by Birkinshaw (2002). For example, Ericsson had a central R&D laboratory for radio in Sweden. Because of personnel shortages in Sweden and the need to access lead customers, a second R&D unit for radio was established in the UK. Being granted relative isolation from the rest of the organization and heavily interacting with lead customers, this unit developed its own capabilities and grew. While we find many examples of such transitions in either direction, which is the way we have portrayed our model, we would expect this sequence between creation and dissemination to continue in line with the innovation needs of the unit. However, as depicted in stage 4, the MNC may also decide to integrate the unit and not allow another creation mode.

The logic of change inherent in our model follows the pattern of a punctuated equilibrium, with longer periods of stability punctuated with periods of relatively short dramatic change (Gersick, 1991; Tushman and Romanelli, 1985). In line with the extant research on ambidextrous organizational designs, we believe that the transitions between the different stages are difficult processes and demand a high level of flexibility – if not a schizophrenic approach. As we cannot make process predictions from a theoretical point, we suggest future studies to explore this transition in more detail.

Building on the above, the essential conclusions of our model are, that, first, knowledge flows are discontinuous, and there are merits in this discontinuous pattern. Second, high knowledge flows are favourable for a dissemination mode, whereas low knowledge flows are suited to a creation mode. Third, units evolve through different stages, but evolution does not follow a linear path and instead is driven by an innovation logic. While these insights are incorporated in the proposed model of discontinuous knowledge flows, future studies need to investigate the empirical details of this pattern.

Our model certainly has some important limitations. Referring to the assumptions mentioned earlier, we assumed a rather simple case, where knowledge creation takes place locally. Situations where the locus of competitive advantage is global, such as in transnational teams, or where innovative units are highly interdependent because of modular technologies, are more complex and require different models. The number of stages and the timing of multiple creation and dissemination modes depend on the specificities of the task as well as on headquarters' ability to coordinate these activities. It is a highly abstract sketch of how knowledge flows could be organized, which would need to be adjusted to the specific operational styles and project requirements of every firm. Moreover, this chapter is concerned with innovative units. While we do not limit this characteristic to R&D units, we acknowledge that not all organizational units are preoccupied with innovation.

A NEW RESEARCH AGENDA FOR KNOWLEDGE FLOWS IN MNCs

The purpose of this chapter was to identify some of the misconceptions of the current knowledge management literature and to propose a model of discontinuous knowledge flows that incorporates novel ideas of how to conceive of and organize knowledge flows in the MNC. The model as such is a rough first idea, and includes several new directions that have to be elaborated and strengthened by future research. Thus, in line with our model, we suggest a new research agenda for knowledge flows in MNCs as a conclusion of this chapter. In particular, three topics warrant attention.

Conceptualizing Knowledge Flows

The central proposition of our chapter was that knowledge is wrongly conceptualized as continuously flowing. Although we acknowledge the difficulty of measuring and comparing knowledge flows, we advocate a general change of direction. To assign more validity to measures, it is necessary to include more contextual information to identify the current stage of the unit. An option may be to focus on specific events or even on problem-solving situations (e.g. Nickerson and Zenger, 2004). A common 'pitfall' of past research, such as Szulanski's (1996) study on best practices, was to include only transfer events and to ignore situations where no knowledge flows were taking place. But to shed light on general dynamics, the only solution seems to be to conduct qualitative longitudinal studies with rich insights into the contingencies of knowledge flows.

Different Aims of Knowledge Transfer

In line with our critique of the lack of distinction between creation and exploitation, we argue that it is necessary to clearly distinguish between the different aims of knowledge transfer. As theory suggests many diverse outcomes of knowledge flows, such as replication (e.g. Winter and Szulanski, 2001), winning a bid (Haas and Hansen, 2005) or limiting new product development time (Hoopes and Postrel, 2002) studies should be very clear on which issue they want to address. This certainly impacts research in two ways: first, to clarify in the theoretical positioning where and through which means value creation can take place, and second, through choosing the appropriate measures for these phenomena (for a related discussion see Chini and Ambos, 2005; Andersson et al., 2006). If we revert to the simpler logic of knowledge flows to create versus flows to exploit, it is important to shed light on the different nature of these flows. In particular, the questions of whether they generally have a different nature (e.g. observability, mobility) and whether they are transferred via different tools and mechanisms must be addressed.

Transitions and Inflection Points

Probably the most novel issue for knowledge management is the timing of knowledge flows. A critical point that could not be sufficiently addressed in our model, which is based in theoretical reasoning and anecdotal empirical evidence, is how the transitions between the different stages can be mastered. It is clear that these transitions are difficult to manage, but we do not know much more than that. The most compelling existing insights in this area come from a simulation study (Siggelkow and Levinthal, 2003), but it would be interesting to explore these processes in practice – in particular, the question of who initiates the transition and how the reorientation in the unit takes place are critical. Again the only feasible way to address these issues is through longitudinal tracking of inflection points.

CONCLUSION

As we have argued in this chapter, three misconceptions have held up progress in the field of intra-organizational knowledge transfer: the notion that knowledge flows continuously, that transfer is an undisputed aim in itself, and that all knowledge flows create new knowledge. We suggested a more dynamic perspective on knowledge flows, which may help future research to more critically interpret prior findings as well as develop alternative approaches to address these pertinent problems. By drawing on insights from literature on innovation, subsidiary evolution, and ambidexterity, we attempted to sketch out an organizational model of discontinuous knowledge flows, which may serve as a basis for future theory development and empirical testing.

REFERENCES

Adler, P., B. Goldoftas and D.I. Levine (1999), 'Flexibility versus efficiency? A case study of model changeovers in the Toyota production system', *Organization Science*, **10** (1), 43–68.
Ambos, B. (2005), 'Foreign direct investment in industrial research and development: a study of German MNCs', *Research Policy*, **34**, 395–410.
Ambos, B. and T.C. Chini (2005), 'Multinationals' location strategies in R&D: an empirical investigation', paper presented at the Strategic Management Society Annual Meeting, Orlando, FL, USA, 23–26 October 2005.

Ambos, B. and W. Reitsperger (2004), 'Offshore centers of excellence: social control and success', *Management International Review*, **44** (2), 51–65.

Ambos, B. and B. Schlegelmilch (2005), 'In search for global advantge', *European Business Forum*, **21**, 23–4.

Andersson, U., R. Mudambi and M. Persson (2006), 'Activity structure and centralization: impacts on performance dimensions of inter-unit knowledge transfer in MNCs', paper presented at the EIBA Annual Conference, Fribourg, Switzerland, 7–9 December 2006.

Asakawa, K. (2001), 'Evolving headquarters–subsidiaries dynamics in international R&D: the case of Japanese multinationals', *R&D Management*, **31** (1), 1–14.

Bartlett, C.A. and S. Ghoshal (1988), 'Organizing for worldwide effectiveness: the transnational solution', *California Management Review*, **41** (1), 54–74.

Bartlett, C.A. and S. Ghoshal (1989), *Managing across Borders: The Transnational Solution*, Boston, MA: Harvard Business School Press.

Birkinshaw, J. (1997), 'Entrepreneurship in multinational corporations: the characteristics of subsidiary initiatives', *Strategic Management Journal*, **18**, 207–29.

Birkinshaw, J. (2002), 'Managing internal R&D networks in global firms', *Long Range Planning*, **35** (3), 245–67.

Birkinshaw, J. and N. Fry (1998), 'Subsidiary initiatives to develop new markets', *Sloan Management Review*, **39** (3), 51–61.

Birkinshaw, J., N. Hood and S. Jonsson (1998), 'Building firm-specific advantages in multinational corporations: the role of subsidiary initiative', *Strategic Management Journal*, **19**, 221–41.

Brown, S.L. and K.M. Eisenhardt (1997), 'The art of continuous change: linking complexity theory and time-paced evolution in relentlessly shifting organizations', *Administrative Science Quarterly*, **42** (1), 1–34.

Brusoni, S., P. Criscuolo and A. Geuna (2005), 'The knowledge bases of the world's largest pharmaceutical groups: what do patent citations to non-patent literature reveal?', *Economics of Innovation & New Technology*, **14** (5), 395–415.

Buckley, P.J. and M.J. Carter (2004), 'A formal analysis of knowledge combination in multinational enterprises', *Journal of International Business Studies*, **35**, 371–84.

Buckley, P.J. and M.C. Casson (1976), *The Future of the Multinational Enterprise*, London: Macmillan.

Caves, R.E. (1982), *Multinational Enterprise and Economic Analysis*, Cambridge: Cambridge University Press.

Chiesa, V. (1996), 'Managing the internationalization of R&D activities', *IEEE Transactions on Engineering Management*, **43**, 7–23.

Chini, T.C. (2004), *Effective Knowledge Transfer in Multinational Corporations*, Houndsmills: Palgrave Macmillan.

Chini, T.C. and B. Ambos (2005), 'Choosing the dependent variable in empirical studies on knowledge flows', paper presented at the 31st Annual JIBS/CIBER Emerging Research in International Business Conference, Rotterdam, The Netherlands, 28–30 September 2005.

Darr, E.D. and L. Argote (1995), 'The acquisition, transfer, and depreciation of knowledge', *Management Science*, **41** (11), 1750–63.

Doz, Y.L., J. Santos and P. Williamson (2001), *From Global to Metanational: How Companies Win in the Knowledge Economy*, Boston, MA: Harvard Business School Press.

Duncan, R.B. (1976), 'The ambidextrous organization: designing dual structures for innovation', in R.H. Kilmann, L.R. Pondy and D.P. Slevin (eds), *The Management of Organization Design*, vol. 1, New York: Elsevier North-Holland, pp. 167–88.

Forsgren, M. (1990), 'Managing the international multi-center firm', *European Management Journal*, **8** (2), 261–7.

Frost, T., J. Birkinshaw and P. Ensign (2002), 'Centers of excellence in multinational corporations', *Strategic Management Journal*, **23** (11), 997–1119.

Gersick, C.J.G. (1991), 'Revolutionary change theories: a multilevel exploration of the punctuated equilibrium paradigm', *Academy of Management Review*, **16** (1), 10–36.

Ghoshal, S. and P. Moran (1996), 'Bad for practice: a critique of the transaction cost theory', *Academy of Management Review*, **21** (1), 13–47.

Ghoshal, S. and N. Nohria (1993), 'Horses for courses: organizational forms for multinational corporations', *Sloan Management Review*, **34**, 23–35.

Gupta, A.K. and V. Govindarajan (1991), 'Knowledge flows and the structure of control within multinational corporations', *Academy of Management Review*, **16** (4), 768–92.

Gupta, A.K. and V. Govindarajan (1994), 'Organizing for knowledge flows within MNCs', *International Business Review*, **3** (4), 443–57.

Gupta, A.K. and V. Govindarajan (2000), 'Knowledge flows within multinational corporations', *Strategic Management Journal*, **21**, 473–96.

Haas, M.R. and M.T. Hansen (2005), 'When using knowledge can hurt performance: the value of organizational capabilities in a management consulting company', *Strategic Management Journal*, **26**, 1–24.

Hansen, M.T. (1999), 'The search-transfer problem', *Administrative Science Quarterly*, **44**, 82–111.

He, Z.-L. and P.-K. Wong (2004), 'Exploration vs. exploitation: an empirical test of the ambidextertiy hypotheses', *Organization Science*, **15** (4), 481–94.

Hedlund, G. (1994), 'A model of knowledge management and the N-form corporation', *Strategic Management Journal*, **15**, 73–90.

Hoopes, D.G. and S. Postrel (1999), 'Shared knowledge, "glitches", and product development performance,' *Strategic Management Journal*, **20**, 837–65.

Hymer, S.H. (1976), *The International Operations of National Firms: A Study of Direct Foreign Investment*, Cambridge, MA: MIT Press.

Inkpen, A.C. and A. Dinur (1998), 'The transfer and management of knowledge in the multinational corporation: considering context', Carnegie Bosch Institute working paper.

Kogut, B. and U. Zander (1992), 'Knowledge of the firm, combinative capabilities, and the replication of technology', *Organization Science*, **3**, 383–97.

Kogut, B. and U. Zander (1993), 'Knowledge of the firm and the evolutionary theory of the multinational corporation', *Journal of International Business Studies*, **24** (4), 625–45.

Kuemmerle, W. (1999), 'The drivers of foreign direct investment into research and development: an empirical investigation', *Journal of International Business Studies*, **30** (1), 1–24.

Leonard-Barton, D. (1992), 'Core capabilities and core rigidities: a paradox in managing new product development', *Strategic Management Journal*, **13** (5), 111–25.

Leonard-Barton, D. (1995), *Wellsprings of Knowledge*, Boston, MA: Harvard Business School Press.

McDonough, E.F. III and R. Leifer (1983), 'Using simultaneous structures to cope with uncertainty', *Academy of Management Journal*, **26** (4), 727–35.

Mahnke, V., T. Pedersen and M. Venzin (2004), 'Does knowledge sharing pay? A MNC subsidiary perspective on knowledge outflows', paper presented at the EIBA Annual Meeting, Lubljana, Slovenia.

March, J.G. (1990), 'Exploration and exploitation in organizational learning', *Organization Science*, **2**, 71–87.

Martinez, J.I. and J.C. Jarillo (1989), 'The evolution of research on coordination mechanisms in MNCs', *Journal of International Business Studies*, **20**, 489–514.

Minbaeva, D., T. Pedersen, I. Bjorkman, C.F. Fey and H.J. Park (2003), 'MNC knowledge transfer, subsidiary absorptive capacity, and HRM', *Journal of International Business Studies*, **34** (6), 586–99.

Monteiro, L.F., N. Arvidsson and J. Birkinshaw (2004), 'Knowledge flows within multinational corporations: why are some subsidiaries isolated?', *Academy of Management Best Paper Proceedings*, B1–B6.

Mudambi, R. and R. Navarra (2004), 'Is knowledge power? Knowledge flows, subsidiary power and rent-seeking within MNCs', *Journal of International Business Studies*, **35** (5), 385–406.

Mudambi, R. and T. Pedersen (2006), 'Subsidiary power in multinational corporations: technological vs. marketing knowledge', paper presented at the Nordic Workshop in International Business, Weybridge, UK, 31 May–2 June.

Nickerson, J.A. and T.R. Zenger (2004), 'A knowledge-based theory of the firm – the problem-solving perspective', *Organization Science*, **15** (6), 617–32.

Nobel, R. and J. Birkinshaw (1998), 'Innovation in multinational corporations: control and communication patterns in international R&D operations', *Strategic Management Journal*, **195**, 479–96.

Nonaka, I. and H. Takeuchi (1995), *The Knowledge Creating Company: How Japanese Companies Create the Dynamics of Innovation*, New York: Oxford University Press.

Paterson, S.L. and D.M. Brock (2002), 'The development of subsidiary-management research: review and theoretical analysis', *International Business Review*, **11**, 139–63.

Schulz, M. (2003), 'Pathways of relevance: inflows of knowledge into subunits of multinational corporations', *Organization Science*, **14** (4), 440–59.

Siggelkow, N. and D.A. Levinthal (2003), 'Temporarily divide to conquer: centralized, decentralized, and reintegrated organizational approaches to exploration and adaptation', *Organization Science*, **14** (6), 650–69.

Szulanski, G. (1996), 'Exploring internal stickiness: impediments to the transfer of best practice within the firm', *Strategic Management Journal*, **17** (special issue), 27–43.

Szulanski, G. and R. Jensen (2006), 'Presumptive adaptation and the effectiveness of knowledge transfer', *Strategic Management Journal*, **27** (10), 937–57.

Taggart, J.H. (1997), 'Autonomy and procedural justices: a framework for evaluation of subsidiary strategy', *Journal of International Business Studies*, **28** (1), 51–76.

Teece, D.J. (1998), 'Capturing value from knowledge assets: the new economy, markets for know-how and intangible assets,' *California Management Review*, **40** (3), 55–79.

Tsai, W. (2001), 'Knowledge transfer in intraorganizational networks: effects of network position and absorptive capacity on business unit innovation and performance', *Academy of Management Journal*, **44** (5), 996–1004.

Tushman, M. and C. O'Reilly (1997), *Winning through Innovation: A Practical Guide to Leading Organizational Change and Renewal*, Cambridge, MA: Harvard Business School Press.

Tushman, M.L. and E. Romanelli (1985), 'Organizational evolution: a metamorphosis model of convergence and reorientation', in L.L. Cummings and B.M. Straw (eds), *Research in Organizational Behavior*, Greenwich, CT: JAI Press, pp. 171–222.

White, R.E. and T.A. Poynter (1984), 'Strategies for foreign-owned subsidiaries in Canada', *Business Quarterly*, **49**, 59–69.

Winter, S.G. and G. Szulanski (2001), 'Replication as strategy', *Organization Science*, **12** (6), 730–43.

Yamin, M. and J. Otto (2004), 'Patterns of knowledge flows and MNC innovative performance', *Journal of International Management*, **10**, 239–58.

Zaltman, G., R. Duncan and J. Holbeck (1973), *Innovations and Organizations*, New York: John Wiley & Sons.

9. Building and leveraging knowledge capabilities through cross-border acquisitions

Manuel Portugal Ferreira

The volume and magnitude of cross-border acquisition over the past decade led some authors to refer to this 'CEO's favorite growth strategy' (Hitt et al., 2001, p. 384) as a merger mania. This mania was not limited to an idiosyncratic group of countries or a few industries, rather it was so widespread that according to recent United Nations reports the volume of mergers and acquisitions accounted for about 80 percent of worldwide foreign direct investment (FDI) flows (UNCTAD, 2000). Notwithstanding the overwhelming share of cross-border acquisitions in FDI flows – cross-border acquisitions have surpassed alternative entry modes as the vehicle through which firms exercise their internationalization strategies (Zollo, 1998) – few studies have examined cross-border acquisitions per se. Rather, the majority of the studies relegate cross-border acquisitions to comparisons with alternative entry modes, such as between acquisitions and greenfield startups or acquisitions and joint ventures (Hennart and Park, 1993; Barkema and Vermeulen, 1998), in the analysis of foreign expansion. Other studies contrast entry modes in terms of the degree of ownership (Anderson and Gatignon, 1986; Woodcock et al., 1994) but do not distinguish the foreign entry modes. To my knowledge, no other study has assessed the degree of equity ownership in cross-border acquisitions as a reflection of the multinational corporations' (MNCs) capabilities and knowledge strategies.

Recent studies propose that some firms expand abroad to augment their own resources and knowledge-based capabilities (Dunning, 1993; Makino et al., 2002). These studies depart from the traditional focus on market imperfections (Teece, 1981) and from analyses contrasting alternative governance forms (Anderson and Gatignon, 1986). The recent focus is on firms' international strategies as ways to explore, learn about and possibly transfer internally the knowledge captured (Bresman et al., 1999), more than to exploit home country advantages or leverage experiential advantages (Dunning, 1993). This view configures MNCs as learning networks (Nohria and Ghoshal, 1997), whereby MNCs increasingly seek certain locations – countries or industry clusters – to access location-specific knowledge (Kogut and Chang, 1991; Porter, 1998). This view underlies the current focus on acquisitions as learning opportunities for MNCs seeking to build their capabilities.

In this chapter, I assess how the knowledge characteristics, or knowledge strategy, of the MNC for a focal cross-border acquisition[1] fit within the MNC's already held (knowledge-based) capabilities[2] and how these influence the ownership structure of the deal, and specifically the degree of equity ownership acquired in a cross-border acquisition. This chapter advances our understanding on the use of cross-border acquisitions as a foreign entry mode, the use of knowledge capabilities by MNCs, and how knowledge strategies influence the foreign entry structures. Existing research has assumed that MNCs pursuing an exploitation strategy do so using greenfield startups (Hymer, 1976), and that the exploration for new knowledge is better achieved through partnerships or acquisitions (Vermeulen and Barkema, 2001), but this need not be the case. Moreover, research on acquisitions has emphasized mostly financial or stock market performance, and has lacked the ability to provide explanations based on firms' capabilities and structural outcomes. Focusing solely on cross-border acquisitions, I clarify the use of cross-border acquisitions as an entry mode for different knowledge strategies.

A KNOWLEDGE-BASED MODEL OF CROSS-BORDER ACQUISITIONS

MNCs do not only base their strategies on leveraging existing capabilities but also seek to augment these capabilities. Tallman and Fladmoe-Lindquist (2002) refer to capability leveraging and capability building as reflections of the MNC's strategy. I further suggest that knowledge exploiting, or capability leveraging, MNCs will tend to acquire larger equity stakes in foreign subsidiaries than will knowledge exploring, or capability building, MNCs. MNCs pursuing an exploitation strategy tend to use their existing knowledge capabilities, which I distinguish into component and architectural capabilities, through full (or majority) ownership structures. The use of fully owned subsidiaries is consistent with prior research on entry modes and on the internalization of proprietary knowledge. Conversely, MNCs seeking to access new knowledge in a foreign country or unrelated business are likely to prefer a partial equity stake in a subsidiary. This preference is consistent with the research on shared equity arrangements as good governance forms for the transfer of knowledge between partners (Hennart, 1988).

In constructing a knowledge-based model of cross-border acquisitions I examine three dimensions: (1) the capabilities held by the focal MNC; (2) the extent of knowledge exploration involved in each deal; and (3) the manner in which the acquirer MNC structures the acquisition (Figure 9.1). I argue that the knowledge strategy of the MNCs will partly drive the structural form (here subsumed to the degree of equity ownership, for simplification purposes) of the acquisition, and also moderate the direct impact of the MNCs' specific capabilities on the structural form. The knowledge strategy for each deal determines the extent to which MNC-specific capabilities will be utilized. Hence the value of the MNC's capabilities is strategy dependent, and even a capabilities-rich MNC may select different structural forms when seeking to leverage or to build its capabilities. This view adapts Chandler's (1962) view that strategic choices precede the selection of structural forms.

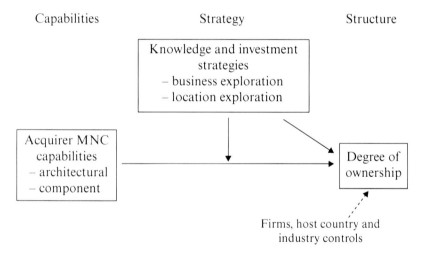

Figure 9.1   Conceptual model of capabilities, strategy and structure

Degree of Equity Ownership in Cross-border Acquisitions

Cross-border acquisitions are a form of governance of transactions in which an MNC expands its boundaries by internalizing activities that were formerly executed by the target firm. While most existing studies assume that cross-border acquisitions refer to full acquisitions,[3] an acquisition may actually involve any equity stake from 1 to 100 percent. Acquisitions per se do not represent a model of organizational integration and do not tell us how and whether control is exercised, rather the degree of equity acquired confers on the acquirer a continuum of control options and of levels of integration of the target.[4] Different degrees of ownership also provide different levels of resource commitment, access to resources, independence and autonomy in decision-making, exposure to political, economic and business risk, and diverse levels of learning. Hence, the degree of ownership not only influences the level of control and integration (structure and governance) but is also the outcome of a strategy.

Existing resource- or capabilities-based research suggests that capabilities-rich MNCs are more likely to try to leverage their physical and knowledge resources across product and geographic markets (Buckley and Casson, 1976; Makino et al., 2002), in a market-seeking orientation (Dunning, 1993). According to Hymer (1976), MNCs prefer higher, possibly whole, ownership modes to transfer headquarters' knowledge, competitive advantages and routines to the subsidiary to capture the future rents from their abilities and technologies. Whole ownership protects MNCs from losing proprietary knowledge. Andersen and Gatignon (1986) noted that MNCs with higher research and development (R&D) expenditures were more likely to enter through wholly-owned modes, seeking to preserve their capabilities and to prevent unintended transfers of knowledge. Full acquisitions may thus be preferred mechanisms to exploit capabilities held, rather than to explore new capabilities. Moreover, full acquisitions are more likely to involve lower post-acquisition integration hazards (Vermeulen and Barkema, 2001) than partial acquisitions because the acquirer will seek essentially to transfer its resources and capabilities. In addition, because MNCs pursuing exploitation strategies base their competitiveness on internally held component and architectural capabilities (Tallman and Fladmoe-Lindquist, 2002), they possibly engage in a lower frequency of novel experimentation, and more often in internal search behaviors.

In some cases, however, even strong MNCs will engage in less than the full acquisition of the target firm. Knowledge exploration strategies, in particular, are possibly better exercised through partial ownership stakes to prevent disruption of the target's resources and because some resources are indivisible from the firm and cannot be efficiently fully integrated. Thus even a resource-rich MNC may not wish to acquire the totality of the target's resources when its purpose for the specific acquisition is to learn from the target or from the target's location. Particularly when the intent is to 'learn in place', full acquisition may alienate other players in the local market – competitors, allies, workers – that provide the very skills desired.

The degree of equity ownership is a structural approach to the degree of autonomy conferred on the target firm post-acquisition. When the target holds valuable resources, the acquirer may prefer either to confer a higher degree of autonomy on the subsidiary (Haspeslagh and Jemison, 1991), or to acquire only a partial equity stake in the target. Partial equity stakes are advisable when higher integration does not guarantee internal transfer. By undertaking a partial acquisition, the acquirer preserves the value of the target's resources, avoiding disruptions in the system of skills, routines, procedures and technologies of the target firm (Haspeslagh and Jemison, 1991) that would possibly destroy the value of the acquisition. Some resources are highly embedded and indivisible from the firm and cannot be efficiently integrated (Mitchell, 1994; Anand and Delios, 1997), cannot be acquired in the factor market (Barney, 1991), and cannot be accessed by fully integrating the target firm. Indeed, Dyer et al. (2004) noted that many target firms lose their CEOs, most qualified personnel and clients post-acquisition. Therefore, it seems reasonable to suggest that the higher the value of the resources, the more likely the acquirer will avoid full integration. Moreover, by acquiring a partial ownership stake, the acquirer minimizes country risks and uncertainty, while it learns about the host country and industry.

The stake of equity ownership is an important structural dimension because if an MNC could minimize the equity acquired and still realize its strategy, it could reduce risks, free up financial resources that might be used to expand in other businesses and locations and increase the odds it will have a foothold in next generation technologies and markets. Moreover, the ownership stake acquired should reflect both the interest of the acquirer MNC in the target's resources and the transferability of the acquirer's capabilities to additional operations.

The Acquirer MNC's Capabilities

Many scholars have advanced research on capability-based strategies and how these capabilities are developed and renewed (Prahalad and Hamel, 1990; Senge, 1990). Learning theory, for example, suggests that by engaging in continuous learning activities, MNCs ensure that their capabilities are created and grow (built), are shared and leveraged. In international business, the traditional emphasis has been on MNCs' international diversification strategies supported by resources and capabilities that are transferable to foreign locations and permit the MNCs to obtain additional returns (Hymer, 1976; Anand and Delios, 1997). FDI, and notably cross-border acquisitions, occur because the markets for these resources are imperfect (Teece, 1981). The MNCs' knowledge capabilities (e.g. international experience, acquisition experience) are the primary sources of value and of sustained competitive advantage, and possibly among the most resistant to exploitation by opportunistic partners (Hennart, 1988).

In this chapter, I distinguish the capabilities of the acquirer MNC into architectural and component capabilities, following Matusik and Hill (1998) and Tallman and Fladmoe-Lindquist (2002). I further disaggregate component and architectural capabilities into business- and location-related knowledge, as reflected in Table 9.1 and explained in the following sections.

Table 9.1   Types of (knowledge-based) capabilities

	Architectural capabilities	Component capabilities
Business knowledge	*Business architectural capability* Knowledge about acquisitions (total experience in entry modes)	*Business component capability* Business knowledge in operating in a specific business. Business and technology specialized or diversified MNC
Location knowledge	*Location architectural capability* Knowledge about international business: – general international experience (number of markets, variety of markets, size of non-home market operations, etc.) – regional/national experience	*Location component capability* Business knowledge in operating in a specific location (previous/current experience in specific or proximate locations)
	Architectural capabilities (AC) relate to overall business and international experience. AC are reflected in the skills at integrating new and/or different businesses and in experiential skills at understanding how to go about entering or operating in any unfamiliar setting	Component capabilities (CC) relate to operating or expanding in existing businesses and locations. CC are distinct from AC because the former relate to operating in a specific business and experience in a specific market or a very similar one

Architectural Capabilities

Architectural knowledge involves a broader understanding of how the components can be brought together, knowing who is who and how firms are connected, and understanding the intricacies of institutional influences and the importance of local embeddedness. Tallman et al. (2004) and Matusik and Hill (1998) extended the concept of architectural knowledge from the traditional innovation-related understanding (per Henderson and Clark, 1990) and conceptualized architectural knowledge at the firm level. Hence architectural capabilities 'are developed in the process of operating the firm, so they are strictly firm-specific and tied closely to the administrative history of the firm' (Tallman and Fladmoe-Lindquist, 2002, p. 120). This perspective also configures what Tallman and Fladmoe-Lindquist (2002) suggested being an architectural capability for managing global operations or for managing a diversified corporation that may influence the MNCs' ability to expand and compete through their component capabilities in other contexts.

Business-related Architectural Capabilities

In the context of cross-border acquisitions business-related architectural capabilities are well depicted by the MNCs' foreign acquisition capability. MNCs with prior acquisition experience develop an *acquisition capability* (Haleblian and Finkelstein, 1999; Hayward, 2002) that is not deal specific, but rather is usable in all, or most, acquisition deals. Reuer and colleagues (2004, p. 23) suggested that acquisition 'experience may help MNCs to obtain more pertinent information on potential targets' and lead to a better execution of the acquisition. An acquisition capability also entails skills in post-acquisition management, management of personnel, interactions with the host country institutions, and so forth, hence increasing the likelihood that these skills will be further utilized in future acquisitions (Zollo, 1998). Therefore, MNCs that have undertaken acquisitions in the past are likely to continue using acquisitions in the future (Hitt et al., 2001), and be successful in future acquisitions (Haleblian and Finkelstein, 1999). Furthermore, MNCs are likely to develop confidence in their ability to realize acquisitions (Hayward and Hambrick, 1997) and, hence to possibly engage more often in full acquisitions. Consistent with the view that MNCs exercise their capabilities using structural forms that provide them accrued control over foreign operations (Chatterjee, 1990), perhaps by virtue of managerial confidence (Hayward and Hambrick, 1997) in the competence for carrying out the deal, a cross-border acquisition capability is likely to influence the equity stake acquired in additional acquisitions, and specifically to drive the acquirer MNC to seek high equity stakes.

Location-Related Architectural Capabilities

The level of the MNC's location-related architectural capabilities is often evidenced by the extent of international experience, and may be expressed in terms of foreign assets, foreign sales or the geographical dispersion of the subsidiaries (Annavarjula et al., 2005). MNCs with operations in multiple countries – internationally diversified – develop the ability to identify target countries and industries, and the potential benefits from operating in those environments.

Existing research has been notably scant on how prior international experience influences the equity stake acquired in cross-border acquisitions. However, the research on the effect of multinationality on the selection of entry modes provides insights. For instance, Caves and Mehra (1986) found that more internationally experienced MNCs were less likely to enter through acquisition, perhaps because for more experienced MNCs additional learning is less salient. Kogut and Singh (1988) did not find any effect of prior experience on the choice between greenfield and acquisition, possibly because both modes were considered as wholly owned. Notwithstanding, Tallman and Fladmoe-Lindquist (2002) suggested that MNCs develop an architectural capability for managing global operations, which may indicate that internationally experienced MNCs are less sensitive to post-acquisition integration hazards and better able to manage geographically dispersed subsidiaries.

The likelihood that an MNC will acquire a larger equity stake in the target firm increases with the level of international experience. MNCs' proprietary competitive and knowledge advantages were noted as antecedents of multinationality (Hitt et al., 1997) suggesting that specific advantages and capabilities drive some foreign expansions for the exploitation of those advantages (Chatterjee, 1990). The internationalization process school (Johanson and Vahlne, 1977) posits that internationally inexperienced MNCs could lower the initial perceived risks committing fewer resources, and as international experience increases MNCs engage in more committing entry modes. Similarly, less/more experienced MNCs in foreign operations or in a specific country may engage in partial/full acquisitions.

Component Capabilities

Component knowledge capabilities are built essentially from the pool of business- and location-related experiences of the MNC. However, contrary to architectural capabilities, rather than being specific to a firm, component capabilities are largely independent of individual firms and are shared by all firms operating in a certain business or location. Component capabilities are more technical, largely acontextual (Tallman et al., 2004), and probably have a narrower scope of potential application beyond the immediate purpose for which they were developed.

Business-related Component Capabilities

The MNC's business-related component capabilities are essentially technical and are built on prior business experience. Business component capabilities relate to, for example, manufacturing and underlying technical understandings of a product and manufacturing process. Business component capabilities are specific to operating in a certain business but they may be transferable to similar businesses in foreign locations because they are, at least in their majority, largely independent of the geographical context (Tallman et al., 2004). Business-related component knowledge comprises elements such as industry R&D and advertising expenditures, skills requirements of the industry and the understanding of the networks of firms in the industry. Therefore, the greater the MNC's business component capabilities, the more likely it will acquire a larger share of the equity of the target firm.

Location-related Component Capabilities

In addition to the business component capabilities, MNCs may also hold a capability of operating in a specific location. A location component capability may consist of an understanding of local accounting practices, local advertising and distribution, how to deal with the local regulatory agents, and so forth. This capability is built up from prior experience in that, or a similar, location, and probably has limited, even if some, applicability outside the specific location in which it was developed. For example, an MNC with operations in Portugal will have a relative advantage in further operations in Portugal, but the location knowledge acquired also may be beneficial for a new entry in Spain because of these countries' cultural, institutional, legal and labor similarities. MNCs entering countries that are similar to countries where they are already present are more likely to be seeking to deepen their capabilities possibly through structural modes that protect and favor the exploitation of the capabilities, such as the full acquisition of the target, that warrant the MNC control over the operations.

In general, the greater the MNC's component and architectural capabilities (business- and location-related) the more likely it is it will acquire a larger share of the equity of the target firm.

KNOWLEDGE AND INVESTMENT STRATEGY

The strategy of the firm consists, according to Chandler (1962), of the goals and objectives that preside over the allocation of firm's resources. Strategies address many facets of the firms' behaviors, but in this chapter I focus specifically on knowledge strategies. Knowledge strategies address the extent to which a focal deal is knowledge explorative. The knowledge strategies are often discussed as market-seeking (exploitation) and strategic asset-seeking (exploration) strategies (Dunning, 1993).

MNCs may augment their knowledge capabilities through global exploration strategies (Tallman and Fladmoe-Lindquist, 2002) by entering additional related and unrelated businesses and geographies. Hence, firms' knowledge strategies (March, 1991) are better examined at the level of each specific deal, rather than conceptualized at the organizational level and made dependent on the firms' resources and capabilities. An MNC may follow different knowledge strategies simultaneously (March, 1991). That is, the characteristics of the deal seem a more accurate depiction of the knowledge benefits and knowledge strategy of the MNC for each foreign deal – that is, the extent to which it entails higher or lower knowledge exploration.

The knowledge strategy of the MNC may not only have a direct effect on the structural form for each deal (structure, see Chandler, 1962), but also moderate the relationship between the MNC's capabilities and the structural form employed. For example, MNCs may seek to locate in knowledge abundant locations (e.g. industry clusters) regardless of their knowledge capabilities, so as to gain access to the locations' knowledge endowments (Tallman et al., 2004), to benefit from status and reputation spillovers, or to increase notoriety to potential clients (Porter, 1998). Hence, when the MNC is essentially seeking to deepen, or exploit, its business component knowledge (or existing technological capabilities), the full integration of the target is less likely to render post-integration hazards, as I suggested previously. In these cases, it is the resources/capabilities of the acquiring MNC, rather than those of the target, that matter for the execution of the MNC's strategy, and the MNC is probably less interested in integrating than it is in superimposing its own skills and capabilities. In other instances, however, the cross-border deal will depart more substantially from the MNC's knowledge capabilities held. In these cases, the acquiring MNC heads off from its existing capabilities to access either/both technical knowledge and the more tacit and locally embedded knowledge that differs from its core understandings (March, 1991). The structural form adopted will need to preserve the value of the knowledge resources accessed in a manner that is consistent with a learning objective. In sum, explanations based on the MNC's pool of resources or capabilities may not be enough, and we need to incorporate the effect of the acquirer's knowledge strategy pursued in each deal.

Exploring for Business Knowledge

MNCs seeking novel business knowledge will diversify into new (un)related industries or markets. The relative business knowledge novelty of a deal is dependent on the business component capabilities already held or, in other words, on the MNCs' prior businesses experiences. Prior business experience reduces hazards in evaluating the target. Moreover, MNCs with a heterogeneous pool of prior experiences face fewer cognitive accuracy challenges and will be better able to evaluate the benefits from infusions of new business knowledge. These MNCs have higher absorptive capacity (Cohen and Levinthal, 1990) across a variety of businesses, suggesting that prior business component knowledge endows MNCs with the ability to identify targets and markets to enter to raise the odds of accessing novel business knowledge.

The extent to which a deal is exploratory is partly driven by the applicability of the MNC's capabilities outside its core business and into more unrelated businesses. Coff (1999) suggested that the more similar the knowledge requirements of the target and acquirer businesses, the more familiar the acquirer will be with the target's resources, buyers and suppliers, management capabilities, and so forth. According to Capron (1999), in absolutely related acquisitions most technical resource transfers are from the acquirer to the target. Therefore, the more related the acquirer and target's businesses, and the more similar their assets, the fewer integration hazards (Chatterjee and Wernerfelt, 1991) and the more potential for synergies (Chatterjee, 1990) there will be.

I noted how resource-rich MNCs are traditionally assumed to prefer wholly-owned foreign entries to protect the value of their resources and as a means to exploit their capabilities across borders. It is apparent from Capron (1999) that how related the acquisition is *vis-à-vis* the acquirer MNC matters when engaging in business-related acquisitions. These transfers from the acquirer are probably transfers of business knowledge, which are subsequently exploited in the host market. MNCs pursuing exploitation strategies will tend to select modes that permit full control over the operations to prevent unintended diffusion of knowledge, because in related acquisitions the partners share a large similarity (technological, market, geographic presence, etc.) with the acquirer MNC (Chatterjee, 1990; Capron, 1999).

Conversely, when the knowledge requirements and skills of the target and the acquirer industries vary considerably, there are larger information asymmetries regarding the target's resources. Acquisitions in non-core, and more unrelated, businesses are more likely to face evaluation hazards because the acquirer MNC 'will be less familiar with targets and less knowledgeable about the value of their underlying resources' (Reuer et al., 2004, p. 22). MNCs entering novel businesses may access business knowledge they do not yet hold. The more distinct the industries, the more likely the acquirer may misevaluate the transferability of the target's resources and the synergistic potential for resource combinations. The selection of the target firm is more hazardous for acquisitions in non-core and unrelated businesses than in core and related businesses. Hence, the shorter the business knowledge distance of the acquisition the closer it is to a business knowledge exploitation strategy and the greater the degree of equity likely to be acquired. Conversely, the larger the knowledge distance between acquirer and target, the closer to a business knowledge exploration strategy it is and the lower the equity stake acquired.

Exploring for Location Knowledge

MNCs also acquire firms in different locations, not only in different industries. A significant body of research on industry clusters, for example, has highlighted the benefits from accessing location-specific knowledge that is often 'in the air' (Marshall, 1920). Some locations have unique technological paths, knowledge bases, orientations towards science, innovation systems (Cantwell and Iammarino, 1998), institutions, political, social and economic profiles, and cultures that endow them with a comparative advantage (Porter, 1998). It is likely that the cultural distance (Kogut and Singh, 1988) between home and host country is a reasonable proxy for how novel the knowledge is that the MNC will be accessing (Reuer et al., 2002).

Equity investments may be essential to access location knowledge. Some countries' knowledge-based endowments are not transferable away from the location (Anand and Delios, 1997), such as in the case of the country's 'general knowledge' (Coff, 1999). As Anand and Kogut (1997) put it, not all resources and capabilities are fungible across borders. Some of these endowments are location-specific and non-transferable. The transferability, or lack of it, justifies cross-border acquisitions because they ease access to 'host country knowledge, resources and capabilities' (Anand and Delios, 1997, p. 581), but also requires the selection of the structural form most likely to guarantee the access to, and absorption of, this knowledge.

The evaluation of the location knowledge exploration strategy of the acquirer warrants examination of the acquirer's location architectural capabilities and the accrued knowledge accessed. A number of studies have considered how prior foreign experience provides benefits for the MNC, and the importance of prior experience for entry decisions (e.g. Haleblian and

Finkelstein, 1999). Furthermore, prior international experience in general should give some benefits, prior experience in a region should give more, and prior investment in a specific target country should provide even more. These benefits relate to, for example, the identification and evaluation of the knowledge accessed, of the specific target firm, and of the assessment of the institutional, social, economic and regulatory environments. That is, in considering the MNC's capabilities of operating in foreign territories, we should observe how relevant those capabilities are for a focal acquisition. The greater the relevance of prior foreign experiences in terms of proximity to the target host country, the higher the likelihood the MNC already possesses a large part of the knowledge that the acquisition permits access to, and therefore the higher the likelihood the acquirer MNC will seek a larger equity stake. In sum, the closer the MNC's foreign experiences are to the focal target country, the more likely it is it will expand through wholly-owned acquisitions.

Interaction of Business and Location Knowledge

Business and location knowledge possibly interact to form the pool of global knowledge that the acquirer MNC accesses in each cross-border acquisition. The ability to exploit specific business technologies should influence the extent to which the MNC is able to improve performance in subsequent internationalizations. Some research on international diversification suggests an interaction between product and international diversification (Tallman and Li, 1996; Hitt et al., 1997). Hitt and colleagues (1997) proposed that the curvilinear effect of international diversification was moderated by product diversity to determine MNCs' performance. These studies resulted in a lack of empirical support for an interactive effect, which may be a result of either the measures employed (overall levels of diversification) or the lack of measures of the actual strategy pursued. Barkema and Vermeulen (1998) also discussed conceptually how MNCs' multinational diversity and product diversity influence their technological capabilities, and how these capabilities influence the choice of entry mode. These studies adopted an asset-exploiting perspective not including the potential for MNC learning. Nevertheless, such interaction suggests a non-linear effect of the knowledge on the degree of equity acquired.

INTERACTIONS BETWEEN STRATEGY AND ARCHITECTURAL CAPABILITIES

It is also possible that an MNC entering a new market to exploit its existing business-specific component knowledge capability might need to take on a partner (joint equity mode, such as a partial acquisition) to access new market-specific location knowledge. This MNC holds business capabilities but lacks knowledge on the specific location of the new entry. A shared equity mode, such as a partial acquisition, provides the MNC with a foothold in the host market and facilitates learning about the specific aspects of doing business in that market, the institutional settings, local culture, income profile, and so forth. The likelihood of a full acquisition increases with national closeness. That is, not only does business knowledge exploration matter per se, but the extent to which the MNC is entering a country with which it is familiar, or is similar to other countries where it already has operations also matters.

Furthermore, when accessing distinctively new location knowledge, the scripts used in the past may not be substantively relevant for a new entry. For example, these may be the routines used in contracting and implementing the deal. They may also be skills at entering foreign countries in a manner that minimizes the hazards of foreignness. That is, for very novel entries, the benefits emerging from the MNC's architectural capabilities may be minimal. By proposing this interaction I am advancing that there is a limit to the scope of applicability of the MNC's capabilities and that we need to take into account the knowledge strategy and how this should be construed to build the capabilities.

CONCLUSION

This chapter contributes to our understanding of the use of capabilities and knowledge strategies by MNCs, particularly in the context of cross-border acquisitions. I sought to overcome recurrent shortcomings that emerge when contrasting entry modes or equity ownership as independent events. For example, foreign entry mode research generally does not distinguish between partial and full ownership within each entry mode, and often relies on dichotomous choices between modes. I focus on equity ownership within the cross-border acquisition mode, rather than across modes. I advance that MNCs may structure the deal in a manner that pursues different strategic motivations: exploitation or exploration. Furthermore, the inadequate assessment of MNCs' capabilities and their knowledge strategy, or a poor design of the structural form, may partly explain why acquisitions tend to be poor performers (Lubatkin, 1987) and are likely to be divested (or to fail). The knowledge strategy for the acquisition needs to be considered to evaluate the success of the acquisition.

Cross-border acquisitions are important to the MNC's competitive strategy because they entail a large commitment of resources, and also through cross-border acquisitions MNCs may reshuffle the competitive landscape and change their strategic resources and capabilities. If well selected, an acquisition may open the door to entirely new knowledge, which then may be leveraged in combination with other resources held by the firm. Conversely, if poorly integrated, firm-specific resources may be captured by competitors or remain unexploited.

The model I developed in this chapter entails some features that are novel. First, the focus on an often overlooked dimension: the structural form. I suggest that more attention needs to be placed on the structural forms. Second, I consider that specific knowledge strategies are determined primarily by the characteristics of the deal, rather than over-relying on the capabilities of the MNC. This is consistent with March's (1991) idea that firms may pursue different strategies simultaneously for different deals. Third, I set guidelines for the empirical operationalization of the capabilities constructs: component and architectural capabilities, at both the business and the location level. While I focused on knowledge access, several scholars in international strategy have already examined how MNCs access knowledge for posterior internal transfer (e.g. Kogut and Zander, 1993; Gupta and Govindarajan, 2000). Future research may explore which structural forms ease the internal transfer of knowledge, and how some structures may be better than others *vis-à-vis* the different types of knowledge accessed.

It is notable that although the dominant train of thought has been suggesting that cross-border acquisitions are entry modes for learning and the exploration of market and technological opportunities, a large number of cross-border acquisitions are occurring between firms in related product areas and in similar countries. These investments are likely to be means of exploiting resources the MNCs already possess rather than being resource-exploring investments. In this chapter I engage this tension and examine both the MNC's capabilities held and the knowledge strategy to investigate learning opportunities. To this aim I specify the knowledge-based and experiential architectural and component capabilities, and their specific influence on foreign expansion. These capabilities may be, for MNCs, the most important intangible, path dependent, causally ambiguous and non-imitable asset of contemporary MNCs.

NOTES

1. A cross-border acquisition occurs when one firm (the acquirer) acquires part or the totality of the equity of another firm (the target) in a foreign country.
2. I refer simply to capabilities, rather than knowledge-based capabilities, since all capabilities are knowledge-based in some respect.
3. By *full acquisition* I mean the acquisition of the totality of the target firm's equity.

4. Although it is worth noting that these choices may not be completely voluntary, such as when host country restrictions on foreign investment force the acquirer into a partial acquisition.

REFERENCES

Anand, J. and A. Delios (1997), 'Location specificity and the transferability of downstream assets to foreign subsidiaries', *Journal of International Business Studies*, **28**, 579–603.

Anand, J. and B. Kogut (1997), 'Technological capabilities of countries, firm rivalry and foreign direct investment', *Journal of International Business Studies*, **28**, 445–65.

Anderson, E. and H. Gatignon (1986), 'Modes of foreign entry: a transaction cost analysis and propositions', *Journal of International Business Studies*, **17**, 1–26.

Annavarjula, M., S. Beldona and F. Sadrieh (2005), 'Corporate performance implications of multinationality: The role of firm specific moderators', *Transnational Management*, **10** (4), 5–33.

Barkema, H. and F. Vermeulen (1998), 'International expansion through start-up or acquisition: a learning perspective', *Academy of Management Journal*, **41** (1), 7–26.

Barney, J. (1991), 'Firm resources and sustained competitive advantage', *Journal of Management*, **17**, 121–54.

Bresman, H., J. Birkinshaw and R. Nobel (1999), 'Knowledge transfer in international acquisitions', *Journal of International Business Studies*, **30** (3), 439.

Buckley, P. and M. Casson (1976), *The Future of the Multinational Enterprise*, London: Macmillan.

Cantwell, J. and S. Iammarino (1998), 'MNCs, technological innovation and regional systems in the EU: some evidence in the Italian case', *International Journal of the Economics of Business*, **5** (3), 383–408.

Capron, L. (1999), 'The long-term performance of horizontal acquisitions', *Strategic Management Journal*, **20** (11), 987–1018.

Caves, R. and S. Mehra (1986), 'Entry of foreign multinationals into the US manufacturing industries', in M. Porter (ed.), *Competition in Global Industries*, Boston, MA: Harvard Business School Press, pp. 449–81.

Chandler, A. (1962), *Strategy and Structure*, Cambridge, MA: MIT Press.

Chatterjee, S. (1990), 'Excess resources, utilization costs, and mode of entry', *Academy of Management Journal*, **33** (4), 780–800.

Chatterjee, S. and B. Wernerfelt (1991), 'The link between resources and type of diversification: theory and evidence', *Strategic Management Journal*, **12** (1), 33–48.

Coff, R. (1999), 'How buyers cope with uncertainty when acquiring firms in knowledge-intensive industries: caveat emptor', *Organization Science*, **10**, 144–61.

Cohen, W. and D. Levinthal (1990), 'Absorptive capacity: a new perspective on learning and innovation', *Administrative Science Quarterly*, **35**, 128–52.

Dunning, J. (1993), *Multinational Enterprises and the Global Economy*, Reading, MA: Addison-Wesley Publishing Company.

Dyer, J., P. Kale and H. Singh (2004), 'When to ally and when to acquire', *Harvard Business Review*, July–August, 1–8.

Gupta, A. and V. Govindarajan (2000), 'Knowledge flows within multinational corporations', *Strategic Management Journal*, **21** (4), 473–96.

Haleblian, J. and S. Finkelstein (1999), 'The influence of organization acquisition experience on acquisition performance: a behavioral learning theory perspective', *Administrative Science Quarterly*, **44**, 29–56.

Haspeslagh, P. and D. Jemison (1991), *Managing Acquisitions: Creating Value through Corporate Renewal*, New York: Free Press.

Hayward, M. (2002), 'When do firms learn from their acquisition experience? Evidence from 1990–1995', *Strategic Management Journal*, **23** (1), 21–39.

Hayward, M. and D. Hambrick (1997), 'Explaining the premiums paid for large acquisitions: evidence of CEO hubris', *Administrative Science Quarterly*, **42** (1), 103–27.

Henderson, R. and K. Clark (1990), 'Architectural innovation: the reconfiguration of existing product technologies and the failure of established firms', *Administrative Science Quarterly*, **35**, 1–30.

Hennart, J.-F. (1988), 'The transaction cost theory of equity joint ventures', *Strategic Management Journal*, **9**, 361–74.

Hennart, J.-F. and Y. Park (1993), 'Greenfield vs. acquisition: the strategy of Japanese investors in the United States', *Management Science*, **39**, 1054–70.

Hitt, M., R. Hoskisson and H. Kim (1997), 'International diversification: effects on innovation and firm performance in product diversified firms', *Academy of Management Journal*, **40** (4), 767–98.

Hitt, M., R. Ireland and J. Harrison (2001), 'Mergers and acquisitions: a value creating or value destroying strategy?', in M. Hitt, R. Freeman and J. Harrison (eds), *Handbook of Strategic Management*, Oxford: Blackwell Business, pp. 384–408.

Hymer, S. (1976), *The International Operations of National Firms: A Study of Direct Foreign Investment*, Cambridge, MA: MIT Press.

Johanson, J. and J.-E. Vahlne (1977), 'The internationalization process of the firm: a model of knowledge development and increasing foreign market commitment', *Journal of International Business Studies*, **9**, 22–32.

Kogut, B. and S. Chang (1991), 'Technological capabilities and Japanese foreign direct investment in the United States', *The Review of Economics and Statistics*, **73** (3), 401–14.

Kogut, B. and H. Singh (1988), 'The effect of national culture on the choice of entry mode', *Journal of International Business Studies*, **19**, 411–32.

Kogut, B. and U. Zander (1993), 'Knowledge of the firm and evolutionary theory of the multinational corporation', *Journal of International Business Studies*, **24**, 625–45.

Lubatkin, M. (1987), 'Merger strategies and stockholder value', *Strategic Management Journal*, **8**, 39–53.

Makino, S., C. Lau and R. Yeh (2002), 'Asset exploitation versus asset seeking: implications for location choice of foreign direct investment', *Journal of International Business Studies*, **33** (3), 403–21.

March, J. (1991), 'Exploration and exploitation in organizational learning', *Organization Science*, **2** (1), 71–87.

Marshall, A. (1920), *Principles of Economics*, 8th edn, London: Macmillan.

Matusik, S. and C. Hill (1998), 'The utilization of contingent work, knowledge creation and competitive advantage', *Academy of Management Review*, **23**, 680–97.

Mitchell, W. (1994), 'The dynamics of evolving markets: the effects of business sales and age dissolutions and divestitures', *Administative Science Quarterly*, **39**, 575–602.

Nohria, N. and S. Ghoshal (1997), *The Differentiated Network: Organizational Multinational Corporations for Value Creation*, San Francisco: CA: Jossey-Bass Publishers.

Porter, M. (1998), 'Clusters and the new economics of competition', *Harvard Business Review*, **76** (6), 77–90.

Prahalad, C.K. and G. Hamel (1990), 'The core competence of the corporation', *Harvard Business Review*, **68**, 79–91.

Reuer, J., K. Park and M. Zollo (2002), 'Experiential learning in international joint ventures: the role of experience heterogeneity and venture novelty', in F.J. Contractor and P. Lorange (eds), *Cooperative Strategies and Alliances*, Amsterdam, The Netherlands: Elsevier.

Reuer, J., O. Shenkar and R. Ragozzino (2004), 'Mitigating risk in international mergers and acquisitions: the role of contingent payouts', *Journal of International Business Studies*, **35** (1), 19–32.

Senge, P. (1990), *The Fifth Discipline: Five Practices of the Learning Organization*, New York: Doubleday.

Tallman, S. and K. Fladmoe-Lindquist (2002), 'Internationalization, globalization, and capability-based strategy', *California Management Review*, **45** (1), 116–35.

Tallman, S., M. Jenkins, N. Henry and S. Pinch (2004), 'Knowledge, clusters, and competitive advantage', *Academy of Management Review*, **29** (2), 258–71.

Tallman, S. and J. Li (1996), 'Effects of international diversity and product diversity on the performance of multinational firms', *Academy of Management Journal*, **39** (1), 179–96.

Teece, D. (1981), 'The multinational enterprise: market failure and market power considerations', *Sloan Management Review*, **22**, 3–17.

UNCTAD (2000), *World Investment Report 2000: Cross-borders Mergers and Acquisitions and Development*, Geneva and New York: United Nations.

Vermeulen, F. and H. Barkema (2001), 'Learning through acquisitions', *Academy of Management Journal*, **44** (3), 457–76.

Woodcock, C., P. Beamish and S. Makino (1994), 'Ownership-based entry mode strategies and international performance', *Journal of International Business Studies*, **25** (2), 253–73.

Zollo, M. (1998), 'Knowledge codification, process routinization, and the creation of organizational capabilities', unpublished doctoral dissertation, University of Pennsylvania.

10. Non-transitive decision making about partner selection in international R&D alliances

Dan Li

Knowledge protection is critical for partner firms in research and development (R&D) alliances. R&D alliances have become a popular vehicle for building and leveraging technological capabilities for firms competing in dynamic and knowledge-intensive environments (Duysters and Hagedoorn, 1996; Narula and Duysters, 2004). While enjoying access to their alliance partners' technological assets, firms place their own valuable technological assets at risk of appropriation, thus firms need to achieve an effective balance between maintaining open knowledge exchange to further the alliance's technological development goals and controlling valuable knowledge flows to avoid unintended leakages (Kale et al., 2000; Oxley and Sampson, 2004).

The number of international R&D alliances has grown rapidly over the past 15 years (Narula and Duysters, 2004). International R&D is motivated not only to exploit firms' technological assets in various markets simultaneously[1] (Doz and Hamel, 1998; Kuemmerle, 1999), but also to acquire technological assets that may be specific to particular locations (Cantwell, 1989; Casson, 1991; Florida, 1997; Kuemmerle, 1997). Regardless of the motivation for international R&D activities, these alliances are more complicated than domestic ones. Both the more complex business environment and higher unfamiliarity between international alliance partners are factors behind the greater perceived risk of opportunism in international than in domestic R&D alliances (Brouthers, 1995; Dunning, 1995). Thus alliance partners typically have more concerns about knowledge leakage in international than in domestic R&D alliances.

Previous research has suggested two solutions to protect firms' valuable technological assets in R&D alliances. Transaction cost economics (TCE) theorists argue that equity-based governance structures can promote knowledge sharing and protect core technologies from appropriation by opportunistic partners better than non-equity-based structures (Oxley, 1999; Pisano, 1989). Narrowing the scope of R&D alliances can also reduce opportunism (Khanna, 1998; Oxley and Sampson, 2004). Moreover, the decisions on governance structure and alliance scope are not mutually exclusive. Under an equity-based governance structure, partner firms are more likely to broaden their alliance scope in order to achieve more synergies; on the other hand, when the alliance scope is narrow, there is less need for an expensive equity-based governance structure (Oxley and Sampson, 2004).

However, in certain circumstances, even the most protective governance structure and the most restricted alliance scope fail to reduce knowledge leakage concerns. Neither provides the level of knowledge sharing needed to achieve the objectives of an international R&D alliance and to protect partners' interests. A classic example of protection failure through narrow scope occurred during the development of the Apple Macintosh from 1982 to 1984. Apple engaged Microsoft to develop spreadsheet, database, and graphical applications for the Mac. As a direct result, Microsoft acquired critical knowledge about Apple's GUI (Graphical User Interface) products that enabled its engineers to develop the Windows operating system. Apple eventually recognized that it was losing its distinctive advantage in the marketplace and brought a lawsuit against Microsoft. The lawsuit was unsuccessful; Microsoft was later awarded a registered trademark for the name 'Windows'. Moreover, in today's globalized economy, many companies, particularly medium- and small-sized firms, hesitate to enter emerging markets such as China and India because of knowledge leakage concerns, although equity-based alliances exist and are even encouraged by host governments.

I argue that partner selection is a third, alternative mechanism whereby firms in an international R&D alliance can control the threat of knowledge leakage and retain their core proprietary assets, and that there are three important types of potential alliance partners based on the intensity of their prior interactions: friends and acquaintances (which I define as prior partners) and strangers. The literature has assumed a *transitive* preference regarding partner selection, such that the level of trust developed between alliance partners increases monotonically with the number of prior alliances. Because the firm's degree of trust in new partners is typically less than in its prior partners, under conditions where knowledge leakage costs are high, one might a priori expect that prior partners would be preferable to new partners. Preference *transitivity* in partner selection would therefore imply that friends would be preferable to acquaintances, which were preferred to strangers.

Yet, assuming preference transitivity in partner selection may be too simplistic. The approach of equating prior ties with trust suffers from substantial conceptual and methodological shortcomings. It is time to dispel this myth in the field. The number of prior partnerships has two potential confounding effects on partner selection: decreasing information asymmetry (which discourages selection of prior partners) and increasing trust between the partners (which encourages selection of prior partners). The tension between trust building and information asymmetry is at the core of my explanation for the firm's possible *non-transitive* decision making about partner selection in international R&D alliances. That is, when knowledge leakage costs are high, the firm might prefer new partners to prior partners. This chapter explores the tension between trust building and information asymmetry to explain the firm's possible *non-transitive* decision making about partner selection in international R&D alliances for the purposes of knowledge protection.

PRIOR RESEARCH ON PARTNER SELECTION IN R&D ALLIANCES

Firms must make three decisions when forming an R&D alliance: with *whom* to ally (partner selection), *how* to allocate responsibilities and authority between partners (governance structure), and *what* activities to perform (alliance scope). In order to prevent opportunistic behavior, firms can choose partners about whom they have more knowledge and trust rather than those about whom they have little or no knowledge. Firms can also design a protective governance structure such as an equity-based joint venture to create a mutual-hostage situation designed to reduce the probability of opportunism (e.g. Hennart, 1982; Oxley, 1999; Pisano, 1989; Teece, 1992). Alternatively, firms can limit the contact with their partners by restricting joint activities; that is, they choose a more narrow alliance scope for the R&D collaboration rather than combining R&D with other vertical operations (Oxley and Sampson, 2004). These three alternatives are interrelated in that each decision is likely to affect the other two.

When determining how to protect valuable knowledge from leakage in an R&D alliance, the extant literature has largely focused on selecting a secure governance structure and, most recently, on narrowing the alliance activity scope. However, the selection of partners has always been treated as exogenous. Partner selection as an alternative means of controlling opportunistic behavior in alliances has not been emphasized, despite work emphasizing that partner selection is the first critical decision in alliance formation (see, for example, Brouthers et al., 1995; Geringer, 1991; Ireland et al., 2002).

There are various advantages of forming R&D alliances with prior partners. First, alliances with prior partners ease knowledge transfer. A common theme in previous work on absorptive capacity is that prior interactions between partner firms facilitate more efficient and effective knowledge flow from one party to the other (e.g. Kogut and Zander, 1992; Mowery et al., 1998; Szulanski, 1996). The stickiness of knowledge and the causal ambiguity surrounding knowledge transfer can be reduced and overcome through repeated interactions between the knowledge source and the recipient (Kale et al., 2000; Szulanski, 1996; von Hippel, 1994). That is, the transfer of technologies between alliance partners can be eased by decreasing the information asymmetry between partner firms.

Second, alliance experience can generate trust between partner firms (Gulati, 1995b), and trust can reduce transaction costs and uncertainties involved in information sharing and transfer (Beckman et al., 2004; McEvily et al., 2003). In the context of technology protection, the major concern for firms entering R&D alliances is the predictability of partners' behavior. Behavioral codes defining the core activities for each party are difficult to specify, typically incomplete, and costly to enforce (Contractor and Lorange, 2002). Even if partner firms can clearly identify the boundary of their proprietary assets, a complete contract is impossible to write beforehand, particularly in R&D alliances where intense interaction and exchange of knowledge are required to achieve the goal of developing new technologies. Therefore, trust is necessary for the parties to make a good-faith effort toward achieving mutual goals and not to take excessive and unilateral advantage of each other, even when the opportunity to do so is available. Furthermore, the trustworthiness of partners established through prior interactions ensures salient benefits of smooth technology exchange when the technologies exchanged in the R&D cooperation are more sophisticated (Carson et al., 2003; Szulanski et al., 2003).

Third, through earlier alliances, jointly held social capital can affect partners' managerial philosophies. Partner firms that have engaged in multiple prior partnerships will have developed common decision-making rules and behaviors and internalized common principles and values (Barney and Hansen, 1994). An exchange partner behaves in a trustworthy manner because to do otherwise would violate values, standards and principles of behavior.

There are also disadvantages to forming R&D alliances with prior partners. First, while reduced information asymmetry can ease technology transfer between alliance partners, it can also place partner firms in vulnerable positions. Because prior partners understand each other's know-how, operating routines and managerial practices through earlier interactions, they can appropriate the firm's core technologies quickly and effectively if they choose to do so. Similar concerns have been expressed in the literature (Arrow, 1974; Heiman and Nickerson, 2002, 2004). For instance, knowledge management practices (KMPs) such as high bandwidth communication channels and co-specialized communication codes can facilitate the transfer of tacit knowledge between partners but generate contracting hazards once behavioral opportunism is considered (Heiman and Nickerson, 2002, 2004).

Second, repeated interactions with a limited number of partners can reduce a firm's flexibility in partner selection for new alliances. Although it is desirable for firms to build trust through multiple cooperative relationships, severely limiting the number of alliance partners can lock them into established relationships (Gulati, 1995a). For instance, concerns about search costs can prevent firms from looking beyond their own existing pool of social relationships (Davies and Ellis, 2000).

Finally, path-dependent learning may prevent the collaboration between prior partners from achieving the goal of developing radical innovations; that is, fundamental changes that represent a clear departure from existing practices through revolutionary changes in technology. Novelty is critical for developing radical innovations (Dewar and Dutton, 1986; Hart and Christensen, 2002; Sheremata, 2004). However, partner firms that have had multiple interactions may have developed similar mental maps for innovation. Beckman et al. (2004) argue that new partners can bring more new information to the alliance than prior partners and therefore may be preferred when a company faces firm-specific uncertainties such as new market entry. Forming R&D alliances with prior partners that share similar learning patterns can slow expansion into novel technological domains over time.

FRIENDS, ACQUAINTANCES, AND STRANGERS

A firm can choose from among three important types of potential alliance partners – friends, acquaintances and strangers – based on the intensity of their prior cooperation. The common definition of a friend is someone you know, like and trust. In an alliance context, I define *friends* as potential alliance partners, with which the firm has developed strong-form trust through multiple previous interactions. Strong-form trust exists between firms that share a unique history of interactions. With strong-form trust, partners are trustworthy, independent of whether or not exchange vulnerabilities or governance mechanisms exist (Barney and Hansen, 1994). The common definition of an acquaintance is someone you know and about whom you have some but limited knowledge. I define *acquaintances* as potential partner firms that know each other through a limited number of prior interactions; trust between them is semi-strong or weak. The limited prior interaction is highly unlikely to yield strong-form trust. A stranger is someone who is unknown to you; I define *strangers* as potential alliance partners that are unknown to each other. Therefore, the trust between strangers is weak. Friends, acquaintances and strangers are expected to vary along a continuum related to the level of implicit trust embedded in the relationship.

Numerous definitions of trust have been presented in the literature (e.g. Bradach and Eccles, 1989; Lewicki et al., 1998). I adopt Sabel's (1993) definition of trust – the mutual confidence that no party to an exchange will exploit another's vulnerabilities – as most appropriate for the research questions. Being vulnerable in a transaction, as suggested by Sabel's definition, implies that there is something of importance to be lost. While trust is the mutual confidence that one's vulnerabilities will not be exploited in an exchange or a transaction, the degree of trust varies between different exchange partners and in various situations. Repeated interactions over time have been used as a proxy for trust (Gulati, 1995b; Zucker, 1986); prior partners are likely to understand and trust each other more than strangers (Ring and Van de Ven, 1994). The repeated interactions over time afford knowledge of the partner and increase the ability to predict its behaviors in an alliance. In support of this conclusion, Parkhe (1993) observes that a prior history of cooperation between firms reduces their expectation of opportunistic behavior in new alliances.

Firms forming R&D alliances with prior partners benefit from the smoothness of technology transfer (as a result of reduced information asymmetry) and the reduction in opportunistic hazards (as a result of increased trust). The smooth transfer of technologies and the reduction of partner opportunism together suggest that the focal firm's partner selection decision should be *transitive*; that is, friends should be preferred to acquaintances, and acquaintances should be preferred to strangers.

Viewing this from a different perspective, the repeated interactions that reduce information asymmetry for smooth technology transfer also generate vulnerabilities for partner firms. While firms may be more likely to expose their valuable knowledge to prior partners than to strangers, risks of appropriation still exist and are even higher in certain circumstances. Because of information asymmetry between partner firms, appropriation by strangers can be avoided or delayed by informal methods that afford intellectual property protection such as lead time and learning curves. Prior partners, through earlier interactions, understand each other's know-how, operating routines and managerial practices. Armed with this knowledge, they can more easily overcome the informal methods of intellectual property protection. It is easier for prior partners than for strangers to appropriate the firm's core technologies if prior partners choose to behave opportunistically.

I posit that as the number and depth of prior relationships increases between two firms, the pace at which trust is developed will be much slower than the pace at which information asymmetry between them is reduced. Information asymmetry can be reduced quickly, particularly where knowledge assets are public in nature; however, it may take multiple close collaborations to build strong-form trust between partner firms (Barney and Hansen, 1994). This suggests that acquaintances should be characterized by a low level of information asymmetry and a low level of trust. Partnering with acquaintances creates a serious situation for firms in terms of worrying about whether their acquaintances may behave opportunistically, because it is likely that acquaintances will succeed in stealing their partners' core technologies if they choose to do so. Therefore, appropriation concerns are more salient for acquaintances than for strangers and friends.

In sum, previous research has shown that more prior alliances are positively associated with building more trust between the alliance partners. This suggests that the focal firm's partner selection preferences should be transitive; that is, friends should be preferred to acquaintances, and acquaintances should be preferred to strangers. However, I argue that this approach is too simplistic. Prior partnerships reduce information asymmetries, causing vulnerabilities that can lead the focal firm to select a stranger over a prior partner. I explore below the factors that can affect information asymmetry, the degree of vulnerability, and the firm's partner selection choices when forming international R&D alliances.

PARTNER SELECTION AND KNOWLEDGE PROTECTION IN INTERNATIONAL R&D ALLIANCES

How well technological assets can be protected is partly based on the degree of technological exposure in an international R&D alliance. International R&D projects can be of different types, ranging from incremental modifications of existing technology to meet the needs of host markets, to ambitious projects seeking to make radical changes in technology to develop the 'next generation' of products that may target both host and home markets. Therefore, the level of partner firms' exposure of their valuable knowledge varies in international R&D alliances depending on the type of innovations (incremental vs. radical) desired. I should expect more protection from opportunism when there is extensive exposure of partner firms' core technologies.

Innovation Radicality

There are at least two types of innovations that R&D alliances can develop – radical and incremental (Dewar and Dutton, 1986; Sheremata, 2004). In general, radical innovations are based on new design concepts that break existing paradigms, whereas incremental innovations are based on minor changes or improvements in the current technology. Radical innovations fundamentally represent a distinct departure from existing practices through revolutionary changes in technology. Firms committed to developing radical innovations seek to locate entrepreneurial opportunities that can shift the basis of competition in the industry (Ireland et al., 2003). In contrast, incremental innovations largely sustain the status quo (Sheremata, 2004). Incremental innovations help incumbent firms derive maximum value from their current capabilities by providing customers with similar products or services in different countries at a lower cost and/or with easier accessibility.

International R&D alliances focused on developing incremental innovations produce fewer risks of technology leakage than those targeting radical innovations, for at least two reasons. First, the pre-existence of a product or process technology enables parties to delineate property rights at the origin of an alliance with far less ambiguity than when the relevant technology does not exist (Pisano, 1989). Because incremental innovations are usually based on pre-existing knowledge, it is possible for partner firms to specify the technologies that will be exposed and those that will not be.

However, it is almost impossible to specify beforehand the knowledge requirements when the objective of an international R&D project is to develop novel paradigms (radical innovation). Therefore, it is difficult for both parties to know what to specify in contractual form. As a result, international cooperation to develop radical innovations entails higher risk of technology leakage than partnerships targeting the development of incremental innovations. As such, efforts to control partners' opportunistic behavior are more necessary for international R&D alliances focused on radical innovations than those focused on incremental innovations.

Second, radical innovations usually require new, subtle insights into customer needs and extensive coordination between alliance partners across national borders. Radical designs frequently take advantage of new process technology, but also require coordination with a company's advanced process technology development efforts. The increased number of contacting points between partner firms leads to more concerns about knowledge leakage during the collaboration. Incremental product developments, on the other hand, require relatively less direct coordination with customers and the engineers working on process technology or manufacturing. Customer requirements with the current or similar products tend to be well understood and codified, and the innovation usually remains within established specifications.

Previous work has suggested that forming alliances between prior partners can reduce the potential for opportunism (Gulati, 1995b; Sabel, 1993). However, the extent to which this occurs is contextual. Thus, alliance relationships are affected by various contingencies. While strangers are more likely to bring new information to the alliance (Beckman et al., 2004), for protection of partner firms' valuable technologies, it is important to form alliances with trustworthy partners when the R&D project aims to develop radical innovations. This is the case for partners that are friends. However, the conditions are different when partners are acquaintances.

Acquaintances may avoid collaborating with each other in an international R&D alliance targeting the development of radical innovations. In contrast to strangers, acquaintances are more familiar with their partner firms' technological assets, and thus are able to appropriate their valuable knowledge more easily. Therefore, firms are highly vulnerable in such situations without either the governance of strong-form trust or the informal barriers stemming from unfamiliar technologies. In such circumstances, firms may intentionally avoid acquaintances to protect their technological assets and other operation-related assets from potential opportunistic behaviors. Additional interactions are necessary for acquaintances to build strong-form trust between each other as the foundation for alliances involving valuable technologies. Therefore, I conclude that, the more radical the innovation goals of an international R&D alliance, the more likely it is that partner selection will be non-transitive: friends are preferred to strangers and strangers are preferred to acquaintances.

Intellectual Property Rights (IPR) Protection

Partner firms in an international R&D alliance also rely on formal protection (such as patents and copyrights) of their proprietary assets. For instance, Beckman et al. (2004) argue that when the formal IPR protection is weak, firms are more likely to form new alliances with their existing partners to reinforce their networks. However in some situations the formal protection is ineffective, or at least not as effective as desired, leaving firms to manage the residual opportunism by carefully selecting partners.

Ineffective market protection occurs for at least two reasons. First, firms seeking protection for technology transferred across national borders often encounter a variety of complicated legal rules and procedures (Oxley, 1999). Although member countries of the Paris Convention for the Protection of Industrial Property agreed to grant foreign firms the same intellectual property protection as domestic firms, the convention does not specify the standards of protection required. Consequently, the level of IPR protection varies significantly across countries (Oxley, 1999). For example, the effective duration of patent protection is almost 20 years in most European countries, while the protection lasts merely 5 years in several Latin American countries. Second, fundamental shifts in technology are rapidly making the current system of intellectual property protection obsolete and ineffective. The current worldwide convention on intellectual property protection, which was designed more than 100 years ago, may have been effective when most patents were granted for new mechanical devices during the early 1900s. However, current knowledge-intensive industries, and the nature of the patents flowing from firms competing in them, pose far more complex challenges. As posited by Thurow (1997), the invention of a new gene cannot be handled in the same way as the invention of a new gearbox. The changes in the nature of technology shift the duty (also the costs) from the market to partner firms with respect to protecting advanced knowledge.

Firms operating in environments with weak intellectual property protection are more vulnerable and therefore have more concerns regarding the safety of their technological assets in international R&D alliances, compared with those operating in markets where intellectual properties are well protected. Consistent with the literature, I argue that in such situations friends are preferred alliance partners because the strong-form trust ensures that partner firms will not appropriate each other's valuable technologies during the collaboration even if the opportunities are present to do so.

However, acquaintances have to be considered differently. Because of fewer information asymmetries between acquaintances, partner firms are even more vulnerable in an environment where their intellectual properties cannot be effectively protected, because strong-form trust has not yet been developed. Therefore, acquaintances represent the worst scenario in a market where intellectual properties are not well protected – low information asymmetry and low trust. In contrast, opportunistic behaviors by strangers can be delayed by informal learning barriers stemming from technologies per se. Thus I conclude that, the weaker the intellectual property rights protection, the more likely that partner selection will be non-transitive in an international R&D alliance: friends are preferred to strangers, and strangers are preferred to acquaintances.

Innovation Radicality and IPR Protection

I have argued that both high radicality and weak IPR protection cause high vulnerability, which can trigger preference intransitivity in partner selection. This suggests that the combination of high radicality and weak IPR protection should reinforce each other. Moreover, strong IPR protection can offset the effects of high radicality. Even though information asymmetries decrease as the number of prior alliances increases, thereby providing the opportunity for opportunistic behavior, strong property rights protection discourages taking advantage of this opportunity. Therefore, firms are less likely to rely on social relationships to structure the international R&D cooperation in a strong-protection environment than in a weak-protection environment.

At the same time, low innovation radicality can offset the effects of weak IPR protection. Even though legal protection is too weak to discourage opportunistic behavior, the gains from doing so are small when the goals of the alliance emphasize incremental innovation. Moreover, because incremental innovations are usually based on pre-existing knowledge, partner firms are able to specify the boundary of technologies involved in the collaboration, thereby preventing partners from further 'invasion'. These arguments suggest that innovation radicality interacts with IPR protection to affect the vulnerability of the firm in an alliance, and thereby the interaction affects partner selection. Together, these arguments imply that alliance innovation goals interact with IPR protection to affect partner selection in an international R&D alliance. That is, high radicality of alliance innovation goal and weak IPR protection reinforce each other in triggering preference intransitivity of partner selection.

DISCUSSION AND CONCLUSION

The literature has assumed a *transitive* preference regarding partner selection such that the level of trusts developed between alliance partners increases monotonically with the number of prior alliances. However, assuming preference transitivity in partner selection may be too simplistic. This chapter explored the tension between increased trust and decreased information asymmetry between alliance partners through prior interactions to explain the firm's possible *non-transitive* decision making about partner selection in international R&D alliances. When the innovation goal of an international R&D alliance is radical and/or the IPR protection provided by the host market is weak, non-transitive decision making about partner selection is likely; that is, friends are preferred to strangers, and strangers are preferred to acquaintances.

This chapter extends our knowledge of organizational learning and transaction cost economics applied to partner selection decisions in alliances. Most previous work emphasized the importance and value of organizational learning. However, this chapter calls for a caveat. Some knowledge that is gained through limited prior contacts may actually be harmful. The knowledge gained from a prior alliance helps partners learn about the firm's routines along with some information regarding its core technology. As a result, it would be easier for the partner to act opportunistically by using this knowledge than if the partner was a stranger with no prior knowledge. The prior knowledge of partners increases risk in terms of exposing a firm's core knowledge on which its competitive advantage is based if the previous relationships were inadequate to establish trust between the firms, particularly firms from different countries. Thus this work contributes to an emerging research stream aimed at understanding the relationship between strategy and efficient economic organization. Firms that are able to benefit from international R&D collaboration while simultaneously protecting their own valuable knowledge increase the likelihood of maintaining their competitive advantage as the foundation for success in the global marketplace.

As argued earlier, the three questions in R&D alliance formation – *whom* (partner selection), *how* (governance structure), and *what* (alliance scope) – are interrelated, with each choice probably affecting the other two. This set of decisions comprises a dynamic and endogenous system. Therefore, it will be productive to investigate whether the relationships among the knowledge protection mechanisms are substitutive or complementary in R&D alliances, and whether the substitutive/complementary relationships remain intact in international R&D collaborations where the knowledge leakage concerns are more serious.

A research avenue worth noting is how partner selection for knowledge protection purposes varies across different types of international R&D alliances. One complication arises when we consider partner firms' nationalities. The international R&D alliance literature has focused primarily on two-firm, equity-based alliances (e.g. joint ventures) formed between a home-country firm and a local (host-country) firm. However, other types of international R&D alliances exist, since the international alliance partner could be another firm from the same home country or possibly from a third country. For instance, we can differentiate the three types of international R&D alliances: home–host alliances (HSAs), home–home alliances (HHAs), and home–foreign alliances (HFAs). To my knowledge, the effects of *partner nationality* on the alliance scope, governance structure, and partner selection decisions for an international R&D alliance have not been investigated in the alliance literature and deserve more scholarly attention, given the increasing number of international R&D alliances during the past decade.

NOTE

1. That is, to adapt and tailor products for foreign markets and to provide technical support to offshore manufacturing operations.

REFERENCES

Arrow, K.J. (1974), *The Limits of Organization*, New York: Norton.

Barney, J.B. and M. Hansen (1994), 'Trustworthiness as a source of competitive advantage', *Strategic Management Journal*, **15**, 175–90.

Beckman, C.M., P.R. Haunschild and D.J. Phillips (2004), 'Friends or strangers? Firm-specific uncertainty, market uncertainty, and network partner selection', *Organization Science*, **15** (3), 259–76.

Bradach, J.L. and R.G. Eccles (1989), 'Price, authority, and trust: from ideal types to plural forms', *Annual Review of Sociology*, **15**, 97–118.

Brouthers, K.D. (1995), 'The influence of international risk on entry mode strategy in the computer software industry', *Management International Review*, **35** (1), 7–28.

Brouthers, K.D., L.E. Brouthers and T.J. Wilkinson (1995), 'Strategic alliances: choose your partners', *Long Range Planning*, **28** (3), 18–25.

Cantwell, J. (1989), *Technological Innovation and Multinational Corporations*, Oxford: Basil Blackwell.

Carson, S.J., A. Madhok, R. Varman and G. John (2003), 'Information processing moderators of the effectiveness of trust-based governance in interfirm R&D collaboration', *Organization Science*, **14** (1), 45–56.

Casson, M. (1991), *Global Research Strategy and International Competitiveness*, Oxford: Basil Blackwell.

Contractor, F. and P. Lorange (2002), 'The growth of alliances in the knowledge-based economy', *International Business Review*, **11**, 485–502.

Davies, H. and P. Ellis (2000), 'Porter's competitive advantage of nations: time for the final judgement?', *Journal of Management Studies*, **37** (8), 1189–213.

Dewar, R.D. and J.E. Dutton (1986), 'The adoption of radical and incremental innovations: an empirical analysis', *Management Science*, **32** (11), 1422–33.

Doz, Y.L. and G. Hamel (1998), *Alliance Advantage: The Art of Creating Value through Partnering*, Boston, MA: Harvard Business School Press.

Dunning, J.H. (1995), 'Reappraising the eclectic paradigm in an age of alliance capitalism', *Journal of International Business Studies*, **26** (3), 461–91.

Duysters, G. and J. Hagedoorn (1996), 'Internationalization of corporate technology through strategic partnering: an empirical investigation', *Research Policy*, **25**, 1–12.

Florida, R. (1997), 'The globalization of R&D: results of a survey of foreign-affiliated R&D laboratories in the USA', *Research Policy*, **26** (1), 85–104.

Geringer, J.M. (1991), 'Strategic determinants of partner selection criteria in international joint ventures', *Journal of International Business Studies*, **22** (1), 41–62.

Gulati, R. (1995a), 'Social structure and alliance formation patterns: a longitudinal analysis', *Administrative Science Quarterly*, **40** (4), 619–52.

Gulati, R. (1995b), 'Does familiarity breed trust? The implications of repeated ties for contractual choices in alliances', *Academy of Management Journal*, **38** (1), 85–112.

Hart, S. and C.M. Christensen (2002), 'Driving innovation from the base of the global pyramid', *MIT Sloan Management Review*, **44** (1), 51–6.

Heiman, B.A. and J.A. Nickerson (2002), 'Towards reconciling transaction cost economics and the knowledge-based view of the firm: the context of interfirm collaborations', *International Journal of the Economics of Business*, **9** (1), 97–116.

Heiman, B.A. and J.A. Nickerson (2004), 'Empirical evidence regarding the tension between knowledge sharing and knowledge expropriation in collaborations', *Managerial and Decision Economics*, **25** (6–7), 401–20.

Hennart, J.-F. (1982), *A Theory of the Multinational Enterprise*, Ann Arbor, MI: University of Michigan Press.

Ireland, D., M.A. Hitt and D.G. Sirmon (2003), 'A model of strategic entrepreneurship: The construct and its dimensions', *Journal of Management*, **29** (6), 963–89.

Ireland, R.D., M.A. Hitt and D. Vaidyanath (2002), 'Alliance management as a source of competitive advantage', *Journal of Management*, **28** (3), 413–46.

Kale, P., H. Singh and H. Perlmutter (2000), 'Learning and protection of proprietary assets in strategic alliances: building relational capital', *Strategic Management Journal*, **21** (3), 217–37.

Khanna, T. (1998), 'The scope of alliances', *Organization Science*, **9** (3), 340–55.

Kogut, B. and U. Zander (1992), 'Knowledge of the firm, combinative capabilities, and the replication of technology', *Organization Science*, **3**, 383–97.

Kuemmerle, W. (1997), 'Building effective R&D capabilities abroad', *Harvard Business Review*, **75** (2), 61–70.

Kuemmerle, W. (1999), 'The drivers of foreign direct investment into research and development: An empirical investigation', *Journal of International Business Studies*, **30** (1), 1–24.

Lewicki, R.J., D.J. McAllister and R.J. Bies (1998), 'Trust and distrust: new relationships and realities', *Academy of Management Review*, **23** (3), 438–58.

McEvily, B., V. Perrone and A. Zaheer (2003), 'Trust as an organizing principle', *Organization Science*, **14**, 91–103.

Mowery, D.C., J.E. Oxley and B.S. Silverman (1998), 'Technological overlap and interfirm cooperation: implications for the resource-based view of the firm', *Research Policy*, **27** (5), 507–23.

Narula, R. and G. Duysters (2004), 'Globalisation and trends in international R&D alliances', *Journal of International Management*, **10**, 199–218.

Oxley, J.E. (1999), 'Institutional environment and the mechanisms of governance: the impact of intellectual property protection on the structure of inter-firm alliances', *Journal of Economic Behavior and Organization*, **38**, 283–309.

Oxley, J.E. and R.C. Sampson (2004), 'The scope and governance of international R&D alliances', *Strategic Management Journal*, **25**, 723–49.

Parkhe, A. (1993), 'Strategic alliance structuring: a game theoretic and transaction cost examination of interfirm cooperation', *Academy of Management Journal*, **36** (4), 794–829.

Pisano, G. (1989), 'Using equity participation to support exchange: evidence from the biotechnology industry', *Journal of Law, Economics and Organization*, **5** (1), 109–26.

Ring, P.S. and A.H. Van de Ven (1994), 'Developmental processes of cooperative interorganizational relationships', *Academy of Management Review*, **19** (1), 90–118.

Sabel, C.F. (1993), 'Studied trust: building new forms of cooperation in a volatile economy', *Human Relations*, **46** (9), 1133–70.

Sheremata, W.A. (2004), 'Competing through innovation in network markets: strategies for challengers', *Strategic Management Journal*, **29** (3), 359–77.

Szulanski, G. (1996), 'Exploring internal stickiness: impediments to the transfer of best practice within the firm', *Strategic Management Journal*, **17** (Winter), 27–43.

Szulanski, G., R. Cappetta and R. Jensen (2003), 'When and how trustworthiness matters: knowledge transfer and the moderating effect of casual ambiguity', *Organization Science*, **15** (5), 600–613.

Teece, D.J. (1992), 'Competition, cooperation, and innovation: organizational arrangements for regimes of rapid technological progress', *Journal of Economic Behavior and Organization*, **18** (1), 1–25.

Thurow, L.C. (1997), 'Needed: a new system of intellectual property rights', *Harvard Business Review*, **75** (5), 94–103.

von Hippel, E. (1994), '"Sticky information" and the locus of problem solving: implications for innovation', *Management Science*, **40** (4), 429–39.

Zucker, L.G. (1986), 'Production of trust: institutional sources of economic structure, 1840–1920', *Research in Organizational Behavior*, **8**, 53–111.

11. Evolution of outcomes in international strategic alliances

Anupama Phene

A significant stream of strategy research focuses on the growing proliferation of strategic alliances as routes to improve firm performance; to gain access to products, markets and knowledge, and to establish competitive advantage. The importance of the strategic alliance in the international arena highlights the utility of this mechanism in overcoming the liability of foreignness. International alliances enable the firm to get a toehold and subsequently establish a dominant position in a foreign market, as well as providing capabilities that can be leveraged worldwide. International alliances are distinct from domestic alliances since they necessarily involve cooperation between partners with very different orientations, skill sets and institutional environments. Consequently, they pose challenges to the achievement of alliance objectives and influence alliance outcomes. International alliances are more tenuous and are likely to demonstrate greater variation in outcomes.

Alliance outcomes have been scrutinized at great length in the strategy literature. Alliances by their nature are temporary arrangements to achieve certain objectives. They may be restructured in response to internal or external pressures, or once the allying partners have reached their goals the arrangement may simply end. Termination is a natural outcome. In some situations, a firm may acquire its ally if it expects value from the assimilation and integration of its partner's capabilities within its own hierarchical set up. Alliances are therefore viewed as flexible arrangements demonstrating instabilities (Inkpen and Beamish, 1997) and are subject to change. Alliance partners re-evaluate the alliance agreement and renegotiate and restructure the alliance if their objectives are not achieved. However, it is not clear from a static, outcome-oriented perspective why such instabilities should be resolved in any particular manner in any particular conditions.

This research adopts a process-based approach to international alliances and examines the evolution of outcomes subsequent to the establishment of the alliance. I present an evolutionary process of international alliance outcomes that is a consequence of firm learning behavior and differences in national environments. I take an organization learning perspective and use the concepts of experience and performance outcomes to predict alliance outcomes. I attempt to explain why certain outcomes may be anticipated at a particular stage of the alliance process. The research presents a framework that covers three stages in the alliance – early, intermediate and mature stages – and considers four distinct outcomes – commitment to status quo, renegotiation, termination and acquisition. The study also evaluates the moderating effects of prior country experience and prior partner experience of the focal firm on the evolutionary process of outcomes, and provides implications for management of the alliance process.

A THEORY OF ALLIANCE EVOLUTION

Research on international strategic alliances has focused on how organizations learn from their partners and develop new competencies (Simonin, 1997). National institutional environments have a significant influence on firm skill sets. Stinchcombe's (1965) imprinting concept points to the enduring effects of the location, industry and time when a firm is created. Therefore firms from different nations display heterogeneity across their capabilities and knowledge. This in turn creates motivation for the formation of international strategic alliances as a route to access new skills (Contractor and Lorange, 1988), for both partners and to overcome liability of foreignness (Zaheer, 1995) on the part of the foreign partner.

National differences, in addition to creating an opportunity for firm learning, also create obstacles specific to international alliances. Hitt et al. (2004) found evidence of significant differences between Chinese and Russian firms' attitudes towards alliance partner selection. These differences also emerge in the contrasting criteria for partner selection in international alliances between emerging market and developed market firms (Hitt et al., 2000). Hitt et al. (1997) in their evaluation of top executives' strategic orientation find significant differences in the types of criteria used by US and Korean executives. Hitt et al. (1997) conclude that success in international alliances may be contingent on an understanding of the strategic orientation of allying partners. Thus international alliances present a more complex phenomenon when compared with domestic alliances because of the influences of the different national institutional contexts on partner behaviors, attitudes and orientations. The lack of transparency or an ability to clearly gauge partner expectations and objectives in this context would suggest that international alliances are inherently more fragile and unstable.

There has been relatively less emphasis on process-related questions in the alliance literature (Simonin, 1997; Doz, 1996). 'Although alliances are known to be highly evolutionary and unstable, it is still unclear why and how changes take place in an alliance' (Das and Teng, 2002, p. 726). Inkpen (2005) proposes that while alliances offer valuable opportunities, the process of realizing these opportunities is one fraught with difficulties and frustrations for the allying partners, therefore the alliance must necessarily evolve through a series of changes to respond to the needs and challenges that the partners face. A dominant view of alliances is that of a dynamic system that tends to adapt and evolve (Arino and de la Torre, 1998; Ring and Van de Ven, 1994). Inkpen and Currall (2004) demonstrate how initial joint venture conditions evolve as partners better understand each other. In order for a firm to achieve the expected objectives from an alliance relationship and create value, Reuer (2000) suggests that firms must, among other things, adapt the alliance relationship and manage the endgame. These issues become particularly important in international alliances, since success is contingent on successful adaptation to allow for partner differences and management of the endgame to reconcile distinct objectives. Yan and Zeng (1999) suggest that a focus on the process of international joint venture development will reveal the dynamic evolution of the venture and the causes of this evolution. I therefore utilize a process-based approach to examine how and why the evolutionary process unfolds across the different stages of an international alliance.

What are the causes of changes in partner behavior as they adapt to manage the alliance relationship? I draw on the organizational learning perspective, particularly the concepts of experience and performance outcomes of prior actions, to examine how partners react and respond at each stage in the alliance, which in turn leads to a particular alliance outcome. As partners accumulate experience and knowledge of outcomes, their responses adapt to this additional information and the outcomes change and evolve. In summary I propose a process-based approach to present a framework of evolving outcomes in international alliances. The evolution of outcomes is determined by organizational learning.

EVOLUTION OF OUTCOMES

Research has classified stages of alliance in fine-grained or more aggregated terms, encompassing a firm's choice of a governance structure, partner selection, negotiation and actual operation (Reuer, 2000). This study focuses on the alliance subsequent to its establishment and evaluates the evolution of the alliance from this point on. Prior research has identified different outcomes of the alliance process. Dussauge et al. (2000) examine four likely outcomes in the alliance process: continuation, reorganization, takeover and dissolution. Das and Teng (2000) propose that alliance termination typically results in a merger or an acquisition, dissolution, or a redefinition of the alliance. I follow these approaches and examine outcomes as (1) a commitment to the status quo, (2) renegotiation, (3) acquisition of a partner, and (4) dissolution.

I turn to the organizational learning perspective to present an evolution of outcomes in international alliances. Organizational learning occurs as firms engage repeatedly in an activity, encoding their learning in routines (Nelson and Winter, 1982) that are utilized to guide future behavior (Levitt and March, 1988). Argote (1999) suggests that experience creates knowledge that improves productivity, thus routines enable the creation of expertise and capability through repetition. Experience is therefore an important source of learning. Recent research on organizational learning (Haleblian et al., 2006) points to another source of learning in addition to experience; that is, performance outcomes of prior actions (Greve, 2003). While routines are susceptible to inertia (Szulanski, 1996) and may persist despite poor performance outcomes, firms also rely on performance cues to guide future behavior. I propose that firm ability to rely on a particular source of learning at each stage of the alliance process defines the outcome.

The initial stages of an international alliance are expected to result in maintenance of the status quo. Participants have yet to develop established routines and cannot draw on prior experience to guide their actions. At this stage, firms will rely on their original investment in setting up the alliance, such as partner screening and choice, governance choice, and splitting up of day-to-day responsibilities, as adequate to achieve the alliance objectives and continue with their commitment to the original alliance arrangement. Allying partners will still be in the process of assessing each other and figuring out ways to establish routines and make the alliance work. Participants are also limited in the second source of learning, performance outcomes. In the early stages, benefits or concerns have not emerged and therefore the firm cannot rely on performance feedback to guide its actions. In the absence of learning to guide its behavior the firm may rely on the status quo. Fichman and Levinthal (1991) term this early stage a honeymoon period that buffers firms from alliance instability. This commitment to the status quo is particularly critical in international alliances. The international environment poses significant hurdles to alliances, related to the complexity of navigating foreign environments, higher costs of partner search and selection, difficulties of understanding partners and limited knowledge of alternatives. A lack of performance outcomes in conjunction with these hurdles may lead to inertia, as participants cannot assess whether their investments are likely to be successful. Further, firms would not venture to renegotiate the alliance at this stage since benefits or concerns have not clearly emerged. An acquisition may also not be a viable strategy in the initial stages since firms may not have adequate information to assess the value of the partner. Similarly, termination in the early stage is unlikely since the firm does not have any cues it can utilize regarding partner commitment or alliance performance. Therefore, as a result of the lack of learning either through experience or performance outcomes, compounded by the significant costs of international alliances, I expect that international alliances will demonstrate commitment to the status quo in these early stages.

As the alliance progresses, partners can draw on experience as they refine and develop various routines to manage interactions with partners and effectively share and integrate capabilities. They can also utilize performance outcome cues since they will be better able to perceive partner objectives, contributions and future potential. Further, benefits and costs of the alliance can be realistically determined. This will cause partners to revisit the original assumptions of the alliance formation. At the intermediate stage, therefore, the status quo does not seem a likely option. Delios et al. (2004) point to the existence of escalation in international alliances because of the presence of high termination and sunk costs. Even though firms may realize that the alliance is not achieving their objectives, they opt to persist with it for various reasons.

First, they may have gained enough experience with their partner to improve and redesign routines in the belief that it would lead to fulfillment of alliance objectives. In a case study of contracts between two firms in the computer industry, Mayer and Argyres (2004) find evidence of incremental and gradual learning by partners to better govern projects through contracts. Firms may expect a similar process of learning and adjustment and adaptation to occur, thereby resorting to renegotiation.

Second, a foreign firm may be reluctant to dissolve the alliance as it may not have enough knowledge about alternative partners that could help it navigate the still unfamiliar environment. The logical approach would be to postpone a dissolution decision until the firm has a viable alternative.

Third, alliances are typically characterized by appropriation concerns and allying firms' attempts to wall off technologies to prevent misappropriation. This may limit a firm's ability to assess the potential of the partner as a target firm for the purposes of acquisition. Further it may also limit a firm's ability to have effectively assimilated its partner's capabilities at the intermediate stage. A domestic firm may therefore be reluctant to terminate the alliance or commit to the status quo (similar to the foreign partner, but with different intentions) and may choose to renegotiate in order to recoup some benefits from its investment in the alliance. Thus, in the intermediate stages, performance outcomes, although available (and sometimes adverse), are not expected to outweigh experience. Instead, participants are likely to use performance outcomes to determine modifications to existing routines leading to renegotiation of alliance terms.

Why do participants rely on renegotiation in contrast to acquisition or termination? This occurs for two reasons. First is the persistence of routines, in that firms may believe refinement of routines will eventually lead to better performance. Second, even though current performance outcomes may be adverse, enough ambiguity exists about the future performance of the alliance and the possible potential of the partner. Given the significant investments made by the participants in the alliance, renegotiation is the most likely outcome. I therefore expect alliances in the intermediate stages to renegotiate.

As the alliance matures, one possible outcome is that both firms demonstrate changed positions that are a direct consequence of learning from experience – the foreign partner gains clearer knowledge of operating in the local environment and of the local partner from the shared interaction, making the alliance less critical to its ability to tap the domestic market. Similarly, the domestic partner will have gained knowledge about the foreign firm's capabilities, so reducing the need for inter-firm cooperation with this particular partner. Performance outcomes can be clearly assessed and firms can determine if the outcomes represent progress towards the achievement of objectives. Success towards the achievement of objectives, whether this is navigating the foreign market or accessing partner capabilities, results in a situation where participants feel the alliance has reached its end state and the collaboration has fulfilled its purpose. Consequently the alliance may be terminated or the partner may be acquired. Another outcome in some instances is the lack of effective progress for one or both of the partners. This may happen for multiple reasons: a participant may be very effective at restricting and preventing access to critical knowledge, the firms may not share a common knowledge base that permits assimilation of the partner's knowledge, or the knowledge sought may be context specific and harder for a partner to transfer. Given their earlier investments in renegotiation at the intermediate stage, partners may perceive that the utility of the alliance is limited, particularly in the context of poor performance outcomes, and in order to achieve its objectives a firm may have to pursue alternative mechanisms.

Given either of the outcomes – success or poor performance – the firm will not continue with or modify existing routines. At this stage the firm relies almost solely on performance outcomes to guide its behavior, in contrast to the earlier stages. This is because in the situation of successful performance, continuation of routines cannot result in additional performance gains. In the other alternative, the poor performance outcomes can no longer be ignored, as the evidence adds up and the firm has no choice but to discard routines rather than modifying them. Therefore alliances in the mature stages are likely to result in termination or acquisition.

How do firms decide between termination or acquisition in the latter stage? The choice between termination and acquisition is contingent on the perceived partner value. A firm may perceive that partner value is low and that it has effectively learned all it could from the alliance. The choice in this case would be dissolution of the alliance and a subsequent search for alternative partners in its pursuit of unfulfilled objectives. Thus, in the latter stages, dissolution of the alliance is likely in a situation of low perceived ' value of the alliance partner. When this value is low, the firm may decide to cut its losses (in contrast to escalation at the intermediate stage) and opt out of the alliance. Alternatively the firm may perceive high partner value, because it still offers an avenue for acquisition of skills. However the firm may recognize the limitations of the alliance mechanism in assimilating these skills. An alliance may not allow it to exert enough control to gain access to skills and it may not permit exclusivity of access to its partner. The firm therefore may decide to gain access to these skills through an acquisition since a hierarchy may be more useful in this regard. Thus, when the perceived value of the partner is high, the firm may choose to use an acquisition to gain better control, but the international alliance is more likely to end in termination when perceived partner value is low.

THE ROLE OF EXPERIENCE

The proposed process of outcomes suggests an ordered increase in the extent of change in the outcome, with the most stable outcome observed at the initial stages and the most disruptive (to the alliance and not necessarily the firm) observed at latter stages. However, in some situations this neatly ordered process of outcomes may not be observed. I draw attention to one of the participants in the alliance, termed the focal firm, to illustrate the effects of prior experience in skewing the evolutionary process of outcomes. The focal firm in an international alliance is defined as the firm that is venturing overseas and is faced with the liability of newness. I posit that focal firm experience will influence the evolving process and moderate the ordered relationship between alliance stages and alliance outcomes. So far the discussion has concentrated on the focal firm's ability to draw on experience related to a particular collaboration with a specific partner. However the focal firm may have an ability to utilize either its experience in the foreign country (to overcome some of the hurdles of searching for alternatives, complexity of environment) or prior experience with the specific partner in other collaborations.

Country Experience

A focal firm may already have some experience in the country, through alliances with other firms, its own operations, or other routes.[1] Experience in the country is likely to reduce the time spent by the focal firm in commitment to the status quo in the early stages of the alliance. Experience is likely to have led to an accumulation of country-specific knowledge and mitigation of many of the hurdles of dealing with a distinct national environment. The focal firm has a larger stock of knowledge that it can use to better gauge the possible performance outcomes of the alliance (even in the initial stages), and superior information about possible alternatives to the alliance. Therefore it is likely to be in a stronger position to renegotiate earlier and more effectively compared with an inexperienced firm. In addition to the shortening of the period spent in the status quo, the experience is also likely to reduce the renegotiation phase. The arguments about better information, assessment and alternatives apply to the second phase as well and the focal firm is likely to make a faster decision regarding termination or acquisition. Consequently focal firm experience in the country is likely to enable it to move quickly rather than delay decision making, so speeding up the evolutionary process and propelling the firm through the outcomes much more rapidly.

Experience with Partner

A firm may also have experience with the specific foreign partner in the host country. Research suggests that firms tend to ally with past partners in new alliances (Gulati, 1995) since they are better able to assess partner capabilities (Gulati and Gargiulo, 1999). Therefore if a firm has prior experience with a foreign partner, it has probably accurately assessed the possible contribution of the partner and the potential benefits from the alliance. Prior experience between partners (Gerwin and Ferris, 2004) also builds trust. Krishnan et al. (2006) suggest that in international alliances, trust between partners reduces behavioral uncertainty relating to the ability to anticipate and understand partner actions, so enabling better alliance performance. Prior experience suggests that partners are comfortable with each other and therefore are likely to have already worked through issues that may be detrimental to novice alliances. Therefore prior experience with a foreign partner suggests two benefits: better assessment of performance outcomes of the alliance, and established routines that can be used to guide the current collaboration. In such alliances, I expect that renegotiation will be eliminated completely or reduced to a significant extent in the intermediate stage when the partners have prior experience with each other. Alliances will demonstrate commitment to the status quo in the early and intermediate stages, and a termination or acquisition in the latter stage.

DISCUSSION AND CONCLUSIONS

Research on inter-organizational dyadic ties has explained the formation or dissolution of these ties as discrete events rather than as a sequence of events that unfold over time (Kim et al., 2006). Kim et al. term this as a content-based perspective, in contrast to a process-based perspective that examines the developmental process of inter-organizational relationships. This study makes a contribution to the alliance literature by focusing on process-related questions. It adopts an evolutionary perspective and examines alliance outcomes as process that can be examined over the duration of the alliance by evaluating a sequence of early, intermediate and latter stages. It evaluates the process by which international alliance outcomes are determined, by examining firms' reliance on experience and performance outcomes to guide their response to the alliance through commitment, renegotiation, termination or acquisition.

As Lavie (2006) points out, the emphasis on alliance formation and performance has left a theoretical gap between traditional theories of the firm and the behavior and performance of interconnected firms. By using the organizational learning perspective to evaluate outcomes, this research seeks to bridge this theoretical gap and explain how firm learning patterns and behavior can be used to explain alliance outcomes. It also complements the current research in the organizational learning field (Haleblian et al., 2006) that examines the interaction between the two sources of learning, experience and performance outcomes, in shaping future firm behavior. In this study, I evaluate when one source of learning dominates the other and has a greater influence on future firm behavior. Thus I theorize that neither source is important in the early stages, as firms do not have the necessary experience or information on performance outcomes. In the intermediate stages, experience is expected to be more important than performance outcomes because of the uncertainty and ambiguity regarding current and future performance. Finally, in the latter stages, performance outcomes are more important than experience, as firms can no longer delay their response to poor performance outcomes. These ideas have important implications for recognizing when firms can overcome the inertial force of routines reflected in firm experience.

The focus on the international arena also fills an existing gap in the understanding of international joint ventures and alliances. Yan and Zeng (1999) suggest that one of the most promising areas for future research is to explain the process of international joint venture development and offer implications for managing organizational change on an ongoing basis. This research highlights the inherent risks in international alliances and their implications for outcomes and their progression. It also presents managerial prescriptions for effectively managing these risks and the expected process of outcomes by accumulating experience within the country or with a specific partner to achieve desired alliance outcomes.

NOTE

1. Experience with current partner is not included in this context but is considered separately.

REFERENCES

Argote, L. (1999), *Organizational Learning: Creating, Learning and Transferring Knowledge*, Boston, MA: Kluwer Academic Publishers.

Arino, A. and J. de la Torre (1998), 'Learning from failure: towards an evolutionary model of collaborative ventures', *Organization Science*, 9 (3), 306–26.

Contractor, F. and P. Lorange (1988), 'Competition v/s cooperation: a benefit/cost framework for choosing between fully owned investments and cooperative relationships', *Management International Review*, 28 (4), 5–18.

Das, T. and B. Teng (2000), 'Instabilities of strategic alliances: an internal tensions perspective', *Organization Science*, 11 (1), 77–101.

Das, T. and B. Teng (2002), 'The dynamics of alliance conditions in the alliance development process', *Journal of Management Studies*, 39 (5), 726–46.

Delios, A., A. Inkpen and J. Ross (2004), 'Escalation in international strategic alliances', *Management International Review*, 44 (4), 457–79.

Doz, Y. (1996), 'The evolution of cooperation in strategic alliances: initial conditions or learning processes', *Strategic Management Journal*, 17 (7), 55–83.

Dussauge, P., B. Garrette and W. Mitchell (2000), 'Learning from competing partners. Outcomes and durations of scale and link alliances', *Strategic Management Journal*, 21 (2), 99–127.

Fichman, M. and D. Levinthal (1991), 'Honeymoons and the liability of adolescence: a new perspective on duration dependence in social and organizational relationships', *Academy of Management Review*, 16 (2), 442–69.

Gerwin, D. and J. Ferris (2004), 'Organizing new product development projects in strategic alliances', *Organization Science*, 15 (1), 22–38.

Greve, H. (2003), *Organizational Learning from Performance Feedback*, New York: Cambridge University Press

Gulati, R. (1995), 'Does familiarity breed trust? The implications of repeated ties for contractual choice in alliances', *Academy of Management Journal*, **38** (1), 85–112.

Gulati, R. and M. Gargiulo (1999), 'Where do interorganizational networks come from?', *American Journal of Sociology*, **104** (5), 1439–43.

Haleblian, J., J. Kim and N. Rajagopalan (2006), 'The influence of acquisition experience and performance on acquisition behavior: evidence from the U.S. commercial banking industry', *Academy of Management Journal*, **49** (2), 357–70.

Hitt, M., D. Ahlstrom, T. Dacin, E. Levitas and L. Svobodina (2004), 'The institutional effects on strategic partner selection in transition economies: China v/s Russia', *Organization Science*, **15** (2), 173–85.

Hitt, M., T. Dacin, E. Levitas, J. Arregle and A. Borza (2000), 'Partner selection in emerging and developed market contexts: resource based and organizational learning perspectives', *Academy of Management Journal*, **43** (3), 449–67.

Hitt, M., T. Dacin, B. Tyler and D. Park (1997), 'Understanding the differences in Korean and U.S. executives' strategic orientations', *Strategic Management Journal*, **18** (2), 159–67.

Inkpen, A. (2005), 'Learning through alliances: General Motors and NUMMI', *California Management Review*, **47** (4), 114–36.

Inkpen, A. and P. Beamish (1997), 'Knowledge, bargaining power and the instability of joint ventures', *Academy of Management Review*, **22** (1), 177–202.

Inkpen, A. and S. Currall (2004), 'The coevolution of trust, control and learning in joint ventures', *Organization Science*, **15** (5), 586–99.

Kim, T., H. Oh and A. Swaminathan (2006), 'Framing interorganizational network change: a network inertia perspective', *Academy of Management Review*, **31** (3), 704–20.

Krishnan, R., X. Martin and N. Noorderhaven (2006), 'When does trust matter to alliance performance', *Academy of Management Journal*, **49** (5), 894–917.

Lavie, D. (2006), 'The competitive advantage of interconnected firms: an extension of the resource-based view', *Academy of Management Review*, **31** (3), 638–58.

Levitt B. and J. March (1988), 'Organizational learning', *Annual Review of Sociology*, **14**, 319–40.

Mayer, K. and N. Argyres (2004), 'Learning to contract: evidence from the personal computer industry', *Organization Science*, **15** (4), 394–410.

Nelson R. and S. Winter (1982), *The Evolutionary Theory of the Firm*, Cambridge, MA: Harvard University Press.

Reuer, J. (2000), 'Parent firm performance across international joint venture life cycle stages', *Journal of International Business Studies*, **31** (1), 1–20.

Ring, P. and A. Van de Ven (1994), 'Developmental processes of cooperative organizational relationships', *Academy of Management Review*, **19** (1), 90–118.

Simonin, B. (1997), 'The importance of collaborative know-how. A test of the learning organization', *Academy of Management Journal*, **40** (5), 1150–75.

Stinchcombe, A. (1965), 'Social structure and organizations', in J.G. March (ed.), *Handbook of Organizations*, Chicago: Rand McNally, pp. 142–93.

Szulanski, G. (1996), 'Exploring internal stickiness: impediments to the transfer of best practice within the firm', *Strategic Management Journal*, **17** (Special Issue), 27–44.

Yan, A. and M. Zeng (1999), 'International joint venture instability: a critique of previous research, a reconceptualization, and directions for future research', *Journal of International Business Studies*, **30** (2), 395–414.

Zaheer, S. (1995), 'Overcoming the liability of foreignness', *Academy of Management Journal*, **38** (2), 341–64.

PART III

Location in the modern globalizing world

12. Is it all a matter of grouping? Examining the regional effect in global strategy research

**Ruth V. Aguilera, Ricardo G. Flores
and Paul Vaaler**

For several decades now, discussion across scientific fields about the significance of the concept of region has not yielded systematic conclusions. For example, building on the idea that regions have become specially important within the global strategy (GS) and international business (IB) fields, scholars have found evidence supporting regional effects in multinational corporations' (MNCs) decision-making processes (Hoffman, 1987), as well as in the performance of international joint ventures (IJVs) (Delios and Beamish, 2004). Rugman and colleagues have even claimed the triumph of 'regional' over 'global' strategy (usually described as the globalization vs. regionalization debate) as the main strategic choice of most multinational corporations (Rugman and Verbeke, 2007), concluding that these choices imply the emergence of 'regional multinationals' because of their 'liability of regional foreignness' (Rugman and Verbeke, 2004).

In spite of the frequent use of the term 'region', surprisingly there is no unambiguous and agreed definition of what countries each region encompasses. For instance, the region of 'Western Europe,' commonly used in global strategy research, seems quite straightforward, particularly for the core group of countries. Yet, when it comes to defining the specific boundaries of this region, agreement and consistency are rarely achieved. In this line, Evans and Newnham (1990) question whether Iceland should be included, where the eastern fringe lies, and similarly, whether Turkey is part of the greater Europe (at least now that it has not yet joined the European Union) or instead part of some region in Asia.

Given this debate on the specific definitions of commonly discussed regions, one probably would need to reconsider the implications of the studies emphasizing the importance of regional effects on the strategic intent of MNCs and global strategies more generally. In this sense, Stevens and Bird (2004) state that Rugman and Verbeke's (2004) argument needs to be judged carefully and might be misleading because their definition of the European region contains countries that geographically fall into Africa and the Middle East. Similarly, Rugman and Verbeke include in the Asian region countries that are geographically in the Oceania continent. Based on these discrepancies, it is fair to ask: how should a '*region*' be defined? Can the same *regional* categorization be used systematically across research projects? Are different regional categorizations likely to offer different insights and conclusions?

In this chapter, we make several contributions to the internationalization literature, location choice research, and overall IB and GS research. First, we uncover the lack of a consistent definition and treatment of the term region across different disciplines, and specifically in the IB and GS realms. Second, even though we find that empirical evidence within these fields reveals regional-level effects for different global strategic behaviors, most of these studies have not systematically controlled for lower-level effects (i.e. country variables), thus casting some doubt on whether the regional effects offered are truly regional in essence or are merely reflecting some country-level effects. Lastly, we engage in the regionalism–globalization debate by empirically exploring whether US MNCs have changed (expanded or retracted) the foreign location choices of their capital investments in the last two decades.

In developing these arguments, the chapter is organized as follows. First, we review how the term region has been defined and used across four different paradigmatic perspectives: economic, socio-cultural, institutional and geographical-centered. Second, we critically assess how researchers within the IB and GS realms have used this term. Third, we evaluate, as an illustrative example, the effects of drawing on different regional definitions in determining the location choice patterns of US MNCs in the last two decades. We finish with a discussion of the implications of this chapter for future work within IB and GS.

REGIONAL SCHEMES: PARADIGMATIC CONCEPTUALIZATIONS

The term *region* is defined as a 'fairly large area of a country or of the world, usually without exact limits' (*Longman Dictionary of Contemporary English*, 1995). This definition connotes physical nearness, however different scholars have come to define and use regional schemes that do not follow this core concept. Instead, they have grouped countries based on homogeneity in a particular dimension of interest. For instance, the world can be divided into countries that share the same religion, the same language, or a commonality on a certain socio-cultural dimension. Also, countries can be grouped by other institutional similarities, such as a common political regime or the same legal system. Regions can even be defined based on economic criteria, such as grouping countries that have signed certain trade agreements (trading blocs); or by the economic wealth level of each country (using indicators such as per capita income).

Given this myriad of potential regional groupings, we provide a comprehensive list of the different regional schemes used in different scholarly fields (see Table 12.1 for a summary). Then, we review specifically which of these regional schemes has been more commonly used within the international business and global strategy fields, and what effects those choices might have for different research projects within those fields.

The Economic Perspective

The most common approach for grouping countries into categories has focused on economic dimensions (Rugman and Verbeke, 2004). This view relies fundamentally on the idea that when studying the strategic actions of multinational corporations, it is important to consider how home and host countries of these organizations are economically related to one another. Several studies emphasize the need to look at the outcomes of regional economic integration (Frankel, 1997). One of the forerunners of this approach was Ohmae's (1985) work. He moved away from culturally or perception-based groupings, and proposed a more radical view of the global market by noting that a reduced set of countries had become the economic center of the world, based on their political power as well as their economical and social institutions. Ohmae grouped these countries into three regions, Japan, North America and Europe (mainly France, Germany and the United Kingdom), and claimed that MNCs that managed to achieve a prevalent position in these three regions would improve their likelihood of survival and success in the new global economy. Building on Ohmae's arguments, Rugman and his colleagues note that the most important regional groupings are integrated by those countries participating in trading blocs such as the North American Free Trade Agreement (NAFTA), the Association of Southeast Asian Nations (ASEAN) and the European Union (EU) (Rugman, 2005; Rugman and Verbeke, 2004).

Extending the economic view beyond trade agreements, other researchers have noted that MNCs' strategic actions may be more affected by issues linked to economic development (i.e. advanced economies vs. developing countries) or differences in national income levels (Dunning, 1998). Finally, researchers have highlighted the relevance of countries' membership in key

Table 12.1 Key regional schemes by scholar field

Dimension	Year	Author/ source	Number of countries included	Dimensions/methodology	Resulting regions	Detailed country list per region
Economic	1985	Ohmae	NA	Economic, technological and historical analysis of top MNCs. Assumed advantages of three regional blocs	Japan, North America and West Europe	No
	2004	Rugman & Verbeke	NA	Extend in general terms Ohmae's arguments	Asia-Pacific, EU, North America	No
	2004	World Bank	190	Income level (GDP per capita)	High income OECD, other high income, upper-middle, lower-middle, low income	Yes
	2005	UNCTAD	40	Trading agreements/blocs	ANDEAN, ASEAN, CARICOM, EFTA, EU, MERCOSUR, NAFTA	
Culture	1980	Hofstede	53	Questionnaire to IBM employees/ hierarchical clustering of 4 cultural dimensions	12 clusters (Hofstede, 2001, p. 62)	Yes
	1985	Ronen & Shenkar	45	Synthesis of previous cultural work on differences among countries	Anglo, Arab, Far Eastern, Germanic, Independent, Latin American, Latin European, Near Eastern, Nordic	Yes
	2002	Gupta et al.	61	Discriminant analysis of GLOBE data (see House et al., 2002 for details of GLOBE project)	South Asia, Anglo, Arab, Germanic Europe, Latin Europe, Eastern Europe, Confucian Asia, Latin America, Sub-Saharan Africa and Nordic Europe	Yes

	Year	Source	Number	Description	Classification	
Institutions	1998	La Porta et al.	49	Comparison of legal institutions as they focus on protection of share and debt holders/grouping based on historical root of the country's legal system	Rooted in common-law; French civil law; German civil law; Scandinavian civil law	Yes
	2006	CIA-World FactBook	Not applicable	Comparison of political systems	Communist, constitutional monarchy, democracy, parliamentary democracy, military-controlled republic, monarchy, theocratic republic	Yes
Geographic	2006	UN SD	190	UN regional division	19 regions	Yes
	2006	UN SD	190	UN continental division	America, Europe, Asia, Africa, Oceania	Yes
	2000	McNamara & Vaaler	Not applicable	Geographical regions	Western Europe–North America; Central–Eastern Europe; Africa–Middle East; Asia–Pacific; & Latin America	No

transnational organizations such as the Organisation for Economic Co-operation and Development (OECD) (Buckley and Ghauri, 2004).

One important issue to highlight about regional schemes based on the economic view is that all of them are quite fluid, since the membership of these multinational organizations or the classification of certain countries according to their income is much more likely to change over time than other categorizations based on physical location or cultural belief.

The Socio-cultural Perspective

A second approach to dividing the world into regional schemes is to group countries according to common socio-cultural dimensions, such as language and religious affiliation of the majority of a country's population. Though language and religion have not been widely used as primary criteria to designate regions, they are often included with other socio-cultural variables when distinguishing and grouping countries in multiple studies such as Chetty et al. (2006), Dow and Karunaratna (2006), and Leung et al. (2005).

The most common regional criteria used by scholars grouping countries according to some socio-cultural dimension are the values and beliefs (culture) held by a given country's inhabitants (see Earley, 2006; Hofstede, 2006; Javidan et al., 2006; Smith, 2006 for current debate over culture in international business). These studies draw on a statistical technique (i.e. hierarchical clustering) for grouping similar responses to a set of belief-centered questions from individuals representing a particular set of countries. The most common cultural construct is the one developed by Geert Hofstede (2001 [1980]). He surveyed IBM employees to derive cultural dimensions in 53 countries. Hofstede's regions based on cultural traits have received empirical support in a myriad of studies and have been used in explaining outcomes at the individual, group/firm and country level of analysis (see Kirkman et al., 2006 for a review of Hofstede's framework). Using hierarchical clustering in four cultural dimensions (power distance, uncertainty avoidance, masculinity/femininity and individualism/collectivism) Hofstede found evidence of the existence of a 12-group regional structure (Hofstede, 2001 [1980], p. 62). Building on the work of Hofstede and other studies focused on cultural dimensions across countries, Ronen and Shenkar (1985) also offered their own grouping of 45 countries in nine clusters. A similar, but much more focused analysis centered on work ethic, achievement motivation and competitiveness among young individuals in 41 countries came up with five world regional groups (Furnham et al., 1994).

More recently, a large-scale project on cultural values, the World Values Survey (Abramson and Inglehart, 1995), has gained legitimacy and is starting to be used in GS and IB research. This survey has been administered in multiple iterations since the early 1980s to individuals from 43 nations (Inglehart, 1997; Inglehart et al., 2004). Several investigators have already used these rich datasets sometimes as a substitute for Hofstede's instrument. For instance, Wan and Hoskisson (2003) show that national trust levels, one key cultural dimension extracted from the World Values Survey, capture the degree to which MNC managers can rely on the business practices of local individuals. In the same line, Knack and Keefer (1997) show that countries' general level of trust facilitates the operation of firms because societies with a high level of trust enhance impersonal business transactions.

A third body of research providing country level cultural data is the so-called GLOBE project (House et al., 2002). The data coming from this project are not without criticism,[1] but it is certainly relevant because of its potential usefulness in creating country groupings sharing common cultural characteristics. Indeed, Gupta et al. (2002) used data from the GLOBE project and through discriminant analysis found a seven-region grouping of the 61 countries involved in the GLOBE project. More restrictive analysis of Europe (Brodbeck et al., 2000) and Latin America (Lenartowicz and Johnson, 2003) has also offered regional schemes based on the GLOBE project to study different global strategic outcomes.

The Institutional Perspective

Another way of grouping countries around the globe is to rely on the commonalities of their institutional environments such as the legal or the labor market systems (Aguilera and Jackson, 2003; La Porta et al., 1999). For instance, La Porta et al. (1998) examine the specific way legal institutions protect share and debt holders in 49 countries contingent on their civil or common law legal traditions. Their analysis ends with a four-region clustering that traced back the original root of the legal system of each country (i.e. English, French, German, or Scandinavian legal system). This partitioning of the world according to the legal institutions prevalent in each country has been used by numerous researchers. For instance, Aguilera and Cuervo-Cazurra (2004) find evidence that countries with legal systems that strongly protect shareholder rights are likely to develop codes of good corporate governance. Still other scholars have grouped countries based on the different types of capitalism in which they are embedded, such as liberal market economies versus coordinated market economies, and infer distinct firm behavior contingent on the system (Hall and Soskice, 2001). It is important to emphasize that when drawing on institutional and socio-cultural regional schemes, it should not be presumed that they are necessarily fixed over time, as values and beliefs, institutional systems, and social structures might change and evolve, particularly when examining long periods of time.

The Geographic Perspective

Conceptualizing regions exclusively in terms of physical contiguity is the most straightforward use of regional grouping. In this view, the grouping of countries is made under the presumption that physical immediacy is a precondition for a sense of unity or shared properties. Dividing the world into the five continents (i.e. Europe, Asia, America, Africa and Oceania) is a common geographic regional grouping used in GS and IB research. For instance, Kwok and Tadesse (2006) use a continental division of the world when exploring the antecedents of the degree of market orientation of the financial systems of 41 countries. Similarly, Katrishen and Scordis (1998) find that multinational insurers have different likelihoods of achieving economies of scale according to their continent of origin. Geringer et al. (1989) also control by continent of origin when assessing the influence of diversification strategy and internationalization extent on the performance of 200 MNCs.

The United Nation's Statistics Division offers a more fine-grained partition of this geographically centered scheme, breaking up the world into 19 regions (i.e. Australia and New Zealand, Caribbean, Central America, Eastern Africa, Eastern Asia, Eastern Europe, Melanesia, Middle Africa, Northern Africa, Northern America, Northern Europe, South America, South-Central Asia, South-Eastern Asia, Southern Africa, Southern Europe, Western Africa, Western Asia, Western Europe). This regional scheme has not been widely used, although Flores and Aguilera (2007) have shown that it might bring new insights to the analysis of the foreign location choices of US MNCs in the last two decades. The geographical view of regional grouping is invariant over time, which may provide an advantage over the other regional categories.

REGIONAL EFFECTS: EMPIRICAL EVIDENCE FROM GLOBAL STRATEGY AND INTERNATIONAL BUSINESS RESEARCH

Our review of the empirical literature related to regional effects within IB and GS reveals a clear differentiation between studies where regional effects are designed as complementary to the main focus of a given study versus other research streams where regional effects are at the core of the study. Within the former research stream, studies uncover empirical evidence showing that key issues on the research agenda of IB and GS may be influenced by effects at the region level of analysis (see Table 12.2 for a summary). For example, 20 years ago Hoffman (1987) demonstrated that regional clusters had important effects on MNCs' actions. Specifically, he found that the relationship between power bases and strategic decisions within MNCs is moderated by the regional location of the MNCs' units. More recently, Delios and Beamish (2004) found that joint ventures of Japanese multinationals outperform their counterparts when operating in the Asian region. Another example of significant regional effect is displayed by the findings of Kolk (2005) when studying environmental reporting practices of 203 firms working in Europe, North America and Asia. Kolk demonstrates that these practices have substantial differences among these three different regions. Similarly, Vaaler and McNamara (2004) find evidence of significant regional effects on the way rating agencies evaluate sovereign credit rates. They illustrate that the regional specialization or regional focus of the rating agencies influences their sovereign risk ratings, even during a national crisis period. Zaheer and Zaheer (2001) offer another example of regional effects on MNCs' actions by finding evidence that the microstructure of the inter-bank business-to-business currency market responds to a clustering scheme for countries of the world that divides the globe into three regions. Unfortunately, a common component across all these studies is that they do not directly discuss the logical reasons behind their respective choices of the specific country grouping used. The immediate result of this lack of detail raises questions about whether that particular region or any another grouping would generate the same results. Also, one wonders whether these regional effects represent a meaningful outcome beyond the country level, or whether they are merely a reflection of other country-level variables not considered.

A second set of studies specifically target their research towards examining whether certain regions have become more or less important for the activities of MNCs around the world in the last few decades. There are two clearly defined sets of works within the so-called regionalists versus globalists debate. In this debate, one side presents an argument claiming that multinationals have become completely regionally focused (Rugman, 2005; Rugman and Verbeke, 2004, 2007). The contrasting position portrays MNCs as globally involved organizations (Bird and Stevens, 2003; Clark and Knowles, 2003; Stevens and Bird, 2004). The regionalist arguments are mostly based on empirical evidence of foreign sales from the top 500 Global Fortune firms (Rugman and Verbeke, 2004). Delios and Beamish (2005) tested this idea for a large sample of Japanese MNCs, finding support for the regionalist arguments. Empirical research by Grosse (2005), which

Table 12.2   IB and GS studies uncovering regional effects in MNCs' actions

Year	Authors	Journal	Countries included	Regions	Detailed country list per region	Regional type	Firms analyzed	Regional effect
1987	Hoffman	JIBS	87	Anglo, Germanic; Nordic; Latin European; & Latin American	No	Clusters (Ronen & Shenkar, 1985)	Managers in 8 countries	Regional clusters moderate the relationship between power bases and influence strategic decisions
2000	McNamara & Vaaler	JIBS	52	Western Europe–North America; Central–Eastern Europe; Africa–Middle East; Asia–Pacific; & Latin America	No	Geographic & economic development	Nationally recognized statistical rating organization	Regional specialization affects sovereign risk-ratings done by NRSROs
2001	Zaheer & Zaheer	SMJ	Not available	Asian, European & American (time zone)	No	Geographic	100 most active banks	Banks from same cluster compete for the same customers
2004	Vaaler & McNamara	OS	53	North American–Caribbean; Latin American, Western Europe, Central–Eastern Europe; Africa–Middle East; & Asia	No	Geographic	5 agencies (Moody's, S&P, DCR, Thomson & IBCA)	Regional focus accentuates downward pressure on ratings, resulting in more negative ratings for more regionally focused agencies in crisis period

Year	Author	Journal	No.	Regions	Yes/No	Definition	Sample	Finding
2004	Rugman & Verbeke	JIBS	Not available	North-America; Asia-Pacific; Europe	No	Ohmae (1985) & firms' definition	Top 500 MNCs	Most top MNCs pursue home TRIAD region-oriented strategies. MNCs are regional not global
2004	Delios & Beamish	MIR	135	Asia; North America–Europe	No	Geographic institutional	Japanese JV subsidiaries	JV in Asia had a moderately better performance than elsewhere
2005	Delios & Beamish	MIR	Not available	Asia, Africa; Europe, Middle East; North America; Oceania; South America	No	Geographic	1229 Japanese MNCs	50%+ of the firms pursue home-oriented international strategy. Yet the largest firms with bi-regional or global strategies outperform others
2005	Grosse	MIR	Not available	USA; Europe; Japan; other Asia; elsewhere	No	Geographic	10 financial institutions	None of these institutions is truly global, but rather bi-regional
2005	Kolk	MIR	Not available	USA; Japan; Europe	No	Ohmae (1985)	203 firms from TRIAD	Environmental reporting varies substantially according to regions
2007	Dunning et al.	JIBS	25	Americas; Europe; Asia; & other/ Anglo; Latin European; Nordic & Germanic; Latin American; Far Eastern; other	Yes	Geographic/ mod. Ronen & Shenkar clusters	Not applicable	Increased geographical dispersion of (foreign-based) MNE activities as well as increasing importance of 'intra-region' effect

Note: JIBS: *Journal of International Business Studies;* OS: *Organization Science;* MIR: *Management International Review.*

focuses on the top ten world financial institutions, also seems to support the regionalist argument. Thus a first overarching conclusion of our review of the regional effects within IB and GS is that the commonly used regional classifications seem to be linked to quite specific perceptions, attitudes, behaviors or institutional characteristics of the countries included in each region. Even using the broader culturally based clusters such as those derived from Hofstede (2001 [1980]) and Ronen and Shenkar (1985) as theoretically driven groupings is questionable. Perhaps more importantly, the studies reviewed here have not consistently controlled regional groupings with country-level variables, thus casting some doubts on the accuracy of their respective interpretations of the regional effects.

A second issue arising from our review is the lack of common ground between the different country groupings. In fact, this overcrowding of potential clusters might bring about the opposite effect for research examining regional effects, since there seems to be no clear criterion for deciding which scheme is the most relevant for a particular research project. Even within the globalization/regionalization debate, a pivotal point of contention is the lack of a rigorous definition of those regional groupings where arguably MNCs have intensified their activities (Dunning et al., 2007; Stevens and Bird, 2004). Indeed, Stevens and Bird (2004) note that Rugman and Verbeke's (2004) regional definition might be misleading because the European region includes some African and Middle Eastern countries, and the Asian region includes countries from Oceania.

In view of these criticisms, we ask how we can determine whether MNCs have become more or less globalized if a clear regional definition is lacking. In the next section we provide an illustration of how different definitions of 'region' can lead to different outcomes by looking at the foreign location choice of US MNCs over a 20-year period (Flores and Aguilera, 2007).

An Illustration of the Effects of Differential Regional Definitions: FDI Location Choices

As an illustration of the potential effects that different regional definitions might have in a particular research project, we examine whether there has been a change in the location choices of the largest US MNCs between 1980 and 2000 and use different regional categorizations to answer this research question. Determining whether these choices have become more geographically widespread or regionally concentrated is the key point of dispute between the regionalists and the globalists (Rugman and Verbeke, 2004, 2007; Stevens and Bird, 2004). The largest American MNCs seem to be a particularly relevant set of organizations to study in order to strengthen our understanding of this issue, as these firms engage in the highest percentage of foreign direct investment (FDI) around the world (Ghemawat and Ghadar, 2006) and they commonly have a corporate governance system that facilitates full-fledged global strategies (Aguilera and Yip, 2004). Also, US firms such as Coca-Cola, or Exxon-Mobil are usually seen as 'the Janus Face' of the globalization process (Eden and Lenway, 2001).

We use archive data on the foreign location choices of the largest 100 US MNCs ranked by revenues (Fortune 500) in 1980 and 2000 (Flores and Aguilera, 2007). The firms in this sample represented 3.1 trillion US dollars in combined assets and employed more than six million individuals in 2000. They encompass 27 different two-digit SIC industry codes from oil and gas exploration to pharmaceuticals manufacturers.

The dependent variable, *foreign location choice*, is a dichotomous variable that captures whether a US-based MNE has substantial direct capital investment in a given country as reported by the *Directory of American Firms Operating in Foreign Countries* (Angel, 2001, p. i). Our operationalization of US foreign location choice addresses, at least partially, some of the criticisms of drawing on sales as an overarching measure to capture MNC activities overseas (Dunning et al., 2007).

US firms in this sample had on average substantial direct capital investment in 22.9 countries in 1980 and 28.9 countries in 2001. The total number of substantial foreign capital investments for the 100 MNCs was 2288 and 2891 in 1980 and 2000, respectively, showing an increase of 26 percent. Within this sample of MNCs, IBM had the highest number of foreign wholly or partially owned subsidiaries, affiliates or branches in 1980 (80 countries), and Xerox had the highest (108 countries) in 2000. The total number of countries receiving significant capital investments from one or more of the largest US MNCs in either 1980 or 2000 is 147. Australia, Canada and the United Kingdom were the three countries with the largest amount of direct capital investment from the 100 largest US MNCs in 1980 (with an average presence of 81 companies), and Canada, the United Kingdom and Japan were the respective countries in 2000 (with an average presence of 84 companies).

To explore whether different regional schemes might change the conclusion regarding the changes in the location choices of this set of US MNCs, we analyze several groupings from each of the economic, socio-cultural, institutional and geographic views presented above. We start by reviewing the economically based regionalist arguments. We find that the number of capital investment units by US MNCs abroad increased 26 percent from 1980 to 2000. More importantly, we show that the percentage change in US foreign investments over time is the greatest for countries outside the TRIAD (Europe, the USA and Japan). We find similar results when using Rugman and Verbeke's (2004) regional definition; that is, an increase of foreign subsidiaries in this 20-year period, as well as a significant percentage of US MNC investments going outside their core regions (EU, North America and Asia-Pacific), with an increase in the presence of US MNCs in the Asia-Pacific region (52 percent increase from 1980 to 2000). Our results also illustrate that US foreign capital investment has changed between 1980 and 2000 when viewing it through the scheme of regional grouping based on the income level of countries around the globe. Lastly, if we group the countries into the main trading blocs in 2000, we find that countries within the ASEAN and EU blocs have received more capital investments in 2000 compared to that received in 1980 from the largest US firms. However the largest expansion in percentage and in absolute value has been in those countries that are not members of the active trading blocs analyzed here. An interesting feature of grouping countries by their membership of certain trading blocs is that it brings new insights into the expansion of US foreign investments. Like no other economically-based regional grouping, the trading bloc partition illustrates that the expansion of US companies might have been in fact not a complete and pure enlargement of their international presence. Instead, some redeployment of resources may have occurred, as shown by the decrease in their capital investments in at least one of these regional trade blocs (CARICOM).

Examining the foreign location choices of the largest US firms according to a socio-cultural view of the world leads to different insights and conclusions. For instance, when we draw on culturally-based regional clusters, the expansion of these firms' activities can be described as irregular or widespread rather than concentrated within a particular cluster. Unfortunately, if one evaluates the location choices of the firms in our sample of the largest US MNCs, using Ronen and Shenkar's (1985) and Hofstede's (2001 [1980]) regional schemes, in both cases a significant portion of the investments of US firms overseas, regardless of the year, is found outside the countries included in these clusters. This trend seems to strengthen over time. Despite these drawbacks, these two regional schemes depict again a widespread expansion and some redeployment of resources in the period under analysis. Similar conclusions could be extracted if we design regions according to the religion embraced by most inhabitants of the respective countries. Even when the investments of these firms have been historically concentrated in Christian countries, in 2000 countries with a majority of Buddhist and Muslim individuals have gained foreign investments from firms in this sample.

If we take a regional definition based on countries with common legal and political systems, we find that these regional schemes expose a high concentration of US investments in countries with a civil legal system and/or embracing democracy as their political system. We also see a growing presence of US firms in countries with a communist legal system or communist political system, probably as a consequence of the institutional/policy changes in those countries (e.g. China and Vietnam).

Finally, there are different ways to group countries into geographically centered regions, from the crude five continent criteria to the more fine-grained regional division used by the UN's Statistical Division. The key insights from analyzing the location changes by using geographic regional groupings is that we can uncover different patterns contingent on the category used. Thus, when taking a coarse continental partition, one can see a clear redeployment of resources, with African countries receiving fewer investments from the firms in this sample. In contrast, Asian countries are much more likely to be chosen as locations for those capital investments. A more detailed examination of these changes shows that the movement away from African countries is not equally spread across that continent. Indeed, we find that the southern part of the continent (Southern Africa region) is receiving a higher level of investments in 2000. A similar situation could be singled out for Europe where even when the Western European region shows no significant increases in the investments received, the Eastern, Northern and Southern European regions are chosen more often as recipients of capital investments. In addition, we uncover that Eastern Europe, Eastern, South-Eastern and Western Asia have become important host countries, while Africa, Central America and the Caribbean have turned out to be less desirable for US MNCs' investments.

CONCLUSION, DISCUSSION, AND IMPLICATIONS FOR FUTURE RESEARCH

This chapter examined the different categories of regions used in GS and IB research to show that there is a need for a more systematic use of regions in our research designs. We described how 'regions' are defined to answer whether the same regional definitions could be used for completely different research projects, and to explore whether using different regional definitions might lead to different insights.

We undertook this endeavor by examining one specifically relevant research problem within the IB and SG realms: the changes in the foreign location choices of US MNCs. Our findings are consistent with recent reports by UNCTAD (2005) regarding the growing importance of some Asian and European locations for FDI coming from the USA. These results show that different regional categories have important implications for understanding certain phenomena within the global strategy and international business research agenda.

Our findings have significant implications for the regionalist–globalist debate since they seem to depict a growing presence of substantial US capital investments beyond the TRIAD or 'New TRIAD' (Rugman and Verbeke, 2004) regions. They also indicate that the extent of global expansion of FDI coming from the USA is much less widespread than it is generally assumed by globalist arguments. For instance, countries within the Caribbean or Middle Africa are the recipients of fewer substantial capital investments by US firms in the year 2000.

Another implication of our study is the need in future research to clearly tease out regional-level from country-level effects. Most studies we reviewed here have reported and discussed regional effects even when those effects were not controlled for by country-level variables. It seems necessary when going forward in the research agenda of GS and IB to make sure that researchers avoid confounding regional effects with effects related to other levels of analysis, such as differences in cultural values, the political system or language.

More generally, the different implications one might draw from using various regional definitions emphasize the need for further work defining which regional grouping may provide researchers with the most effective division of the globe. In this sense, we conclude by sharing the overall judgment offered by Allen et al. (1998, p. 2) when noting that 'There is no complete portray of a region. They only exist in relation to a particular criteria [...] they are our constructions.' Future research thus would be well-advised to work toward finding regional schemes that are effective groupings for the problem at hand, instead of continuing to use previously defined regional schemes close to one's preferred paradigmatic view. One possible way of adopting this new philosophy of 'looking for' the 'best' regional scheme for each research project would be to find some kind of computational procedure that minimizes the overall unexplained variance in the statistical models used (Vaaler et al., 2007).

In the end, no matter which methodology a particular research team decides to use for a particular project, the findings presented here show evidence of how pivotal the regional definition could be. Thus we hope that this work has at least raised awareness of the potential confounding effects that using only one regional definition may have in the conclusions one might derive from any particular research project analyzing regional effects.

NOTE

1. The GLOBE project has been contested by Hofstede recently. He argues that this survey is a better reflection of researchers' minds than of the respondents', and consequently his

original cultural model emerges strengthened by the data collected in this project (Hofstede, 2006). Leaders of the GLOBE project have quickly answered Hofstede's concerns (Javidan et al., 2006), but as noted by other scholars, this discussion seems to be far from finished (Earley, 2006; Smith, 2006).

REFERENCES

Abramson, P.R. and R. Inglehart (1995), *Value Change in Global Perspective*, Ann Arbor, MI: University of Michigan Press.

Aguilera, R.V. and A. Cuervo-Cazurra. (2004), 'Codes of good governance worldwide: what is the trigger?', *Organization Studies*, **25** (3), 415–43.

Aguilera, R.V. and G. Jackson (2003), 'The cross-national diversity of corporate governance: dimensions and determinants', *Academy of Management Review*, **28**, 447–65.

Aguilera, R.V. and G. Yip. (2004), 'Corporate governance and globalization', in A. Ariño, P. Ghemawat and J.E. Ricart (eds), *Creating Value through Global Strategy*, London: Palgrave Macmillan.

Allen, J., D. Massey, A. Cochrane and J. Charlesworth (1998), *Rethinking the Region*, London: Routledge.

Angel, J.L. (ed.) (2001), *Directory of American Firms Operating in Foreign Countries*, 16th edn, New York: Simon & Schuster.

Bird, A. and M.J. Stevens (2003), 'Toward an emergent global culture and the effects of globalization on obsolescing national cultures', *Journal of International Management*, **9** (4), 395–427.

Brodbeck, F.C., M. Frese, S. Akerblom, G. Audia, G. Bakacsi and H. Bendova (2000), 'Cultural variation of leadership prototypes across 22 European countries', *Journal of Occupational and Organizational Psychology*, **73**, 1–29.

Buckley, P.J. and P.N. Ghauri (2004), 'Globalization, economic geography and the strategy of multinational enterprises', *Journal of International Business Studies*, **35** (2), 81–98.

Chetty, S., K. Eriksson and J. Lindbergh (2006), 'The effect of specificity of experience on a firm's perceived importance of institutional knowledge in an ongoing business', *Journal of International Business Studies*, **37**, 619–712.

CIA – World FactBook (2007), 'The world factbook', available online at http://www. cia.gov./cia/publications/factbook/index.html (accessed 15 December 2006).

Clark, T. and L.L. Knowles (2003), 'Global myopia: globalization theory in international business', *Journal of International Management*, **9**, 361–72.

Delios, A. and P.W. Beamish (2004), 'Joint venture performance revisited: Japanese foreign subsidiaries worldwide', *Management International Review*, **44** (1), 69–91.

Delios, A. and P.W. Beamish (2005), 'Regional and global strategies of Japanese firms', *Management International Review*, **45** (Special Issue), 19–36.

Dow, D. and A. Karunaratna (2006), 'Developing a multidimensional instrument to measure psych distance stimuli', *Journal of International Business Studies*, **37**, 578–602.

Dunning, J.H. (1998), 'Location and the multinational enterprise: a neglected factor?', *Journal of International Business Studies*, **29** (1), 45–66.

Dunning, J.H., M. Fujita and N. Yakova (2007), 'Some macro-data on the regionalization/globalization debate: a comment on the Rugman & Verbeke Analysis', *Journal of International Business Studies*, **38**, 177–99.

Earley, P.C. (2006), 'Leading cultural research in the future: a matter of paradigms and taste', *Journal of International Business Studies*, **37**, 922–31.

Eden, L. and S. Lenway (2001), 'Introduction to the symposium multinationals: the Janus face of globalization', *Journal of International Business Studies*, **32** (3), 383–400.

Evans, G. and J. Newnham (1990), *The Dictionary of World Politics: A Reference Guide to Concepts, Ideas and Institutions*, New York: Harvester Wheatsheaf.

Flores, R. and R. Aguilera (2007), 'Globalization and location choice: an analysis of US multinational firms in 1980 and 2000', *Journal of International Business Studies*, forthcoming.

Frankel, J.A. (1997), *Regional Trading Blocs in the World Economic System*, Washington, DC: Institute for International Economics.

Furnham, A., B. Kirkcaldy and R. Lynn (1994), 'National attitudes to competitiveness, money and work amongst young people: first, second and third world differences', *Human Relations*, **47**, 119–32.

Geringer, J.M., P.W. Beamish and R.C. daCosta (1989), 'Diversification strategy and internationalization: implications for MNE performance', *Strategic Management Journal*, **10** (2), 109–19.

Ghemawat, P. and F. Ghadar (2006), 'Global integration? Global concentration', *Industrial and Corporate Change*, **15** (4), 595–623.

Grosse, R. (2005), 'Are the largest financial institutions really "global"?', *Management International Review*, **45** (Special Issue), 129–44.

Gupta, V., P.J. Hanges and P. Dorfman (2002), 'Cultural clusters: methodology and findings', *Journal of World Business*, **37**, 11–15.

Hall, P.A. and D. Soskice (eds) (2001), *Varieties of Capitalism: The Institutional Foundations of Comparative Advantage*, New York: Oxford University Press.

Hoffman, R.C. (1987), 'Political versus rational sources of decision power among country clusters', *Journal of International Business Studies*, **18**, 1–14.

Hofstede, G. (2001 [1980]), *Culture's Consequences: Comparing Values, Behaviors, Institutions and Organizations across Nations*, 2nd edn, Thousand Oaks, CA: Sage.

Hofstede, G. (2006), 'What did GLOBE really measure? Researchers' mind versus respondents' minds', *Journal of International Business Studies*, **37**, 882–96.

House, R., M. Javidan, P.J. Hanges and P. Dorfman (2002), 'Understanding cultures and implicit leadership theories across the globe: an introduction to project GLOBE', *Journal of World Business*, **37**, 3–10.

Inglehart, R. (1997), *Modernization and Postmodernization: Cultural, Economic, and Political Change in 43 Societies*, Princeton, NJ: Princeton University Press.

Inglehart, R., M. Basanez, J. Diez-Medrano, L. Halman and R. Luijkx (2004), *Human Beliefs and Values: A Cross-cultural Sourcebook Based on the 1999–2002 Values Surveys*, Delegacion Coyocan, Mexico: Siglo Veintiuno Editores.

Javidan, M., R. House, P. Dorfman, P.J. Hanges and M. Sully de Luque (2006), 'Conceptualizing and measuring cultures and their consequences: a comparative review of GLOBE's and Hofstede's approaches', *Journal of International Business Studies*, **37**, 897–914.

Katrishen, F.A. and N.A. Scordis (1998), 'Economies of scale in services: a study of multinational insurers', *Journal of International Business Studies*, **29**, 305–23.

Kirkman, B.L., K.B. Lowe and C.B. Gibson (2006), 'A quarter century of *Culture's Consequences*: a review of empirical research incorporating Hofstede's cultural values framework', *Journal of International Business Studies*, **37**, 285–320.

Knack, S. and P. Keefer (1997), 'Does social capital have an economic payoff? A cross-country investigation', *The Quarterly Journal of Economics*, **112** (4), 1251–88.

Kolk, A. (2005), 'Environmental reporting by multinationals from the TRIAD: convergence or divergence?', *Management International Review*, **45** (Special Issue): 145–66.

Kwok, C.C-Y. and S. Tadesse (2006), 'National culture and financial systems', *Journal of International Business Studies*, **37**, 227–47.

La Porta, R., F. Lopez-de-Silanes, A. Shleifer and R.W. Vishny (1998), 'Law and Finance', *Journal of Political Economy*, **106** (6), 1113–55.

La Porta, R., F. Lopez-de-Silanes, A. Shleifer and R.W. Vishny. (1999), 'The quality of government', *Journal of Law, Economics and Organization*, **15** (1), 222–79.

Lenartowicz, T. and J. P. Johnson (2003), 'A cross-national assessment of the values of Latin American managers: contrasting hues or shades of gray', *Journal of International Business Studies*, **34**, 266–81.

Leung, K., R. Bhagat, N.R. Buchan, M. Erez and C.B. Gibson (2005), Culture and international business: recent advances and their implications for future research', *Journal of International Business Studies*, **36**, 357–78.

Longman Dictionary of Contemporary English (1995), 3rd edn, Harlow: Longman.

McNamara, G. and P. Vaaler (2000), 'The influence of competitive positioning and rivalry on emerging market risk asessment', *Journal of International Business Studies*, **31** (2), 337–47.

Ohmae, K. (1985), *Triad Power: The Coming Sharp of Global Competition*, New York: The Free Press.

Ronen, S. and O. Shenkar. (1985), 'Clustering countries on attitudinal dimensions: a review and synthesis', *Academy of Management Review*, **10** (3), 435–54.

Rugman, A.M. (2005), *The Regional Multinationals: MNEs and 'Global' Strategic Management*, Cambridge: Cambridge University Press.

Rugman, A.M. and A. Verbeke (2004), 'A perspective on regional and global strategies of multinational enterprises', *Journal of International Business Studies*, **35**, 3–18.

Rugman, A.M. and A. Verbeke (2007), 'Liabilities of regional foreignness and the use of firm-level versus country-level data: a response to Dunning et al. (2007)', *Journal of International Business Studies*, **38**, 200–5.

Smith, P.B. (2006), 'When elephants fight, the grass gets trampled: the GLOBE and Hofstede projects', *Journal of International Business Studies*, **37**, 915–21.

Stevens, M.J. and A. Bird (2004), 'On the myth of believing that globalization is a myth: or the effects of misdirected responses on obsolescing an emergent substantive discourse', *Journal of International Management*, **10**, 501–10.

UN (SD) (2006), 'Regional scheme', available online at http://unstats.un.org/unsd/methods/m49/m49regin.htm (accessed 15 December 2006).

United Nations Conference on Trade and Development (UNCTAD) (2005), *World Investment Report: Transnational Corporations and the Internationalization of R&D*, New York: United Nations.

Vaaler, P., R. Aguilera and R. Flores (2007), 'Simulated annealing and the impact of country regional groupings on us multinational corporate investment decisions', in D.J. Ketchen and D.D. Bergh (eds), *Research Methodology in Strategy and Management*, Amsterdam: Elsevier.

Vaaler, P. and G. McNamara (2004), 'Crisis and competition in expert organizational decision making: credit-rating agencies and their response to turbulence in emerging economies', *Organization Science*, **15** (6), 687–703.

Wan, W.P. and R.E. Hoskisson (2003), 'Home country environments, corporate diversification strategies and firm performance', *Academy of Management Journal*, **46** (1), 27–45.

World Bank (2004), *World Develoment Report 2005: A Better Investment Climate for Everyone*, Washington, DC: The World Bank and Oxford University Press.

Zaheer, S. and A. Zaheer (2001), 'Market microstructure in a global B2B network', *Strategic Management Journal*, **22**, 859–73.

13. Global cities and multinational corporation investment

Anthony Goerzen

The trend towards economic globalization has become a central issue in public and academic debate. Multinational corporations (MNCs) have been identified as the key drivers of this process that fosters increased economic interdependence among national markets (UNCTAD, 2000). For this reason, the impact of investment location has become of renewed interest; in fact, as suggested by Ricart et al. (2004), location is the distinctive component of international business research. In fact, Buckley and Ghauri (2004) state that the deepening international division of labour arising from the changing ownership strategies of MNCs and the resulting effect on the world economy is the 'big question' that faces international business scholars, requiring a focus on economic geography.

The tradition in international business scholarship is to examine the nation state as the basic unit of analysis. If we were to look at such diverse literature streams as those on geographic scope, culture, entry mode, and others, we would see that virtually all work examines the impact of national political boundaries. Yet, as argued by previous authors, 'states aren't really the right geographical units' to shed light on the critical phenomenon of economic globalization and the role of MNCs – the relevant geographic unit of observation is at the city level (Feldman and Audretsch, 1999; Krugman, 1991, p. 57).

In an era in which MNCs act as centrifugal forces, 'offshoring' their operations (Bhagwati et al., 2004, Harrison and McMillan, 2006), expanding their worldwide networks of alliances and subsidiaries (Goerzen, 2005a, 2005b; Goerzen and Beamish, 2005), and moving their back-office operations from urban centres to outlying suburbs (Sassen, 2001), some observers have suggested that cities are becoming obsolete (Scott et al., 2001). It is true that economic globalization has led to a severe decline in many once-great industrial centres as well as many minor ones (e.g. see *The Economist*, 2005). As described by Sassen (1996b), however, state-of-the-art infrastructure and the specialized managerial expertise required to make these systems, facilities and processes function appear to be agglomerating in 'global cities' (e.g. New York, London, Tokyo) and are providing a countering centripetal force.

How many global cities there are and how they fit into an international hierarchy are all under current debate (Beaverstock et al., 1999; Derudder et al., 2003; Short et al., 2000; Taylor et al., 2002). Nonetheless, a growing consensus is emerging among political scientists, economic geographers and urban planners that certain key cities in both hemispheres are rising in importance as centres of economic coordination and control.

Although managers rarely see their businesses in terms of inter-organizational clusters (Porter, 2000), the concept of the global city is also important to management scholars, MNC executives and government policy officials, for several reasons. First, the systematic grouping of certain types of firms in specific places suggests that much of competitive advantage lies outside a given company or even outside its industry, residing instead in the locations of its business units. Therefore, there is a 'compelling need to reorient our thinking about corporate strategy in a way that sees location … as integral to a firm's success' (Porter, 2000, p. 254). Second, if the concept of the global city is a useful way of analysing the ways and means by which MNCs establish their production networks, then this shifts the character of the debate of the relationship between MNCs and local governments; rather than a contest between large, resourceful MNCs and increasingly powerless local governments (Sassen, 1996a; Vernon, 1971), the global city concept highlights the notion that MNCs are attracted to specific places that vary with firms' individual needs for specialized managerial expertise as well as transportation and communication infrastructures.

As competition globalizes, the geographic or location-specific sources of competitive advantage are becoming more, not less, important (Scott, 1998) and it appears that MNCs increasingly are using the logic of clustering in their investment and location decisions (Enright, 1998, 1999). Yet there has been very little research in the management literature on MNC behaviour specifically as it relates to the concept of global cities, despite the fact that significant streams of research on the world city concept exist. This chapter, therefore, is designed to review some of the major underpinnings in the world city literature to provide a bridge to management research. Subsequently, I examine a large data set on MNC subsidiary location to provide a nuanced description of the relationships of global cities to MNC investment. At the outset, however, it may be worthwhile to briefly consider how previous scholars have viewed the global city concept.

WHAT IS A GLOBAL CITY?

Major cities have been of interest for years to researchers from a variety of disciplines and, as a result of the diversity of perspectives, many labels have been derived to describe them, including mega-cities, great industrial cities, world cities, imperial cities, global capitalist cities, primate cities, and global cities. Essentially, the study of major cities can be decomposed into two basic approaches; one is a demographic tradition that focuses on the sizes of cities and the second is a functional tradition that examines the role of cities within larger systems. The demographic approach is primarily interested in the human and ecological implications of the concentration of human populations. The functional tradition, on the other hand, examines cities that appear to be integral to contemporary globalization processes. It is research in this latter stream that I use in this examination of global cities and MNC investment.

Beginning with the work of Hall (1966), there has been broad consensus as to which cities are at the top of the world city hierarchy based on an examination of the centrality of geoeconomic power in the world system. Yet, below this top tier of global cities there has been a wide range of opinion on which other cities qualify for this elite status. According to Beaverstock et al. (1999), some of this variety relates to the fact that there are at least four major approaches, with different criteria being used to identify world cities, as briefly reviewed below.

The earliest approach to identifying world city status (e.g. Hall, 1966) was to identify the functional capabilities of cities with respect to their power and influence in politics, trade, communications, finance, education, culture and technology. This work was originally an extension of ideas on urbanization or cosmopolitanism rather than a reflection of the establishment of unique concentrations of power in the global economy.

A second approach, also building upon the work of Hall (1966), but even more so on that of Hymer (1972), centred on the decision-making corporate activities and power of MNCs, in the context of an emerging view of an international division of labour. Among the more important contributions in this stream are Cohen (1981) and especially Friedman (1986), who developed the concept of primary and secondary cities in core and semi-peripheral countries. His world city hierarchy was based on an analysis of several key criteria including the existence of a major financial centre, headquarters for MNCs and other international institutions, the rapid growth of the business services sector, an important manufacturing centre, a major transportation node, and population size.

A third approach to the study of world city status, pioneered by Sassen (1991, 1994, 1996b, 1997, 2001), has focused on the rapid growth, specialization and agglomeration of producer services. From this perspective, the concept of the global city has emerged because of the globalization of economic activity and the organizational structure of the producer service and finance industry. Thus major cities take on renewed importance as sites for certain types of production, servicing, marketing and innovation, as well as the management and coordination of economic power in the global economy.

Finally, a fourth approach identifies major cities and their relative positions through rankings of international financial centres, a perspective initiated by Reed (1981). On the basis of a series of banking, financial and related cultural, economic, geographical and political variables, Reed (1981) developed a taxonomy of financial centres that included 'supranational', 'international' and 'host international financial centres'. This perspective on world city status has been adopted in the popular press including, for example, *The Economist*, which published a series of articles in 1998 entitled 'Capitals of capital'.

An overarching problem with the collection of approaches described above is that the variety of criteria used ranges from objective to quite subjective and perhaps even vague. Beaverstock et al. (1999), therefore, compiled a list of world cities from 15 sources drawn from all four approaches described above. Of the 79 cities that were identified, 25 were mentioned by just one source and only 4 were unanimously endorsed (i.e. London, New York, Paris and Tokyo).

Based on Sassen's (1991, p. 126) argument that advanced producer services (i.e. 'post-industrial production sites ... that have a specific role in the current phase of the world economy') are the distinctive feature of contemporary world city formation, Beaverstock et al. (1999) developed a new roster of world cities based on the 'global capacity' (i.e. concentrations of expertise and knowledge) of cities in terms of the services they provide in accounting, advertising, banking and law. Cities are evaluated as global service centres in each of these sectors, and aggregation of these results provides a measure of each one's global capacity or the extent to which it can be considered a global city.

As summarized in Table 13.1, there is a hierarchy of 10 'Alpha' world cities, 10 'Beta' world cities and 35 'Gamma' world cities, with 68 cities clearly indicating world city formation characteristics (i.e. 'delta' world cities). In the empirical section of this chapter, I adopt Beaverstock et al.'s (1999)[1] approach as it is comprehensive, theoretically directed and empirically transparent. To this list of world cities I added a group of 437 that had more than one million inhabitants (i.e. million+ cities). This group of large urban agglomerations was intended to determine whether MNC behaviour was influenced as much by a given city's size as by its world city stature and

Table 13.1 Roster of world cities

Alpha world cities (n = 10)		Beta world cities (n = 10)			Gamma world cities (n = 35)			Delta world cities (n = 67)		
Group α₁ (n = 4)	Group α₂ (n = 6)	Group β₁ (n = 4)	Group β₂ (n = 4)	Group β₃ (n = 2)	Group γ₁ (n = 15)	Group γ₂ (n = 5)	Group γ₃ (n = 15)	Group δ₁ (n = 11)	Group δ₂ (n = 26)	Group δ₃ (n = 30)
London	Chicago	San Francisco	Brussels	Moscow	Amsterdam	Bangkok	Atlanta	Auckland	Abu Dhabi	Adelaide
New York	Frankfurt	Sydney	Madrid	Seoul	Boston	Beijing	Barcelona	Dublin	Almaty	Antwerp
Paris	Hong Kong	Toronto	Mexico City		Caracas	Rome	Berlin	Helsinki	Athens	Arhus
Tokyo	Los Angeles	Zurich	Sao Paulo		Dallas	Stockholm	Buenos Aires	Luxembourg	Birmingham	Baltimore
	Milan				Düsseldorf	Warsaw	Budapest	Lyon	Bogotá	Bangalore
	Singapore				Geneva		Copenhagen	Mumbai	Bratislava	Bologna
					Houston		Hamburg	New Delhi	Brisbane	Brazilia
					Jakarta		Istanbul	Philadelphia	Bucharest	Calgary
					Johannesburg		Kuala Lumpur	Rio de Janeiro	Cairo	Cape Town
					Melbourne		Manila	Tel Aviv	Cleveland	Colombo
					Osaka		Miami	Vienna	Cologne	Columbus
					Prague		Minneapolis		Detroit	Dresden
					Santiago		Montreal		Dubai	Edinburgh
					Taipei		Munich		Ho Chi Ming City	Genoa
					Washington		Shanghai		Kiev	Glasgow
									Lima	Gothenburg
									Lisbon	Guangzhou
									Manchester	Hanoi
									Montevideo	Kansas City
									Oslo	Leeds
									Rotterdam	Lille
									Riyadh	Marseille
									Seattle	Richmond
									Stuttgart	St Petersburg
									The Hague	Tashkent
									Vancouver	Tehran
										Tijuana
										Turin
										Utrecht
										Wellington

233

resources. The reason behind my choice of cities of a million people or more follows the common practice among city demographers to use that figure as a threshold (e.g. see United Nations, 2001). The city list was obtained from Brinkhoff (2006), based on official censuses and estimations.

WHAT IS THE RELATIONSHIP BETWEEN GLOBAL CITIES AND MNC INVESTMENT?

To assess the extent to which global cities are relevant in the study of MNC investment, I compiled a data set on the locational choices of 3486 MNCs that owned 17 804 foreign subsidiaries in 104 countries in 2000.[2] The primary source of these data is a survey published by *Kaigai Shinshutsu Kigyou Souran*, a publication of Toyo Keizai Shinposha (Toyo Keizai, 2000). Toyo Keizai (which translates to Oriental Economist) was formed in 1895 and currently publishes more than 100 volumes annually as well as a variety of data covering economic conditions, stock markets and Japanese corporations. The surveys, which were sent to the subsidiaries through their parent firms, were completed by the subsidiary general managers with a response rate of 60 per cent. The survey requested basic facts such as subsidiary location, foundation date, industry, annual revenue, capital invested and equity partner identities (if any).

My data on MNC subsidiaries were coded as being either within a given city on my designated list or not. Many subsidiaries, however, were often not within the city but were instead part of the urban agglomerations that sprawl adjacent to official city boundaries. This fact is usually accommodated by considering locations within the area of contiguous urban density (e.g. the surrounding metropolitan area) as part of the focal city (e.g. see Brinkhoff, 2006; United Nations, 2001). In fact, the concept of the 'global city-region' is considered by many to be a more relevant unit of analysis, since researchers are usually less interested in technical city boundaries and more interested in the impact of major urban agglomerations on the world economy (Sassen, 2001; Scott et al., 2001). For these reasons, I coded my data to include both global cities, strictly defined, as well as global city metropolitan regions as described below.

As summarized in Table 13.2, global cities are clearly related to MNC investment behaviour. The MNCs in my sample had 3552 subsidiaries, or 20 per cent of the total, in the set of alpha world cities alone (i.e. London, Chicago, New York, Frankfurt, Paris, Hong Kong, Tokyo, Los Angeles, Milan, Singapore). Further, if their metropolitan areas are considered, more than 26 per cent of all MNC subsidiaries are located in alpha world cities. According to Beaverstock et al.'s (1999) definition of bona fide global cities (alpha, beta and gamma cities), the MNCs in my sample had 55 per cent of their subsidiaries in these 55 world cities. In contrast, only 16 per cent of MNC subsidiaries were located in my list of 437 million+ cities, and all other locations (i.e. a virtually infinite list of all other locations not identified as a global or a million+ city) attracted only 19 per cent of the overall total of 17 804 subsidiaries in 2000. These results are more striking when you consider the fact that there are only 10 alpha cities and a total of 55 global cities in the world.

Table 13.2   MNC investment location

Investment location	City type		Metropolitan city type	
	Frequency	Per cent	Frequency	Per cent
Alpha world cities (*n* = 10)	3 552	20.0	4 664	26.2
Beta world cities (*n* = 10)	879	4.9	1 331	7.5
Gamma world cities (*n* = 35)	3 317	18.6	3 707	20.8
Delta world cities (*n* = 67)	1 355	7.6	1 845	10.4
Million+ cities (*n* = 437)	2 324	13.1	2 916	16.4
All other locations (*n* = ∞)	6 377	35.8	3 341	18.8
Total	17 804		17 804	

The overwhelming majority of MNC investments in Asia (by Japanese MNCs) are in global cities. Over 70 per cent of the total of 8597 subsidiaries are in these locations whereas 20 per cent are in million+ cities and only 9 per cent are in all other places.[3] In North America, however, while a majority of MNC investments are still in global cities (54 per cent) a much larger proportion of subsidiaries are found outside global and million+ cities; almost 30 per cent of the total of 4021 subsidiaries are found in other locations. Similarly in Europe, MNC investment in global cities is 67 per cent of the total (2273 subsidiaries) and 29 per cent are in these other locations. In part, this may be because of the fact that the economies of North America and Europe are more developed and, as a result, the amenities and resources required by MNCs are more widely dispersed as compared with Asian countries.

In the case of the regions that are outside the economic triad (i.e. South America, Oceania, Africa and the Middle East) each appears to have a different story. In South America, for example, while a majority of investments are still in global cities (i.e. 51 per cent) a significant number are located in million+ cities (29 per cent) and fewer in other locations (20 per cent). In contrast, MNC investments in Africa take on a very different pattern, with only 24 per cent in global cities (not surprisingly given that there are few) and 47 per cent in million+ cities and a full 30 per cent in other locations. Taken together, it is clear that each region is quite different and that generalization across economic zones that vary widely in their levels of economic development is problematic. It appears that MNC investments outside the key economies of the triad (Europe, Japan and the US) may be based on quite different considerations, perhaps in keeping with Dunning's (1993) suggestion that the strategic motivations of MNC investments may vary based on their desire to capture strategic assets, markets, resources, and/or lower factor costs.

The figures above indicate that that there are regional effects on MNC propensity to invest inside global cities that may relate, for example, to the level of economic development as well as to MNC strategic objectives. I also examine the extent to which industry membership plays a role. My data suggest, for example, that the manufacturing sector (SIC 2000–3999) is heavily represented by the MNCs, making up a total of 64 per cent of foreign subsidiaries, followed distantly by the wholesale and retail trade with 23 per cent. Based on this overview of MNC investment worldwide, we see that a full 40 per cent of all foreign subsidiaries are manufacturers located in global cities. Further, based on the difference between global cities and global cities in the case of manufacturers (i.e. 14 per cent versus 40 per cent, respectively), it appears that manufacturers are attracted by global cities yet do not locate centrally, preferring the outlying metropolitan areas. This may be to avoid the higher costs associated with central cities as well as providing greater ability to move and grow in the nearby suburbs.

It is also valuable to take a closer look into investment behaviour by MNCs within their primary industry. Whereas the figures above showed that investment in agriculture, forestry and fishing (SIC 100–900) was relatively sparse, my data indicate that a significant share (i.e. 39 per cent) of these subsidiaries are nonetheless located in global cities. Further, MNCs in that industry appear to divide their investments fairly equally among global cities, million+ cities and other locations – an effect that might be related to an equal need to locate close to both their sources of production and their major consuming markets. In construction (SIC 1000–1500), manufacturing (SIC 2000–3999), transportation and communication (SIC 4000–4900), wholesale trade (SIC 5000–5900) and services (SIC 7000–8700) there appears to be a fairly consistent story in which most MNCs invest overwhelmingly in global cities (82 per cent, 62 per cent, 78 per cent, 69 per cent and 69 per cent, respectively). In contrast, investment in million+ cities is comparatively modest; in manufacturing and services, for example, only 15 per cent and 17 per cent, respectively, of subsidiaries are located in these population centres, with only 22 per cent and 14 per cent located in all other places combined. An even more striking example of the draw of global cities can be found in the case of finance, insurance and real estate (SIC 6000–6700), where 89 per cent of all subsidiaries are located in global cities, and 45 per cent within the central cities themselves. The corresponding figures for million+ cities as well as for all other locations are low, with only 11 per cent of all financial services subsidiaries combined.

Thus far, the description of MNC investment by location and industry I have provided has focused on the MNC's primary industry. In the section below, therefore, I provide a breakdown of investment characteristics based on the subsidiaries' activities. The subsidiary general managers characterized their local activities as either manufacturing, wholesale/retail, or services. Of the 17 804 foreign subsidiaries in my sample, 44 per cent listed themselves as manufacturers, and of these 3943 firms, 51 per cent were located in global cities, 24 per cent in cities with more than one million inhabitants, and 25 per cent in all other locations. Even more striking are the group of subsidiaries engaged in wholesale/retail activities, 78 per cent of which are located in global cities, with only 8 per cent and 14 per cent in million+ cities and all other locations, respectively.

According to my figures, there appears to be no difference in the nominal amount of capital invested in subsidiaries across location types, yet the operations established in million+ cities and to a lesser extent all other cities, are somewhat larger employers, with an average of 159, 293 and 230 employees, respectively. Further, MNC subsidiaries in global cities tend to have a higher number of expatriates, particularly as a ratio of expatriates to total employees. Finally, subsidiaries established in global cities tend to be somewhat older that those established in other locations, perhaps not surprisingly since these cities tend to have long histories as commercial centres.

When I compare subsidiary ownership patterns, it is evident that there are significant differences in the propensity of MNCs to enter into joint ventures (JVs) versus wholly-owned subsidiaries. This effect is most pronounced in Asia where 55 per cent of MNC subsidiaries located in global cities are joint ventures, as compared with 72 per cent in million+ cities. Similarly, in North America, 83 per cent of MNC investments in global cities are wholly owned, versus 67 per cent in other cities (i.e. neither global nor million+ cities). In the North American context, however, there is little difference in the propensity to establish wholly-owned operations when comparing global and million+ cities (83 per cent versus 80 per cent) yet there is a significant gap in these locations in terms of joint ventures (17 per cent versus 33 per cent). In Europe there are significant differences in the propensity to establish wholly-owned operations when comparing global cities, million+ cities and all other cities (82 per cent, 77 per cent and 70 per cent, respectively) as well as joint ventures (18 per cent, 23 per cent, and 30 per cent, respectively). While the differences suggest that regional effects are also at play, in all cases we see a greater propensity to enter into wholly-owned subsidiaries in global cities versus non-global cities, as well as a lower propensity to enter into joint ventures in global versus non-global cities. This may be the result of superior resources available in global cities, or perhaps more capable firms that do not require the capabilities of partners to invest abroad.

To this point my description has related to MNC subsidiaries, yet it is also important to examine the characteristics of the parent firms. Based on the firms in my sample, it appears that 'global city-centric' firms (i.e. those with more than 75 per cent of their subsidiaries in global cities) appear to be somewhat different from other MNCs. They are somewhat smaller in terms of both average assets and revenues. Similarly, global city-centric firms average 2066 employees versus 2888 for all other MNCs in my sample (see Table 13.3).

Table 13.3   Comparison of global city-centric MNCs

	Global city-centric MNCs	Other MNCs
Assets ($US million)	$212.4	$307.6
Sales ($US million)	$176.5	$294.9
Employees	2066	2888
R&D intensity	0.8%	1.4%
Advertising intensity	1.5%	0.9%
Product diversity entropy score	1.0	1.3
No. of nations	10.7	11.8
No. of subsidiaries	19.6	31.5
No. of JVs	9.7	19.6
JV ratio	46.2%	53.0%
Repeat ratio	29.5%	37.8%

Whereas proprietary assets are often seen as the primary drivers of foreign investment, these data indicate that global city-centric firms tend to spend somewhat less on technical assets (i.e. R&D intensity is 0.8 per cent versus 1.4 per cent for other MNCs), but somewhat more on advertising assets (i.e. advertising intensity is 1.5 per cent versus 0.9 per cent). Further, not only are global city-centric firms more focused – as indicated by their product diversity entropy score of 1.0 versus 1.3 for other MNCs, they also have far fewer subsidiaries, fewer JVs, a lesser propensity to enter into JVs, and a reduced propensity to enter into JVs with repeat partners.

Although the descriptive findings discussed above suggest that global city attributes are major considerations in MNC investment, prior studies rarely indicate that managers are explicitly aware of the global city phenomenon. However, interviews with several senior managers at InBev SA, the world's largest brewer, suggested that some firms are developing a clear focus on global cities as an investment platform, as described below.

GLOBAL CITIES AS AN INVESTMENT PLATFORM – AN EXAMPLE

As InBev (created by the merger of Interbrew and Companhia de Bebidas das Américas) developed its global brewing plans with strong local brands in addition to successful global brands, managers applied several strategic filters to yield a smaller set of attractive opportunities. The first filter that any initiative had to pass through was an analysis of either a large and/or a growing market. This screen had the net effect of eliminating sparsely populated and rural areas, focusing instead on urban centres where critical mass would be more easily achieved. The second screen was an analysis of margins that would remain attractive after the initial investment was made. This screen also led to an increasing focus on cities that were relatively more affluent, where margins tend to respond to concentrated promotional spending. The third filter that initiatives had to pass through was whether or not a committed local partner was available that could attain good distribution and was willing to co-invest. Given that distribution systems were more highly developed in major population centres, this screen had a similar effect to the previous two in that it shifted InBev's focus towards large urban areas. The final screen was the determination that the investment would increase leverage in other local and regional markets. InBev's previous experience had shown that success in national markets such as the UK, Central Europe, and the USA often could be traced back to a market pull following on the heels of a successful market push in a key, trend-setting city.

Once filtered through these strategic market development screens, this approach led InBev away from a national market perspective and their plans began to take shape around a city-centric view of their potential investment opportunities. Thus the evolving global development plan required much more careful planning on a city-by-city basis, moving away from the more traditional national market perspective. Among the demands of this new approach were that promotional efforts and the funding to support them would have to be both centrally stewarded and locally tailored to reflect the unique local environments. The corporate group would thereby be charged with the responsibility to identify top priority markets and guidelines for local execution, and to allocate resources to achieve the objectives.

In the mid-1990s, for example, InBev began its efforts to establish Stella Artois as a global brand[4] first by focusing on certain key major cities in which Interbrew already had a strong position (e.g. London, Brussels, New York, etc.), subsequently moving to such large, high potential markets as Moscow, Los Angeles and Hong Kong, and then various key Central European cities including Budapest, Zagreb, Bucharest and Sofia. The success of InBev's global development experience appeared to be derived from the careful and concentrated targeting of urban centres where demand pull for their products from outlying areas followed a successful market push in key cities.

A FINAL WORD

One of the basic ideas that underpins the global city concept in its functional role in the global economy is that the resources and capabilities of cities interact with those of MNCs to create forces that attract (or repel) investment in particular locations, yet previous streams of research that include MNC investment, expatriate management and entry mode, to name a few, have generally used the country as a basic unit of analysis. Based on a descriptive analysis of my data, however, it appears clear that different echelons of global cities vary in their relationships with MNC investment behaviour, and that these variances are also dependent on region. While my data examine only Japanese MNCs, I suspect that firms from other countries of origin have varying needs and, therefore, probably different responses to the attractions of global cities.

The work of Beaverstock et al. (1999) used in this chapter is a systematic, multi-sector assessment of cities that produced an inventory of contemporary world cities, but, if this list is inadequate or incomplete, it may be worthwhile to examine the distinguishing features of cities that emphasize other aspects that are important for MNC investment. Urban agglomerations, such as global cities, may take varying forms, but most include end-product or service companies; suppliers of specialized inputs, components, machinery and services; financial institutions; and firms in related industries. According to Porter (2000, p. 254), they also often include firms in downstream industries, producers of complementary products, and specialized infrastructure providers, as well as a number of institutions including government that provide specialized training, education, information, research and technical support. Finally, many clusters include trade organizations and other collective private sector bodies that support cluster members. This suggests that other locational configurations, including traditional downtown centres, newer business centres, 'edge' cities and various specialized subcentres may be more meaningful in a given research context.

In addition to the managerial relevance of global cities, this topic also has public policy implications; if MNCs choose global cities, then they are involved in a process of increasing inequality, a proposition discussed by Sassen (1994) and by Hymer's (1972) 'law of uneven development'. This phenomenon has been recently described by Pezzini (2003) who found that between 1975 and 1995, regional unemployment rates in OECD countries differed by more than 30 per cent from national ones, and in some countries by even more than 60 per cent. Through this process of unequal economic development, Sassen (1997) and others have suggested that global cities are disconnecting from their regions; as a result, New York City might have more in common with Tokyo than it does with other more proximate communities in the state of New York. Similarly, in Canada for example, Toronto, Montreal and Vancouver generate more than half of the economic output of their respective provinces. Thus vast territories are becoming more peripheral, excluded from the processes that fuel growth. Formerly important economic centers have spiralled downward, while activities ancillary to certain sectors (e.g. hotels, upscale boutiques and elite restaurants that surround the financial sector) succeed. Specific downtown areas and business centers receive massive investments in real estate and telecommunications, while low-income areas continue to be starved of resources. Certain industries produce superprofits and others barely survive. Highly educated workers see their incomes rise to stratospheric levels, while less skilled workers see their opportunities and wages spiral downwards.

Although there has been extensive literature on the impact of MNCs on host economies that include employment, training, technology transfer, contribution to the balance of payments, supply of foreign exchange, creation of demand expectations, stimulation of entrepreneurship and provision of spillovers to suppliers, customers and competitors (e.g. see Dunning, 1993), there are also numerous opportunities for future research on the connection between public micropolicy (i.e. governance of global cities) and private firms such as MNCs. Some topics that emerge relate to the development of the physical infrastructure, human capital, technology base and inter-firm cooperation that are viewed as necessary to support cluster growth and internationalization (Enright, 1999).

One possible result of the tension between globalization and agglomerations at the city level is that we might end up with firm configurations that include tight coupling across geographically separated clusters, so that a few linked 'hub locations' or 'technology districts' could dominate the world in a particular industry (Storper, 1991; Zaheer and Manrakhan, 2001).

While the logic of MNC investment appears to be influenced by the local characteristics of location, it is an empirical question as to the performance benefits for those entities that are willing and able to participate in global cities. In theory, they may receive a boost by being part of tightly linked and spatially concentrated clusters, not only because clustering greatly mitigates transactions costs, but also because of the flexibility and information effects. Also, as described by Scott et al. (2001), creativity and innovation in global cities may be enhanced because of the variety of skills and experiences within the labour force.

Location has been described as the central question that defines international business research. The descriptive results in this chapter, coupled with the work of Enright (1998, 1999), Porter (2000), Sassen (1991, 1994, 1996a, 1996b, 1997, 2001), Saxenian (1990) and others, suggests clearly that urban agglomerations such as global cities should be an important part of future study on MNC behaviour and performance.

NOTES

1. For a detailed description of their methodology, see Beaverstock et al. (1999).
2. My sincere thanks go to Takehiko Isobe (Kobe U) who very generously shared important parts of this data.
3. To conserve space, the detailed tables are not provided in this chapter. However, those interested are welcome to contact the author to obtain more detail on the figures that support this discussion.
4. For more information, see 'Global Branding of Stella Artois' (case no. 9B00A019), available from Ivey Publishing at http://cases.ivey.uwo.ca/

REFERENCES

Beaverstock, J., R. Smith and P. Taylor (1999), 'A roster of world cities', *Cities*, **6**, 445–58.

Bhagwati, J., A. Panagariya and T. Srinivastan (2004), 'The muddles over outsourcing', *Journal of Economic Perspectives*, **18**, 93–114.

Brinkhoff, T. (2006), 'The principal agglomerations of the world', http://www.citypopulation.de: accessed on 28 January 2006.

Buckley, P. and P. Ghauri (2004), 'Globalization, economic geography and the strategy of multinational firms', *Journal of International Business Studies*, **35**, 81–98.

Cohen, R. (1981), 'The new international division of labour, multinational corporations and urban hierarchy', in M. Dear and A. Scott (eds), *Urbanisation and Urban Planning in Capitalist Society*, London: Methuen.

Derudder, B., P. Taylor, F. Witlox and G. Catalano (2003), 'Hierarchical tendencies and regional patterns in the world city network: a global urban analysis of 234 cities', *Regional Studies*, **37**, 875–86.

Dunning, J. (1993), *Multinational Enterprises and the Global Economy*, Wokingham: Addison-Wesley.

The Economist (2005), 'The human cost of cheaper towels', 23–29 April, 30.

Enright, M. (1998), 'Regional clusters and firm strategy', in A. Chandler, O. Solvell and P. Hagstrom (eds), *The Dynamic Firm: The Role of Technology, Strategy, Organization, and Regions*, Oxford: Oxford University Press.

Enright, M. (1999), 'Globalization, regionalization and the knowledge-based economy of Hong Kong', in J. Dunning (ed.), *Regions, Globalization and the Knowledge-based Economy*, Oxford: Oxford University Press.

Feldman, M. and D. Audretsch (1999), 'Innovation in cities: science-based diversity, specialization, and localized competition', *European Economic Review*, **11**, 283–96.

Friedmann, J. (1986), 'The world city hypothesis', *Development and Change*, **17**, 69–83.

Goerzen, A. (2005a), 'Managing alliance networks: emerging practices of multinational corporations', *Academy of Management Executive*, **19**, 94–107.

Goerzen, A. (2005b), *Networks and Location: Organizing the Diversified Multinational Corporation for Value Creation*, New York: Palgrave McMillan.

Goerzen, A. and P. Beamish (2005), 'The effect of alliance network diversity on multinational enterprise performance', *Strategic Management Journal*, **26**, 333–54.

Hall, P. (1966), *The World Cities*, London: Heinemann.

Harrison, A. and M. McMillan (2006), 'Dispelling some myths about offshoring', *Academy of Management Perspectives*, **20** (4), 6–23.

Hymer, S. (1972), 'The multinational corporation and the law of uneven development', in J. Bhagwati (ed.), *Economics and World Order from the 1970s to the 1990s*, New York: Collier-Macmillan.

Krugman, P. (1991), *Geography and Trade*, Cambridge, MA: MIT Press.

Pezzini, M. (2003), *Main Trends and Policy Challenges in OECD Regions: Metropolitan Regions in a Global Context*, Paris: OECD.

Porter, M. (2000), 'Locations, clusters, and company strategy', in G. Clark, M. Gertler and M. Feldman (eds), *The Oxford Handbook of Economic Geography*, Oxford: Oxford University Press.

Reed, H. (1981), *The Preeminence of International Financial Centers*, New York: Praeger.

Ricart, J., M. Enright, P. Ghemawat, S. Hart and T. Khanna (2004), 'New frontiers in international strategy', *Journal of International Business Studies*, **35**, 175–200.

Sassen, S. (1991), *The Global City: New York, London, Tokyo*, Princeton, NJ: Princeton University Press.

Sassen, S. (1994), *Cities in a World Economy*, Thousand Oaks, CA: Pine Forge/Sage.

Sassen, S. (1996a), *Losing Control? Sovereignty in an Age of Globalization*, New York: Columbia University Press.

Sassen, S. (1996b), 'Whose city is it? Globalisation and the formation of new claims', *Public Culture*, **8** (2), 205–23.

Sassen, S. (1997), 'Global cities: a challenge for urban scholarship', http://www.columbia.edu/cu/21stC/issue-2.4/sassen.html, accessed on 18 May 2005.

Sassen, S. (2001), 'Global cities and global city-regions: a comparison', in A. Scott (ed.), *Global City-regions: Trends, Theory, Policy*, Oxford: Oxford University Press.

Saxenian, A. (1990), 'Regional networks and the resurgence of Silicon Valley', *California Management Review*, **33**, 89–111.

Scott, A. (1998), 'The geographic foundations of industrial performance', in A. Chandler, O. Solvell and P. Hagstrom (eds), *The Dynamic Firm: The Role of Technology, Strategy, Organization, and Regions*, Oxford: Oxford University Press.

Scott, A., J. Agnew, E. Soja and M. Storper (2001), 'Global city-regions', in A. Scott (ed.), *Global City-regions: Trends, Theory, Policy*, Oxford: Oxford University Press.

Short, J., C. Breitbach, S. Buckman and J. Essex (2000), 'From world cities to gateway cities', *City*, **4**, 317–40.

Storper, M. (1991), 'The limits to globalization: technology districts and international trade', *Economic Geography*, **68**, 60–93.

Taylor, P., D. Walker and J. Beaverstock (2002), 'Firms and their global service networks', in S. Sassen (ed.), *Global Networks, Linked Cities*, New York: Routledge.

Toyo Keizai (2000), *Kaigai Shinshutsu Kigyou Souran-kuni Betsu*, Tokyo: Toyo Keizai Ltd.

UNCTAD (2000), *World Investment Report*, New York: United Nations.

United Nations (2001), *World Urbanization Prospects: The 2001 Revision*, New York: United Nations.

Vernon, R. (1971), *Sovereignty at Bay: The Multinational Spread of US Enterprises*, New York: Basic Books.

Zaheer, S. and S. Manrakhan (2001), 'Concentration and dispersion in global industries: remote electronic access and the location of economic activities', *Journal of International Business Studies*, **32**, 667–87.

14. Cultural and institutional determinants of agglomeration

Robert Salomon and Zheying Wu

Location choice is an integral, yet often overlooked, facet of firm strategy (Porter, 2000). Through its impact on operating costs and revenues, a firm's choice of location can have lasting effects on performance, survival and success. Moreover, location decisions can influence the development of a firm's competitive advantage.

Although scholars from various disciplines recognize the importance of location to performance (e.g. Marshall, 1920; Pouder and St John, 1996; DeCarolis and Deeds, 1999), less attention has been devoted to the determinants of location choice. In particular, we understand less than we should about how national culture and the institutional environment affect location choice within and across countries. To fill this gap, we examine the cultural and institutional determinants of agglomeration – that is, the choice to locate in a geographic cluster of industrial activity. The decision to agglomerate probably varies across national contexts, and culture and institutions play an important role in that decision. Specifically, we believe that a firm's incentives to agglomerate vary with the cultural and institutional context of a given country.

Moreover, because foreign investments into a particular country come from countries that do not share the same cultural and institutional environment, we consider how home and host country characteristics have an influence on the location decisions of firms making foreign investments. Since a foreign entrant is subject to the cultural and institutional environment of the host country, and that of its home country, we theorize that the location choices of foreign direct investments (FDIs) are impacted by the cultural norms and the institutional uncertainty of both countries.

This chapter makes several contributions to the extant strategy, international business and economics literatures. Theoretically, it sheds light on the cultural and institutional antecedents of location choice. Though industrial organization and strategy scholars have studied the impact of natural endowments, resource scarcity, and firm-specific characteristics on location choice, to our knowledge no study has focused on its macro-level cultural and institutional determinants. Moreover, where most studies that examine agglomeration continue to use data from a single economy, we argue that cross-country panel data can be fruitfully exploited to test cultural and institutional effects. We therefore propose practical suggestions to operationalize and test the phenomena. Finally, this chapter reminds us of the central role that cultural and institutional environments can play in business activities.

The chapter is organized as follows: we first review prior literature on the determinants of location choice. Based on this review we develop propositions related to the cultural and institutional determinants of agglomeration. We subsequently offer suggestions to test the propositions. The final section concludes.

LITERATURE REVIEW

Because the outcomes of location decisions are long-lasting and often irreversible, location choice can have enduring implications for firm performance. Firms are impacted by the resources available within their local environment; therefore, they tend to carefully consider such decisions. Recognizing this, scholars in different disciplines have studied the antecedents to location choice. Economics scholars have predominantly focused on what causes firms to select particular geographical locations in the first place. On the input side, economic geographers note that resource endowments and the availability (scarcity) of human capital can facilitate (restrict) a firm's development. For this reason, firms should favor sites that are rich with various input factors in order to minimize costs (Ghosh and Rushton, 1987; Weber, 1929). Work in industrial organization, by contrast, maintains that firms should maximize their proximity to customers, yet keep their distance from competitors so as to avoid head-to-head competition (Hotelling, 1929).

Building on this latter insight, research on firm location choice in the strategy literature has centered on whether firms choose to locate geographically proximal or distal to one another. This phenomenon has been referred to as agglomeration (see Shaver and Flyer, 2000, for a review). Agglomeration, or the geographical clustering of firms, can have both positive and negative consequences for these firms. On the one hand, an agglomeration of firms can generate beneficial externalities. For example, Marshall (1920) argued that the clustering of similar firms creates a pool of specialized labor that can be shared among members of the agglomeration. Firms in the agglomeration benefit from specialized suppliers that increase the competitiveness of the industry (Porter, 2000). Moreover, locating close to similar firms affords firms the opportunity to share knowledge with others or absorb knowledge through competitive spillovers (Marshall, 1920). Firms can learn from their competitors' experiences, and competition may improve the performance of firms within the agglomeration (Shaver and Flyer, 2000; Chung and Song, 2004). Therefore, such positive externalities motivate firms to agglomerate.

On the other hand, scholars note that agglomerating does not come without costs. As the number of firms requiring similar resources in an agglomeration increases, competition intensifies, which leads to a corresponding increase in firm failure (Hannan and Carroll, 1992; Hannan et al., 1995). Moreover, competition for similar inputs and markets can be especially intense among firms in an agglomeration, especially if they produce homogeneous goods (Fischer and Harrington, 1996). Such competition can lead to increased human resource costs and land rents, and may result in entrenchment (Hoen, 2001; Porter, 1998; Schmutzler, 1999). Firms located closely together may also suffer from 'groupthink' – that is, they may become resistant to new ideas and innovation (Hoen, 2001). For these reasons, firms that are similar to their competitors may strategically avoid collocating with them and therefore have a disincentive to agglomerate (Baum and Haveman, 1997).

The aforementioned literature suggests that firms decide whether or not to agglomerate by assessing the advantages and disadvantages given the specific external market conditions they face and their individual internal characteristics. This supports a contingent view of agglomeration; that is, agglomerating may be better for some firms than for others. Moreover, agglomerating may be better in certain contexts than in others. For example, Shaver and Flyer (2000) argued that although firms benefit from inward knowledge spillovers in an agglomeration, they also contribute knowledge to the agglomeration by generating outward spillovers. Therefore, to avoid information leakage, firms with better technology or stronger capabilities are less likely to agglomerate. Similarly, Chung and Song (2004) discovered that firms with little or no experience are more likely to locate their early ventures close to competitors. They argued that investment reflects a learning process in which firms with less experience disproportionately benefit from proximity to their competitors. Furthermore, Sorenson and Audia (2000) found that location choice is influenced by social networks. They studied the location pattern of new ventures in the US footwear industry and, despite intense competition, they found that entrepreneurial ventures were more likely to agglomerate because the local area provided social resources for these firms. That is, even in the face of fierce competition, entrepreneurs felt they benefited from having ties to their existing social networks and therefore preferred not to risk losing those ties by locating farther away. Taken together, these studies demonstrate that firms do not uniformly decide to agglomerate, but instead they must carefully weigh concerns about firm characteristics and the environment.

In summary, research in strategy and economics has examined the antecedents to, and consequences of, agglomeration. Although many of these studies examine agglomeration within the context of a specific country, there are few studies of agglomeration using multi-country samples. Moreover, one important antecedent of location choice remains relatively understudied. To our knowledge, there has been little examination of the impact of culture and institutions on agglomeration patterns. Cultures and institutions normalize firm activities and shape the environment in which firms are embedded. These forces stand to moderate the impact of agglomeration externalities on firms; that is, in certain cultural and institutional environments, firms may benefit more from agglomerating, while in other environments firms may benefit less. In the next section we discuss how culture and institutions are likely to affect a firm's decision to agglomerate.

THEORY

Culture

Firms are embedded in a social context. One of the most important factors in this context is national culture. Culture normalizes the behavior of organizational actors within societies (Hofstede, 2001). As a product of the societies from which they are born, firms are inherently imprinted with societal norms. Conforming to these norms benefits firms by helping to justify their existence and increasing their chances for survival (DiMaggio and Powell, 1983; Meyer and Rowan, 1977). Thus culture deeply influences firm behavior.

Prior literature has investigated the impact of national culture on firm behavior. For example, national culture has been shown to have a significant effect on managerial goals, management processes and organizational values (Hofstede, 1985, 1994; Hofstede et al., 2002). Similarly, Kogut and Singh (1988) found that cultural distance impacts the behavior of firms entering new markets. Although these studies do not focus on location choice per se, they imply that national culture impacts the decisions and activities of firms. We likewise expect culture to have a significant impact on firm behavior with respect to agglomeration.

Though national culture has multiple dimensions (Hofstede, 2001), we focus on the continua of individualism/collectivism and uncertainty avoidance as the cultural factors most likely to influence agglomeration. Individualism/collectivism addresses the relationship between individual members of a society and its groups. Because an agglomeration is formed by a group of similar firms, this cultural dimension is likely to influence an individual firm's desire to join the group. By contrast, uncertainty avoidance captures societal attitudes toward risk, ambiguity and unpredictability. Firms often face a great deal of uncertainty when making location decisions and will factor this uncertainty into their decision processes. The level of uncertainty avoidance in a society may therefore influence a firm's location preference. Though the other cultural dimensions (i.e. masculinity, power distance, and long-term orientation) describe important features of national culture, we believe they are less relevant to explaining a firm's likelihood to join an agglomeration.

Individualism refers to the extent to which decisions are made independent of larger group interests and norms, while collectivism encompasses the willingness to cooperate, an emphasis on relationships, and subordination to larger group goals (Hofstede, 2001; Morris et al., 1994; Triandis, 1995). An important attribute of collectivism is the power of social norms (Triandis, 1995). While an individualist culture encourages social members to preserve and protect individual values and norms, a collectivist culture places greater emphasis on the adoption of group norms. Because cultural expectations normalize behavior (DiMaggio and Powell, 1983; Hofstede, 2001), a firm in a collectivist culture is likely to follow the norms set by the majority. By contrast, decisions that deviate from those of the group are more socially acceptable in an individualist culture.

Following the above logic, we can plausibly expect firms in countries characterized by collectivist cultures to be more likely to join an agglomeration. From an economic perspective, it could be that the positive externalities associated with agglomeration are enhanced (diminished) in a collectivist (individualist) culture, while the negative consequences of agglomeration are diminished (enhanced). Collectivist cultures put greater emphasis on relationships, harmony and within-group cooperation (Chen et al., 2002). Therefore, in a collectivist country, firms within an agglomeration may be more willing to share their resources and knowledge in order to help each other. In other words, an agglomeration in a collectivist environment may generate more spillovers, and transmit the spillovers more fluently, than an agglomeration in an individualist environment. This is because collectivism suppresses free riding, mitigates opportunistic behavior, induces individuals to sacrifice for the good of the group, and dampens competition within a group (Earley, 1989; Chen et al., 2002). Collectivism thereby acts as a mechanism that increases trust (decreases opportunistic behavior) among group members and reduces transaction costs for firms within the agglomeration. Therefore, although Krugman (1991) and Sorensen and Audia (2000) found that agglomerations are generally characterized by intense competition, the severity of the competition is likely to vary across contexts; that is, collectivist cultures may moderate the intensity of competition among members of the agglomeration. Consequently, firms may have more to gain and less to lose from agglomerating in a country with a collectivist culture.

From a sociological perspective, firms might obtain greater legitimacy by joining an agglomeration in countries characterized by collectivism. Because an agglomeration is a manifestation of group preference, joining an agglomeration may be regarded as rational, efficient and legitimate (Meyer and Rowan, 1977). Therefore, to prevent loss of legitimacy and to enhance chances for survival, firms in a collectivist culture are more likely to adopt societally accepted norms and imitate the location behavior of firms that resemble them. Otherwise stated, because collectivist cultures value conformity with group norms over independent behavior (Morris et al., 1994), firms face greater social pressure to conform, and agglomerating probably represents the most legitimate location choice for these firms. Individualist cultures, by contrast, more readily support independent behavior. In such cultures, deviation from group norms is more socially acceptable. Therefore, choosing a location far away from an agglomeration is more likely to be viewed as socially legitimate as compared to taking the same action in a collectivist culture.

For the reasons stated above, we expect firms in countries characterized by collectivist cultures to be more likely to agglomerate than firms in countries characterized by individualist cultures.

In addition to individualism/collectivism, we believe that uncertainty avoidance represents an important cultural determinant of location choice. Again, uncertainty avoidance refers to responses to unpredictable or ambiguous situations (Hofstede, 2001). Greater values of uncertainty avoidance are associated with higher levels of risk aversion. To cope with uncertainty, individuals in high uncertainty-avoidance cultures often adhere to norms or patterns of behavior to reduce risk (Hofstede, 2001). By contrast, low uncertainty-avoidance cultures are less risk averse and more comfortable operating with ambiguity. Individuals from such cultures generally will not go to extraordinary lengths to mitigate or avoid risk.

By their nature, location decisions involve uncertainty. Firms often put substantial sums of money at risk and make long-term commitments to specific locales. Not only do firms make monetary and time commitments to particular geographic locations, but they are also strongly influenced by the institutions and resources available within the specific environment. One way in which firms can mitigate their exposure to location risk is by agglomerating, which represents the less risky option because specialized inputs are more readily available within an agglomeration (Marshall, 1920). Furthermore, information about inputs such as labor, suppliers, raw materials and infrastructure may be known within the agglomeration, or at the very least be more predictable than in alternative locations in which no similar firms exist.

For these reasons, we expect firms in high uncertainty-avoidance cultures, versus their counterparts in low uncertainty-avoidance cultures, to be more likely to agglomerate. Firms from high uncertainty-avoidance countries see the specialized inputs available within an agglomeration as a means to reduce risk given the input uncertainties faced in alternative locations. That is, firms from high uncertainty-avoidance cultures value those inputs more highly than do firms from low uncertainty-avoidance cultures. By contrast, in countries with low uncertainty-avoidance cultures, firms are more likely to accept the risks that go along with investing in a riskier site.

Institutional Factors

Besides cultural factors, a country's institutional environment also stands to have an impact on firm strategy. Although uncertain market conditions and policies can discourage firms from making investments in the first place (Williamson, 1979), if firms are to invest in particular locations they may strategically locate facilities to mitigate the risks of operating under such uncertainty. We are interested in whether firms agglomerate as a response to uncertainty in the institutional environment.

Political uncertainty can strongly impact firm behavior (Henisz, 2002). Although uncertain political conditions often discourage investment in a particular country (Henisz and Delios, 2001; Henisz and Macher, 2004), firms can develop strategies to decrease risk after making a commitment in a politically uncertain country. For example, one way to decrease risks is to generate more accurate expectations of probable policy changes (Arrow, 1972; Henisz, 2002). To improve expectations, the firm needs a better information set. Because agglomerations generate spillovers of other firms' private knowledge of the political environment (Mariotti and Piscitello, 1995), a firm may choose to agglomerate to better understand and adapt to the political environment. These spillovers of information are likely to be more important to firm performance and survival in an uncertain political environment. A firm may therefore choose to agglomerate in order to preserve proximity to information sources and to obtain better information on policy issues that are of interest to industry participants.

Additionally, a firm may choose to agglomerate in order to increase the power of its industry group vis-à-vis local and national policy makers. A powerful interest group's collective action affords more opportunities to influence policy changes in its favor (Laffont and Tirole, 1991; Olson, 1965). Although industry trade associations mainly lobby on behalf of the group in matters of national-level policy (Porter, 2000), networks established within an agglomeration may have an impact on local, and perhaps national, policies. Furthermore, closely connected groups can coordinate collective actions more efficiently than loosely connected ones (Olson, 1965). Because geographic proximity enables firms to interact with each other more routinely, firms within the agglomeration may have more power to impact policy makers than dispersed firms. As a result, in an uncertain political environment, a firm may agglomerate in order to better mobilize action, if necessary.

In summary, in an environment characterized by uncertain political conditions, agglomerating benefits a firm by allowing it insight into its competitors' policy information, thereby enhancing the positive externalities associated with agglomeration. Moreover, as an interest group, the firms in an agglomeration may be in a better position to influence policy in their favor. We therefore predict that firms will be more likely to locate within an economic agglomeration when political environments are uncertain.

Another source of uncertainty lies in a country's economic institutions. When product-market prices are unpredictable, whether because of a lack of market openness, distortions brought about by regulatory intervention, or inefficient government, the quality of the information that can be gleaned from the market decreases (Hayek, 1945). In such cases, firms have greater difficulty understanding and predicting future economic states of the environment and must rely on information from other sources. One important source of such information lies in the knowledge spillovers generated by firms within an agglomeration. This information, transmitted through the interaction among firms within the agglomeration, is likely to be richer and more reliable than information available in the market (Burt, 1992; Uzzi, 1997). This externality is especially important when firms face greater levels of economic uncertainty, as they may prefer to co-locate to share vital information about the general economic environment. Information sharing among geographically proximal firms may therefore help them cope in the presence of economic uncertainty.

Economic uncertainty may also result from inefficient capital markets. When capital markets are incomplete and financial information is less transparent, banks are reluctant to offer loans to firms whose quality is not readily observable, as unknown quality increases bank risk. In such situations, banks generally rely on social relations and environmental cues (Uzzi and Lancaster, 2003). For example, with limited resources and information, banks generally restrict loans to firms about which they have better information and with which they share ties – for example, those with shared board members or social connections, or from the same geographic area (Gerlach, 1992; Lamoreaux, 1994). Therefore, in countries with weak external capital markets, firms can obtain financial resources on better terms by signaling their quality to banks. One observable and persuasive signal is whether the firm is associated in some way with other reputable corporations (Stuart et al., 1999). A firm may signal its association with or similarity to other reputable corporations by agglomerating. Because the agglomeration includes many similar and related firms, a bank can recognize the common traits of these firms and better infer information about each. As such, banks have better information about the whole. Furthermore, the agglomeration of similar and related firms may motivate local banks to offer these firms specialized service, which will lower their cost of capital, and would be more difficult to acquire from distant banks.

By integrating the above arguments, we contend that in uncertain economic environments, firms can benefit by agglomerating. This strategy may enable firms to obtain information from competitors, signal their quality to external capital markets, and attract specialized financial resources.

To summarize, we propose that firms adapt to the external environment. They internalize cultural and societal norms. Moreover, they anticipate the level of uncertainty in the political and economic environment. As a result, firms make strategic decisions with respect to agglomeration. Figure 14.1 illustrates these effects.

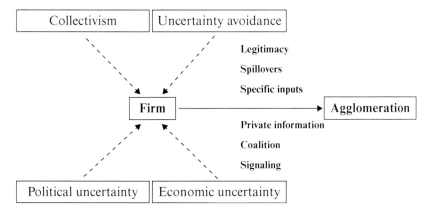

Figure 14.1   External factors and agglomeration

Foreign Direct Investment and Agglomeration

In considering the above arguments regarding culture and institutions, we did not distinguish domestic firms from foreign firms. Foreign firms generally act differently from domestic firms with regard to location choice (Shaver, 1998). These differences may arise for various reasons such as, but not limited to, technological heterogeneity, market segmentation, and the spillover impacts of foreign entry (Shaver, 1998). For our purposes, however, the interesting issue is that foreign firms may act differently from domestic firms because foreign entrants are from nations where the cultural and institutional environments differ from those in the host country.

While purely domestic firms face a constant national context, foreign firms face a more complex environment. On the one hand, subsidiaries of multinational firms are influenced by the forces within the destination country and, as such, are subject to the demands of the local market. On the other hand, foreign subsidiaries are managed by a parent that often originates from a very different cultural and institutional context (Rosenzweig and Singh, 1991; Westney, 2005). Foreign subsidiaries are therefore subject to various cultural and institutional pressures emanating from both the home, and host, countries. The question that follows is whether foreign firms, in deciding whether or not to agglomerate, adapt to those forces in the host country, or preserve patterns of behavior exhibited in their home country.

Scholars in the international business literature suggest that foreign firms face disadvantages relative to domestic firms operating in their home environment. This disadvantage has come to be referred to as the 'liability of foreignness' (Hymer, 1960). Firms that invest abroad face additional costs because of information asymmetries, cultural differences, coordination difficulties, and local biases (Hymer, 1960; Zaheer, 1995; Caves, 1996; Martin and Salomon, 2003a). Empirical results consistent with this theory show that foreign firms take longer to set up (Salomon and Martin, 2006), face higher employee costs (Mincer and Higuchi, 1988; Lipsey, 1994), are subject to more lawsuits than domestic firms (Mezias, 2002), suffer from lower profitability (Zaheer, 1995), and experience a higher probability of failure (Zaheer and Mosakowski, 1997).

To overcome the liability of foreignness, it is important for foreign entrants to establish legitimacy in the domestic environment (Kostova and Zaheer, 1999). The foreign entrant faces greater difficulty than domestic firms because host country governments often impose greater challenges and requirements (Kostova and Zaheer, 1999). One way in which foreign firms may achieve legitimacy in the local market is by adapting to the demands of the local environment, and by imitating the behavior of local firms (Zaheer, 1995; Rosenzweig and Singh, 1991). With respect to location decisions, we believe that this will manifest as an adherence to the cultural and institutional norms of the host environment. That is, we might plausibly expect firms to be more likely to locate within an economic agglomeration when investing abroad if the host country is characterized by a more collectivist culture, a more uncertainty avoiding culture, greater economic uncertainty, or greater political uncertainty.

Although foreign firms have strong incentives to follow host country norms when making location decisions, foreign entrants are also imprinted by their home country's cultural and institutional norms. These norms guide firm behavior, even when entering new markets.

One of the basic premises of research in international business is that in order to succeed abroad, a firm must possess some advantageous, intangible assets and capabilities (Hymer, 1960; Buckley and Casson, 1976). Firms generally develop these capabilities in their home country (Caves, 1996; Martin and Salomon, 2003b). Although these capabilities are born from internal firm resources and routines, they are influenced, and shaped, by the cultural and institutional context within the home country (Kogut, 2005).

When firms expand abroad, they transfer advantages developed in the home country to multiple country markets. Because the practices developed in the home country have been shaped by its cultural and institutional environment, they carry over to its overseas operations (Kogut, 2005; Dicken et al., 1994; Dicken, 2000). For example, foreign subsidiaries often adopt the routines of their parent company (Martin and Salomon, 2003b). Routines develop over time as a result of ongoing interaction between a firm and its environment (Nelson and Winter, 1982). Because routines are slow to evolve and difficult to change (Cyert and March, 1963), they have a stable and durable impact on firm behavior. Consistent with these ideas, empirical evidence shows that firms from different countries differ markedly with respect to their routines, activities and strategies (Dicken, 2000). Moreover, firms generally rely on, and extend, their domestic organizational practices to foreign markets, especially in the early stages of internationalization (Kogut, 2005).

For these reasons, when investing abroad, foreign entrants are likely to imitate location patterns exhibited in the home country. Although foreign firms face pressures to conform to the local cultural and institutional context, they are also influenced, and shaped, by their experience in the home country, and the systematic patterns of behavior exhibited in that country. Therefore, arguments likewise support the view that firms are likely to locate within an economic agglomeration when investing abroad if the home country is characterized by a more collectivist culture, a more uncertainty-avoiding culture, greater economic uncertainty, or greater political uncertainty.

In this section, we suggested that multinational firms are impacted by cultural and institutional forces in both the host and home country environments. These forces exert pressure on firms entering foreign markets, and these pressures are likely to influence their location choice – whether to agglomerate – in the host country. Figure 14.2 illustrates these effects.

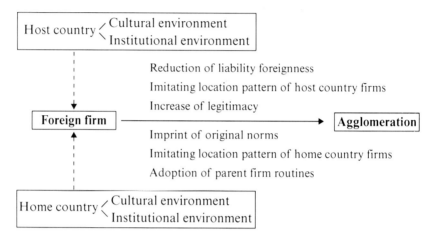

Figure 14.2   The effects of acculturation

DIRECTIONS FOR FUTURE RESEARCH

This chapter suggests a relationship between the cultural and institutional environment of a given country and firm location choice (i.e. the choice to agglomerate in an area of industrial activity). According to our theory, firms internalize cultural and societal norms with respect to location choice. Moreover, they anticipate the uncertainty of operating in a particular environment. As a result, firms make strategic decisions with respect to agglomeration. We also argued that multinational firms (compared with their purely domestic counterparts) face competing pressures with respect to location choice. On the one hand, they are impacted by the cultural and institutional environment of the host nation. On the other, they are influenced by the cultural and institutional environments within their home country. This leads to an interesting tension for firms making investments in foreign countries as it is unclear, a priori, whether firms would be more likely to make location decisions based on patterns exhibited in their home country or in the host country.

We believe that a global industry setting would be most appropriate to test the proposed effects. Global industries are characterized by the exchange of goods across borders and investments in diverse national markets (Martin and Salomon, 2003b). This would afford ample variance across countries, cultures and institutional contexts to test our theory. In addition, because we are likely to observe greater levels of foreign investment in global industries, we can more reasonably test the predictions with regard to foreign investments.

We likewise believe that panel data from a range of countries, as opposed to cross-sectional data from a single economy, would provide the most comprehensive test of our theory. A panel of this sort offers the most detailed view of location activity across various countries over time. Moreover, the panel would allow us to examine agglomeration patterns within countries over time, and to better isolate how changes in the independent variables of interest, versus other sources of heterogeneity, influence agglomeration.

With respect to the dependent variable, research demonstrates that agglomerations are a meaningful and valuable unit of measurement for the economic analysis of location choice (e.g. Porter, 1990). Among the various measures of agglomeration used in previous literature, we suggest adopting a definition of agglomeration as a city or geographical region that contains a collection of neighboring firms (e.g. Baum and Haveman, 1997). This definition allows a consistent, and meaningful, application of the agglomeration construct across countries. Once an agglomeration is identified in this manner, a firm's location choice can be operationalized by its proximity to the nearest agglomeration, and/or based on whether it joins the agglomeration.

To effectively proxy for the independent variables of interest, we need indicators that capture cultural and institutional contexts. For example, both Hofstede (2001) and Schwartz (1994) offer comprehensive indexes of culture that provide a reasonable starting point to capture the underlying cultural dimensions described above. To proxy for the uncertainty associated with political and economic environments, the PRS Group, Freedom House and the Heritage Foundation have spent decades assessing political risk, economic risk, corruption, and other indicators of country-specific institutional risk. In addition, Henisz (2002) developed the POLCON index to capture volatility in political systems across countries over time. Likewise, La Porta et al. (1998) used a set of variables to measure different characteristics of a country's legal system. More generally, we suggest adopting multiple, time-varying institutional and cultural measures wherever possible. This would provide complementary tests of the underlying phenomena and serve to validate the impact of the cultural and institutional factors on agglomeration.

In order to test our theory, the customary approach would be to regress our measure(s) of agglomeration on the institutional and cultural indicators of interest while controlling for other factors that stand to impact the dependent variable. To test the propositions regarding foreign versus domestic investments, however, more involved procedures are required. That is, we would need to focus on the subset of investments made by foreign firms. For these firms, variance exists across home and host country cultural and institutional variables. We would then regress the measure of agglomeration on the institutional and cultural indicators of both the host and home countries for this subset of firms and compare them with those from the full sample.

CONCLUSION

Although the extant strategy and economics literatures demonstrate that location choice is dependent on external market factors and internal firm characteristics, we understand far less about how national culture and institutions influence firm location decisions. To fill that gap, this chapter focused on the impact of cultural and institutional factors on the agglomeration pattern of firms. We argued that firms internalize cultural and societal norms and agglomerate in cultures characterized by collectivism and uncertainty avoidance. In addition, firms anticipate the uncertainty of operating in a particular institutional environment and take those factors into account when making location decisions. Specifically, we suggested that firms are more likely to agglomerate in countries characterized by political and economic uncertainty. We also argued that multinational firms face greater pressures than domestic firms with respect to location choice. This is because foreign firms are impacted by forces in both their home and host countries. Foreign firms must find a balance among those competing pressures when entering new markets. Taken together, we ultimately advance that the cultural and institutional context affects firms' incentives to agglomerate.

This study holds important implications and suggests several avenues for further research. Perhaps most obvious is the scope for empirical validation. We encourage research meant to empirically validate (or invalidate) the claims made herein. More generally, we encourage scholars to explore the connections between firm strategy and location choice precisely because location choice is a relatively understudied area. If we assume that location decisions are ultimately tied to performance, future research would be well served to examine the relationship among location choice, its fit with cultural and institutional factors, and performance. We would expect firms that agglomerate in countries with more collectivist cultures and in countries characterized by economic and political uncertainty to perform better than firms that do not.

This chapter demonstrates the importance of cultural and institutional conditions on the choice of location and, specifically, on the decision to agglomerate with other industry participants. Admittedly, we have presented only a first pass at what is surely a much more complicated phenomenon. Nevertheless, we hope others will follow in exploring the interplay among culture, institutions and location. Given the theoretical importance of these issues, further conceptual and empirical research in this area seems well warranted.

REFERENCES

Arrow, K.J. (1972), 'The value of and demand for information', in C.B. McGuire and R. Radner (eds), *Decision and Organization*, Amsterdam and London: North Holland, pp. 131–9.

Baum, J.A. and H.A. Haveman (1997), 'Love thy neighbor? Differentiation and agglomeration in the Manhattan hotel industry, 1989–1990', *Administrative Science Quarterly*, **42** (2), 304–38.

Buckley, P. and M.C. Casson (1976), *The Future of the Multinational Enterprise*, London: Holmes & Meier.

Burt, R. (1992), 'The social structure of competition', in N. Nohria and R. Eccles (eds), *Networks and Organizations*, Boston, MA: Harvard Business School Press, pp. 57–91.

Caves, R.E. (1996), *Multinational Enterprise and Economic Analysis*, New York: Cambridge University Press.

Chen, C.C., M.W. Peng and P.A. Saparito (2002), 'Individualism, collectivism and opportunism: a cultural perspective on transaction cost economics', *Journal of Management*, **28** (4), 567–83.

Chung, W. and J. Song (2004), 'Sequential investment, firm motives, and agglomeration of Japanese electronics firms in the United States', *Journal of Economics and Management Strategy*, **13** (3), 539–60.

Cyert, R. and J. March (1963), *A Behavioral Theory of the Firm*, Englewood Cliffs, NJ: Prentice Hall.

DeCarolis, D.M. and D.L. Deeds (1999), 'The impact of stocks and flows of organizational knowledge on firm performance: an empirical investigation of the biotechnology industry', *Strategic Management Journal*, **20**, 953–68.

Dicken, P. (2000) 'Places and flows: situating international investment', in G.L. Clark, M.P. Feldman and M.S. Gertler (eds), *The Oxford Handbook of Economic Geography*, New York: Oxford University Press.

Dicken, P., M. Forsgren and A. Malmberg (1994), 'The local embeddedness of transnational corporations', in A. Amin and N. Thrift (eds), *Globalization, Institutions and Regional Development in Europe*, Oxford: Oxford University Press.

DiMaggio, P.J. and W.W. Powell (1983), 'The iron cage revisited: institutional isomorphism and collective rationality in organizational fields', *American Sociological Review*, **48** (2), 147–60.

Earley, P.C. (1989), 'Social-loafing and collectivism: a comparison of the United States and the People's Republic of China', *Administrative Science Quarterly*, **34** (4), 565–81.

Fischer, J.H. and J. Harrington Jr (1996), 'Product variety and firm agglomeration', *Rand Journal of Economics*, **27** (2), 281–309.

Gerlach, M. (1992), *Alliance Capitalism: The Social Organization of Japanese Business*, Berkeley: University of California Press.

Ghosh, A. and G. Rushton (1987), *Spatial Analysis and Location-allocation Models*, New York: Van Nostrand Reinhold.

Hannan, M.T. and G.R. Carroll (1992), *Dynamics of Organizational Populations: Density, Legitimation, and Competition*, New York: Oxford University Press.

Hannan, M.T., G.R. Carroll, E.A. Dundon and J.C. Torres (1995), 'Organizational evolution in a multinational context: entries of automobile manufacturers in Belgium, Britain, France, Germany, and Italy', *American Sociological Review*, **60** (4), 509–28.

Hayek, F.A. (1945), 'The use of knowledge in society', *American Economic Review*, **35** (4), 519–30.

Henisz, W.J. (2002), 'The institutional environment for infrastructure investment', *Industrial and Corporate Change*, **11** (2), 355–89.

Henisz, W.J. and A. Delios (2001), 'Uncertainty, imitation, and plant location: Japanese multinational corporation, 1990–1996', *Administrative Science Quarterly*, **46** (3), 443–77.

Henisz, W.J. and J.T. Macher (2004), 'Firm- and country-level trade-offs and contingencies in the evaluation of foreign investment: the semiconductor industry, 1994–2002', *Organization Science*, **15** (5), 537–54.

Hoen, A. (2001), 'Clusters: determinants and effects', CPB Netherlands Bureau for Economic Policy Analysis, CPB Memo.

Hofstede, G. (1985), 'The interaction between national and organizational value systems', *Journal of Management Studies*, **22** (4), 347–57.

Hofstede, G. (1994), 'Management scientists are human', *Management Science*, **40** (1, Focused Issue: Is management science international?), 4–13.

Hofstede, G. (2001), *Culture's Consequences: Comparing Values, Behaviors, Institutions, and Organizations across Nations*, 2nd edn, Thousand Oaks, CA: Sage.

Hofstede, G., C.A. Van Deusen, C.B. Mueller, T.A. Charles and Business Goals Network (2002), 'What goals do business leaders pursue? A study in fifteen countries', *Journal of International Business Studies*, **33** (4), 785–803.

Hotelling, H. (1929) 'Stability in competition', *The Economic Journal*, **39** (153), 41–57.

Hymer, S.H. (1960), 'The international operations of national firms: a study of direct foreign investment', doctoral dissertation, MIT (Published by MIT Press in 1976).

Kogut, B. (2005), 'Learning, or the importance of being inert: country imprinting and international competition', in S. Ghoshal and D.E. Westney (eds), *Organization Theory and the Multinational Corporation*, 2nd edn, New York: Palgrave Macmillan, pp. 106–22.

Kogut, B. and H. Singh (1988), 'The effect of national culture on the choice of entry mode', *Journal of International Business Studies*, **19** (3), 411–32.

Kostova, T. and S. Zaheer (1999), 'Organizational legitimacy under conditions of complexity: the case of multinational enterprise', *Academy of Management Review*, **24** (1), 64–81.

Krugman, P.R. (1991), *Geography and Trade*, Cambridge, MA: MIT Press.

La Porta, R., F. Lopez-de-Silanes, A. Shleifer and R.W. Vishny (1998), 'Law and finance', *Journal of Political Economy*, **106** (6), 1113–55.

Laffont, J.-J. and J. Tirole (1991), 'The politics of government decision-making: a theory of regulatory capture', *Quarterly Journal of Economics*, **106** (4), 1089–127.

Lamoreaux, N.R. (1994), *Insider Lending: Banks, Personal Connections, and Economic Development in Industrial New England*, New York: Cambridge University Press.

Lipsey, R.E. (1994), 'Foreign-owned firms and US wages', National Bureau of Economic Research Working Paper 4927.

Mariotti, S. and L. Piscitello (1995), 'Information costs and location of FDIs within the host country: empirical evidence from Italy', *Journal of International Business Studies*, **26** (4), 815–41.

Marshall, A. (1920), *Principles of Economics*, London: Macmillan.

Martin, X. and R.M. Salomon (2003a), 'Knowledge transfer capacity and its implications for the theory of multinational corporation', *Journal of International Business Studies*, **34**, 356–73.

Martin, X. and R.M. Salomon (2003b), 'Tacitness, learning, and international expansion: a study of foreign direct investment in a knowledge-intensive industry', *Organization Science*, **14** (3), 297–312.

Meyer, J.W. and B. Rowan (1977), 'Institutionalized organizations: formal structure as myth and ceremony', *American Journal of Sociology*, **83**, 340–63.

Mezias, J.M. (2002), 'Identifying liabilities of foreignness and strategies to minimize their effects: the case of labor lawsuit judgments in the United States', *Strategic Management Journal*, **23**, 229–44.

Mincer, J. and M. Higuchi (1988), 'Wage structures and labour turnover in the US and Japan', *Journal of the Japanese and International Economies*, **2**, 97–133.

Morris, M.H., D.L. Davis and J.W. Allen (1994), 'Fostering corporate entrepreneurship: cross-cultural comparisons of the importance of individualism versus collectivism', *Journal of International Business Studies*, **25** (1), 65–89.

Nelson, R.R. and S. Winter (1982), *An Evolutionary Theory of Economic Change*, Cambridge, MA: Belknap Press.

Olson, M. (1965), *The Logic of Collective Action*, Cambridge, MA: Harvard University Press.

Porter, M.E. (1990), *The Competitive Advantage of Nations*, New York: Free Press.

Porter, M.E. (1998), *On Competition*, Boston, MA: Harvard Business School.

Porter, M.E. (2000), 'Locations, clusters, and company strategy', in G.L. Clark, M.P. Feldman and M.S. Gertler (eds), *The Oxford Handbook of Economic Geography*, New York: Oxford University Press, pp. 253–74.

Pouder, R. and C. St John (1996), 'Hot spots and blind spots: geographic clusters of firms and innovation', *Academy of Management Review*, **21** (4), 1192–225.

Rosenzweig, P.M. and J.V. Singh (1991) 'Organizational environments and the multinational enterprise', *Academy of Management Review*, **16** (2), 340–61.

Salomon, R.M. and X. Martin (2006), 'Learning, knowledge transfer, and technology implementation performance: a study of "time-to-build" in the global semiconductor industry', New York University Working Paper.

Schmutzler, A. (1999), 'The new economic geography', *Journal of Economic Surveys*, **13** (4), 355–79.

Schwartz, S.H. (1994), 'Beyond individualism/collectivism: new cultural dimensions of values', in U. Kim, H.C. Triandis, C. Kagitcibasi, S.-C. Choi and G. Yoon (eds), *Individualism and Collectivism: Theory, Method and Application*, Newbury Park, CA: Sage, pp. 85–119.

Shaver, J.M. (1998), 'Do foreign-owned and U.S.-owned establishments exhibit the same location pattern in U.S. manufacturing industries?', *Journal of International Business Studies*, **29** (3), 469–92.

Shaver, J.M. and F. Flyer (2000), 'Agglomeration economies, firm heterogeneity and foreign direct investment in the United States', *Strategic Management Journal*, **21** (12), 1175–93.

Sorenson, O. and P.G. Audia (2000), 'The social structure of entrepreneurial activity: geographic concentration of footwear production in the United States, 1940–1989', *American Journal of Sociology*, **106** (2), 324–62.

Stuart, T.E., H. Hoang and R.C. Hybels (1999), 'Interorganizational endorsements and the performance of entrepreneurial ventures', *Administrative Science Quarterly*, **44**, 315–49.

Triandis, H.C. (1995), *Individualism and Collectivism*, Boulder, CO: Westview Press.

Uzzi, B. (1997), 'Social structure and competition in interfirm networks: the paradox of embeddedness', *Administrative Science Quarterly*, **42**, 35–67.

Uzzi, B. and R. Lancaster (2003), 'Relational embeddedness and learning: the case of bank loan managers and their clients', *Management Science*, **49** (4), 383–99.

Weber, A. (1929), *Theory of Location of Industries*, Chicago: University of Chicago Press.

Westney, D.E. (2005), 'Institutional theory and the multinational corporation', in S. Ghoshal and D.E. Westney (eds), *Organization Theory and the Multinational Corporation*, 2nd edn, New York: Palgrave Macmillan, pp. 47–67.

Williamson, O.E. (1979), 'Transaction cost economics: the governance of contractual relations', *Journal of Law and Economics*, **22**, 233–62.

Zaheer, S. (1995), 'Overcoming the liability of foreignness', *Academy of Management Journal*, **38** (2), 341–63.

Zaheer, S. and E. Mosakowski (1997), 'The dynamics of liability of foreignness: a global study of survival in financial service', *Strategic Management Journal*, **18** (6), 439–64.

15. Local clusters with non-local demand: an exploratory study of *small ethnic worlds* in the Indian IT industry[1]

Florian A. Täube

This chapter combines one theoretical question with two striking features of recent global economic development in. First, entrepreneurship is a rising phenomenon in emerging markets: India, for instance, according to the Global Entrepreneurship Monitor, holds the second place in the Total Entrepreneurial Activity (TEA) index among 37 countries in the world (Manimala et al., 2002). Second, the Indian IT industry attracts increasing scholarly interest, with software being a major investment target of venture capital (VC), as well as the most active sector in the Indian economy. This chapter explicitly focuses on the analysis of geographical concentrations of the IT industry and the co-evolution of supportive socio-institutional conditions. Third, this is interesting because these Indian IT clusters have developed far away from their main demand markets. It is primarily the last issue that makes this a highly relevant and theoretically intriguing case study.

It is well established that industry clusters can provide a competitive advantage for the firms located in them (Porter, 1990; Tallman et al., 2004). A steadily increasing number of western firms from various industries enter industry clusters in emerging markets like the Indian city of Bangalore to benefit from capabilities available locally at a fraction of the cost of their respective home countries. It is doubtful that cost advantages can be sustained after more than a decade of such offshoring and outsourcing, in particular when one employs a more dynamic perspective; cost differentials alone seem to become eroded rather quickly. In fact, it is less the cost savings than the benefits of locating in a cluster that attract firms. Therefore, these clusters and firms in these clusters must be able to offer something beyond cost advantages. Surprisingly, Bangalore is successful without the typical high degree of local knowledge flows, as it relies principally on export markets. How can an industry cluster be successful if most of its turnover is exports?

One main component of a cluster – per definition – is close interaction with the customers. In the case of local (or regional) demand, local networks are one of the conduits of knowledge transfer as a major competitive advantage of clusters. Firms located in a cluster away from the main markets do not necessarily compete for the same customers, at least not as fiercely; their main competition is for input factors and resources (Baum and Mezias, 1992). Thus a location not proximate to the market reduces competitive effects, thereby positively enhancing the beneficial agglomeration effects of a cluster. On the other hand, in a cluster located away from the market there must be some other mechanisms that provide for interaction with customers. It seems that social networks may become more important the further away firms get from the market. Ethnic networks can be interpreted as a *small world*-type of social networks that can play this role of providing high local clustering and short global separation (Watts, 1999). They seem to be particularly suited to non-local networking since the shared experience necessary to breed trust can hardly be higher than through a common origin. In most network studies, the net value of a network structure configured by closure versus structural holes is usually determined as the benefits less the cost of creating and maintaining the relevant ties. Here we argue that ethnic networks are latent in the sense there is no upfront investment required in order to 'create' a tie. Hence, the value of ethnic networks immediately becomes much larger. We introduce the notion of *small ethnic worlds* where the structural holes between local clusters within the network are bridged by the boundary-spanning diaspora.

The purpose of this study is to uncover the links through which firms in a cluster that is distant from the main market gain access to important interactions with customers and maintain a competitive advantage. From the firm perspective, this is relevant for at least two reasons. First, what kinds of network are important for high-tech firms in industries like software? Second, and related to the first, how can a cluster of firms emerge and prosper without sophisticated local demand? Interweaving interview material with archival and quantitative sources, this empirically grounded research combines perspectives from business and other social sciences that build on a network rationale – exemplified in the Indian IT industry and sub-sectors thereof. The chapter is structured as follows. The next section describes methods and research design. The main theoretical part reviews literatures on clusters, demand and networks, respectively, and develops propositions on each one. The chapter ends with some summarizing conclusions.

METHODS

This chapter uses a mixed methodology by combining the grounded theory approach of an exploratory study of firms clustered in one metropolitan region (qualitative interviews and historic accounts) with quantitative data (industry statistics, etc.) The former includes semi-structured interviews conducted at the premises of firms, educational institutions and government bodies in Bangalore during the winter of 2003. The latter consists of content analysis of primary and secondary materials at firm, industry and regional level.

Between November and December 2003, I visited the Indian Institute of Science, Bangalore and conducted 36 interviews – 23 with private firms (15 Indian and 2 foreign SMEs, 2 Indian and 4 foreign MNCs), 8 with public sector units, and 5 with universities; three double counts resulting from multiple affiliations of one contact were cancelled out. The sample selection was designed to reflect both randomness and networks. (However, an element of chance, spontaneously bumping into people working in the IT industry – which is almost unavoidable, being in Bangalore for one month – helped in understanding the context and deducing relationships.) A random sample is used in order to obtain a differentiated picture of the Indian IT industry in Bangalore, and was selected from a directory of the National Association of Software and Services Companies (NASSCOM). The diverse nature of predominantly small and medium-size enterprises (SMEs) but also multinational corporations (MNCs) of both Indian and foreign ownership is reflected through this selection. Among the Indian companies, some large firms complement the medium and very small companies that are represented. Moreover, there are hardware and software companies in both service and product sectors of IT. A chain of personal contacts through networks was used where it was necessary to learn from key decision makers (Bewley, 2002).

Most interviews were conducted at the interviewee's office. However, some were more informal, visiting people at their homes, or meeting them in a coffee shop. Three interviews were arranged spontaneously, meeting people on the campus of the Indian Institute of Science or at private socializing events. The average length of an interview was 45 minutes, ranging from 20 to 150 minutes. Since most of the people interviewed were company founders, CEOs or other senior executives, I decided to conduct the interviews in a semi-structured way, instead of going through the set of questions one by one; this left considerably more time and space for open answers on the part of these industry insiders. Bewley (1999, p. 16) finds that 'respondents were most informative when they talked freely and the discussion wandered'. I used a questionnaire of more than 30 questions as a guideline to the interviews. The questions addressed issues related to general company information, employees and recruiting, local networks, regional networks and international networks, and policy. In general, all topics have been covered in these open discussions.

Qualitative evidence from 16 semi-structured interviews with senior executives of Indian SMEs and MNCs in Germany conducted in Frankfurt between October and November 2002 complements the findings from Bangalore, and was used to triangulate information gathered on the international dimensions of networks.

THEORETICAL BACKGROUND

This chapter focuses on two key elements of most agglomeration theories, which are related to the knowledge spillover argument – the role of networks and of 'sophisticated and demanding buyers' (Porter, 1990, p. 89). Agglomeration theories, mainly in economic geography, but also in international business (Tallman et al., 2004), organization theory (Baum and Mezias, 1992) and more recently revived in strategy (Folta et al., 2006) explain cluster evolution, and implications for firms. Given the multi-faceted approaches to agglomeration phenomena, the diversity of explanations comes as no surprise. Factors contributing to firm clustering include knowledge spillovers, factor market pooling, lowering consumer search costs, and so on (Porter, 1990).

Entrepreneurship and Clusters

Most of the literature on entrepreneurship and clusters is concerned with advanced economies, therefore this review will be mainly confined to these countries as well; differences from emerging markets will be added by focusing on the Indian context. It is not possible to cover all the relevant literature, nor do I intend to debate the virtues or otherwise of other approaches to the same issue; here the goal is to bring together developments from the related literatures of the economics of location and entrepreneurship. Theoretical definitions of entrepreneurship range from risk taking to merely founding a new venture, whereas some agreement has been established about the individual micro-level nature of the entrepreneurial process (Carroll and Khessina, 2005). In this chapter, I employ the narrowly defined notion of firm founding. This concentration of entrepreneurship is more than proportionate for industries engaged in knowledge-intensive activities (Audretsch and Keilbach, 2004). There is considerable evidence in the extant literature suggesting that such firm founding is regionally concentrated in clusters. Sorenson and Audia (2000, p. 426) maintain that, 'dense local concentrations of structurally equivalent organizations increase the pool of entrepreneurs in a region, thereby increasing founding rates'.

Most work on agglomerations, be it in the cluster tradition or in related strands, emphasizes the role of local networks (formal and informal) and the role of user–producer interaction: in other words, the role of demand in quantitative and qualitative terms as an important positive factor for the innovation potential of the cluster. However, more recent research also emphasized the importance of non-local linkages for clusters (Britton, 2004) and possible upgrading of clusters (Grote and Täube, 2006). According to traditional location choice theories – mostly developed in relation to manufacturing industries – firms were expected to locate close to either their customers or their suppliers in order to minimize transport costs; services were so-called 'non-tradables', therefore they had to be 'produced' at the locus of consumption. Nowadays many services have become 'tradable' (i.e. they can be transported), often because it is possible to digitize them, as in the case of software. Options for location choices become much wider, and theoretically 'production' of services can happen anywhere. One such option seems to be the tapping of resources in clusters in order to benefit from a variety of received cluster benefits.

Clusters are established in the literature as important places for learning, innovation and economic development (Romanelli and Khessina, 2005). Different agglomeration theories such as Porter's (1990) cluster, the industrial district, the innovative milieu or the learning region commonly emphasize a regional concentration of firms, in most cases SMEs, and supporting institutions. Besides the traditional Marshallian externalities, external economies like knowledge spillovers (Almeida and Kogut, 1999) derive from collective efficiency, social capital or some other form of social cohesiveness (Uzzi, 1997).

Hence, one would expect higher value-added activities to be localized in those existing clusters exhibiting features such as labour markets with experience specific to the requirements of foreign firms. In particular, the knowledge residing within a cluster is a target of firms entering that cluster. However, in this case, the good or service offered – software – is mobile and has very low physical transportation costs. Although one could argue that labour is relatively mobile in the service sector – even more so in high-technology industries like software – capital is still the input factor with the greatest mobility. This localness of human capital is responsible for knowledge spillovers – theoretically the most interesting yet under-researched agglomeration mechanism. Bangalore is home to the highest number of engineering schools and students in India, both absolute and relative to the population (see Table 15.1). In Bangalore, like in other technology clusters, human capital is the most important factor, in particular engineering talent. An intuitive agglomeration channel is the local concentration of the labour market, since it is easier for both parties to find the matching counterpart if both are located within the same geographical boundaries; even with the rise of the internet, search costs can never be fully eliminated. Hence, a concentrated labour market serves to reduce uncertainty for supply and demand of labour.

Table 15.1   *Number of engineering colleges and enrolment compared to population*

Region	Engineering colleges[1]		Enrolment[1]		Population[II]
	No.	National share (%)	Sanctioned capacity	National share (%)	National share (%)
Central	50	7.54	9470	6.05	–
East	25	3.77	4812	3.07	25.8
North	140	21.12	25449	16.26	31.3
West	140	21.12	34165	21.83	19.6
South	308	46.46	82597	52.78	23.2
Total	663	100.00	156493	100.00	100.00

Sources: [1] Arora and Athreye (2002), [II] Dossani (2002).

Nevertheless, the economics of clustering are not sufficient to explain the positive impact on innovation of geographic proximity. Economic geography has broadened the range of concepts of proximity used by including social, organizational and cultural proximity, among others (Boschma, 2005). In fact, it is claimed that geographic proximity per se is neither a necessary nor a sufficient condition for collective learning (van Dijk and Sverrison, 2003). However, geographical proximity facilitates the development of other forms of proximity and thereby strengthens interactive learning and innovation.

This chapter shares some similarity with recent studies that combine cluster-level with firm-level processes. But whereas other scholars (e.g. Giuliani, 2005; Tallman et al., 2004) explicitly theorize that the knowledge bases of firms are heterogeneous, the focus here is on the diversity of individual employees in firms, and the access of firms to the ensuing heterogeneous knowledge bases. Another difference is this chapter's emphasis on non-local network relations, compared with others that focus on intra-cluster relations. Giuliani (2005) finds knowledge spillovers to be unevenly distributed among firms in a cluster. In other words, the benefits of clustering differ between firms, depending on the relative absorptive capacities of the firms in a cluster. Similarly, Alcacer (2003) shows that most advanced firms do not locate in a cluster in order to prevent knowledge leakages. Hence, we expect firms conducting research and development (R&D) not to co-locate with less sophisticated firms. One foreign firm for instance, engaging in R&D for various sub-units, operates in so secluded a manner that it was not even possible to get in contact with this firm. Oerlemans and Meeus (2005) find geographical proximity (i.e. co-location) improves firm performance in R&D-related networks in the Netherlands relative to firms with few ties to buyers and suppliers, thereby supporting the knowledge spillover argument. Analyzing Canadian information technology firms, Globerman et al. (2005) obtained strong evidence of locational clustering effects on firm growth, but less on survival.

Two clarifications are important for an understanding of the Indian context. First, since most of the Indian IT industry consists of software services firms, it might be useful to have a broad conceptualization of innovation: in this context, innovation must extend beyond product innovation to include mainly process innovation; but one should also include organizational innovation acknowledging the role Indian IT firms have played in the diffusion of new organizational forms. Second, one should know that the 'Indian' software industry also is composed of a host of MNCs located in various Indian technology centres, most importantly Bangalore. Using this definition, the IT industry in India has put forward some innovative products.

The secluded R&D-intensive foreign firm mentioned above is at the top end of knowledge-based firms; and the higher the degree of knowledge used in 'production', the higher the risk of knowledge leakage to the cluster. Based on empirical evidence from fieldwork, I maintain that in sub-sectors of IT that are more knowledge-intensive (i.e. software products or hardware), the degree of local networking is reduced to minimize the risk of leakage. On the other hand, when the risk of knowledge leakage is relatively low, like in software services, there is a higher degree of local networking. The more knowledge-intensive an industrial sector, the higher the risk of knowledge leakage, and the lower the degree of local networking.

IT CLUSTERS IN INDIA: DOES THE INDIAN CONTEXT DIFFER?

There are factors that seem to be idiosyncratic to different institutional contexts of emerging economies; some of them might even be special in the Indian case. One idiosyncrasy of the Indian IT sector is that in the starting years domestic markets were not targeted; orientation of IT entrepreneurs was initially almost exclusively towards foreign markets. Moreover, their founding entrepreneurs tended to be young and, hence, their intrinsic motivation a critical factor to rely on. There is ample evidence of emerging economies with underdeveloped product and factor markets exhibiting parallel or informal economies and scope for large integrated conglomerates (Khanna and Palepu, 2000; Ahlstrom and Bruton, 2006). The motive put forward by Sorensen and Audia (2000) appears to have particular relevance in an economy in which the institutional framework seems different in terms of social safety nets. Here, social networks play an even bigger role. Findings from my fieldwork suggest an important role of socio-institutional factors for the emergence and growth of the IT industry as well as its geographical distribution. Two key factors, as mentioned by my interview partners, are the openness and diversity of a society:

> One of the most important location factors is the very cosmopolitan nature of the city. (co-founder and COO, Indian SME)
> Cosmopolitan nature has created mentality to connect with foreigners. (Director, Indian SME)
> Innovation happens when there's a high level of diversity. (co-founder and Director, Indian MNC)

Diversity and openness are among the most crucial location factors for knowledge workers of the creative class (Florida, 2002). Florida, takes a multivariate measure to test for location factors relevant to Bohemians, and he calls it the three Ts – technology, talent and tolerance. In this work, I specifically look at the correlation between technology, on the one hand, and some indicators of talent and tolerance on the other. While talent is relatively easy to assess given the data in India are much better than in other emerging economies, it becomes more difficult for tolerance. Openness at the firm level is as much a necessary condition as a constant inflow of new knowledge and ideas is necessary in order to maintain a certain degree of innovativeness (Laursen and Salter, 2006). A cluster with a culture of openness helps each firm in it, because knowledge diffuses once it has entered the cluster through one firm (Tallman et al., 2004). Openness has been found to impact the overall climate of a location together with other amenities (Florida, 2002). According to my interview partners, Bangalore is

> A place high tech professionals want to be part of. (CEO, MNC spin-off, product company), with the
> Quality of life at heart in IT. (co-founder and Director, Indian MNC).

Local and Global Market Demand – and Openness

Sophisticated and demanding buyers (Porter, 1990, pp. 89–91), similar to 'lead users' (von Hippel, 1986), play a key role in most prominent formulations of cluster theories. They are supposedly an integral component of a successful cluster. Geographical proximity to such lead users is supposed to enhance innovation capability through increased interaction. The argument relates to knowledge spillovers found on the supply side of cluster theories, and can be linked to both market and technological knowledge. From this perspective, it is paradoxical that the Indian IT industry has almost no local or even national demand – certainly not at the time when clusters started to emerge and evolve and only to a negligible extent once clusters matured. This is even more surprising given the fact that the Indian IT industry in the early years consisted basically of customized software project firms. On the one hand, their so-called 'body-shopping' moderated the effect of a lack of local demand; programmers were simply flown to the sites of a firm's customers (usually in the USA). On the other hand, then, it remains startling why so many firms chose the *same* few locations in distant India, with the majority locating in Bangalore.

In industries where a product or service is easily transportable because it is digitizable, one could expect a decrease in clustering compared with manufacturing sectors. Nevertheless, in spite of the ease of transportability, and the implied dispersion of industries, we do still witness a high degree of clustering in high-tech industries (e.g. Stuart and Sorenson, 2003; Tsang, 2005). Yet for Bangalore an important missing component is the absence of producer–user interaction, with users as a relevant source of innovation (von Hippel, 1986). Given the absence of the demand side in Bangalore, explanations for clustering in software must either lie with the supply side or with information channels connecting to the non-local demand. I emphasize the latter aspect. Indian IT firms usually have other firms as their customers, but there is no convincing argument for why corporate customers should have less relevance to new product development than end-consumers. In some industries, communication with users is possible over a distance; and, in fact, this was the case in the customized software development business of the early years of the Indian IT industry. Recent evidence shows that geographical proximity and face-to-face communication are not enough to stimulate innovation-generating knowledge exchange; the more relevant knowledge rather comes through relational ties (van Dijk and Sverrison, 2003), for instance, face-to-face or email (Ganesan et al., 2005). While initial site visits probably were always necessary, in the later stages of many projects the physical distance between firms and their customers might well have been overcome by other forms of proximity.

In an industrial cluster where knowledge is a valuable and scarce resource, access to novel sources of knowledge is a competitive advantage. The focal firm is the primary beneficiary from access to wider networks – and the entire population of firms in this cluster benefits through the circulation of new ideas within the locality. In order to allow for such an inflow of new ideas, clusters are expected to have some degree of openness to be successful on a sustainable basis (Laursen and Salter, 2006), even more so for clusters that have to bridge the distance to the non-local demand. Successful clusters without local demand are expected to demonstrate a higher degree of openness towards new ideas.

One such source of openness in a traditional and masculine (Hofstede, 1980) society like India is the attitude towards women (Kantor, 2002). Analysing female university enrolment rates of 13 large Indian area-states, the mean of female enrolment percentages in South and West India (45.08 per cent) is higher than in North and East India (37.62 per cent); in fact taking only South and North India the difference increases to 46.32 per cent, compared with 33.89 per cent. In addition, the variance is much lower in the South and West (7.63) compared to the North and East (8.80), too. Again, this difference is slightly higher comparing only South (9.45) and North (10.70). In other words, except for one state in the North (Punjab), one finds the highest percentages for female enrolment in the four states of South India – Andhra Pradesh, Karnataka, Kerala, Tamil Nadu – plus the two West Indian states Gujarat and Maharashtra (see Table 15.2); that is, in those states where the lion's share of the IT industry is located.

Table 15.2   State-wise female enrolment

Female percentage of state-wise student enrolment (2002–2003)			
South (S) and West (W) India		North (N) and East (E) India	
Andhra Pradesh (S)	39.3	Bihar (N)	23.81
Gujarat (W)	44.21	Haryana (N)	41
Karnataka (S)	40.86	Orissa (E)	35.69
Kerala (S)	60	Punjab (N)	52.68
Maharashtra (W)	41	Rajasthan (N)	32.33
Tamil Nadu (S)	45.1	Uttar Pradesh (N)	38.4
		West Bengal (E)	39.4
Mean South and West	45.08	Mean North and East	37.56
Mean South	46.32	Mean North	37.57
		Mean North (excl. Punjab)	34.55
Variance	7.63	Variance	8.80
Variance South	9.45	Variance North	10.70

Source: Own calculations, based on Kapur and Mehta (2004).

Nevertheless, in all networks (local and non-local, face-to-face, phone or online) there is one common concern to address in every transfer of knowledge or even information: how trustworthy is the source of this new information? Presumably, trust in online communities where both ends of a communication link are initially unknown to each other, is much more difficult to establish than in 'real' communication. The latter has the advantage of additional means of signalling and monitoring, such as body language, voice, and so on. However, this issue of trust will be dealt with below.

Networks and Diversity

Taking a network perspective on industry clusters, one must consider a host of factors; however this chapter is not intended to review the network literature. In principle, the benefits of different network relations or structures have to be distinguished, but for the present study, basic conceptual differences and similarities (strong vs. weak ties, dense vs. loose networks, etc.) should suffice. Ahuja (2000), for example, identifies three types of social network structures that have differing effects on innovative processes in firms: direct ties, indirect ties, and structural holes. Dense networks of direct ties give the focal firm access to knowledge and resources, and the same applies to firms in a dense network of indirect ties, although to a lesser extent. On the other hand, networks characterized by structural holes; that is, focal actors in a network with non-redundant ties that bridge previously unconnected actors (Burt, 1992), provide focal firms with the benefit of increased information and knowledge flows (Ahuja, 2000). In the related stream of organizational learning literature, these networks are related to exploration and exploitation of firms (March, 1991). In order to learn, diverse and heterogeneous networks serve firms best.

In this chapter, we focus on the knowledge and information spillovers networks can provide, rather than on the resource-sharing aspects of social networks. Ahuja (2000, p. 432) finds diametrically opposed conclusions regarding the relevance of structural holes depending on whether emphasis is laid on resource sharing or knowledge spillovers as the main benefit of a network. Moreover, in the context of this chapter, networks are seen as relational rather than structural constructs, because the emphasis is on interpersonal networks as knowledge conduits (Grabher and Ibert, 2006). In the regional development literature there has been a long debate about whether specialized (Marshall, 1920 [1890]) or diversified (Jacobs, 1969) industrial structures better promote growth at the regional level. In both cases, a major channel for information and knowledge flows is through formal and informal personal networks (Tallman et al., 2004). At the firm level the corresponding argument is that diversified firms can have access to broader or multiple knowledge bases, thereby increasing innovative performance; on the other hand, diversification can also imply greater bureaucratization, hence a reduction in innovative output (Ahuja, 2000, p. 445).

Analysing the geographical nature of knowledge spillovers, it is well established that they are almost always confined locally, or regionally at most (e.g. Audretsch and Feldman, 1996). McEvily and Zaheer (1999) find that firms in geographical clusters with fewer non-redundant ties (structural holes) acquire fewer competitive capabilities. A distinct feature of geographic clusters conferring a competitive advantage on firms within the cluster is the increased flow of information through a higher frequency of both formal and informal meetings. Thus the questions arise as to whether and how firms should try to tap non-local sources of knowledge. The first is easily answered by deduction: given that a more diverse network is beneficial for learning processes both at firm and cluster level, the number of (outside) ties should increase the knowledge stock within the cluster and hence for all the firms located there. Even more so, when outside knowledge, for example that pertaining to non-local demand, is unavailable otherwise. In the context of technological knowledge, this might be acquired by firms through exploration beyond local search. Explicitly including the geographical dimension, alliances and mobility of inventors is a useful mechanism (Rosenkopf and Almeida, 2003). In addition, the knowledge relevant to these firms ideally comes from lead users. Given the nature of Indian IT, their corresponding networks would be rather non-local. Therefore, trust becomes an issue again. On a local level, trust building can be achieved through assimilation (Marini, 2004) by investing in embedding in localized social networks to benefit from the legitimacy of a population.

Maskell (2001) provides an excellent explanation for why spatial clustering cannot be inferred from a reduction in transaction costs alone. His contribution towards a 'knowledge-based theory of the cluster' asserts that internalization alone would result in single firms benefiting from resources, including knowledge, available in the cluster. But it is the variation in the knowledge bases of a multiplicity of firms that gives the cluster its competitive edge.

Transfer of tacit knowledge needs communication channels that are based on proximity and trust (Dosi, 1988). Potential channels for this kind of knowledge transfer are alliances and the mobile researchers and scientists (Rosenkopf and Almeida, 2003) that are instrumental for firms gaining competitive advantage.

This learning is assumed to happen through spillovers that can take place through 'both formal and informal interactions by firms and individuals in networks' (Mahmood and Rufin, 2005, p. 342). 'People almost always have more, *more diverse*, and stronger ties to contacts in the geographic region in which they reside. This suggests that the form of social capital most valuable in the resource mobilization process is to a large extent a geographically localized currency' (Stuart and Sorenson, 2003, p. 249).

Diversity is a broad and ambiguous concept, with at least three aspects to it: variety, separation, and disparity (Harrison and Klein, 2007). Diversity can also be technical or cognitive, both of which reinforce each other. Whereas diversity in the sense of variety confers benefits on the group analysed, separation and disparity are rather detrimental to a group's effectiveness and efficiency. The benefits of diversity in terms of a diversified industrial base in a region (Jacobs, 1969), different educational backgrounds or gender in teams are relatively straightforward (Visser and Boschma, 2004; Harrison and Klein, 2007).

Evidence grounded in our fieldwork shows that for hardware and software product firms, network relations seem to be more crucial in the knowledge spillover realm, which conforms to the findings of Britton (2004). Regarding the sourcing of knowledge, von Hayek (1945) has established the fact of dispersion of knowledge in society. Thus access to multiple entry points of the knowledge base is beneficial to firms dependent on multitude types of information and knowledge. For firms in knowledge-intensive industries, having diverse network ties as sources of ideas is more important than specific types of diversity.

Ethnic Networks

The benefits of diversity in terms of ethnicity are less straightforward than in other types of diversity. Moreover, ethnic diversity has not yet played a prominent role in network theory. However, taking the step from knowledge spillovers to idea generation and learning makes this much clearer. Here, the distinction between technical and cognitive comes into play; whereas the former is almost a necessary condition of learning, the sufficient condition for '[...] learning requires an act of will – a conscious decision to deviate from one's preferences, to collect and process new information, and to change one's perceptions of how the world looks' (Visser and Boschma, 2004, p. 794). In a context of mental models, one can distinguish between first-order and second-order learning; whereas the former consists of learning within one's established cognitive context, or mental model, the latter implies changing a mental model as a result of communication with others. First-order learning is thus described as small error-eliminating learning, while second-order learning generates more radical product or process innovations.

The benefits of ties across different ethnicities, or people from various regional backgrounds, are that people in different regions develop different cognitive structures (Visser and Boschma, 2004, p. 796; Johansson, 2004, p. 47). Ethnicity and hence ethnic diversity are ambiguous concepts; in social science 'ethnicity' or 'ethnic group' has increasingly been used to identify people according to their cultural instead of biological similarity of race (Tsui-Auch, 2005).

Depending on the level of interaction with other people, anthropologists have found a 'contingent dynamic and relativity of structurally opposing groups' based on Evans-Pritchard's (1940) analysis of the Nuer. In other words, people usually feel closer to ever more distant groups the further they are from their home environment.[2] In the case of India, Indians abroad might identify themselves as Indians, but in a place like Silicon Valley with many other Indians, they might resort to regional differences; and when in India they will probably use an even more fine-grained self-identification based on, say, language or dialect. Hence, ethnicity is a multi-layered concept, and assuming intra-ethnic homogeneity can only be justified at more grounded levels but not, for example, at the level of 'being Indian'. Using such a broad construct of ethnicity and co-ethnicity, Agrawal et al. (2004) find evidence for stronger knowledge flows between co-inventors sharing 'Indian' ethnicity.

There are only a few studies on ethnic Indian sub-groups (Täube, 2004), particularly compared with those on overseas Chinese networks (Tan, 2002); for example, on ethnic entrepreneurs in Singapore (Tsui-Auch, 2005), Punjabi and Gujarati immigrants in London and Chicago (Frederking, 2004; Basu and Goswami, 1999), Gujaratis in Texas (Kalnins and Chung, 2006). Interestingly, kin-based networks simultaneously provide extensive and strong ties (Lin, 2001, p. 110). Arguably, the strength of such ties is rather latent, particularly in societies like the Chinese, Indian or other Asian ones where the concept of family extends beyond the core family. In these societies, there are no grounds for assuming a generally strong connection between all members of the same kin, let alone the same ethnicity. Hence, they combine the positive features of a small-world-type network characterized by both high local clustering and short global separation through boundary-spanning individuals in the diaspora who bridge structural holes (Watts, 1999). Therefore, such kin, and to a lesser extent all ethnic networks, allow for the inflow of filtered (i.e. trustworthy) information and knowledge into a localized cluster. Ethnic network ties confer at least two advantages on a population of firms in an industry or cluster. First, they provide those in a location distant from important markets with the relevant information and knowledge on consumer needs; second, this information and knowledge have already passed social filter and screening mechanisms. Therefore, ethnic network ties are considered to be *more reliable conduits of information* than other networks characterized by structural holes, and ethnic network ties are *able to channel thicker information* than other strong ties. Further, we can deduce an additional advantage that an ethnically *diverse* labour force has for clusters and firms located in clusters: it guarantees access to a diversity of ideas and knowledge that have been through the screening processes of ethnic networks (Alesina and La Ferrara, 2005; Ottaviano and Peri, 2006).

CONCLUSIONS, LIMITATIONS AND FURTHER DIRECTIONS

Entrepreneurs in emerging markets often face the problem of little knowledge about the demand side that is located far away. This exploratory chapter is a first step towards an understanding of the links between knowledge-intensive industry clusters *without* sophisticated local demand and social networks. Based on inductive fieldwork, it theoretically establishes propositions about clusters, demand interaction and ethnic networks and diversity. The latter are shown by deduction to be a valuable resource for firms in emerging markets located away from the main markets. The principal aim of the chapter is to advance the literature by connecting theories of location choice and social networks in knowledge-based industries.

Obviously, this study has some limitations; similar to Stuart and Sorenson (2003) who confine their study to explaining the evolution of an industry in locales once a biotech firm has been founded, not why the first firm has been established there, my aim is not to explain the emergence but the subsequent development of a cluster. Another interesting question that is beyond the scope of this chapter concerns the regional distribution of users (and their communities); are they as localized as firms are in many clustered industries – maybe even in the same location? Also, I ignore a host of other mechanisms at work, not because they are not important, but rather to sharpen the focus of the present theorizing, given its exploratory and interpretive nature. Such issues include a more nuanced investigation of export intensity (Britton, 2004), the role of the global demand structure, the actual process of (local) knowledge spillovers, or a comparative study of multiple locations.

The main contribution of this chapter lies in the integration of ethnic networks as a small world of social networks. We introduce the notion of *small ethnic worlds* where the boundary-spanning diaspora bridges the structural holes between local clusters within the network. Hence, one finding is the usefulness of ethnic ties, because there is a latency of trust to peers of one's own ethnicity as well as a broad reach through the global spread of these networks such as the Indian Diaspora. In other words, there are trustworthy connections to both these contacts and other non-local customers on the demand side. Therefore, ethnic networks combine positive characteristics of networks characterized by both cohesion and structural holes. Thus ethnic networks can support clusters without local demand by bridging structural holes and providing access to a larger pool of knowledge and information. By inference, ethnic diversity can enhance a cluster's knowledge base by increasing the number of beneficial ethnic network ties and allowing for a greater influx of different knowledge and ideas on the supply side. Further research into how such ethnic ties can be fruitfully used by the entrepreneurial firm seems worthwhile. In particular, emerging markets such as India and China seem to be able to benefit from their global diasporas as did Taiwan over the last decades.

NOTES

1. I would like to thank Linus Dahlander, Greg Fairchild, Michael Grote, Alexander Klein, Miguel Meuleman and Marc Umber, three anonymous referees and conference participants at the AOM 2006 meeting for helpful comments and suggestions, and my interview partners for sharing their thoughts and time with me. All remaining errors are my own.
2. Thanks are due to Burkhart Schnepel, anthropologist formerly at the University of Frankfurt, who pointed this out to me.

REFERENCES

Agrawal, A., Kapur, D. and McHale, J. (2004), 'Defying distance: examining the influence of the Diaspora on scientific knowledge flows', mimeo.
Ahlstrom, D. and Bruton, G. (2006), 'Venture capital in emerging economies: networks and institutional change', *Entrepreneurship Theory and Practice*, **30** (2), 299–320.
Ahuja, G. (2000), 'Collaboration networks, structural holes and innovation: a longitudinal study', *Administrative Science Quarterly*, **45**, 425–55.
Alcacer, J. (2003), 'Location choices across the value chain: how activity and capability influence agglomeration and competition effects', ssrn.com/abstract=460621.
Alesina. A. and La Ferrara, E. (2005), 'Ethnic diversity and economic performance', *Journal of Economic Literature*, **43** (3), 762–800.
Almeida, P. and Kogut, B. (1999), 'Localization of knowledge and the mobility of engineers in regional networks', *Management Science*, **45**, 905–17.
Arora, A. and S. Athreye (2002), 'The software industry and India's economic development', *Information Economics and Policy*, **14** (2), 253–73.
Audretsch, D.B. and Feldman, M. (1996), 'R&D spillovers and the geography of innovation and production', *American Economic Review*, **86**, 630–40.
Audretsch, D.B. and Keilbach, M. (2004), 'Does entrepreneurship capital matter?', *Entrepreneurship Theory and Practice*, **28** (5), 19–29.

Basu, A. and Goswami, A. (1999), 'Determinants of South Asian entrepreneurial growth in Britain: a multivariate analysis', *Small Business Economics*, **13** (1), 57–70.

Baum, J.A.C. and Mezias, S.J. (1992), 'Localized competition and organizational failure in the Manhattan hotel industry, 1989–1990', *Administrative Science Quarterly*, **37**, 580–604.

Bewley, T. (1999), *Why Wages Don't Fall During a Recession*, Cambridge, MA and London: Harvard University Press.

Bewley, T. (2002), 'Interviews as a valid empirical tool in economics', *Journal of Socio-Economics*, **31**, 343–53.

Boschma R.A. (2005), 'Proximity and innovation: a critical assessment', *Regional Studies*, **39**, 61–74.

Britton, J. (2004), 'High technology localization and extra-regional networks', *Entrepreneurship and Regional Development*, **16**, 369–90.

Burt, R. (1992). *Structural Holes: The Social Structure of Competition*, Cambridge, MA: Harvard University Press.

Carroll, G. and Khessina, O. (2005), 'The ecology of entrepreneurship', in S.A. Alvarez, R. Agarwal and O. Sorenson (eds), *Handbook of Entrepreneurship Research: Disciplinary Perspectives*, New York: Springer, pp. 167–200.

Dosi, G. (1988), 'Sources, procedures, and microeconomic effects of innovation', *Journal of Economic Literature*, **XXVI**, 1120–71.

Dossani, R. (2002), *Chinese and Indian Engineers and their Networks in Silicon Valley*, Stanford, CA: Asia/Pacific Research Center.

Evans-Pritchard, E.E. (1940), 'The Nuer of the Southern Sudan', in M. Fortes and E.E. Evans-Pritchard (eds), *African Political Systems*, London: Oxford University Press, pp. 272–96.

Florida, R. (2002), 'Bohemia and economic geography', *Journal of Economic Geography*, **2**, 55–71.

Folta, T.B., Cooper, A.C. and Baik, Y.S. (2006), 'Geographic cluster size and firm performance', *Journal of Business Venturing*, **21** (2), 217–42.

Frederking, L. (2004), 'A cross-national study of culture, organization and entrepreneurship in three neighbourhoods', *Entrepreneurship and Regional Development*, **16**, 197–215.

Ganesan, S., Malter, A.J. and Rindfleisch, A. (2005), 'Does Distance Still Matter? Geographic Proximity and New Product Development', *Journal of Marketing*, **69**, 44–60.

Giuliani, E. (2005), 'The structure of cluster knowledge networks: uneven and selective, not pervasive and collective', DRUID Working Paper No. 05–11.

Globerman, S., Shapiro, D. and Vining, A. (2005), 'Clusters and intercluster spillovers: their influence on the growth and survival of Canadian information technology firms', *Industrial and Corporate Change*, **14** (1), 27–60.

Grabher, G. and Ibert, O. (2006), 'Bad company? The ambiguity of personal knowledge networks', *Journal of Economic Geography*, **6** (3), 251–71.

Grote, M. and Täube, F. (2006), 'Offshoring the financial services industry: implications for the evolution of Indian IT clusters', *Environment and Planning A*, **38** (7), 1287–305.

Harrison, D. and Klein, K. (2007), 'What's the difference? Diversity constructs as separation, variety, or disparity in organizations', *Academy of Management Review*, forthcoming.

Hofstede, G. (1980), *Culture's Consequences: International Differences in Work-related values*, Beverly Hills, CA: Sage.

Jacobs, J. (1969), *The Economy of Cities*, New York: Vintage.

Johansson, F. (2004), *The Medici Effect: Breakthrough Insights at the Intersection of Ideas, Concepts, and Cultures*, Boston, MA: Harvard Business School Press.

Kalnins, A. and Chung, W. (2006), 'Social capital, geography, and survival: Gujarati immigrant entrepreneurs in the U.S. lodging industry', *Management Science*, **52** (2), 233–47.

Kantor, P. (2002), 'Gender, microenterprise success and cultural context: the case of South Asia', *Entrepreneurship Theory and Practice*, **26** (4), 131–43.

Kapur, D. and Mehta, B. (2004), 'Indian higher education reform: from half-baked socialism to half-baked capitalism', working paper, Harvard University.

Khanna, T. and Palepu, K. (2000), 'Is group affiliation profitable in emerging markets? An analysis of diversified Indian business groups', *Journal of Finance*, **55** (2), 867–91.

Laursen, K. and Salter, A. (2006), 'Open for innovation: the role of openness in explaining innovation performance among U.K. manufacturing firms', *Strategic Management Journal*, **27** (2), 131–50.

Lin, N. (2001), *Social Capital. A Theory of Social Structure and Action*, Cambridge: Cambridge University Press.

McEvily, B. and Zaheer, A. (1999), 'Bridging ties: a source of firm heterogeneity in competitive capabilities', *Strategic Management Journal*, **20** (12), 1133–56.

Mahmood, I.P. and Rufin, C. (2005), 'Government's dilemma: the institutional framework for imitation and innovation', *Academy of Management Review*, **30** (2), 338–60.

Manimala, M., Gopal, M. and Sridhar, P. (2002), *Global Entrepreneurship Monitor India Report 2002*, Bangalore: Indian Institute of Management.

March, J.G. (1991), 'Exploration and exploitation in organizational learning', *Organization Science*, **2** (1), 71–87.

Marini, M. (2004), 'Cultural evolution and economic growth: a theoretical hypothesis with some empirical evidence', *Journal of Socio-Economics*, **33**, 765–84.

Marshall, A. (1920 [1890]), *Principles of Economics*, London: Macmillan.

Maskell, P. (2001), 'Towards a knowledge-based theory of the geographical cluster', *Industrial and Corporate Change*, **10**, 921–41.

Oerlemans, L. and Meeus, M. (2005), 'Do organizational and spatial proximity impact on firm performance?', *Regional Studies*, **39** (1), 89–104.

Ottaviano, G. and Peri, G. (2006), 'The economic value of cultural diversity: evidence from U.S. cities', *Journal of Economic Geography*, **6** (1), 9–44.

Porter, M.E. (1990), *The Competitive Advantage of Nations*, New York: Free Press.

Romanelli, E. and Khessina, O. (2005), 'Regional industrial identity: cluster configurations and economic development', *Organization Science*, **16** (4), 344–58.

Rosenkopf, L. and Almeida, P. (2003), 'Overcoming local search through alliances and mobility', *Management Science*, **49** (6), 751–66.

Sorenson, O. and Audia, P.G. (2000), 'The social structure of entrepreneurial opportunity: geographic concentration of footwear production in the United States, 1940–1989', *American Journal of Sociology*, **106**, 424–62.

Stuart, T. and Sorenson, O. (2003), 'The geography of opportunity: spatial heterogeneity in founding rates and the performance of biotechnology firms', *Research Policy*, **32**, 229–53.

Tallman, S., Jenkins, M., Henry, N. and Pinch, S. (2004), 'Knowledge, clusters, and competitive advantage', *Academy of Management Review*, **29** (2), 258–71.

Tan, J. (2002), 'Culture, nation and entrepreneurial strategic orientations: implications for an emerging economy', *Entrepreneurship Theory and Practice*, **26** (4), 95–111.

Täube, F. (2004), 'Transnational networks and the evolution of the Indian software industry: the role of culture and ethnicity', in D. Audretsch, D. Fornahl and C. Zellner (eds), *The Role of Labour Mobility and Informal Networks for Knowledge Transfer*, Dordrecht: Kluwer, pp. 97–121.

Tsang, D. (2005), 'Growth of indigenous entrepreneurial software firms in cities', *Technovation*, **25**, 1331–6.

Tsui-Auch, L. (2005), 'Unpacking regional ethnicity and the strength of ties in shaping ethnic entrepreneurship', *Organization Studies*, **26** (8), 1189–216.

Uzzi, B. (1997), 'Social structure and competition in interfirm networks: the paradox of embeddedness', *Administrative Science Quarterly*, **42** (1), 35–67.

van Dijk, M.P. and Sverrisson, A. (2003), 'Enterprise clusters in developing countries: mechanisms of transition and stagnation', *Entrepreneurship and Regional Development*, **15**, 183–206.

Visser, E.-J. and Boschma, R. (2004), 'Learning in districts: novelty and lock-in in a regional context', *European Planning Studies*, **12**, 793–808.

von Hayek, F.A. (1945), 'The use of knowledge in society', *American Economic Review*, **35**, 519–30.

von Hippel, E. (1986), 'Lead users: A source of novel product concepts', *Management Science*, **32** (7), 791–805.

Watts, D.J. (1999), 'Networks, dynamics and the small world phenomenon', *American Journal of Sociology*, **105** (2), 493–527.

16. Technology as a remedy for political risks[1]

Veneta Andonova

Most research that focuses on the impact of the institutional environment on global business strategy assumes more or less explicitly that firms treat institutions or 'the rules of the game' as constraints, not as choice variables. This is especially true for political institutions that are related to the ability of governments to guarantee private investment. We argue, first, that political risks can be mitigated by technological choices and, second, that the technological choices of multinational companies affect host countries' development and institutions. We illustrate our argument by looking at the case of mobile telecommunication services. The implementation of technologies to make key institutions less important might allow companies to follow consistent international strategies across different developing countries, spurring the catch-up effect in international development.

Today's emerging economies are under constant observation. Business executives compare nations' potential by referring to indices of competitiveness, quality of government, corruption perceptions or political constraints. It seems, however, that most of them still prefer to keep an eye on developing countries while actually investing their capital in well-established capitalist systems. According to Khanna et al. (2005), by the end of 2002, American corporations chose to invest in Brazil, China, India and Russia a combined 2.5 percent (equivalent to $173 billion) of the total investments American companies held during that year. At the same time, American companies held assets in the United Kingdom worth $1.6 trillion and in Canada worth $514 billion.

Foreign investors are frequently kept away from developing economies by what have been called institutional voids (Khanna and Palepu, 1997). These are flaws in a country's market institutions that range from a lack of contract-enforcement mechanisms to an ill-controlled branch of the government. More generally, institutional voids arise in the absence of providers of specialized services (such as specialized intermediators in buyers' and sellers' markets, generally resulting in a reduction in the cost of doing business) or of contract-enforcing mechanisms. These institutional voids, however, are hard to compensate for as it takes considerable time to build a reliable judicial system or to create political checks and balances. Institutional voids therefore persist because they are characterized by path-dependency and embeddedness. Sometimes, entrepreneurs are able to find business models to avoid institutional voids, but it can be argued that the remedy is often as damaging for the incipient market institutions as the problem it is supposed to solve. This is the case of the Indian and Chilean business groups (Khanna and Palepu, 1999a, 1999b)[2] and the Mexican bankers in the 1970s (del Angel, 2006).[3] In addition, composite indices that are supposed to warn investors of the dangers of institutional voids in different countries frequently disguise important differences in business friendliness across developing nations (Khanna et al., 2005).

On the other hand, performing top-down institutional reforms that eliminate institutional voids is a costly process with a remarkably low success rate. One reason is that many of these reforms are perceived as coerced by different stakeholders in developing countries (Henisz et al., 2005). An alternative has been revealed by the *Doing Business* project initiated by the World Bank in an attempt to generate a race to the top among developing nations to eliminate institutional voids and to facilitate market transactions and foreign investment. It is clear now that the elimination by law of bureaucratic hurdles does not necessarily have an impact because enforcement mechanisms, whose effectiveness is often hard to measure, are deeply entrenched in old practices. As a result, institutional voids keep foreign investment away and contribute to a growing gap in international development.

We propose here that suitable technologies can change the local context and reduce the impact of a number of 'inappropriate' institutions, in particular political risks, which by western standards are labeled institutional voids. We identify several characteristics that can improve the fit of technologies in the developing country context: asset mobility, redeployability, low cost and labor-intensiveness (in contrast to capital-intensiveness). As an example, the knowledge economy has given rise to a situation in which human capital, not physical assets, is the principal source of competitive advantage (Rivette and Kline, 2000). The knowledge economy is enabled by the new information and communication technologies (ICT), so that an underdeveloped telecommunications infrastructure dramatically limits the competitiveness of emerging economies. Saunders et al. (1994) argue that newly industrialized countries such as Singapore, the Republic of Korea and Hong Kong (China) managed telecommunications as an indispensable part of their development strategies. Waverman and Roller (2001) find that the expansion of telecommunications networks in the OECD countries accounted for one-third of their output growth between 1970 and 1990. In addition, modern competitive strategies often involve information-intensive production, outsourcing and management of multiple locations, all of which rely heavily on telecoms infrastructure. In sum, good telecommunications infrastructure improves growth opportunities and competitiveness for emerging economies and makes them more attractive for foreign investment. The problem for developing countries is that investment in telecommunications infrastructure is argued to be extremely sensitive to institutional voids. The established view is that cross-country differences in access to ICT reflect differences in the severity of institutional voids, implying that institutional reforms are a necessary condition for investment in telecoms infrastructure.

A conjecture made here is that modular and mobile technologies requiring low initial investment are a viable business opportunity in institutionally underdeveloped countries (Hart and Christensen, 2002). Moreover, we speculate that companies can alter the parameters of the institutional environment by making a conscious decision to invest in cheaper mobile technologies in developing countries, instead of entering the frequently saturated markets of developed nations using expensive processes that require western-style supporting institutions. Tentatively, improvement in the environment for foreign investment can come into being as a byproduct of companies' quest for profit, whenever there are cheap and mobile technologies that are viable in an environment with many institutional voids.

The effect of technological characteristics as mechanisms for reducing the role of political institutions to guarantee private investment has not been studied in the international strategy literature. The majority of researchers looking at institutions assume that most institutional voids, and political risks in particular, are exogenous factors and that their impacts cannot be alleviated by strategic means. However, we argue that such voids may be endogenous and can be mitigated by business strategies. We first show that institutional voids seem to be less important for mobile telecommunications than for other information and communication technologies. Then we discuss the characteristics of mobile telephony that may reduce the importance of certain institutional voids such as the government's ability to guarantee private investment. Next, we consider the implications of our main hypothesis on global and international strategy. Finally, we propose several characteristics of technological processes that, if used in the context of developing countries, reduce the impact of political risk on investment.

INSTITUTIONAL VOIDS AND INVESTMENT IN TELECOMMUNICATIONS

Economists claim that basic infrastructure development in telecommunications is dependent on the quality of countries' institutions (e.g. the severity of institutional voids) and on the political institutions in particular (Esfahani and Ramírez, 2003; Henisz and Zelner, 2001; Levy and Spiller, 1996). The reason, which applies to all utilities sectors, is that the existence of political checks and balances reduces the probability of hold-up or expropriation of the investors by the government. Investment in telecommunications infrastructure is believed to suffer from a number of market imperfections that increase the role of governments, for example economies of scale generated by network externalities. In principle, governments are interested only in regulating these externalities, but occasionally they try to redistribute wealth and expropriate investors in order to obtain political credit. In the case of telecommunications, an opportunistic government could ex post expropriate the heavy capital investment in infrastructure and guarantee at least temporarily cheap service to its citizens, an action that would arguably result in some internal political credit. The chance of this happening is frequently evaluated by looking at measures of institutional voids. These often take the form of indices based on investor surveys such as the International Country Risk Guide or structurally derived indices of the local polity such as the POLCON index proposed by Henisz (2000). In order to avoid the risk of expropriation, investors are advised to avoid the poor institutional settings typical of many developing countries, even when local market conditions for growth advise otherwise (Henisz and Zelner, 2001, p. 132).

We argue that both investors and developing nations can do better if appropriate technologies are available, and investment in telecommunications provides a good example. Despite poor investor protection and lack of institutional reforms, investment in mobile phone services in Africa has been generous. Mobile phones in developing countries become substitutes for fixed telephony, allowing these populations to benefit from better communication in the same way that industrialized economies benefited from fixed telephony. Why are investors willing to take these risks in the case of mobile telephony in spite of the institutional voids?

INVESTMENT SIZE AND ASSET MOBILITY IN TELECOMMUNICATIONS

Fixed line telephony and cellular (mobile) telephony are different technologies that rely on different types of asset. For example, mobile networks can be installed more rapidly than fixed (ITU, 1999, p. 5) because, instead of requiring the installation of new wired lines, they use installed fixed lines for links between cell sites: 'Technically, there are no lines to lay to the subscriber's premises; put in a few base stations and a switch and service is available for anyone with a handset' (ITU, 1999, p. 62). Also, if built today, mobile networks are much cheaper to deploy than fixed networks (ITU, 1999, pp. 61, 83). The differences in the value and in the site specificity of the assets on which the two technologies rely mean that they require different degrees of investor protection. Technologies relying on expensive, site-specific assets are more exposed to possible governmental hold-up, so the diffusion of such technologies would depend more on eliminating institutional voids and, more specifically, on the political predictability of host countries. In fact, countries in which the institutional development does not provide sufficient guarantees for expanding fixed line networks might still be attractive for investment in cellular telephony, given the mobility and the lower cost of assets for the latter.

Econometric evidence exists to support this hypothesis. In a cross-sectional set-up, we find that better institutions for investor protection correlate less strongly with the adoption level of technologies relying on mobile and redeployable modules than with that of technologies built on site-specific assets (Andonova, 2006). In addition, Andonova and Díaz (2006) study the diffusion of telecommunications technologies and institutional proxies for investor protection across 183 countries during the period 1990–2004, showing that telecommunications dependence on superior political institutions is greatly reduced in the case of cellular telecommunications. It is argued that picking the technology that best fits the institutional environment is one of the things that policymakers and investors can do to foster technological adoption and the consequent economic development in developing countries. This is not to say that institutional voids do not matter for investment decisions. However, it is important to understand that institutional voids can be less important than previously thought, given the existence of technologies that rely on cheap, mobile and redeployable assets. Numerous examples from Africa illustrate the main result of these econometric exercises.[4]

In Africa, mobile telephony is a functional substitute for ill-developed fixed phone networks and roads, resulting in lower information asymmetry among economic agents and higher economic development. Investors who spotted the opportunity of mobile telephony in Africa went against the advice of analysts who emphasize institutional voids as a deterrent. The result is that today telecoms companies in Africa are successfully providing services that are much in demand.

In Senegal, Manobi-Senegal owned by Manobi (France) and Sonatel (Senegal) offers a service platform that provides subscribers with real-time price information for a number of agricultural products. The use of the service is associated with a 15 percent increase in the profits (net of the cost of the service) of the subscribed farmers and is also profitable for the provider. Safaricon (Kenya) and MCel (Mozambique) introduced mobile airtime credit swapping services that allow subscribers to transfer money to one another in the form of airtime credit. This works as a lending and repayment mechanism, and substitutes for the underdeveloped financial sector services, allowing mobile operators to cash some of the profits banks could have appropriated. Vodacom Congo has 1.1 million subscribers despite political and security problems in the country. People in the jungle villages in Congo were so willing to be connected that they built a 50-foot-high treehouse in order to capture the signals from the nearest cellphone towers, thus paying for the infrastructure that makes the technology work themselves.

Mobile telecommunications in Africa are able to attract investors even though the great majority of the countries on the continent are textbook examples of poor governance with plenty of institutional voids. Moreover, improvements in telecommunications have had an important social and economic impact beyond the profits of the telecoms. The reduction in information asymmetry helps farmers adjust to demand, and facilitates credit markets and access to technology, all of which have a positive impact on economic development.

In sum, in the case of mobile services in Africa, the private quest for profits resulted in improved prospects for growth, thanks to the cheaper, mobile and modular nature of the assets needed to build the network. In the light of this evidence, it is strange that the literature on global and international strategy, so concerned about institutional voids, has paid little attention to technology and to the nature of assets as a remedy for political risks. One exception is the framework for successful investment in developing countries proposed by London and Hart (2004). They identify the following factors as important for the success of multinational companies in developing countries: scalability, flexibility, decentralization, knowledge sharing, local sourcing, fragmented distribution, non-traditional partners, societal performance and local entrepreneurship. Understanding the effect of institutional voids on technologies with varying degrees of asset specificity and cost is just one way in which international strategy research can shed light on the interplay between company investment strategy and institutions.

EFFECTS OF GLOBAL AND INTERNATIONAL STRATEGY ON INSTITUTIONS

Institutional theory, complemented with transaction cost theory, agency theory and resource-based theory, is arguably the most useful theoretical approach to explain how companies should adapt their global strategies in order to be successful in developing countries (Wright et al., 2005). Using an institutional perspective, for example, Brouthers and Brouthers (2001) study the way cultural and institutional distance affect entry mode. Fey and Bjorkman (2001) study the effect of HRM practices on the performance of foreign companies in Russia. Meyer (2004) looks at the spillover effects a foreign company has on host markets. Delios and Henisz (2000) and Meyer (2001) analyze the importance of experience and capabilities for new market entry in the context of developing countries. All of these studies are labeled 'representative' for the field of international strategy (Wright et al., 2005). At the same time, in the special issue of the *Journal of Management Studies* (2005) on strategy research in emerging economies, the following were identified as two of the most interesting questions in the domain of institutional theory. How do informal institutions complement formal institutions to explain foreign investors' entry strategies? To what extent do problems arising from institutional differences increase transaction and agency costs and lead to exit by foreign entrants (Wright et al., 2005, p. 24)? What all these studies and directions for future research have in common is that they take the rules of the game (the institutions) as given and exogenous to the activities of the companies, and in particular to their investment strategies.

Experts in global and international strategy are in an advantageous position to push the boundaries of institutional theory and create an impact on other social sciences by documenting the mechanisms by which companies investing in developing nations change local institutions, for better or for worse. This is one actionable plan by which we can get beyond the stage of 'the institutions matter' to one where we actually understand institutional change and its direct and immediate impact on companies' investment decisions and internationalization. Some work has already been done in this direction. London and Hart (2004), for example, propose a new model of internationalization, which analyses the assumptions of the transnational model (Tallman, 1991) and questions the assumption that developing nations would necessarily mimic the western-style model of development and institutional environment. They propose that successful multinational companies that target the base-of-the-pyramid market are those that not only develop global efficiency, national responsiveness and worldwide learning, but also achieve social embeddedness; that is, the capability to develop 'a deep understanding of the local environment, and [focus] on generating bottom-up business creation based on identifying, leveraging, and building the existing social infrastructure' (London and Hart, 2004, p. 366). In summary, investment in developing nations should be molded according to the host country's institutions after learning how these particular institutions work. This framework, however, does not include the possibility that foreign investors' strategies will affect developing countries' institutions (rules of the game). Nevertheless, there is evidence that makes the impact of investment strategies on the institutions of many developing countries hard to deny (Khanna et al., 2005, p. 74).

For instance, smallholders in Africa were seen as commercially unattractive because of the inefficiencies stemming from the absence of reliable, useful information. In Africa today, however, cheap and reliable information made available by the telecoms' decision to invest in the continent's mobile network as described above, makes small farmers more productive, increases their bargaining power with intermediaries, improves their access to credit, and eventually transforms the production and exchange process for goods, services and technologies (Eggleston et al., 2002; Davis and Ochieng, 2006), affecting overall productivity and growth and the demand for market-supporting institutions.

Approaching institutions as mechanisms that can be molded by companies' behavior has at least two advantages. First, firms are forced to focus on the long-term impact of their decisions on local institutions and to act responsibly (avoiding, for example, the payment of bribes). This transfers responsibilities from the government, which in the developing country context is frequently ineffective, weak and unaccountable, to private enterprise. Private enterprises, which depend largely on developed countries' markets and are listed on stock exchanges, can be disciplined and made accountable as they have a lot to lose. Second, top–bottom institutional reforms, when necessary, would be designed explicitly not only to include government bodies but also to regulate international investors, or in general, business behavior, recognizing important synergies and interdependencies in governmental and companies' interests.

Again, we propose here that suitable technologies can change the local context and reduce the impact of a number of 'inappropriate' institutions, in particular political risks, which by western standards are labeled institutional voids. In addition, we identify several characteristics that can improve the fit of technologies into the developing country context: asset mobility, redeployability, low cost and labor-intensiveness (in contrast to capital-intensiveness).

Both asset mobility and redeployability reduce the degree of asset specificity.[5] The existence of specific assets gives rise to the hold-up problem we describe above for the case of investment in telecommunication (Williamson, 1985). In essence, if investors reduce their exposure to expropriation by the host country's government or interest groups by using assets that have high value outside this specific contract (because assets are mobile and redeployable), then the lack of western-style investment protection would be less of a deterrent for foreign investment. This mobile and redeployable technology should also be available at relatively low cost, which reduces additionally the investors' exposure to risk. As a result, developing countries can have similar goods and services to those available in developed countries, but will use different technological processes. More optimistically, we can speculate that, if certain technological innovations designed to work in developing countries prove sustainable, they can be exported to developed countries that have their own problems with environmental impact, for example. As conjectured by Hart and Christensen (2002), if distributed energy production is economically and environmentally viable in developing countries, there will be no reason to limit its use to developing countries only.

In order to fit into an environment with multiple institutional voids, mobility and redeployability should be achieved at low cost, thus reducing investors' exposure to business risk while increasing the attractiveness of the investment location. One way to reduce the cost of the technology tailored to the developing country environment is to use the factors of production that are abundant locally. Developing countries tend to have high birth rates and young populations, making them abundant in labor.[6] The literature on factor-saving innovation has studied the effects of factor abundance on the efficiency of choosing labor-intensive versus capital-intensive production technologies. A standard conclusion of these models is that there is sound economic logic for firms to choose capital-intensive technologies when capital is abundant and labor is scarce, while it is rational to choose labor-intensive technologies when labor is abundant and capital is scarce (Zuleta, 2006). This insight has important implications for the framework proposed here. If firms entering developing markets do not adjust their technologies to employ the factor that is locally abundant, they end up with expensive operations (given the host country's factor prices) and require supporting institutions like the ones available where these technologies were initially invented. Considering that firms rarely engage in creating a labor-intensive version of their processes to be used in the developing country environment, we can conclude that companies largely expect that the institutions supporting their technologies will be available locally, and hope that local governments will promote a western-style environment to attract foreign investment. Companies therefore limit their possibilities for investment as there are few developing countries that have managed to transform their environment to the full satisfaction of foreign investors (as Chile or South Korea have done, for example). Companies can considerably increase the number of attractive investment locations if they develop the capability to transform advanced, capital-intensive processes into more basic, labor-intensive operations. This will reduce the size of the capital required for investment, shrinking the exposure to business risk and, more importantly, reducing the need for supporting political institutions to make investment possible in the first place.

CONCLUSION

The impact of the institutional environment on global business strategy has been identified as an important research field (Rumelt et al., 1994; Peng, 2001). Most research efforts in this direction, however, make the implicit assumption that institutions (the rules of the game) and institutional voids are given, and that companies should adapt their strategies to the local context if they find it profitable. This is especially true if we consider political institutions related to the ability of the government to guarantee private investment. If we accept this approach to international and global strategy, we end up with only a short list of developing countries that are attractive investment locations because their governments are relatively effective and manage to alleviate the effect of existing institutional voids. We argue here that companies can expand their international scope and make an impact on international development by adopting technological processes that reduce the importance of western-style institutions and, in particular, the importance of political institutions that limit the risk of expropriation of foreign investors. After analyzing the success of mobile telephony in Africa, we hypothesize that some of the characteristics of these technological processes that fit into the environment of most developing countries are asset mobility and redeployability coupled with low to moderate levels of investment size. We propose that the low cost can be achieved by developing the capability to transform capital-intensive processes into labor-intensive ones.

The success of this strategy is not guaranteed, as it does not take place in a vacuum. As we learnt from the pattern of adoption of information and communication technologies, there are important local socio-economic conditions such as human capital and urbanization that are related to the diffusion of telecommunications. These and other forces will shape investment decision and technological choices, but we should not underestimate the ability of people to adjust to working technologies if these exist and have been sufficiently adapted to the local context. Examples are the villagers in Congo who built a treehouse, and the literate individuals with cell phones in South Africa who receive, read and communicate text messages to those without a cell phone and to those who can't read and write (Gough, 2005).

We know that institutions are important and can create difficulties both for companies' international business strategies and for developing countries' prospects. Finding ways to make certain key institutions less important via technological processes would allow companies to follow consistent international strategies across different developing countries and would spur on the catching-up effect in international development. If companies use this framework when drawing up their international strategies, they will benefit from an increase in attractive investment opportunities. Simultaneously, their profitable investment choices will contribute to more balanced international development and may even have the potential to change the dynamics of complex global phenomena such as international migration.

NOTES

1. I thank Steve Tallman and Hernando Zuleta for their comments and suggestions. All remaining mistakes are mine.
2. Khanna and Palepu (1999b) argue that large business groups in India and Chile continuously strengthen their internal structure and processes, while performing value-enhancing intermediation functions in environments that lack appropriate market institutions. It can be argued, however, that such private institutional arrangements interfere unfavorably with the country's gradual process of institutional development. In fact, Khanna and Palepu (1999c) recognize that business groups enjoy short-term benefits from preventing the development of national market institutions and conjecture but never prove why 'it is not in the long-term interests of companies' to encourage institutional development.
3. From 1940 until 1982, Mexican bankers relied extensively on insider lending and the use of private networks for information exchange. It has been argued that these business practices were optimally adapted to the institutional environment characterized by uncertain property rights and scarce information. These practices arguably helped Mexican bankers to protect themselves from opportunistic behavior by establishing commitments and creating discipline. Nevertheless, this mode of operations limited competition and led to very high concentration in the industry, preventing the development of an effective credit market in the economy (del Angel, 2006).
4. The examples in this section are taken from the award-winning essay 'ICTs as appropriate technologies for African development' by Kristin Davis and Cosmos Ochieng (2006).
5. Specific assets are those whose value is greatly reduced outside a specific transaction.
6. This assertion is true for developing countries on average but there are important exceptions. Most transition countries in Eastern and Central Europe have aging populations.

REFERENCES

Andonova, V. (2006), 'Mobile phones, the Internet and the institutional environment', *Telecommunications Policy*, **30**, 29–45.

Andonova, V. and L. Díaz (2006), 'Political institutions and the development of telecommunications', IZA Working Paper 2569, available at http://ftp.iza.org/dp2569.pdf

Brouthers, K. and L. Brouthers (2001), 'Explaining the national cultural distance paradox', *Journal of International Business Studies*, **32** (1), 177–89.

Davis, K. and C. Ochieng (2006), 'ICTs as appropriate technologies for African development', available at www.ifc.org/competition, consulted on 3 March 2006.

del Angel, G. (2006), 'The corporate governance of the Mexican banking system in historical perspective: 1940–1990', CIDE Working Paper.

Delios, A. and W. Henisz (2000), 'Japanese firms' investment strategies in emerging economies', *Academy of Management Journal*, **43** (3), 305–23.

Eggleston, K., R. Jensen and R. Zeckhauser (2002), 'Information and communication technologies, markets, and economic development', Working Paper, Tufts University, Department of Economics, Medford, MA.

Esfahani, H.S. and M.T. Ramírez (2003), 'Institutions, infrastructure, and economic growth', *Journal of Development Economics*, **70** (2), 443–78.

Fey, C. and I. Bjorkman (2001), 'The importance of human resource management practices on MNC subsidiary performance in Russia', *Journal of International Business Studies*, **32**, 59–75.

Gough, N. (2005), 'Introduction in Vodafone Africa: the impact of mobile phones', Vodafone Policy Paper Series No. 2.

Hart, S. and C. Christensen (2002), 'The great leap. Driving innovation from the base of the pyramid', *MIT Sloan Management Review*, **44** (1), 51–6.

Henisz, W. (2000), 'The institutional environment for economic growth', *Economics and Politics*, **12** (1), 1–31.

Henisz, W., G. Holburn and B. Zelner (2005), 'Deinstitutionalization and institutional replacement: state-centered and neoliberal models in the global electricity supply industry', Best Paper Proceedings 2005, Academy of Management Annual Meeting, Honolulu, HI.

Henisz, W. and B. Zelner (2001), 'The institutional environment for telecommunications investment', *Journal of Economics and Management Strategy*, **10** (1), 123–47.

ITU (1999), 'Mobile cellular', World Telecommunications Development Report.

Khanna, T. and K. Palepu (1997), 'Why focused strategies may be wrong for emerging markets', *Harvard Business Review*, **75** (4), 41–51.

Khanna, T. and K. Palepu (1999a), 'The right way to restructure conglomerates in emerging markets', *Harvard Business Review*, **77** (4), 125–35.

Khanna, T. and K. Palepu (1999b), 'Policy shocks, market intermediaries, and corporate strategy: the evolution of business groups in Chile and India', *Journal of Economics and Management Strategy*, **8** (2), 271–30.

Khanna, T. and K. Palepu (1999c), 'Letters to the Editor', *Harvard Business Review*, **77** (6), 195–6.

Khanna, T., K. Palepu and J. Sinha (2005), 'Strategies that fit emerging markets', *Harvard Business Review*, **83** (6), 63–76.

Levy, B. and P. Spiller (1996), *Regulations, Institutions and Commitment*, Cambridge: Cambridge University Press.

London, T. and S. Hart (2004), 'Reinventing strategies for emerging markets: beyond the transnational model', *Journal of International Business Studies*, **35**, 350–70.

Meyer, K. (2001), 'Institutions, transaction costs, and entry mode choice in Eastern Europe', *Journal of International Business Studies*, **32** (2), 357–67.

Meyer, K. (2004), 'Perspectives on multinational enterprises in emerging economies', *Journal of International Business Studies*, **35** (4), 259–76.

Peng, M. (2001), 'The resource-based view and international business', *Journal of Management*, **27** (6), 803–29.

Rivette, K. and D. Kline (2000), 'Discovering new value in intellectual property', *Harvard Business Review*, **78** (1), 54–67.

Rumelt, R., D. Shendel and D. Teece (1994), 'Fundamental issues in strategy', in R. Rumelt, D. Schendel and D. Teece (eds), *Fundamental Issues in Strategy: A Research Agenda*, Boston, MA: Harvard Business School Press, pp. 9–47.

Saunders, R., J. Warford and B. Wellenius (1994), *Telecommunications and Economic Development*, Baltimore, MD: Johns Hopkins University Press.

Tallman, S. (1991), 'Strategic management models and resourced-based strategies among MNEs in a host market', *Strategic Management Journal*, **12**, 69–82.

Waverman, L. and L.H. Roller (2001), 'Telecommunications infrastructure and economic development: a simultaneous approach', *American Economic Review*, **91** (4), 909–23.

Williamson, O. (1985), *The Economic Institutions of Capitalism: Firms, Markets and Relational Contracting*, New York: The Free Press.

Wright, M., I. Filatotchev, R. Hoskisson and M. Peng (2005), 'Strategy research in emerging economies: challenging the conventional wisdom', *Journal of Management Studies*, **42** (1), 1–33.

Zuleta, H. (2006), 'Factor saving innovations and factor income shares', Universidad del Rosario, Working Paper 6.

17. The role of geographic distance in FDI

Roberto Ragozzino

Geographic distance has received comparatively little attention from research in international business, and for the most part the discourse has considered this variable as a surrogate for cultural or psychic distance (e.g. Johanson and Vahlne, 1977; Kogut and Singh, 1988). There are a few noteworthy exceptions of studies that have investigated the bilateral affinities of source and host countries, pointing to a number of determinants of foreign direct investment (FDI), including the proximity of the two locations. For instance, Yoshihara (1978) and Tsurumi (1976) note the propensity for Japanese firms to expand into Southeast Asia, and similar behaviors have been reported in relation to Swedish, Australian, Italian and French multinationals (e.g. Deane, 1970; Michalet and Delapierre, 1976; Swedenborg, 1979; Onida and Viesti, 1988). Furthermore, Veugelers (1991) has emphasized the importance of proximity in firms' international investment decisions, even in the face of location-specific advantages that may be available in a host country.

A second stream of research has explored the time-dependent choices made by firms expanding internationally, highlighting experiential learning as a determinant of firms' expansion into foreign markets, especially remote ones (e.g. Johanson and Vahlne, 1977; Vernon, 1979). This process-based perspective has found that companies' initial investments abroad tend to be less resource intensive and to be in markets that are geographically and culturally close to the host country's, while firms eventually expand to greater degrees and intensities over time and through experience accumulation (Barkema et al., 1996).

Unfortunately, while noting the relevance of geographic distance as a determinant of firms' investment decisions, these studies have not parceled out the theoretical reasons underlying firms' preferences for neighboring investments. In fact, geographic distance has been mostly discussed in terms of the transportation and logistical costs that crop up in remote investments (e.g. Caves, 1996), and recent work has argued that concerns surrounding the relevance of distance should diminish over time, owing to continued advancements in telecommunication and information technology (e.g. Grosse and Trevino, 1996). In contrast, the bulk of the research in international business investigating entry mode has tended to focus either on micro-level determinants of entry – namely, firm and transaction level characteristics – or it has devoted its attention to other country-level factors of entry mode such as cultural distance and political risk (e.g. Anderson and Gatignon, 1986; Hennart, 1988; Kim and Hwang, 1992).

The apparent omission of geographic distance as an important variable for firms' entry decisions stands in sharp contrast to research in other areas of business, which has shown that proximity, as opposed to remoteness, can directly affect the ability of businesses to organize operations, value prospective investments, acquire resources and even survive (e.g. Lerner, 1995; Audretsch and Feldman, 1996; Chakrabarti and Mitchell, 2006). I draw from this diverse set of theoretical arguments and findings and explore whether geographic distance can help to explain firms' entry mode decisions. First, using insights from financial economics that have considered geographic distance as a proxy for information asymmetry, I develop the proposition that investments located at more distant locations raise the hazard of adverse selection for foreign entrants, and cause them to seek shared-ownership solutions rather than internalization. Second, setting aside the ex ante valuation uncertainty surrounding remote investments, I draw from transaction cost economics theory to argue that geographic distance can also exacerbate the risk of ex post opportunism by foreign partners, because of the reduced ability of entrants to monitor and control operations situated at more distant locations. The prediction that follows, which runs counter to my previous prediction, is that firms will opt to internalize at more remote locations, and engage in inter-firm cooperation otherwise.

Last, I discuss the moderating effects that geographic distance can bring to other country-level determinants of the entry decision, such as cultural distance and political risk. While previous work has studied how these two variables can affect firms' international strategies, I know of no study that has explored whether the available findings are subject to a different interpretation conditional on geographic distance. Given that the extant research has focused on the risk of opportunism that can arise ex post, owing to cultural distance and political risk, and since I argue that distance can hinder the ability of foreign entrants to monitor their investments, I predict that the effects of these two variables will be exacerbated at farther locations, and attenuated otherwise.

GEOGRAPHIC DISTANCE AS A PROXY FOR INFORMATION ASYMMETRY

Although the basic assumption that proximity can yield an information advantage to a party *vis-à-vis* its remote counterpart seems straightforward, there have not been many formal empirical studies to support this idea to date. It has not been until recently that scholars have begun to study geographic distance as a proxy for information asymmetry, and this relatively new stream of research is perhaps a result in part of the increased importance that information economics theory has gained following the reception of the Nobel Prize by Akerlof, Spence and Stiglitz for their work in this area of economics.

Jaffe et al. (1993) have studied the effects of localization on knowledge spillovers for a sample of patents assigned to universities and corporate entities in the United States, and their analysis shows a positive and significant relationship between the locations of patent citations and of the patents being cited, thereby supporting the idea that proximity can result in superior information. As a second illustration, Lerner (1995) examines the role of geographic distance as a determinant of board membership of venture capitalists (VCs) in entrepreneurial firms, finding that proximity significantly increases the likelihood of direct participation by VCs in these firms. In turn, the monitoring function of VCs reduces the risks of agency problems that tend to surface when appropriate controls (such as direct participation on the board) are not in place. As another example, in commercial real estate transactions, research has shown that buyers tend to be local when the extent of the information asymmetry separating the parties is severe (e.g. Garmaise and Moskowitz, 2004). The logic offered by these authors to explain their findings is that proximate investors have better information on local properties, and are more familiar with market conditions, regulations, environmental considerations, and social dynamics than remote buyers.

The effects of geographic distance defined as a proxy for information asymmetry have also been studied in the area of financial investments. Since proximate investors can talk to local firms' stakeholders with regularity and establish personal ties with local executives, they hold superior information with which to value localized investment opportunities (Coval and Moskowitz, 1999; Malloy, 2005), and this benefit results in higher gains realized by investors holding a larger proportion of local firms' stocks in their portfolios (Coval and Moskowitz, 2001). Similar findings have also been reported at the international level. In a recent study, Bae et al. (2005) have investigated a sample of stock analysts from a set of 32 countries, showing that domestic analysts consistently forecast earnings better than their foreign counterparts. Interestingly, this result is inversely related to the information disclosure requirements imposed on firms in their respective countries, suggesting that proximity becomes particularly salient when the existence of private information is pervasive.

The findings illustrated above provide a useful starting point from which to discuss the effects of geographic distance on firms' entry decisions. Absent internal and exogenous constraints, the spectrum of governance solutions available to foreign entrants spans the continuum from outsourcing to wholly-owned operations. Furthermore, the literature that has studied the trade-offs inherent in these alternatives using an information economics lens, as I do here, has tended to use wholly-owned solutions as a benchmark, reasoning that when the magnitude of the information asymmetry becomes severe, firms prefer to engage in intermediate ownership solutions such as strategic alliances (e.g. Balakrishnan and Koza, 1993; Hennart and Reddy, 1997; Reuer and Koza, 2000). To the extent that geographic distance can be used as a proxy for asymmetric information, as discussed in the previous section of the chapter, it is plausible that the same logic can be extended to the entry mode decision facing multinational organizations. For instance, firms situated in more proximate locations to their targeted countries may be able to gain access to information available through direct or indirect contact with prospective partners or their stakeholders (e.g. Tallman and Phene, 2006). This sort of knowledge can not only mitigate the information asymmetry gap separating a firm from a targeted investment, but it can also reduce the uncertainty about the host country's environment, legal system, customs and culture. Therefore, I predict that entrants will shift toward internalization and away from shared-ownership arrangements at more proximate locations, and reverse this strategy when entering more distant countries.

Although the purpose of this chapter is not to provide an empirical investigation of the role of distance on the entry mode decision of firms, I have collected some data that offer descriptive evidence supporting my prediction. Table 17.1 shows a selected sample of countries targeted by US multinationals seeking acquisitions abroad over the time period 1993–2004. These data were collected from the Mergers and Acquisitions module of the Security Data Corporation (SDC) database. Columns I and II present the number of transactions from the US to each respective country, as well as the average percentage of ownership sought. Column III provides the mean distance separating acquirers and sellers in these transactions. An inspection of these data shows that US firms adjusted their ownership decisions based on the distance separating them from the host country. The correlation coefficient between geographic distance and the ownership acquired variable, which ranges from 1 to 100 percent, is in fact positive and significant. Furthermore, a *t*-test aimed at determining whether the mean ownership acquired at distances lower than the average for the sample (3571 miles) differed from the ownership acquired at distances greater than the average was also highly significant (i.e. $p < 0.001$). While these results are not conclusive and they call for further investigation in a multivariate setting, they provide initial evidence of the relevance of geographic distance to the entry mode decision made by multinationals.

Table 17.1   Percentage of equity acquired by country

Host country	I Deal count	II Ownership acquired (%)	III Average distance (miles)
Canada	209	85	1363
United Kingdom	156	82	4061
France	31	72	4199
Netherlands	12	61	4443
Norway	9	71	4478
Italy	8	62	4588
Sweden	13	77	4592
Germany	16	75	4727
Switzerland	9	76	4829
Japan	17	33	6283
Israel	13	76	6494
South Korea	4	18	6716
New Zealand	3	42	7841
Australia	34	57	9058
Mean	–	77	3572

	II–III
$\sigma =$	–59%
Mean ownership acquired at less than the mean distance:	83%
Mean ownership acquired at more than the mean distance:	71%
t-test for ownership acquired differences: 3.88 ($p < 0.001$)	

GEOGRAPHIC DISTANCE AS A MONITORING CONSTRAINT

The reasoning laid out in the preceding section of the chapter focuses on geographic distance as a proxy for information asymmetry. More precisely,

I argue that geographic distance can inherently increase the ex ante costs of entry, and cause firms to choose intermediate governance solutions over wholly-owned alternatives. In contrast, this section of the chapter discusses the costs that can arise in the aftermath of entry, using a transaction cost economics (TCE) lens to examine the role of distance in FDI.

In a nutshell, TCE focuses on the optimal governance choice to be made by a firm when there is risk of opportunistic behavior by prospective partners to a transaction. To the extent that this risk exists and that firms are constrained by bounded rationality and cannot predict how or when opportunism may turn up in the future, and based on the characteristics of a transaction (i.e. the specificity of the asset to be exchanged), firms may choose to internalize or outsource. Thus, while the governance decision is to be made at time zero, it is based on the expectations by the parties of ex post opportunistic behavior by their counterpart(s). In this respect, TCE differs from information economics, because the latter focuses on the risk of misrepresentation by a negotiating party *before* a deal takes place, while the latter centers around the hazards that may occur *after* a deal is consummated. Although it is clearly difficult to disentangle conceptually the problem of adverse selection, which affects the early stages of a deal, from the problems of moral hazard and holdup, which become manifest ex post (Stiglitz, 2000), it is evident that the two hazards are different in nature. While I am not trying to offer a thorough comparative treatment of information economics and transaction cost economics, partly because this gargantuan task is well beyond my abilities, it is important to draw a distinction between these two theoretical frameworks now, for the purpose of the ensuing discussion.

The central question of this section of the chapter is to address whether and how geographic distance might affect the governance decision by foreign entrants, based on TCE logic. Aside from the ex ante valuation problems that distance can introduce, it is apparent that larger distances between entrants' home countries and the host country might introduce higher monitoring and coordination costs for the former, once foreign operations begin. Using transaction cost economics reasoning, these costs will tend to rise when shared-ownership solutions are preferred to full acquisitions, because greater amounts of ownership confer a proportional degree of control over the investment and the ability by the acquirer to implement decisions and resolve disputes that could arise ex post (e.g. Anderson and Gatignon, 1986; Grossman and Hart, 1986). On the contrary, partial ownership may leave partners with differing incentives and opportunities that could not be accounted for in the due diligence stages of a transaction, owing to bounded rationality. As partial evidence of this rationale, a working paper by Chakrabarti and Mitchell (2006) studies the effects of distance on firms' acquisition behavior in the chemical industry and finds that acquirers prefer proximate investments over more remote ones when the integration and monitoring requirements of the target firm are high.

To the extent that opportunistic behavior is more likely to surface when monitoring is costly to implement (e.g. Williamson, 1985, p. 65), and provided that geographic distance can limit the ability of, or raise the costs for business partners to screen and penalize shirking by their counterparts, I predict that, ceteris paribus, TCE considerations will cause foreign entrants to seek higher levels of ownership (i.e. internalizations) when the investment is situated at farther away locations, and lower levels of ownership (i.e. cooperative agreements and outsourcing) otherwise.

GEOGRAPHIC DISTANCE AS A MODERATOR OF CULTURAL DISTANCE AND POLITICAL RISK

Although the previous sections have discussed how geographic distance may directly affect the entry mode decisions of firms, I am also interested in exploring how this variable may moderate the effects of other country-level sources of uncertainty. While research on entry mode has devoted a considerable amount of attention to such hazards as political risk and cultural distance, this work has not fully attended to the need to introduce moderating variables to improve our understanding of the effects of country-level sources of uncertainty on firms' FDI (e.g. Tihanyi et al., 2005). In the ensuing paragraphs, I will discuss how geographic distance might moderate the effects of cultural distance and political risk and therefore provide conditional explanations for how these two hazards might affect firms' entry decisions.

A great deal of work has been done in international business research on cultural distance and its effects on entry mode. Although the findings have not been conclusive and some debate remains on the role of culture (e.g. Erramilli et al., 1997; Tihanyi et al., 2005), the evidence suggests that cultural distance tends to increase the cost of entry and limit firms' ability to transfer core competencies across borders (e.g. Bartlett and Ghoshal, 1989). The upshot is that when firms seek international investments in countries characterized by cultural dissimilarities, they prefer shared-ownership entry modes over wholly-owned subsidiaries (e.g. Kogut and Singh, 1988; Hennart and Larimo, 1998).

Political risk has also been found to affect firms' international investment decisions. First, weaknesses in the institutional environment can endanger the protection and enforcement of property rights laws, and consequently increase the risks embedded in a business exchange (Williamson, 1996).

Additionally, the lack of reliability of incumbent institutions in the host country can cause relationships to change unexpectedly, promised incentives to vanish, and the ability to transfer factors of production to and from the host country to be curtailed. These considerations have been associated with the propensity of firms to calibrate their entry mode strategies to account for political risk (Delios and Beamish, 1999), and the findings indicate that shared-ownership solutions tend to be chosen over wholly-owned subsidiaries when political risk is high in the host country (e.g. Hill et al., 1990; Shan, 1991).

The discussion above suggests that cultural distance and political risk are important country-level dimensions that directly affect firms' entry mode decisions. The question that comes to the fore is whether geographic distance can moderate the effects of these variables. In other words, it is interesting to explore whether the relationship between cultural distance or political risk and the entry mode decision stays constant independent of geographic distance, or if instead it shifts based on the proximity of the host country. As I discuss previously, geographic distance can (1) increase the valuation uncertainty of foreign investments and cause firms to prefer shared-ownership solutions at distant locations, and (2) increase the monitoring and coordination costs that follow entry into a host country, which in turn leads firms to internalize more in remote investments, instead. Given these opposing outcomes, it becomes challenging to predict how distance may affect firms' investment decisions in the face of cultural distance and political risk. On one hand, geographic distance may exacerbate the informational uncertainty created by these two country-level hazards, leading to lower ownership solutions at farther locations, holding cultural distance and political risk constant. However, to the extent that proximity reduces the monitoring and coordinating costs in the aftermath of an investment, firms may also opt to internalize more at distant locations for a given level of cultural distance (or political risk).

In Figure 17.1, I draw from the same data on international acquisitions by US firms between 1993 and 2004 as before. Cultural distance is computed using the method developed by Kogut and Singh (1988), and political risk is calculated from the ratings made available by the International Country Risk Guide (ICRG). The figure offers descriptive statistics that indicate that geographic distance causes acquirers to reduce the amount of ownership in a foreign target more when cultural distance and political risk are high. The first graph in Figure 17.1 shows that when the geographic distance between buyers and sellers in mergers and acquisitions goes from the 2500–5000 mile range to the 5000–10000+ mile range, the drop in ownership acquired is roughly 6 percent when the target country is at a low cultural distance. In contrast, the drop in ownership in countries characterized by high cultural distance is about 16 percent. Similarly, ownership acquired drops by only 7 percent when political risk in the host country is low, whereas buyers buy 10 percent less in far off locations when the political risk is high. Therefore, these findings offer some evidence that distance may exacerbate (rather than mitigate) the effects of cultural distance and political risk. Needless to say, these figures clearly call for a more thorough empirical investigation by future research.

Average percentage acquired by US firms by cultural distance and geographic distance 1993–2004

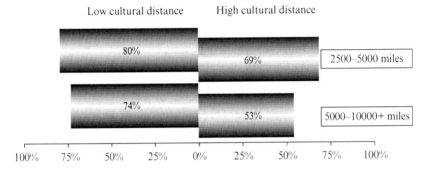

Average percentage acquired by US firms by political risk and geographic distance 1993–2004

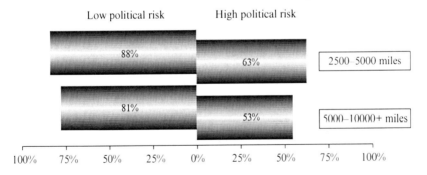

Figure 17.1   Geographic distance interactions

CONCLUSIONS

This chapter discusses the role that geographic distance can play in the entry mode decisions implemented by firms. First, using an information economics framework and drawing from extensive work in other areas of business research, I argue that proximity, as opposed to remoteness, can facilitate the ex ante due diligence stages of a transaction, and therefore cause firms to internalize more in nearer investments, and less when the target location is farther away. Second, turning to the monitoring and coordination costs of foreign investments, and using a TCE perspective, I argue that farther investments raise transaction costs for foreign firms, leading them to internalize at more remote locations, and to opt for shared ownership arrangements otherwise. Clearly, appropriate empirical tests aimed at understanding how these opposing predictions reconcile would be useful. The descriptive statistics I provide seem to underscore the value of proximity as a source of information advantages, but more extensive work is needed to shed some light on this issue.

Aside from the direct effects of geographic distance on firms' investment decisions, I also discuss how this variable might moderate or exacerbate the effects of two other country-level determinants of entry – cultural distance and political risk. Prior work has found that firms resort to intermediate governance solutions when cultural distance or political risk is high in the target country. On one hand, I predict that geographic distance might mitigate the effects of these two hazards on ownership, because remote investments raise the risk of opportunistic behavior by indigenous partners borne by foreign firms. On the other hand, I also argue that the valuation risks inherent in farther away investments can exacerbate the effects of cultural distance and political risk, and lead firms to prefer shared-governance solutions at remote locations, and full ownership in more proximate undertakings.

A number of interesting implications stem from the present discussion on geographic distance. As studies on the effects of distance gain momentum in other areas of research, there is a valuable opportunity to build on the findings coming from related research to explore whether this country-level variable can help to explain firms' entry mode decisions. This work would be particularly helpful given the paucity of research that has investigated how established determinants of firms' international strategies, such as cultural distance and political risk, might play out in conjunction with other under-explored factors, such as geographic distance (Tihanyi et al., 2005). For example, the present discussion raises the possibility that cultural distance may become a relatively small concern in proximate investments, such as a US firm investment in Canada, whereas it may be a much greater hazard for the same US firm investing in Australia, owing to the geographic distance separating the two countries, and despite the similar cultural characteristics shared by Canada and Australia. If proven empirically, this logic could well explain the mixed findings reported on the effects of cultural dissimilarities on MNEs' governance choices. As a second illustration, it may also be possible to draw a direct link between firms' competitive objectives with the hazards presented by geographic distance. For instance, future work may attempt to separate transactions aimed at the attainment of scale economies from others intended to yield strategic flexibility, and then examine how geographic distance affects firms' decisions in either case.

Overall, although geographic distance may be but one of the many challenges faced by multinational firms, this chapter points at further research aimed at understanding how distance can allow firms to obtain resources, develop partnerships abroad, enter new markets, and so on. While some work has argued that improvements in transportation and information technology will reduce the effects of distance over time, it is also true that the level of internationalization and the scope of the geographic operations of firms have also increased in the last few decades. Thus it remains to be explained whether one phenomenon (i.e. improved technology) offsets the effects of geographic distance, or whether the concerns discussed in this chapter stay relevant over time. Further, it would be interesting to explore the sources of performance heterogeneity that can stem from firms' geographic preferences. In other words, future empirical work investigating whether entry decisions made in the face of geographic distance translate into better or worse performance for firms would be very valuable.

REFERENCES

Anderson, E. and H. Gatignon (1986), 'Modes of foreign entry: a transaction cost analysis and propositions', *Journal of International Business Studies*, 17, 1–26.

Audretsch, D. and M.P. Feldman (1996), 'R&D spillovers and the geography of innovation and production', *American Economic Review*, 86, 630–40.

Bae, K.H., R.M. Stulz and H. Tan (2005), 'Do local analysts know more? A cross-country study of the performance of local analysts and foreign analysts', working paper 11697, National Bureau of Economic Research, Cambridge, MA.

Balakrishnan, S. and M.P. Koza (1993), 'Information asymmetry, adverse selection, and joint ventures', *Journal of Economic Behavior and Organization*, 20, 99–117.

Barkema, H., J.J. Bell and J.M. Pennings (1996), 'Foreign entry, cultural barriers, and learning', *Strategic Management Journal*, 17, 151–66.

Bartlett, C. and S. Ghoshal (1989), *Managing Across Borders: The Transnational Solution*, Boston, MA: Harvard Business School Press.

Caves, R. (1996), *Multinational Enterprises and Economic Analysis*, 2nd edn, Cambridge: Cambridge University Press.

Chakrabarti, A. and W. Mitchell (2006), 'Target selection: the role of geographic distance in acquisition decision-making', Unpublished manuscript.

Coval, J.D. and T.J. Moskowitz (1999), 'Home bias at home: local equity preference in domestic portfolios', *Journal of Finance*, 54, 2045–73.

Coval, J.D. and T.J. Maskowitz (2001), 'The geography of investment: informed trading and asset prices', *Journal of Political Economy*, **109**, 811–41.

Deane, R.S. (1970), *Foreign Investment in New Zealand Manufacturing*, Wellington, New Zealand: Sweet and Maxwell.

Delios, A. and P.W. Beamish (1999), 'Ownership strategies for Japanese firms: transactional, institutional, and experience influences', *Strategic Management Journal*, **20**, 915–33.

Erramilli, M.K., S. Agarwal and S.S. Kim (1997), 'Are firm-specific advantages location-specific too?', *Journal of International Business Studies*, **28**, 735–57.

Garmaise, M.J. and T.J. Moskowitz (2004), 'Confronting information asymmetries: evidence from real estate markets', *Review of Financial Studies*, **17**, 405–37.

Grosse, R. and L.J. Trevino (1996), 'Foreign direct investment in the United States: an analysis by country of origin', *Journal of International Business Studies*, **27**, 139–55.

Grossman, S.J. and O.D. Hart (1986), 'The costs and benefits of ownership: a theory of vertical and lateral integration', *The Journal of Political Economy*, **94**, 691–720.

Hennart, J.-F. (1988), 'A transaction cost theory of equity joint ventures', *Strategic Management Journal*, **9**, 361–74.

Hennart, J.-F. and J. Larimo (1998), 'The impact of culture on the strategy of multinational enterprises: does national origin affect ownership decisions?', *Journal of International Business Studies*, **29**, 515–38.

Hennart, J.-F. and S. Reddy (1997), 'The choice between mergers/acquisitions and joint ventures: the case of Japanese investors in the United States', *Strategic Management Journal*, **18**, 1–12.

Hill, C.W., P. Hwang and W.C. Kim (1990), 'An eclectic theory of the choice of international entry mode', *Strategic Management Journal*, **11**, 117–28.

Jaffe, A.B., M. Trajtenberg and R. Henderson (1993), 'Geographic localization of knowledge spillovers as evidenced by patent citations', *Quarterly Journal of Economics*, **63**, 577–98.

Johanson, J. and J.E. Vahlne (1977), 'The internationalization process of the firm', *Journal of International Business Studies*, **8**, 23–32.

Kim, W.C. and P. Hwang (1992), 'Global strategy and multinationals' entry mode choice', *Journal of International Business Studies*, **23**, 29–53.

Kogut, B. and H. Singh (1988), 'The effect of national culture on the choice of entry mode', *Journal of International Business Studies*, **19**, 411–32.

Lerner, J. (1995), 'Venture capitalists and the oversight of private firms', *Journal of Finance*, **50**, 301–18.

Malloy, C.J. (2005), 'The geography of equity analysis', *The Journal of Finance*, **60**, 719–55.

Michalet, C.-A. and M. Delapierre (1976), *The Multinationalization of French Firms*, Chicago: Academy of International Business.

Onida, F. and G. Viesti (1998), *The Italian Multinationals*, London: Croom Helms Ltd.

Reuer, J.J. and M.P. Koza (2000), 'Asymmetric information and joint venture performance: theory and evidence for domestic and international joint ventures', *Strategic Management Journal*, **21**, 81–8.

Shan, W. (1991), 'Environmental risks and joint venture sharing arrangements', *Journal of International Business Studies*, **22**, 555–78.

Stiglitz, J.E. (2000), 'The contributions of the economics of information to twentieth century economics', *Quarterly Journal of Economics*, **115**, 1441–78.

Swedenborg, B. (1979), *The Multinational Operations of Swedish Firms: An Analysis of Determinants and Effects*, Stockholm: Almquist & Wicksell.

Tallman, S. and A. Phene (2006), 'Coordination, appropriation and governance in alliances: the biotechnology case', in A. Ariño and J.J. Reuer (eds) *Strategic Alliances: Governance and Contracts*, New York: Palgrave Macmillan, pp. 67–76.

Tihanyi, L., D.A. Griffith and C.J. Russell (2005), 'The effect of cultural distance on entry mode choice, international diversification, and MNE performance: a meta-analysis', *Journal of International Business Studies*, **36**, 270–83.

Tsurumi, Y. (1976), *The Japanese are coming: A multinational spread of Japanese firms*, Cambridge, MA: Ballinger.

Vernon, R. (1979), 'The product cycle hypotheses in a new international environment', *Oxford Bulletin of Economics & Statistics*, **4**, 255–67.

Veugelers, R. (1991), 'Locational determinants and ranking of host countries: an empirical assessment', *Kyklos*, **44**, 363–82.

Williamson, O.E. (1985), *The Economic Institutions of Capitalism*, New York: Free Press.

Williamson, O.E. (1996), *The Mechanisms of Governance*, New York: Oxford University Press.

Yoshihara, M.Y. (1978), 'Japanese investment in Southeast Asia', Monograph of the Center for Southeast Asian Studies, Kyoto University, University Press of Hawaii, Honolulu, HI, pp. 11, 24–31.

18. Psychic distance and directional equivalence: a theoretical framework

Ronaldo Parente, Daniel W. Baack and Victor Almeida

It has been claimed that international business research is not complete without controlling for the effect of cultural distance (CD) (Cho and Padmanabhan, 2005), and the effect of cultural differences on business activities have been considered since Beckerman (1956) first discussed the concept. Cultural distance captures differences between the cultures of two different countries (Johnson et al., 2006), and is typically measured using the index introduced by Kogut and Singh (1988). The concept has been used to explain various international business activities, including foreign market entry mode decisions (Cho and Padhmanabhan, 2005), differences in multinational performance in foreign markets (Gomez-Mejia and Palich, 1997; Morosini et al., 1998), inter-firm cross-border knowledge transfer (Simonin, 1999; Minbaeva et al., 2003), expatriate adjustment (Black and Mendenhall, 1991), and patterns of foreign direct investment (Grosse and Trevino, 1996; Habib and Zurawicki, 2002).

The 'blind confidence' in Kogut and Singh's (1988) index as a measure of cultural distance has been severely criticized (Shenkar, 2001; Harzing, 2004; Magnusson, et al., 2006). In response to these criticisms, recent research has focused on the difference between psychic and cultural distance measures (Sousa and Bradley, 2006), and has begun to take a broader and more individual based view of the effect of culture on international business (Dow and Karunaratna, 2006). This individual level of analysis moves beyond what has been called a 'simplistic view of culture' (Leung et al., 2005, p. 374), and instead considers individual perception of cultural differences to be dynamic and influenced by contextual variables (Leung et al., 2005; Kirkman et al., 2006).

This chapter adds to this growing psychic distance literature stream by drawing from the psychology literature two potential individual level biases that may affect psychic distance. These biases, assimilation and contrast, are based on levels of familiarity with cultures, a contextual variable, and may cause a disconnection between individual perceptions of cultural risk and the actual risk in the environment. While this flawed perception has important implications for various international business topics, this chapter will focus on the implication for entry mode decisions.

The underlying logic of this work is theory building (i.e. elaboration of constructs and propositions), which involves inducting insights from existing literature and field-based interviews. Using this logic, this chapter contributes to the international business literature in several ways. First, the empirical findings of the effect of cultural distance and psychic distance on entry mode have often been conflicting and inconclusive (e.g. Tihanyi et al., 2005; Magnusson et al., 2006). While it is not assumed that all these problems are a result of assimilation or contrast bias, or level of analysis difficulties, a better understanding of potential biases and a shift of focus to individual decision makers may provide important insight into cultural based risk and entry mode decisions. Second, there is a growing body of literature criticizing cultural distance (e.g. Shenkar, 2001), and this study expands on these criticisms by exploring, both qualitatively and theoretically, their implications. Third, while the literature already acknowledges the lack of symmetry in the Kogut and Singh (1988) measure (Shenkar, 2001), and makes a distinction between national level (cultural distance) and individual level measures (psychic distance) (e.g. Dow and Karunaratna, 2006), the field is only beginning to explore the theoretical and empirical implications of these criticisms. For example, there is little qualitative research investigating psychic distance, and no studies empirically examining Shenkar's (2001) illusion of symmetry, or applying the assimilation and contrast biases to the psychic distance concept. This chapter begins to meet all these research gaps and also begins meet the recent calls in the international business literature for a more dynamic view of culture (e.g. Leung et al. 2005).

To explore these various international business issues, this chapter is organized as follows. First, the importance of the cultural distance concept, especially in terms of internal risk or uncertainty, on the entry mode decision is discussed, and the ambiguous empirical results regarding cultural distance are reviewed. Second, recent criticisms of cultural distance and Kogut and Singh's (1988) computation are discussed, with a focus on the assumption of directional equivalence. Third, the cultural versus psychic distance distinction is reviewed. Fourth, the concepts of assimilation and contrast bias are introduced and applied to the prediction of cost and risk in the entry mode decision. A qualitative exploration of these biases is interwoven throughout the discussion.

CRITICISMS OF CULTURAL DISTANCE AND ENTRY MODE DECISIONS

Entry mode refers to the choice of entry form made by multinational business decision markers when entering a foreign market. Entry mode types range from complete ownership to exporting, with the typical theoretical trade-off being between level of ownership or control and the amount of risk involved. One of the dominant theoretical explanations of entry mode decisions is transaction costs theory (Williamson, 1975). This theory is rooted in the attributes of transactions and in the bounded rationality and opportunism of human actors. Transaction costs theorists posit that cultural differences lead to increased information-gathering costs, increased difficulties in transferring competencies and skills, and increased difficulty in forward thinking. The end result of these difficulties is increased costs and risks (Williamson, 1975; Buckley and Casson, 1998; Anderson and Gatignon, 1986). In response to these increased costs and risks in culturally distant foreign markets, transaction costs theorists typically predict that the more culturally distant the country, the lower the control level of the entry mode (Kogut and Singh, 1988; Agarwal, 1994).

Despite this theoretical foundation, empirical research on cultural distance and entry mode choice has been inconclusive. Some studies find that as the cultural distance between countries increases, the level of ownership and control increases (Pan, 1996; Hennart and Reddy, 1997). Other studies find that the higher the cultural distance the greater the likelihood of joint ventures (Hennart and Larimo, 1998; Brouthers and Brouthers, 2001). Still other studies find that as cultural distance increases, firms are more likely to use low level control modes such as licensing (Arora and Fosfuri, 2000) or lower percentages of equity ownership (Barkema et al., 1997; Barkema and Vermeulen, 1998). Lastly, other studies do not find a relationship between cultural distance and control structure (Li et al., 2001).

These inconclusive findings may be partially rooted in the measure of cultural distance typically used, namely Kogut and Singh's (1988) national level computation. Two contemporary meta-analyses find this measure to be the overwhelmingly most common one used to represent cultural differences, and express concern that the field is overly reliant on it (Tihanyi et al., 2005; Magnusson et al., 2006). This concern is partly rooted in Shenkar's 2001 *Journal of International Business Studies* article that pointedly criticizes the Kogut and Singh (1988) measure by focusing on various assumptions or illusions inherent in the computation, including the illusion of symmetry.

The inconclusive entry mode findings may also be driven by the level of analysis used. There has been growing emphasis in the literature on a distinction between a national level cultural distance measure and an individual level psychic distance measure (Sousa and Bradley, 2006). There is statistical evidence of differences in the effect of culture on entry mode decisions depending on whether individual or national level measures are used (Drogendijk and Slangen, 2005). Recent writings have emphasized that research on the effect of cultural differences on international business 'should ideally be measured by the perceptions of the decision makers at the time the decision is made' (Dow and Karunaratna, 2006, p. 579).

While Shenkar (2001) discusses the potential asymmetry in the cultural distance measure, the article does not propose any drivers for this effect. This chapter, therefore, builds on this 'Illusion of Symmetry' concept by introducing two individual-level biases from the psychology literature. These biases, assimilation and contrast, are potential drivers of asymmetry and directional inequivalence, and at an individual level analysis of the entry mode decision, affect these decisions. As this chapter looks at cultural differences at an individual level, for the rest of the text the term 'psychic distance' is used. Psychic distance is defined as 'the mind's processing, in terms of perception and understanding, of cultural and business differences' (Evans, et al. 2000, p. 375). This definition, and the use of the term psychic distance, shifts the focus away from distant, national level measures of cultural distance, to the more personal, individual level psychic distance measure. This focus on the individual, instead of on reductionist national level values (Hofstede, 1980), allows for the exploration of how individual level biases may influence the perception of culture based risk in entry mode decisions. Moreover, this chapter distinguishes between the existing psychic distance in a cross-cultural relationship and the perception, a potentially biased one, of that distance. This perception component of psychic distance is contained in the definition from Evans et al. (2000), but most writings on cultural differences focus on the national versus individual level distinction, failing to consider the role of faulty, individual level biases.

This chapter introduces a pair of such biases – assimilation and contrast – to the discussion and explores through both theoretical discussion and a qualitative analysis how these biases influence the perceptions of individuals from different cultures. These biases are drawn from social and cognitive psychology writings (e.g. Hart and Diehl, 1994). Assimilation is defined as 'the perception of one's view being closer to another's view than they actually are' (Hart and Diehl, 1994, p. 71). On the other hand, contrast bias is defined as 'when a person holds a view relatively distant from another's' and states that this 'person will likely perceive the opposing view as even more distant than it is in actuality' (Hart and Diehl, 1994, p. 71). These psychological concepts have implications for the perception of psychic distance and for entry mode decisions. To this end, the chapter develops a theoretical framework that incorporates assimilation and contrast bias into a discussion of entry mode decisions and, through this application, provides insight into the inconsistent empirical results regarding the effect of cultural differences on entry mode decisions.

A MODEL OF PERCEIVED PSYCHIC DISTANCE UNDER ASSIMILATION AND CONTRAST BIAS

The development of this chapter's theoretical framework is guided by the culture and entry mode literature in international business and by the psychology literature on assimilation and contrast bias. In addition, a series of interviews were completed with individuals with potential perceptual biases. For these preliminary interviews, three pairs of countries were sampled: the United States/Brazil, the United States/Singapore, and the United States/Taiwan. In each pair of countries, individuals were identified that were representative of potential assimilation or contrast bias in relation to the other country in the pair; that is, these respondents were either extremely familiar with or had very limited exposure to the paired country culture. In total, 24 individuals were interviewed, with 12 potentially having an assimilation bias and 12 potentially having a contrast bias. These interviews provide preliminary insight into the relationships theoretically explored below, particularly on how assimilation and contrast biases affect individual level perceptions of psychic distance. While the results of the interviews are not testable, quotes from the interviews will be interspersed throughout the theoretical framework discussion below to help support and illuminate the points made.

Directional Equivalence

In Shenkar's (2001) article, the Kogut and Singh (1988) measure is criticized for an illusion of symmetry. To quote:

'Distance', by definition, is symmetric: the distance between from point A to point B is identical to the distance from point B to point A. CD symmetry is difficult to defend in the context of FDI. It suggests an identical role for the home and host cultures, for instance, that a Dutch firm investing in China is faced with the same CD as a Chinese firm investing in the Netherlands. There is no support for such an assumption ... there are no studies showing symmetry between the two nor is there a reason to assume one' (p. 523).

In this chapter, we apply this illusion to an individual level of analysis and, as the level of analysis shifts to the individual, we discuss it in terms of 'directional equivalence'. The assumption of directional equivalence is based on the idea that the psychic distance between individuals from two countries does not depend on from which direction it is being observed. In other words, the distance between country A and B perceived by an individual in country A is assumed to be the same as the distance perceived by another individual in country B. Because of the potential for differences and biases in individual perceptions, the assumption of directional equivalence for psychic distance is incorrect. Consider the hypothetical example of a Brazilian, the son of Japanese immigrants and born in the Japanese section of Sao Paulo, who is raised in Brazil but has predominantly the same values and behavior patterns as his Japanese parents. This Japanese-Brazilian is making an entry mode decision for a Brazilian firm entering Japan and has certain assumptions regarding the differences between these two countries' cultures. Now compare the potential psychic distance for this manager with the psychic distance for a Japanese citizen who knows Brazil only from hearing about the Carnival, and maybe the soccer player Pele. Obviously, the directional equivalence assumption does not hold.

The theory of assimilation and contrast (Hart and Diehl, 1994), which suggests that individuals react differently to the same message, depending on the degree of similarity or difference perceived in relation to the originator of the message, provides further support for a lack of directional equivalence. Moreover, our interviews provide anecdotal evidence of problems with the equivalence assumption. Consider the difference between the responses of an American respondent highly familiar with Singaporean culture and the responses of a Singaporean unfamiliar with the United States. The American respondent comments that:

> Singapore is the most western influenced Asian country. The opportunity for conflict is very low due to the trade and economic relationship that the two countries share. In addition, Singapore has long been an ally and a stable Asian country for the USA to leverage. The USA will look to countries like Singapore to continue to push democracy in the region. The economic and political needs will limit conflict.

In comparison, a low familiarity contrast bias Singaporean respondent said that Americans have:

> less hesitation in expressing how one feels; either pleasure or unhappiness. Use more words to communicate by explaining at length. More liberal in terms of values to live by. Greater sense of self rather than community – emphasis on 'I'. In terms of communication, Singaporeans may find someone from the United States more opinionated and assertive. Singaporeans may also regard them to have more self-interest with less regard for group's harmony and disrupting the equilibrium within the group.

These quotes support the above theoretical discussion, and provide further evidence against the assumption of directional equivalence. The American respondent assumes far fewer differences and a far lower potential for cultural conflict than the Singaporean respondent. Based on the above discussion and interview evidence, we therefore propose that psychic distance lacks directional equivalence. That is, there will be differences in the perceived psychic distance between countries A and B as perceived by individuals from the two countries.

Assimilation and Contrast Biases

Research suggests that the assimilation effect or bias will be present when the sender of the message shares something in common with the audience (for example perspectives, values, race, life style, religion, faith, and other cultural characteristics) (Hart and Diehl, 1994). Because of this sense of familiarity, the individual will perceive the messenger as more of an equal, as more trustworthy, and the messenger's point of view will be more easily assimilated (Hart and Diehl, 1994). Alternatively, the contrast effect or bias will be present when the sender of the message shares little in common with the audience. This results in a tendency for exaggeration of the discrepancies between the attitudes of the sender and the attitudes of the audience (Dawes et al., 1972).

While the origins of these effects are in the psychology literature, the biases have been applied to various business issues, including the evaluation of brand alliances (Levin, 2002), print advertising (Yi, 1990; Schmitt, 1994), salespeople (Stafford et al., 1995), and individual performance (Ivancevich, 1983). The literature has found a consistent negative effect from these biases, and, for the contrast bias, it has been linked to an increase in conflict between groups, a skewed perception of the ability to compromise, and lower esteem for the other group or individual. This lowering of esteem in turn increases the contrast effect, making the bias self-perpetuating (Dawes et al., 1972). The effect is also driven by pre-existing expectations or knowledge (Geers and Lassiter, 2005).

Therefore, as the level of familiarity that individuals have with a country's culture is not homogeneous, each individual is biased to some degree in relation to that country. Depending on the degree and type of individual bias (e.g. assimilation or contrast), each individual perceives the psychic distance in the relationship differently. Our interviews provide examples of this difference in familiarity. For the low familiarity contrast bias respondents, there was frequently hesitation to respond and questions regarding their appropriateness as a respondent. One American respondent even stated that 'I know nothing about Taiwan.' This difference in familiarity was then reflected in the responses given. For example, the reluctant, contrast biased American respondent mentioned above stated that, 'While both the US and Taiwan are developed, modern nations with democratic forms of government, I'd assume that nearly all other cultural features are different.' In comparison, the assimilation biased American respondent, who had high levels of familiarity with Taiwanese culture, stated that, 'I think of any industrialized country as a country with westernized culture. I'm not sure that there are many significant differences in countries with westernized ideals.' These two quotes, by individuals from the same national culture but with vast differences in familiarity with Taiwanese culture, reveal how familiarity can lead to bias.

Therefore, based on our theoretical discussion and the anecdotal evidence from our interviews, we argue that assimilation and contrast biases will prejudice perceived psychic distance. In cases where an individual has a high level of familiarity with another country, the individual will perceive the psychic distance between him or herself and individuals from that country as lower than the actual psychic distance between the two countries. On the other hand, in cases where an individual has a low level of familiarity with another country, the perceived psychic distance between that individual and individuals from the other country will be greater than the actual psychic distance.

The above discussion introduced the skewing effect of assimilation or contrast bias in perception of psychic distance between individuals from two countries. It is also important is for us to examine the combined effect of individual biases and to explore how this may affect the relationship between actual and perceived psychic distance. Research finds that assimilation and contrast biases become more pronounced as the differences between the individuals become more extreme (Hart and Diehl, 1994). Moreover, the effects are found to be self-perpetuating and recursive (Dawes et al., 1972). Therefore, in cases of duplicate bias, either bilateral assimilation or contrast, the pairing of like biased individuals will exacerbate the prejudice, and the perceived psychic distance will be more biased.

Our interviews provide some insight into how bilateral contrast or assimilation may increase cultural conflict. Consider the responses of two Brazilians unfamiliar with America, when asked about differences between the countries. The first states that, 'Americans are cold regarding personal relationships. They put too much value/emphasis on work to the detriment of other personal aspects of life ... Americans have little flexibility.' The second respondent showed even more of a conflict bias, claiming that 'Americans are more nationalistic. They think that everything that relates to US is bigger and better. US have a very aggressive capitalism, where everyone is obsessed about making money.' In isolation, these two Brazilian respondents see a large cultural gap and this potential contrast bias will, alone, increase the perceived psychic distance in the relationship. Now consider how the amount of conflict in the relationship would be increased if they were in a business relationship with an American who was unfamiliar with Brazilian culture and wrote: 'US – democratic, free market place, multicultural, multi-religious, generally middle class financially. Brazil – dictatorship, militaristic, mostly Catholic, not free, dangerous surroundings, generally lower class financially.' The cultural conflict in the pairing would obviously be higher than it would be with an American who was more familiar with Brazilian culture and responded that, 'Brazilians are more flexible regarding time and also very friendly. They are very hard working people but they also separate well work and family time. I believe we share a lot of the same values considering both countries are majority Christians.' Comparing the potential conflict with these pairings helps illuminate how the assimilation and contrast bias do not operate in isolation, and if paired together can compound the bias. Therefore, the above discussion leads us to suggest that in cases where both individuals have assimilation bias (bilateral assimilation bias), or are familiar with each other's countries, the perceived psychic distance between the two countries will be far smaller than the actual cultural differences between them. Moreover, in cases where both individuals have contrast bias (bilateral contrast bias), or are unfamiliar with each other's countries, the perceived psychic distance between the two countries will be far greater than the actual psychic distance between them.

Entry Mode Implications

A biased perception of cultural differences, whether assimilation or contrast, results in an overly optimistic or overly pessimistic estimation of the effect of these differences on business actions. This faulty perception is the result of a difference between the perceived psychic distance in a relationship and the actual cultural differences between the individuals. While this bias may be important to many different aspects of international business, this chapter focuses on how biased perceptions skew the estimation of the cultural biased risk and costs involved in entry mode decisions.

Our discussion of the entry mode decision is rooted in the transaction costs theory of the firm. In brief, this theory sees the firm's entry mode decision as a balance between the increased control that comes from internalizing the market and the increased costs and risks associated with that internalization. While the market should be the default choice, market inefficiencies, and the resulting increase in costs, produce a need for hierarchy or internalization (Anderson and Gatignon, 1986; Erramilli and Rao, 1993). The focus of the theory is then on decreasing the costs, both ex ante and ex post, of the transaction through the choice of the most efficient entry mode (Hill and Kim, 1988). While a variety of factors influence these costs, including bounded rationality and opportunism (Pak and Park, 2004), free-riding (Hennart, 1991), transaction-specific assets (Erramilli and Rao, 1993), and external and internal uncertainty (Anderson and Gatignon, 1986), this chapter focuses on the increased risks and costs associated with psychic distance.

The transaction costs perspective sees increased psychic distance as a source of increasing risks and costs (Anderson and Gatignon, 1986). This growth in costs includes increases in communication costs (Pak and Park, 2004), knowledge transfer and knowledge acquisition costs, and the costs associated with the need for more knowledge (Gatignon and Anderson, 1988; Hill and Kim, 1988). Additionally, the price of monitoring and evaluating employees increases, as does the cost of evaluating inputs and results (Erramilli and Rao, 1993). In general, the greater the psychic distance between countries, the higher the transaction costs. Psychic distance not only increases costs but is a core component of the total risk companies face when entering a country (Brouthers, 1995). This increased risk is rooted in an increase in the potential for conflict (Kogut and Singh, 1988) and an increase in the chance of entry failure (Barkema et al., 1996).

While past studies have discussed psychic distance theoretically, only a few have discussed the potential for disparity between the perception by individuals of the differences between cultures and the actual, existing differences between these cultures. Gatignon and Anderson (1988) mention that increased cultural distance leads to an undervaluing of foreign investments, implying a disconnection between perception and reality. More pointedly, Kogut and Singh (1988) refer to managerial perceptions of cultural differences and state that the increased costs from greater cultural distance 'may be perceptual only or accurate appraisals of the increased difficulties of managing a foreign workforce in a culturally distant country' (p. 415). Therefore, this distinction between perceived and actual psychic distance has been hinted at in previous writings, but this is the first attempt to investigate potential causes of this difference.

Overall, transaction costs theorists predict that in response to the increased risk and cost caused by increase psychic distance, a low control level entry mode should be selected (Kogut and Singh, 1988; Agarwal, 1994; Kim and Hwang, 1992; Pak and Park, 2004), though research over the last two decades has failed to consistently support this relationship (see Pan, 1996; Hennart and Reddy, 1997; Erramilli and Rao, 1993; Gatignon and Anderson, 1988).

How then will assimilation and contrast biases affect the theoretical relationships discussed above? In general, the biases result in managers having a skewed estimate of the costs and risks caused by psychic distance. In the case of assimilation bias, individuals will perceive the psychic distance and its associated risks and costs as smaller than the actual psychic distance, resulting in a decision to use a higher control level entry mode than appropriate. In the case of contrast bias, the individuals will perceive the psychic distance as greater than the actual psychic distance, resulting in a lower control level entry mode than appropriate.

Host Country Bias

	ASSIMILATION	CONTRAST
ASSIMILATION	Higher control entry mode than appropriate	Lack of host country opportunities
CONTRAST	High home country resistance	Lower control entry mode than appropriate

Figure 18.1   Perceived psychic distance under conditions of assimilation and contrast bias

In the case of entry mode decisions, there are, in broad terms, two actors or groups of actors, involved in the decision – those from the host country and those from the home country. Each of these actors has different levels of familiarity with the home or host country culture, and, as such, will have either a contrast or an assimilation bias. As shown in Figure 18.1, these different bias pairings will have important and different effects on the entry mode decision. As mentioned earlier, the assimilation or contrast bias in a transaction happens at the individual or group level, and considering the existence of directional inequivalence when these effects are present, we discuss the entry mode implications under four possible bias combinations: lower control level than appropriate, higher control level than appropriate, high home country resistance, and lack of host country opportunities.

The tendency to mistakenly choose a higher control level entry mode than is appropriate will occur under conditions of bilateral assimilation, where both decision makers (home and host countries) have assimilation bias. In this case, the decision maker from the home country may underestimate the risks involved and became overly optimistic, reducing his or her capacity to rationally evaluate uncertainty and the corresponding costs. Therefore, in this case, these individuals will favor the choice of an entry mode with higher levels of control when maybe a lower level of control would be appropriate. To restate, in an environment of bilateral assimilation bias, managers may inappropriately choose a high control level entry mode.

Under conditions of bilateral contrast there is a tendency to mistakenly choose a lower control level entry mode than is appropriate since both decision makers (home and host countries) have contrast bias. This bias leads to an increase in the perceived, but not actual, psychic distance. In this case, the decision maker from the home country may overestimate the risks involved and became overly pessimistic, reducing his or her capacity to rationally evaluate uncertainty and costs, and resulting in the choice of an entry mode with lower levels of control than appropriate. Therefore, in an environment of bilateral contrast bias, managers may inappropriately choose a low control level entry mode.

High resistance will occur when the home country decision maker is under the influence of contrast bias and the host country decision maker is under the influence of assimilation bias. Even though the host country decision maker will be interested in a relationship, the home country decision maker will have a tendency to ignore the host's interest and be reluctant to enter the market. Additionally, the home market decision maker will push for a lower control level entry mode than appropriate. Therefore, in an environment of home country contrast bias and host country assimilation bias, the host country managers will face high resistance to market entry, while the home country managers may inappropriately choose a low control level entry mode.

A lack of opportunities will occur in the case where the home country decision maker is under the influence of assimilation bias and the host country decision maker is under the influence of contrast bias. Because of the differences in perceptions of psychic distance, the home country decision maker will seek a higher control level entry mode than appropriate, while the host country decision maker will try to get all possible safeguards, raising the transaction costs, and making the negotiation process more difficult. Therefore, in an environment of home county assimilation bias and host country contrast bias, home country managers will face a lack of opportunity to enter the host country market and will most likely choose an inappropriately high control level entry mode.

The end result of these biases on the entry mode decision will be an increase in costs and an increase in chance of failure for the entry. These negative results will then result in poor subsidiary performance. This finding has been partially covered previously in writings discussing the psychic distance paradox. In the classic article on this process, O'Grady and Lane (1996) found that Canadian firms entering the American market had high failure rates because of unanticipated cultural problems. Evans and Mavondo (2002) also found empirical support for the psychic distance paradox, reporting that Australian retailers performed better in psychically distant markets than in close markets. Similarly, Pedersen and Petersen (2004) observed firms experiencing a shock effect arising from unanticipated cultural differences in geographically close markets. The results of all of these studies point to a possible link between assimilation and contrast bias and performance, suggesting that increasing levels of contrast or assimilation bias may be associated with decreasing subsidiary performance.

DISCUSSION AND IMPLICATIONS

In this chapter we examined psychic distance in the context of assimilation and contrast bias as it relates to individual perception, and the effect of these biases on the perception of risk and costs for foreign market entry decisions. Overall, our theoretical framework suggests that psychic distance is not directionally equivalent, that there is a separation between the perceived psychic distance of decision makers and the actual psychic distance in the relationship, that one source of this disconnect is assimilation or contrast bias, and that these biases affect entry mode decisions. Our support for these arguments is based on a review of the international management literature as it relates to cultural distance, transaction cost theory, and entry mode selection, and a bridging of this literature with the psychology literature on assimilation and contrast bias. To provide additional support for our discussion, the responses from preliminary qualitative data collected through personal interviews conducted with individuals in four countries: the United States, Brazil, Taiwan and Singapore, are used. Our interviews affirm the importance of considering the bias of the individual decision maker when dealing with international business issues, and suggest that the type and the level of individual bias can affect the perceived psychic distance expected by the decision maker in cross-country issues.

Overall, our interview results suggest that it is important to consider the individual bias of the decision maker in the context of doing business in foreign markets. Our theoretical framework, along with our preliminary qualitative data, supports the idea that individuals under conditions of assimilation bias because of familiarity, and the resulting perceived similarities with regard to the other culture, will be more open and willing to engage in business transactions with individuals from familiar cultures. Moreover, the prior experience and exposure of the decision maker to the other culture will create a sense of familiarity that will in turn be associated with an overly optimist assessment of the cultural differences or psychic distance involved. In turn, individuals less familiar with the culture will have contrast bias resulting in an overly negative estimation of psychic distance and a resistance to engage in business transactions with individuals from unfamiliar cultures. This leads to the central argument of the chapter, namely that assimilation and contrast bias can cause decision makers to be overly optimistic or pessimistic regarding the amount of risk or cost in a foreign market. This potentially biased estimation will affect the selection of entry mode and, therefore, will result in an incorrect selection.

Our proposed framework contributes to the international business field by extending research exploring the role of cultural differences in the entry mode process (Buckley and Casson, 1998; Anderson and Gatignon, 1986). In addition, it provides an opportunity to explore the relationship between psychic distance and cultural risk in the international business environment under conditions of assimilation and contrast bias. Insights from our preliminary interviews suggest that assimilation and contrast bias are important drivers of directional inequivalence and must be incorporated into studies of psychic distance. This insight into the entry mode decision may begin to partially explain the inconclusive empirical results regarding entry mode decisions and cultural distance (Pan, 1996; Hennart and Reddy, 1997; Eramilli and Rao, 1993; Gatignon and Anderson, 1988).

Our findings should help both researchers and practitioners understand the trends in psychic distance research and international business research in general. Our fieldwork seems to support our claim that psychic distance is not directionally equivalent, and that the relationship between perceived psychic distance and the adoption of the appropriate entry mode is mediated by the level and type of individual biases in the transaction. Future research on the topic should consider the theoretical framework presented here within the context of potential asymmetry in cultural distance (Shenkar, 2001), the potential drivers of directional inequivalence, including assimilation and contrast bias, and the negative effect that the difference between perceived and actual psychic distance may have on entry mode choices and the subsequent performance of subsidiaries.

Additionally, this chapter contributes to the international business field by contributing to the extant literature (Shenkar, 2001; Dow and Karunaratna, 2006) by emphasizing perceived psychic distance as a key construct in international business research and incorporating the concept of the 'illusion of symmetry' and other criticisms of Kogut and Singh's (1988) computation. Compared with previous work on the topic, our research is unique in that it focuses on individual perception and it takes a qualitative, in-depth view of psychic distance.

Finally, our discussion has interesting implications for international business education and managerial awareness. Many curricula focus on

increasing cross-cultural awareness, and recent academic articles have begun
to consider the possible negative or positive effect of this increased cross-
cultural competence (Johnson et al., 2006; Magnusson et al., 2006). This
study presents the possibility that increased familiarity with a culture will
lead to assimilation bias and its corresponding faulty decision making. Identification and education regarding this potential bias are the simplest way
to avoid this problem. International business educators need to be certain
to distinguish between knowledge and deep understanding and to limit
the overconfidence of students. Likewise, managers facing an international
investment decision should be aware of their potential biases, depending on
their own psychic distances from target nations, and adjust their decision
processes accordingly.

REFERENCES

Agarwal, S. (1994), 'Socio-cultural distance and the choice of joint ventures: a
contingency perspective', *Journal of International Marketing*, **2** (2), 63–80.
Anderson, E. and H. Gatignon (1986), 'Modes of foreign entry: a transaction cost
analysis and propositions', *Journal of International Business Studies*, **17** (3),
1–26.
Arora, A. and A. Fosfuri (2000), 'Wholly owned subsidiary versus technology
licensing in the worldwide chemical industry', *Journal of International Business
Studies*, **31** (4), 555–72.
Barkema, H.G., J.H. Bell and J.M. Pennings (1996), 'Foreign entry, cultural barriers,
and learning', *Strategic Management Journal*, **17** (2), 151–66.
Barkema, HG., O. Shenkar, F. Vermeulen and J.H. Bell (1997), 'Working abroad,
working with others: how firms learn to operate international joint ventures',
The Academy of Management Journal, **40** (2), 426–42.
Barkema, H.G. and F. Vermeulen (1998), 'International expansion through start-
up or acquisition: a learning perspective', *Academy of Management Journal*, **41**
(1), 7–26.
Beckerman, W. (1956), 'Distance and the pattern of intra-European trade', *The
Review of Economics and Statistics*, **38** (1), 31–40.
Black, J.S. and M. Mendenhall (1991), 'The u-curve adjustment hypothesis revisited:
a review and theoretical framework', *Journal of International Business Studies*,
22 (2), 225–47.
Brouthers, K.D. (1995), 'The influence of international risk on entry mode strategy
in the computer software industry', *Management International Review*, **35** (1),
7–28.
Brouthers, K.D. and L.E. Brouthers (2001), 'Explaining the national cultural
distance paradox', *Strategic Management Journal*, **32** (1), 177–89.
Buckley, P.J. and M.C. Casson (1979), 'Analyzing foreign market entry strategies:
extending the internalization approach', *Journal of International Business Studies*,
29 (3), 539–62.

Cho, K.R. and P. Padmanabhan (2005), 'Revisiting the role of cultural distance in MNCs' foreign ownership mode choice: the moderating effect of experience attributes', *International Business Review*, **14** (3), 307–24.

Dawes, R.M., D. Singer and F. Lemons (1972), 'An experimental analysis of the contrast effect and its implications for intergroup communication and the indirect assessment of attitude', *Journal of Personality and Social Psychology*, **21** (3), 281–95.

Dow, D. and A. Karunaratna (2006), 'Developing a multidimensional instrument to measure pyschic distance stimuli', *Journal of International Business Studies*, **37** (5), 578–602.

Drogendijk, R. and A. Slangen (2005), 'Hofstede, Schwartz, or managerial perceptions? A comparative analysis of the effects of various cultural distance measures on an MNEs establishment choice mode', paper presented at the Academy of International Business meeting, Quebec, Canada, December.

Erramilli, M.K. and C.P. Rao (1993), 'Service firms' international entry-mode choice: a modified transaction-costs analysis approach', *Journal of Marketing*, **57** (7), 19–38.

Evans, J. and F.T. Mavondo (2002), 'Psychic distance and organizational performance: an empirical examination of international retailing operations', *Journal of International Business Studies*, **33** (3), 515–32.

Evans, J., A. Treadgold and F.T. Mavondo (2000), 'Psychic distance and the performance of international retailers – a suggested theoretical framework', *International Marketing Review*, **17** (4/5), 373–91.

Gatignon, H. and E. Anderson (1988), 'The multinational corporation's degree of control over foreign subsidiaries: an empirical test of a transaction cost explanation', *Journal of Law, Economics, and Organization*, **4** (2), 305–36.

Geers, A.L. and G.D. Lassiter (2005), 'Affective assimilation and contrast: effects of expectations and prior stimulus exposure', *Basic and Applied Social Psychology*, **27** (2), 143–54.

Gomez-Mejia, L.R. and L.E. Palich (1997), 'Cultural diversity and the performance of multinational firms', *Journal of International Business Studies*, **28** (2), 309–35.

Grosse, R. and L.J. Trevino (1996), 'Foreign direct investment in the United States: an analysis by country of origin', *Journal of International Business Studies*, **26** (1), 139–55.

Habib, M. and L. Zurawicki (2002), 'Corruption and foreign direct investment', *Journal of International Business Studies*, **33** (2), 291–307.

Hart, B. and V. Diehl (1994), 'Position reversal: isolating the key factor in assimilation and contrast', *The Journal of Psychology*, **128** (1), 71–87.

Harzing, A.W. (2004), 'The role of culture in entry-mode studies: from neglect to myopia?', in J. Cheng and M. Hitt (eds), *Advances in International Management*, Amsterdam: Elsevier.

Hennart, J.-F. (1991), 'The transaction costs theory of joint ventures: an empirical study of Japanese subsidiaires in the United States', *Management Science*, **37** (4), 483–97.

Hennart, J.-F. and J. Larimo (1998), 'The impact of culture on the strategy of multinational enterprises: does national origin affect ownership decisions?', *Journal of International Business Studies*, **29** (3), 515–38.

Hennart, J.-F. and Reddy, S. (1997), 'The choice between mergers/acquisitions and joint ventures: the case of Japanese investors in the United States', *Strategic Management Journal*, **18** (1), 1–12.

Hill, C.W. and W.C. Kim (1988), 'Searching for a dynamic theory of the multinational enterprise: a transaction cost model', *Strategic Management Journal*, **9** (Special Issue), 93–104.

Hofstede, G. (1980), *Culture's Consequences: International Differences in Work-related Values*, Thousands Oaks, CA: Sage.

Ivancevich, J.M. (1983), 'Contrast effects in performance evaluation reward practices', *Academy of Management Journal*, **26** (3), 465–79.

Johnson, J.P., T. Lenartowicz and S. Apud (2006), 'Cross-cultural competence in international business: toward a definition and a model', *Journal of International Business Studies*, **37** (4), 525–43.

Kim, W.C. and P. Hwang (1992), 'Global strategy and multinationals' entry mode choice', *Journal of International Business Studies*, **23** (1), 29–53.

Kirkman, B.L., K.B. Lowe and C.B. Gibson (2006), 'A quarter century of culture's consequences: a review of empirical research incorporating Hofstede's cultural values framework', *Journal of International Business Studies*, **37** (3), 285–320.

Kogut, B. and H. Singh (1988), 'The effect of national culture on the choice of entry Mode', *Journal of International Business Studies*, **19** (3), 411–32.

Leung, K., R.S. Bhagat, N.R. Buchan, M. Erez and C.B. Gibson (2005), 'Culture and international business: recent advances and their implications for future research', *Journal of International Business Studies*, **36** (4), 357–78.

Levin, A.M. (2002), 'Contrast and assimilation processes in consumers' evaluations of dual brands', *Journal of Business and Psychology*, **17** (1), 145–54.

Li, J., K. Lam and G. Qian (2001), 'Family-orientated collectivism and its effect on firm performance: a comparison between overseas Chinese and foreign firms in China', *International Journal of Organizational Analysis*, **8** (4), 364–80.

Magnusson, P., D.W. Baack, S. Zdravkovic and K. Staub (2006), 'Cultural distance in international business: a meta-analytic review', paper presented at the Academy of International Business Conference, Beijing, China.

Minbaeva, D., T. Pedersen, I. Bjoerkman, C.F. Fery and H.J. Park (2003), 'MNC knowledge transfer, subsidiary absorptive capacity, and HRM', *Journal of International Business Studies*, **34** (6), 586–99.

Morosini, P., S. Shane and H. Singh (1998), 'National cultural distance and cross-border acquisition performance', *Journal of International Business Studies*, **29** (1), 137–58.

O'Grady, S. and H. Lane (1996), 'The psychic distance paradox', *Journal of International Business Studies*, **27** (2), 309–33.

Pak, Y.S. and Y.-R. Park (2004), 'Global ownership strategy of Japanese multinational enterprises: a test of internalization theory', *Management International Review*, **44** (1), 3–22.

Pan, Y. (1996), 'Influences on foreign equity ownership level in joint ventures in China', *Journal of International Business Studies*, **27** (1), 1–26.

Pedersen, T. and B. Petersen (2004), 'Learning about foreign markets: are entrant firms exposed to a "shock effect"?' *Journal of International Marketing*, **12** (1), 103–22.

Schmitt, B.H. (1994), 'Contextual priming of visual information in advertisements', *Psychology and Marketing*, **11** (1), 1–14.

Shenkar, O. (2001), 'Cultural distance revisited: towards a more rigorous conceptualization and measurement of cultural differences', *Journal of International Business Studies*, **32** (3), 519–35.

Simonin, B.L. (1999), 'Transfer of marketing know-how in international strategic alliances: an empirical investigation of the role and antecedents of knowledge ambiguity', *Journal of International Business Studies*, **30** (3), 463–90.

Sousa, C.M.P. and F. Bradley (2006), 'Cultural distance and psychic distance: two peas in a pod?', *Journal of International Marketing*, **14** (1), 49–70.

Stafford, T.F., T.W. Leigh and L.L. Martin (1995), 'Assimilation and contrast priming effects in the initial consumer sales call', *Psychology and Marketing*, **12** (4), 321–47.

Tihanyi, L., D.A. Griffith and C.J. Russell (2005), 'The effect of cultural distance on entry mode choice, international diversification, and MNE performance: a meta-analysis', *Journal of International Business Studies*, **36** (3), 270–83.

Williamson, O.E. (1975) *Markets and Hierarchies: An Analysis and Antitrust Implications*, New York: The Free Press.

Yi, Y. (1990), 'The effects of contextual priming in print advertisements', *Journal of Consumer Research*, **17** (2), 215–22.

Yin, R.K. (1984), *Case Study Research: Design and Methods*, Beverly Hills, CA: Sage.

Index

Korea
	FDI 291
	institutional characteristics 87
	international partner selection 196
	telecommunications 283
	US FDI 299

Larsen and Toubro (L&T) 94–5
Latin America
	ANDEAN 212
	global cities 235
	language problems 78
	MERCOSUR 212
	patent protection 189
	regional effects 212, 213, 218
	see also individual countries
Lee, Seung-Hyun 20–39
Lexmark 49
LG Electronics 52
Li, Dan 180–94
Li, Jing 22, 30, 31, 65, 75, 100–17, 174, 310
liability of foreignness *see* foreignness liability
Lincoln Electric 69–70, 76, 77
location choice determinants
	agglomeration definition 257
	agglomeration (geographical clustering) 246–7, 249, 251–2, 253, 254–6, 257–8
	and competitive advantage 247, 249–50, 255
	cultural factors 248–51, 254, 255–6, 257–8, 268
	domestic firms 254, 258
	economic uncertainty 252–3, 255, 257
	and FDI 220–23, 254–7, 258, 282
	and firm strategy 258–9
	future research 256–9
	individualism/collectivism 249–50, 253, 255
	industry membership 252
	institutional factors 251–3, 254, 255–6, 257–8, 268
	and knowledge transfer 247, 251, 252, 253, 267
	liability of foreignness 254–5, 256
	literature review 246–8, 254

local clusters with non-local demand
	see clusters, local, with non-local demands
	and performance 246, 269
	political uncertainty 251–2, 253, 255, 257
	social networks 247–8
	specialization benefits 246–7
	tradables and non-tradables 267
	uncertainty avoidance 249, 250–53, 255–6, 257
	see also clusters
London, as global city 232, 233

Malaysia, R&D 25, 26
management
	cross-border acquisitions 168, 169, 181
	innovation 146–7, 150, 151, 154–5
	international strategic alliances 199
	and internationalization process 76, 77
	joint ventures, international 204
	MNEs 13–16, 111, 114, 127–8, 130
	neoclassical economics 15–16
	and psychic distance 318–19, 321–2
	and R&D internationalization 88, 90, 91, 183, 184, 186
	real options theory 113–14
	see also risk management
Matsushita 25, 26
MCel 287
mergers *see* cross-border acquisitions
Merida 55–6
Mexico
	institutional voids 283
	MNEs 8, 11
Microsoft 51, 92, 181
Middle East, global cities 235
Millennium 94
Mittal 5
MNEs
	corporate downside risk 113
	cross-border acquisitions *see* cross-border acquisitions
	cultural differences 5, 111, 113
	decision-specific experience, past 123–4
	definition 136–7